THE
HISTORY OF HUMAYUN

THE HISTORY OF HUMAYUN:

HUMAYUN-NAMA

GUL-BADAN BEGAM

GYAN

Published by

Gyan Publishing House
5, Ansari Road
Daryaganj, New Delhi-110002
Phone: 011-47034999, 9811692060
E-mail: books@gyanbooks.com

Distribution Network
gyanbooks.com
India, USA, Canada, UK, Australia

ISBN: 978-93-6920-400-7 (PB)

First Published, 1902

2nd Impression 2025

Printed at: Gyan Press, Delhi.

THE HISTORY OF HUMAYUN
Author: GUL-BADAN BEGAM

THE HISTORY OF HUMĀYŪN
(HUMĀYŪN-NĀMA).

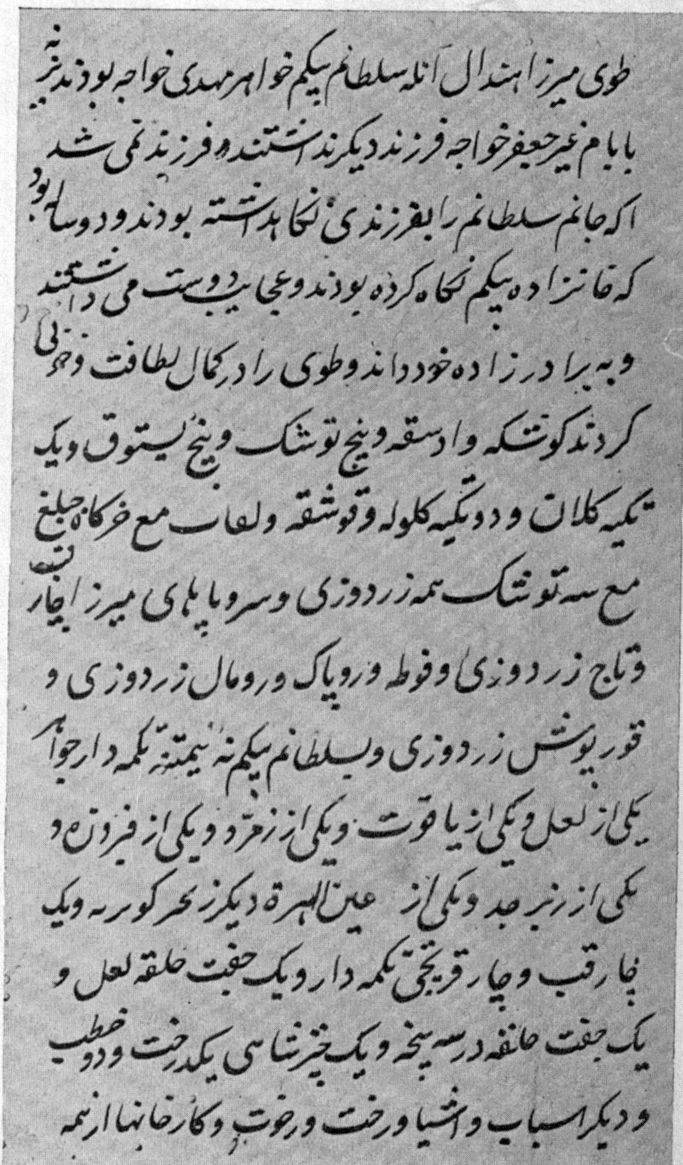

طوی میرزا هندال آنکه سلطانم بیگم خواهر مهدی خواجه بودند نیز
بابام عیر جعفر خواجه فرزند دیگر نداشتند و فرزند نمی شد
آکه جانم سلطانم را بفرزندی نگاهداشته بودند و دو ساله بود
که خانزاده بیگم نگاه کرده بودند و عجایب دوست می داشتند
و به برادرزاده خود داده اند و طوی را در کمال لطافت و خوبی
کردند کوتشکه و ادسقه و پنج توشک و پنج یستوق و یک
تکیه کلان و دو تکیه کلوله و قوشقه و لحاف مع خرگاه جلبغ
مع سه توشک همه زردوزی و سروپاهای میرزا چارقب
و تاج زردوزی و فوطه و رویاک و رومال زردوزی و
قوریوش زردوزی و سلطانم بیگم نه نیمتنه تکمه دار جواهر
یکی از لعل و یکی از یاقوت و یکی از زمرد و یکی از فیروزه و
یکی از زبرجد و یکی از عین الهره دیگر زبحر کورسه و یک
چارقب و چار قریجی تکمه دار و یک جفت حلقه لعل و
یک جفت حانفه در سه بخه و یک خنجر شاهی یکدرخت و دو خطب
و دیگر اسباب و اشیا و رخت و رخوت و کارخانها از همه

PAGE 28*b* OF GUL-BADAN BEGAM'S MS.

[*Frontispiece.*

ORIENTAL TRANSLATION FUND.

NEW SERIES.

I.

THE

HISTORY OF HUMĀYŪN

(HUMĀYŪN-NĀMA).

BY

GUL-BADAN BEGAM (PRINCESS ROSE BODY).

Translated, with Introduction, Notes, Illustrations and Biographical Appendix; and reproduced in the Persian from the only known MS. of the British Museum

BY

ANNETTE S. BEVERIDGE, M.R.A.S.

PRINTED AND PUBLISHED UNDER THE PATRONAGE OF THE ROYAL ASIATIC SOCIETY,

AND SOLD AT

22, ALBEMARLE STREET, LONDON.

1902.

To

MY HUSBAND,

WHO SET MY FEET UPON THE PERSIAN WAY,

AND HAS STREWED IT

WITH OPEN-HEARTED LARGESSE OF HELP AND COUNSEL.

A. S. B.

November, 1901.

PREFACE.

It was in October, 1900, that the late Mr. F. F. Arbuthnot made arrangements with me for the publication of this volume. It has now to put forth bereft of his guidance. I can but trust that he would have given to the finished work the welcome with which he greeted the small portion I was able to show him in print. It is natural to feel towards him what he has expressed in his dedication of the Assemblies of *Al Ḥarīrī* to Chenery, and to hope he may be glad of the fulfilment of this piece of his work.

The little history which is reproduced in this volume has few, if any, compeers, inasmuch as it is the work of a Musalmānī, and lights up her woman's world. She writes colloquially and without pose, and is unaffected and spontaneous. For these reasons I have tried to make an accurate copy of her text, and to preserve her characteristics of orthography and diction; and this the more that the British Museum MS. may be her very own, unique, and autographic. With a few chosen exceptions, I have reproduced all her deflections from common rule without comment; my additions to the MS. are limited to a few *iẓāfats* and other signs of which example is given at some place in the MS..

Princess Rose-body has rendered one essential service to history, by giving precise details of relationship in her own and some contemporary families. Up till now, however, no use has been made of her information, and her book has remained, both in India and Europe, a literary *pardanīshīn*.

The Biographical Appendix, which I have modelled in admiration of Professor Blochmann's in his *Aīn-i-akbarī*, will, I hope, be of use to future writers. It is the outcome of the notes of several years, but it is incomplete and over brief. Nevertheless, it discloses the elements of many a romantic story.

One of an author's most agreeable final touches is the expression of thanks to those who have helped his book on its way. My obligation to my husband is too great to be told. I am much indebted to Mr. A. G. Ellis for his unfailing kindness during the long and pleasant time of my work in the British Museum, and to my friends Mr. E. H. Whinfield and Mr. W. Irvine for the expression of their opinions on several perplexing points. As I have said in writing of the plates, I owe all my illustrations but one to Mr. Bourdillon, B.C.S..

The printing of a book so full as is this one of unfamiliar names and of diacritically-marked letters entails a heavy tax upon proof-readers and compositors. I wish to express my sense of this, and to thank Messrs. Billing, their proof-readers and their compositors for what they have done to accomplish a difficult and tiresome task. My thanks are indeed due and are offered to Messrs. Drugelin for the patience and skill with which they have dealt with Persian copy from my untrained hand.

I now venture to express, in Mr. E. Granville Browne's words, the thought which haunts all who make a book, and to beg my critics to listen to their plea :

'*Now, seeing that to fail and fall is the fate of all, and to claim exemption from the lot of humanity a proof of pride and vanity, and somewhat of mercy our common need ; therefore let such as read, and errors detect, either ignore or neglect, or correct and conceal them, rather than revile and reveal them.*'

TABLE OF CONTENTS.

LIST OF PLATES.

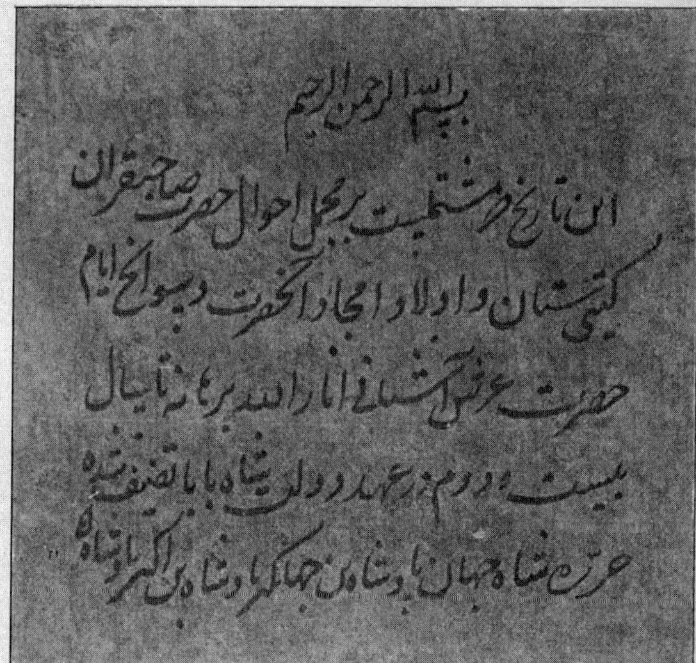
بسم الله الرحمن الرحیم
این تاریخ که مشتمل است بر مجمل احوال حضرت صاحبقران
گیتی ستان و اولاد و امجاد آنحضرت و سوانح ایام
حضرت عرش آشیانی انار الله برهانه تا سال
بیست و دوم از عهد دولت شاه بابا تصنیف شده
حرره شاه جهان پادشاه بن جهانگیر پادشاه بن اکبر پادشاه

AUTOGRAPH NOTE OF SHĀH-JAHĀN.

[*To face p.* xiii.

NOTE ON THE ILLUSTRATIONS.

The page of the MS. selected for reproduction in Plate I. contains several words which I have found difficult, and concerning which explanation will be welcomed. It and Plate No. II. make silent protest against printing, and plead that the sun best shows the grace and beauty of manuscript.

With the exception of the first illustration, all the plates are photographic reproductions from a splendidly illustrated Persian MS., entitled the *Tārīkh-i-khāndān-i-tīmūriya*, which is the choicest volume in the library with which Maulvī Khūda-baksh *Khān Bahādur* has enriched the city of Patna.[1]

The Emperor Shāh-jahān appears to have paid R.8,000 for the illustrations in the volume. The MS. itself is of older date, and Mr. Beveridge has found in it some portions, at least, of the *Tārīkh-i-alfī*. The title-page is wanting.

The volume has a further distinction, inasmuch as it bears on an opening page an autograph note of Shāh-jahān. This is reproduced (as Plate No. II.) on the opposite page, and by its charm and grace is worthy of that royal fount of creative beauty.

The pictures of Bābar's devotion of himself and the triad connected with the birth of Akbar are admirable; they repay close attention and enlargement under a glass.

---

[1] A copy of the Maulvī's catalogue (published while he was Chief Justice in Hydarābād) is in the British Museum, and may be consulted for some details of the book. (p. 110) Mr. Beveridge also gives some particulars about it in the *R.A.S. Journal*, January, 1901, p. 81.

I am indebted for these pictures, first to Mr. Beveridge who, when he examined this *Tārīkh* in 1899, thought of my book, and, secondly, to Mr. Bourdillon, the then Commissioner of Patna, who most kindly photographed them for us.

TRANSLATION OF SHĀH-JAHĀN'S NOTE.

IN THE NAME OF GOD, THE MERCIFUL, THE COMPASSIONATE.

This history, which contains an abridgment of the affairs of his Majesty, *Ṣāḥib-qirān Gītī-sitānī* (Tīmūr), and of his glorious descendants, and of the events of the days of *'Arsh-āshyānī* (Akbar)—May God make clear his proof!—down to the twenty-second year of his reign, was written in the time of Shāh Bābā (Akbar).

Signed: Shāh-jahān Pādshāh, son of Jahāngīr Pādshāh, son of Akbar Pādshāh.

INTRODUCTION.

PART I.

BIOGRAPHICAL ACCOUNT OF THE PRINCESS AND HER FAMILY.[1]

SECTION I.—UNDER BĀBAR.

GUL-BADAN BEGAM (Princess Rose-body) was a daughter of Z̤ahru-d-dīn Muḥammad Bābar, in whom were united the lines of highest Central Asian aristocracy—namely, that of Tīmūr the Tūrk, through his son Mīrān-shāh ; and that of Chingīz the Mughal, through his son Chaghatāi. He was born on February 14th, 1483, and succeeded to his father's principality of Farghāna when under twelve. He spent ten years of early youth in trying to save his small domain from the clutch of kinsmen, but, being forced to abandon the task, went southwards in 1504 to Afghānistān, where he captured Kābul from its Arghūn usurpers.

Princess Gul-badan was born somewhere about 1523 and when her father had been lord in Kābul for nineteen years ; he was master also in Kunduz and Badakhshān ; had held Bajaur and Swat since 1519, and Qandahār for a year. During ten of those nineteen years he had been styled *pādshāh*, in token of headship of the house of Tīmūr and of

[1] In selecting from the mass of material which, without discursiveness, might have been included under the above heading, only that has been used which concerns the begam or is in touch with her interests and sympathies.

This Introduction corrects several errors which occur in an article on the life and writings of the begam, and which was published by me in the *Calcutta Review*, April, 1898.

his independent sovereignty. To translate *pādshāh*, however, as is often done, by the word *emperor* would give a wrong impression of Bābar's status amongst rulers at this height of his rising fortunes. Nevertheless, Gul-badan was born the child of a strong and stable chief, and of one who was better followed in war than his nominal domains would allow, because his army was drawn for the most part from tribes not under his government, and was not territorial and of Kābul but personal and inherited.

Bābar says that he cherished the desire to conquer beyond the Indus for nineteen years. At the date of Gul-badan's birth he was engaged in the attempt, and succeeded when she was about two and a half years old. He then became the first Tūrkī sovereign in Hindūstān, and the founder of its miscalled Mughal dynasty.

If the princess had first seen light in London instead of in Kābul, she would have had Henry VIII for king, and the slumbers of her birth-year might have been troubled as men marched forth at Wolsey's will to fight and lose in France. Her personal vicissitudes were the greater that she was a Tīmūrid and Tūrk. She spent her childhood under her father's rule in Kābul and Hindūstān; her girlhood and young wifehood shared the fall and exile of Humāyūn; and her maturity and failing years slipped past under the protection of Akbar.

Her mother was Dil-dār Begam—the Heart-holding Princess—of whose descent, it is noticeable to observe, neither her husband nor her daughter gives any information. This peculiarity of omission she shares with Māham, the wife of Bābar's affection and the mother of his heir; and with Gul-rukh, the mother of Kāmrān and 'Askarī. All three ladies are spoken of by our begam with the style befitting the wives of a king; all were mothers of children, and for this reason, if for no other, it seems natural that something should be said of their birth. Bābar frequently mentions Māham, and calls her by this name *tout court*. Dil-dār's name occurs in the Tūrkī version of the Memoirs, but not in the Persian, and she is there styled *āghācha*—

i.e., a lady, but not a begam, by birth. Gul-rukh is, I believe, never named by Bābar. This silence does not necessarily imply low birth. It may be an omission of the contemporarily obvious; and also it may indicate that no one of the three women was of royal birth, although all seem to have been of good family.

Three Tīmūrids had been Bābar's wives in childhood and youth. These were: 'Āyisha, who left him before 1504 and who was betrothed to him when he was five; Zainab, who died in 1506 or 1507; and Ma'sūma, whom he married in 1507 and who died at the birth of her first child. Māham was married in Khurāsān, and therefore in 1506; Dil-dār and Gul-rukh probably considerably later, and after the three royal ladies had passed away from the household. The next recorded marriage of Bābar is one of 1519, when a Yusufzāi chief brought him his daughter, Bībī Mubārika, as the seal of submission. She had no children, and was an altogether charming person in the eyes of those who have written of her.

To return now to Dil-dār. She bore five children, three girls and two boys. The eldest was born in an absence of Bābar from Kābul and in Khost. This fixes her birth as occurring somewhere between 1511 and 1515. She was Gul-rang (Rose-hued), named like her sisters from the rose; then came Gul-chihra (Rose-cheeked); and then Abū'n-nāṣir Muḥammad, the Hindāl of history, who was born in 1519; next was Gul-badan (Rose-body); and last a boy, whom his sister calls Alwar, a word which looks like a sobriquet drawn from the Indian town. He died after the migration of the household to Āgra, and in 1529.

Princess Gul-badan was born some two years before Bābar set out on his last expedition across the Indus, so her baby eyes may have seen his troops leave Kābul in November, 1525, for the rallying-place at Jacob's Village (*Dih-i-ya'qūb*). It is not mere word-painting to picture her as looking down from the citadel at what went on below, for she tells of later watching from this view-point which would give the farewell glimpse of the departing army, and, as weeks and years rolled on, the first sight of many a speck on the eastern road which took form as loin-girt runner or mounted courier.

We who live upon the wire, need a kindled imagination to realize what it was to those left behind, to have their men-folk go to India. With us, fancy is checked by maps and books, and has not often to dwell on the unknown and inconceivable. To them, what was not a blank was probably a fear. Distance could have no terrors for them, because they were mostly, by tribe and breeding, ingrain nomads; many of them had come from the far north and thought the great mountains or the desert sands the desirable setting for life. Such experience, however, would not help to understand the place of the Hindūs, with its heats, its rains, strange beasts, and hated and dreaded pagans.

It is not easy to say wherein lies the pleasure of animating the silhouettes which are all that names, without detail of character, bring down from the past. Perhaps its roots run too deep and close to what is dear and hidden in the heart, for them to make way readily to the surface in speech. But it is an undoubted pleasure, and it is what makes it agreeable to linger with these women in Kābul in those hours when our common human nature allows their thoughts and feelings to be clear to us. Sometimes their surroundings are too unfamiliar for us to understand what sentiments they would awaken, but this is not so when there is news of marches, fighting, defeat, or victory. Then the silhouettes round, and breathe, and weep or smile.

Bābar left few fighting men in Kābul, but there remained a great company of women and children, all under the nominal command and charge of Prince Kāmrān, who was himself a child. His exact age I am not able to set down, for Bābar does not chronicle his birth, an omission which appears due to its falling in one of the gaps of the Memoirs. Bābar left the city on November 17th, and was joined on December 3rd by Humāyūn at the Garden of Fidelity (*Bāgh-i-wafā*). He had to wait for the boy, and was much displeased, and reprimanded him severely.

Humāyūn was then seventeen years old, and since 1520 had been governor of Badakhshān. He had now brought over his army to reinforce his father, and it may well be that Māham had something to do with his delayed march from Kābul. She could have seen him only at long intervals since she had accompanied Bābar, in 1520, to console and settle her child of twelve in his distant and undesired post of authority.

Shortly after the army had gone eastwards, disquieting news must have reached Kābul, for three times before the middle of December, 1525, Bābar was alarmingly ill. What he records of drinking and drug-eating may explain this; he thought his illness a chastisement, and set himself to repent of sins which were bred of good-fellowship and by forgetfulness in gay company; but his conflict with them was without victory. He referred his punishment to another cause than these grosser acts, and came to regard the composition of satirical verses as a grave fault. His reflections on the point place him near higher moralists, for he says it was sad a tongue which could repeat sublime words, should occupy itself with meaner and despicable fancies. 'Oh, my Creator! I have tyrannized over my soul, and if Thou art not bountiful to me, of a truth I shall be numbered amongst the accursed.' These are some of the thoughts of Bābar which lift our eyes above what is antipathetic in him, and explain why he wins the respect and affection of all who take trouble to know him.

Not long after January 8th, 1526, a messenger would reach Kābul who took more than news, for Bābar had found manuscripts in the captured fort of Milwat, and now sent some for Kāmrān, while he gave others to Humāyūn. They were valuable, but not so much so as he had hoped, and many were theological. This and other records about books remind one that they were few and precious in those days. How many that we now rank amongst the best of the sixteenth century had not yet been written! There was no *Tārīkh-i-rashīdī*, and the very stuff of the *Tūzūk* was in the living and making.

On February 26th Humāyūn created news which would be as welcome to Māham as it was to Bābar, for he was successful in his first expedition on active service. This occurred at Ḥiṣār-firoza, and the town and district were given to him with a sum of money. News of the victory was despatched to Kābul from Shāhābād; and immediately after Bābar's record of this in the Memoirs, there occurs a passage of varied interest, although it seems to European ears a somewhat strange commemoration of a detail of toilette: 'At this same station and this same day the razor or scissors were first applied to Humāyūn's beard.' Bābar made an entry in June, 1504, of the same act accomplished for himself. It was one which Tūrks celebrated by festivity. The entry quoted above is made as though by Bābar, but it is followed by an explanation that it is inserted by Humāyūn in pious imitation of his father's own. Humāyūn did this in 1553-4, shortly before he set out to recover his father's lost domains in Hindūstān. The date is fixed by his statement that he made the interpolation when he was forty-six.[1]

Humāyūn's little victory would be dwarfed by the next news of the royal army, for April 12th, 1526, brought the battle of Pānīpat and the overthrow of Ibrāhīm *Lodī Afghān*, the Emperor of Hindūstān. The swiftest of runners would carry these tidings to Kābul in something under a month. On May 11th Bābar distributed the treasures of five kings, and left himself so little that he was jestingly dubbed beggar (*qalandar*). He forgot no one, but sent gifts far and wide to kinsmen and friends, and to shrines both in

---

[1] There is a point of great interest about this note of Humāyūn and Mr. Erskine's translation of it. I venture to refer readers who take interest in the Memoirs, as a book, to my article on the Tūrkī text of the Memoirs (*Royal Asiatic Society's Journal*, July, 1899), which contains information gathered from some sources which were not at Mr. Erskine's disposition, and which suggest that another reading is allowable to the concluding words (not mentioned in this text) of Humāyūn's interpolation.

Arabia and 'Irāq. Kābul was specially remembered and a small coin sent for every soul within it. Gul-badan tells what was given to the ladies, beginning with the great begams, the aunts of frequent mention. It was certainly a wonderful day when the curiosities and splendid things of Hind were unpacked for their inspection, and very welcome, too, would be the amīr who escorted the precious caravan. He was Bābar's friend, Khwāja Kilān, who had extorted a most unwilling leave from India on the ground that his constitution was not suited to the climate of that country, a delicate assumption of blame to his own defects which it is to be hoped he conveyed to the ladies as a reassurance. After the gay social fashion of the time, no doubt he helped the ladies to run day into night in the tale-telling they loved. It appears probable that there was no such complete seclusion of Tūrkī women from the outside world as came to be the rule in Hindūstān. The ladies may have veiled themselves, but I think they received visitors more freely, and more in accordance with the active life of much-travelling peoples, than is the case in Hindū or Moslim houses in India at the present day.[1]

The little Gul-badan will have had her present with the rest, and probably, like some others, it was chosen by her father specially for her. He sent a list with the gifts so that each person might receive what he had settled upon. This he is said to have done both in allotting the jewels and the dancing-girls, the latter of whom are mentioned as sent to the great begams. Their novel style of dancing ranks them amongst the 'curiosities of Hind,' but nothing is said about their views of presentation to foreign ladies in Kābul. Certainly Gul-badan will have seen them dance, and she will also have enjoyed the joke played off by Bābar from Āgra on an old dependent called 'Asas (night-guard).

---

[1] I remember a Muḥammadan gentleman astonishing me by a story of a Musalmānī child who died of the shock to her propriety when she was taken out from the *ḥaram*. He was an 'English-educated' man, and the child was his sister.

This and all the begam's stories are left for her to tell, as she does later in this volume.

There came with the gifts an injunction which calls out the remark, that at all crises Bābar gave expression to religious feeling and performed due devotional ceremonies. He had desired Khwāja Kilān to arrange for the ladies to go out of the city to the Garden of the Audience-hall, so that they might there make the prostration of thanks for the success of his arms. They were to go in state, and to remain some days. He must have sighed as he planned an excursion so much to his liking and in which he could not share. The act of thanksgiving would be done under a summer heaven, in an enchanting June garden, of which the snowy hills were the distant girdle. Our princess will have gone out with the rest, and with theirs her small figure, bravely attired, will have bowed forehead to the earth in thanks to the Giver of Victory. Tender thoughts will have travelled to the absent, and especially to him who loved his Kābul as Bābar did.

It is remarkable in him that, longing to return home as he did, he should have had endurance to remain and fight on in Hindūstān. His constitution was assuredly not suited to its climate. His men hated it; his closest friend had left it; Humāyūn and other intimates were soon to follow the khwāja on leave; but he resisted all influences, even when he had become so homesick that he wept at sight of fruit from Kābul. Only love of action, desire to be great, and capacity for greatness, could have held and upheld him at his self-chosen post. It cannot be called a small matter on which the history of hundreds of years turns, and yet it was but the innate quality of one man, and that man very human. Bābar stood fast, and India had Akbar and his splendid followers and all the galaxy of their creations in sandstone and marble.

When Gul-badan was about two years old, and therefore shortly before her father left Kābul, she was adopted by Māham Begam to rear and educate. Māham was the chief lady of the royal household and mother of Bābar's eldest son; she was supreme, and had well-defined rights over other inmates. Perhaps this position justified her in taking from Dil-dār two of her children, Hindāl and Gul-badan, as she did in 1519 and 1525. Before 1519 Māham had lost four children younger than Humāyūn; they were three girls and a boy, and all died in infancy. So it may have been heart-hunger that led to the adoptions she made, or they might be the outcome of affection for Bābar (it is said she was to him what 'Āyisha was to Muḥammad), which determined her, if she could not rear her children for him, at least to give him his children with the stamp of her love upon them. In some cases which are mentioned by Bābar, adoptions were made by a childless wife of high degree from a slave or servant, but no such reason seems behind those from Dil-dār. She is spoken of in terms which preclude the supposition that (as Ḥaidar puts it in another place,) she was outside the circle of distinction.

The story of Hindāl's adoption is briefly this: In 1519 Bābar was away from Kābul on the expedition which gave him Bajaur and Swat, and which brought into the royal household Bībī Mubārika *Yusufzāi*. On January 25th he received a letter from Māham, who was in Kābul, about a topic which had been discussed earlier between them—namely, the adoption by her of a child of which Dil-dār expected the birth. Now she repeated her wishes and, moreover, asked Bābar to take the fates and declare whether it would be a boy or girl. Whether he performed the divination rite himself, or had it done by some of the women who were in camp with the army, (he speaks of it as believed in by women,) it was done, and the result was announced to Māham as promising a boy. The rite is simple: Two pieces of paper are inscribed, one with a boy's name and one with a girl's, and are enwrapped in clay and set in water. The name first disclosed, as the clay opens out in the moisture, reveals the secret. On the 26th Bābar wrote, giving over the child to Māham and communicating the prophecy. On March 4th a boy was born, to whom was given the name of Abū'n-nāṣir with the sobriquet of Hindāl by which he is known in history and which is perhaps to be read as meaning 'of the dynasty of Hind.'[1] Three days after birth he was taken, whether she would or no, from Dil-dār to be made over to Māham.

It is clear that Dil-dār objected; and although the separation could not have been so complete where the real and adoptive mothers are part of one household as it is under monogamous custom, it was certainly hard to lose her firstborn son in this way. She had still her two elder girls. Gul-badan was born four years later and removed from her care at the age of two, by which date, it may be, she had her son Alwar. In after-years Dil-dār, as a widow, lived with Hindāl, and she had back Gul-badan while the latter was still a young and unmarried girl.

Bābar was separated from his family for over three years after he left Kābul in 1525. The tedium of waiting for news or for his return was broken for the ladies by several interesting home events, and by several items of Indian news which must have stirred the whole community in Kābul. On August 2nd, 1526, Māham gave birth to a son who was named Fārūq, but he too died in babyhood and his father never saw him. In December, 1526, there occurred to Bābar what must have roused anger and dread in all Kābul, for he was poisoned by the mother of Ibrāhīm

---

[1] The account of the adoption of Hindāl is given in much abbreviated form both by the Persian and English versions of the Memoirs. The latter has, indeed, an error which is not borne out by the Persian; *i.e.*, it states that several children had been born in 1519. The correct statement is that several had been borne by Māham younger than Humāyūn. The Tūrkī text of Kehr and Ilminsky has a longer account, with curious details which may have been omitted on revision of the Memoirs by Bābar himself in later copies, or may have been omitted by the Persian translator. The former is the more probable suggestion, because if the full passage had occurred in the Elphinstone Tūrkī text used by Leyden and Erskine, it could not have escaped both these careful workers. (This MS. is unfortunately not forthcoming for consultation.) The point is of interest as bearing on the history of the Tūrkī texts. It makes for the opinion that Kehr's source was one of the early copies of the Memoirs, since the passage is one which from its domestic nature would be less likely to be added to, than omitted from a revised version.

Lodī Afghān. How Bābar conveyed the news of this to his people at home can be seen, because he has inserted the letter he wrote to allay anxiety, as soon as recovered strength permitted. Gul-badan has given the main points of the crime. She observes that Bābar had called the 'ill-fated demon,' mother, and had shown her kindness, a sectional view which leaves out the Afghān mourner, Buw'ā Begam, whose son had been defeated and killed, his dynasty overthrown, and herself pitied by the man on whom she tried to avenge herself. Her fate is worth commemorating. She was first put under contribution—*i.e.*, made over for the exploitation of her fortune to two of Bābar's officers—and then placed in the custody of a trusty man for conveyance to Kābul. Perhaps she dreaded her reception there, for she contrived to elude her guards in crossing the Indus, threw herself into the water, and was drowned.

The letter above-mentioned is full of what one likes in Bābar. He quotes, 'Whoever comes to the gates of death knows the value of life,' and says, with thanks to Heaven, that he did not know before how sweet a thing life is. Here, too, he shows that he felt the tie which bound him to the Power in whose hands are the issues of life and death. He, his daughter, and his cousin and literary compeer, Ḥaidar Mīrzā *Dughlāt*, frequently express religious sentiment; and here Bābar exhibits the human graces of kind thought and solicitude to lessen the anxieties of his distant household and people. He forced himself to live again, in words, the horrible experiences of which he wrote while still in retirement, and four days[1] only after their occurrence.

---

[1] This letter bears date December 26th, 1526, and thus provides a detail which is of use when considering the probable time of composition of the Memoirs. Was a copy of the letter kept? Did the original return from Kābul? The impression given by points of evidence is that the book was written down in present form later than the date of this letter. There are in the beginning of it statements which refer its composition or revised version to 1528. The same point is raised by letters of 1529 to Humāyūn and Khwāja Kilān, the date of which may indicate progress in the composition.

All the letters share another ground of interest, which is that, having

Three months later Kābul had news of an uplifting victory, inasmuch as it had been won from men of alien faith, whose overthrow was a plenary religious duty to the Moslim. It was fought on March 13th, 1527, against Hindū Rājpūts under Rānā Sangā, and at Khānwa, on the skirts of the yet uncrowned hill of Sīkrī. It was preluded by dread amongst the Musalmāns, and by solemn acts which should make them more worthy to be the tools of Heaven and to enforce the stern belief that in battle with the pagan there was vengeance of the cause of God. Men declared repentance for sin and took oaths of abstinence; gold and silver drinking-vessels, probably of Persian handicraft and artistic beauty, were broken up and given to the poor; wine was poured out upon the ground, and some was salted into vinegar. Where the libation of penitence was offered, the earth was dedicated to the uses of an almshouse with chambered well. So strengthened, the Musalmāns went into the fight and made great slaughter of valiant foes.

The victory was followed by change in the personnel of Bābar's army, which had long been wearying for home and murmuring against Hindūstān. This was especially so amongst Humāyūn's Badakhshīs, who were accustomed to short service of one or two months, and it was now almost sixteen since they had left even Kābul. Only promise of immediate leave to follow had induced some men to stay for this one fight, and they had been told that when it was over, all who desired it should have freedom to go. Many amīrs had given 'stupid and unformed opinions' against remaining in Hindūstān at all, and down to the humblest followers these views had found acceptance. As has been said, nothing would persuade Bābar's closest friend to stay with him, although before his final decision

---

been composed in Tūrkī, they have been preserved in Tūrkī in the Persian translation. This may be an act of pious deference. The Memoirs were certainly altogether in Tūrkī, but they were not addressed to individuals as were the letters. It is a fact of interest, and open to pleasant interpretation.

was acted on, his master had called a council, and had expressed himself with directness and vigour.

'I told them that empire and conquest could not exist without the material and means of war; that royalty and nobility could not exist without subjects and dependent provinces; that by the labour of many years, after undergoing great hardships, measuring many a toilsome journey, and raising various armies—after exposing myself and my troops to circumstances of great danger, to battle and bloodshed, by the Divine favour I had routed my formidable enemy (Ibrāhīm), and achieved the conquest of numerous provinces and kingdoms which we at present held. And now, what force compels, what hardship obliges us, without visible cause, after having worn out our life in accomplishing the desired achievement, to abandon and fly from our conquests, and to retreat to Kābul with every symptom of disappointment and discomfiture? Let anyone who calls himself my friend never henceforward make such a proposal; but if there is any among you who cannot bring himself to stay, or to give up his purpose of return, let him depart. Having made this fair and reasonable proposal, the discontented were of necessity compelled, however unwillingly, to renounce their seditious purpose.'

After the Rājpūt defeat the time came for the promised leave, but there is no mention in the Memoirs of a general exodus. Humāyūn went with his Badakhshīs, and also, as he seemed 'uncomfortable,' Mahdī[1] Khwāja, Khānzāda's husband. He, but not only he, had been through one hot season in the plains and another was approaching,—a discomposing fact, and one to wing the fancy and the feet to Kābul. He, however, left his son Ja'far in his government of Etāwa, and returned to India himself in 1528.

Humāyūn said farewell on April 16th, 1527, and betook himself to Dihlī, where he broke open the treasury and

---

[1] There are difficulties in tracing the descent of this man, which are discussed in the Appendix. *Cf.* Index, *s.n.* Muḥammad Mahdī.

stole its contents. If he had needed money to pay his men, his act might have taken different colour and have been leniently described; but he had had lavish gifts in money and kind from Bābar, and had been allowed to keep the great diamond which the Rānī of Guāliār had given him as the price of family honour and which, there is good ground to believe, is the *Koh-i-nūr*. Treated as he had been, his act was a crime, and base and mean. Perhaps it may be set to the credit of the older Humāyūn that the record of his theft has survived 1553-4 and his then perusal and annotation of his father's Memoirs. By that time he had suffered many painful consequences of his own acts, and may have concurred with his father's judgment on his younger self. Bābar was extremely hurt by his unexpected conduct and reproached him severely. There was enough now known of Humāyūn's character to awaken doubt of his fitness to rule, and to need all his father's great affection to veil and forgive. From Dihlī he returned to Badakshān, and is next heard of in the autumn of 1528, when he announced the birth of his first-born son, Al-amān. Al-amān was the child of that Bega (*Ḥājī*) Begam of whom the histories all speak, when in 1539 she is captured by Shīr Shāh at Chausa.

Together with the news of Al-amān's birth came that of a marriage of Kāmrān with a daughter of Sulṭān ʿAlī *Begchik*. Bābar sent congratulatory gifts to both sons in response; and he has included his covering letter to Humāyūn in his text. It is frank, fault-finding, and affectionate. It objects to the name given to the child; it urges action: 'The world is his who exerts himself'; it objects to Humāyūn's complaints of the remoteness of Badakhshān, and tells him that no bondage is like the bondage of kings, and that it ill becomes him to complain. It attacks Humāyūn's spelling and composition, and ends this topic with words good to quote: 'You certainly do not excel in letter-writing; and you fail chiefly because you have too great a desire to show off your acquirements. For the future, write unaffectedly, clearly, and in plain words, which will give less trouble to writer and reader.' Some remarks about Kāmrān have a coming interest; Bābar faintly praises him as a worthy and correct young man, and enjoins favour for him, without a hint of suspicion that it could ever be in Kāmrān's power to show favour to Humāyūn. Humāyūn is also desired to make friends with Khwāja Kilān and with Sulṭān Wais of Kūlāb. He failed with the khwāja, who on Bābar's death joined the worthy and correct Kāmrān. Humāyūn kept on better terms with Sulṭān Wais (*Qibchāq Mughal*), and at a later date owed much to his daughter, the inimitable Ḥaram (Khurram), who stands up in history bold, capable, haughty, and altogether strongly outlined.

Something must now be set down about Bābar's third adult son, who was a younger full-brother of Kāmrān and is known in history by his sobriquet of 'Askarī, which indicates a camp as his birthplace. Neither his birth nor Kāmrān's is mentioned in the Memoirs, as we now have them,—an omission which other sources allow to be explained by their falling in one of the gaps of the book. 'Askarī was born in 1516 (922H.), and during a period of storm and of camp life. His name first occurs in the Memoirs as having presents sent to him after the battle of Pānīpat, when he is classed with Hindāl, as suited their ages of nine and seven, and they received various gifts, and not, like their two seniors, sums of money. In 1528 he was in Multān, but there is no entry of an appointment, perhaps because it would fall in the gap which extends from April 2nd to September 18th. On the latter day he was received, in home fashion, by his father in his private apartments at Āgra, and then, having spent till December 2nd with him, he was furnished with munitions of war for a campaign in the eastern districts. Special injunctions were given to the officers to consult with him as to the conduct of affairs. The interest of these details is their relation to the boy of twelve. Few years were needed in those days to support military command. Humāyūn had gone to Badakhshān at eleven; Bābar had been a fighting king at twelve. Boy chiefs were common when fathers were so apt to die by violent means; so were baby figure-heads of armies such as that few-monthed Persian baby who (like an angel's semblance on an ancient battle-ship) led his father's army for Humāyūn's help in 1544.

On December 12th other signs of dignity were bestowed on the boy 'Askarī: not only a jewelled dagger, a belt, and royal dress of honour, but the insignia of high command, the standard, horse-tail, and kettle-drums; excellent horses, ten elephants, mules and camels, the equipage of a royal camp, and leave to hold a princely court and sit at the head of a hall of state. The small boy's mind is clear to us about the horses, for where is the child of twelve whom they would not delight? But what was in it about the elephants? and how did he look when he inspected their bulky line?

He bade farewell to his father on the 21st,—the Emperor being in his bath, a statement which exhales the East,—and after this, though there are many details of his campaigning, nothing of living interest is set down in the Memoirs about him. In the future he was Kāmrān's shadow, and displayed a loyalty to mother-blood which was natural under the difficulty of being loyal to Humāyūn, but which made him a Tīmūrid foe to his house, who initiated nothing and walked always in the bad path marked out for him by the 'worthy and correct' Kāmrān.

Coming back from this excursion into the future, to the simple topic of Bābar's presents to his children, there can be mentioned a set which is quite delightful in its careful choice and appropriateness. It was sent to Kābul in 1528 for Hindāl, and consisted of a jewelled inkstand, a stool inlaid with mother-of-pearl, a short robe of Bābar's own, and an alphabet. What could be better for the royal schoolboy of ten?

In 1528 an order was issued which brought about an event of extreme importance to the ladies in Kābul,—namely, that they should migrate to Hindūstān. There was delay in the execution of the royal command; and having regard to the number of ladies, the difference of opinion as to the advisability of going at all, discussion as to the details of the journey, and also remembering that (as the facts about the migration come out in the Memoirs,) there would be many who thought their family interest might be better served by remaining in Kābul, it is not remarkable that there was delay in starting the cavalcade.

The migration was amply dictated to many of the party by Bābar's wish to see his own people again; but it is clear that the enforced *levée en masse* of the ladies was a result of considerations of policy and peace. The city was full of women who, by birth or marriage, were attached to various branches of the Tīmūrids, and there was conflict of aims and palpable friction. It may well be that Kāmrān's government provoked unrest, because he was the son of a mother of less birth than were very many of the resident begams of Kābul.

The Emperor was put in full possession of the state of affairs by a letter from Khwāja Kilān which reached him in camp on February 6th, 1528, and which was brought by a servant who, in addition to the written words, gave him all the news of Kābul by word of mouth. Bābar replied to the khwāja on February 11th by that letter which those who know the time and writer rank amongst the truly interesting epistles of the world. The tenor of the khwāja's own is clear from it, and in part reply the Emperor writes:

'You take notice of the unsettled state of Kābul. I have considered the matter very attentively and with the best of my judgment, and have made up my mind that in a country where there are seven or eight chiefs, nothing regular or settled is to be looked for. I have therefore sent for my sisters and the ladies of my family into Hindūstān, and, having resolved on making Kābul and all the neighbouring countries and districts part of the imperial domain, I have written fully on the subject to Humāyūn and Kāmrān. . . . Immediately on receiving this letter you will, without loss of time, attend my sisters and the ladies of my family as far as the Nīl-āb (Indus); so that, whatever impediments there may be to their leaving Kābul, they must, at all events, start out within a week after this arrives; for as a detachment has left Hindūstān and is waiting for them, any delay will expose it to difficulty, and the country, too, will suffer.'

Who were these seven or eight chiefs in Kābul? Not men! The fighting chiefs were almost all in India; even Mahdī had rejoined the army before the date of this letter. Bābar's word 'sisters' is a guiding light, and it does not altogether exclude the influence of the men who, though in Hindūstān, were in touch with Kābul and its friction and intrigues. First of sisters was Khānzāda, who had certainly a holding for her support; and who had influence of birth and personal, as having sacrificed herself in her earlier marriage to secure Bābar's safety. She was now the wife of a man, Mahdī Khwāja, who, if the story told of him by the author of the *Ṭabaqāt* is true even in gist, was such as to suggest him as a possible successor of Bābar to the powerful and sensible Khalīfa. There was, since her husband was with Bābar and all great ladies had been left in Kābul, Shahr-bānū, Khānzāda's half-sister, wife of Khalīfa's brother, Junaid *Barlās*, and mother of a son. There was also, it is probable, another of 'Umar Shaikh's daughters, Yādgār.[1]

Besides Bābar's sisters *de facto*, there were others of courtesy. Such was Sulaimān's mother, whose anxieties for his future were, however, about to find happy end by his reinstatement in 1530 in his hereditary government of Badakhshān. There were the families of three men of Tīmūrid birth, grandsons of Sulṭān Ḥusain Mīrzā *Bāyqrā*,

[1] Of the two others who are the complement in girls of his family, it is safe to say that they were absent. Mihr-bānū was the apparently contented wife of an Uzbeg Sulṭān, and Ruqaiya, who, like Mihr-bānū, had been spoil of battle and an Uzbeg wife, was recently dead. Bābar says she died just when he was making the entries about her parentage at the beginning of the Memoirs. This can hardly have been before 1528, because an appointment mentioned on the same page is recorded on its occurrence as made in 1528.

all of whom were in India, and all of whom were men of high pretension. They were,—Muḥammad Sulṭān Mīrzā, the arch-rebel of the future; Qāsim Ḥusain Sulṭān Mīrzā, son of an Uzbeg father; and Muḥammad-zāman Mīrzā, son of Ḥusain's son, Badīʿu-z-zāman. There were in Kābul the people of Yādgār-nāṣir also, Bābar's half-nephew. These instances will suffice to show the reality of the elements of unrest which conflicting family interests and jealousies might and did foment in Kābul; they do not include the many others furnished by Bābar's personal circle, and by his numerous and influential aunts.

Two Tīmūrid ladies, Fakhr-jahān and Khadīja, both paternal aunts of the Emperor, had gone to Hindūstān so early as November, 1527. With whom they went or why they went is not recorded. The first was the wife of a Tīrmīzī sayyid, member of a religious family with which royal alliance was frequent, and she would find relations of her husband in the army. The second, Khadīja, has no man mentioned as her husband, an omission by Bābar and Gul-badan which surprises, and which the chance word of another writer may easily fill up. Perhaps these aunts joined their nephew in response to his invitation of April, 1526, that kinsfolk and friends would come and see prosperity with him. They brought their children, and were met outside the city by Bābar on November 23rd, and by him conducted in a lucky hour to their assigned palace[1] in Āgra.

Fakhr-jahān and Khadīja stayed eleven months, and were bidden good-bye before their return journey to Kābul on September 20th, 1528. After all, Khadīja did not go, having affairs of her own to detain her, and this delay allowed the Emperor to pay her another of the Friday calls which he habitually made, during the time of his

---

[1] Readers who are interested in the Tūrkī and Persian texts of the Memoirs, will like to have attention drawn to the fact of there being a record of this episode in one of the fragments attached to Kehr's MS., and that this varies in detail from his text and from the Persian source of the Memoirs.

occupation of Hindūstān, on his elder kinswomen. On the 17th three sisters of Fakhr-jahān and Khadīja arrived in the suburbs and were welcomed. From all these Bābar could hear the news and gossip of Kābul, and thus add to the impressions which led to his order for the begams to join him in India.

Apropos of the aunts of frequent mention, it may be said that both Bābar and Ḥaidar convey the opinion that deference to elder women was a permanent trait of their age and set. Comings and goings of aunts are set down; houses and incomes provided; advice is sought; troubles are carried to them for sympathy; they are ambassadors of peace; their nephews vie with one another as to who shall entertain them; in short, both the *Tūzūk* and the *Tārīkh* indicate distinct deference to women of an elder generation.

A good deal about the exodus of the ladies can be gleaned from Bābar and from our princess, who now comes on the scene in her small person of five or six. The order for it was given at latest in 1528; this is clear from the royal letter to the khwāja and from the fact that Māham started in January, 1529. Bābar heard on March 22nd that all had really left Kābul, which news, taken with the arrival of the main cavalcade three months after her, suggests that Māham started first and travelled quickly, as being of a small company, and that the rest set off in detachments, as they and their transport were ready. The whole party would get off between January 21st and the end of February; this can be surmised, because the letter of March 22nd would be about a month in reaching Bābar. Most of the journey would be made by horse-litter, and some perhaps by palki with bearers. Men frequently dropped down the Kābul River on rafts, being thus able to do in twelve hours what ten marches covered; but one cannot suppose the ladies would make this adventurous journey, which was attended by risk even when people did not fall off the raft after potations, as some of Bābar's companions had done. Probably the road taken was that by But-khāk (Dust of Idols) and Jagdalik, and by Jalālābād and the Khaibar; but there is no certainty, because there is no information.

Gul-badan travelled with Māham in advance of her sisters, and thus had experiences all her own and a reception by her father unalloyed by numbers. Her liveliness would while away the tedium of the five months' travel, and help to distract Māham's sad thoughts from the loss of Fārūq, her youngest born. Unfortunately, she sets down nothing about the journey until near its end. Letters between the Emperor and the travellers were frequent. One of the couriers, named Shīrak (Little Lion), who was despatched by him on March 5th, carried not only letters to Māham, but was entrusted with a copy of the Memoirs which had been made to send to Samarqand.[1]

On April 1st, and at Ghāzīpūr, Bābar heard that the ladies had been met at the Indus on February 19th by their military escort under his master-of-horse, and by this amīr convoyed to the Chanāb. This might fitly be told of Māham's party, for there are other records of covering the distance to the Indus in about a month.

On the 22nd a servant of Māham brought letters to Arrah from her whom he had left at the Garden of Purity (*Bāgh-i-ṣafā*), near Pind-dādan Khān, and this is the last such entry. Māham reached Agra on June 27th, and Bābar met her outside the city at midnight.

Gul-badan gives amusing particulars of her own arrival, all of which she shall be left to tell. She followed Māham into Āgra on the 28th, not having been allowed to travel with her through the previous night. Then she saw her father. Of him she can have kept only a dim memory, and it is likely enough she would stand in some awe of him and his deeds, but no word he has written suggests that a

[1] This is the earliest recorded copying of the Tūrkī text. This Samarqand MS. and its descendants (if any) may have been written up subsequently; but the points of this early transmission to Central Asia of a copy and the variations of the Russian texts from those found in India, are worth consideration. There is an unexplored MS. in Bukhārā of high reputation.

child needed to fear him, and she soon experienced 'happiness such that greater could not be imagined.' Happy child! and happy father, too! who recovered such a clever and attractive little daughter. It is not only her book that lets us know she had a lively mind, but the fact of its composition at an age when wits are apt to be rusted by domestic peace. Only a light that was strong in childhood would have burned so long to guide her unaccustomed pen after half a century of life, and only a youth of happy thoughts and quick perceptions have buoyed her, still gay and vivacious, across the worries and troubles of Humāyūn's time.

There were pleasant days after the coming to Āgra, when Bābar took Māham, and the child also, to see his works at Dholpūr and Sīkrī. He had always been a builder and a lover of a view, a maker of gardens and planter of trees. Much of the scenery of his new location displeased him; he thought the neighbourhood of Āgra 'ugly and detestable' and 'repulsive and disgusting,' words which do not now link well with that Āgra which he and his line have made the goal of the pilgrim of beauty. It is difficult to go back in fancy to the city without a Tāj, with no Sikundra near and with Sīkrī uncrowned.

Dholpūr and Sīkrī had much to show of work done by the orders of the Emperor,—'my royal father,' as Gulbadan generally calls him, using the home word *bābā* invariably. At Sīkrī, amongst other buildings, was that in which she says he used to sit and write his book, *i.e.*, the *Tūzūk*. There, too, the great battle which had been fought in 1527 will not have been ignored to ears so sympathetic as Māham's. Perhaps here the little girl first learnt dimly what it was to be a Ghāzī, and to fight on the side of Heaven. She says that when these excursions had been made, and three months after her own arrival had sped by, the begams, with Khānzāda as their chief, came within meeting distance of the capital, and that the Emperor went out to welcome them. There is nothing of this in the Memoirs, which are silent after the arrival of Māham as to the doings of the royal ladies. The reunion was soon to be clouded by anxieties and loss.

A brief return in the story of Humāyūn must be made here. In the summer of 1529 he heard in Badakhshān of his father's failing health, and, without asking leave, set off for India. He passed through Kābul, and there, to Kāmrān's surprise, met him, who had just come up from Ghaznī. The two conferred, and persuaded the ten-years-old Hindāl, who was under orders for Āgra, to take up the government of Badakhshān. Humāyūn then continued his march, and arrived in Āgra without announcement to his father.

He came to the presence just when, by a coincidence which Māham may have helped to bring about, his parents were talking of him. It would be natural for the mother, who cannot have been ignorant of her son's coming, to stir gentle thoughts of him and to warm his father's heart towards him before they met, and by this to break the shock of the unpermitted absence from duty.

Bābar was greatly angered by the desertion, which in truth placed Badakhshān in difficulty by withdrawing both troops and control. Its consequences were important, and caused him profound regret. To stand fast across the mountains and to push out the royal holdings beyond the Oxus from the vantage-ground of Badakhshān was a cherished dream, and one which he had taken steps through both Humāyūn and Kāmrān to realize. He wished Humāyūn to return to his post, but the latter, while saying he must go if ordered, was not willing to leave his people again. Bābar then asked Khalīfa to go, but this request was evaded, and there is much to arouse surmise that Khalīfa saw in it the act of someone who wished him absent from the scene of crisis now foreseen as near. In his objection to leave Āgra, affection for his old master would be a natural factor; another was his own supreme influence, the sequel of his character and of Bābar's recent failure in health; and springing from his power was, perhaps the dominant factor of his objection to leave,—a disposition to supplant Humāyūn in the succession by a ruler of less doubtful character.

The fate of Badakhshān was decided by its bestowal on its hereditary chief, Sulaimān Mīrzā, *Mīrān-shāhī*, now a boy of sixteen, while Humāyūn's youthful *locum tenens* was ordered to come to India. Humāyūn betook himself to the idle enjoyments of his *jāgīr* of Sambhal, and was there, in a few months, attacked by illness which threatened life and which led to the remarkable episode of Bābar's self-sacrifice to save him. The narrative of this stands in all the histories and need not be repeated, but for the sake of making our princess' details clear, it is as well to state what was the rite performed by Bābar.

There was and is in the East belief that if offering be made of the thing most precious to the suppliant, and if the offering be accepted, Heaven will give the life of a sick man in exchange. The rite observed is simple: first prayer of intercession is made; then the suppliant walks three times round the sick man's bed. Of Bābar's sincerity there is no doubt; in mind and heart he gave himself; he felt conviction that, after the circuits, he had borne away the illness. Humāyūn was restored and Bābar died,—a return from the gate of death and an entry there which might have occurred without Bābar's rite, but none the less was the self-sacrifice complete because he believed in its efficacy and was willing to die.

His health worsened rapidly after this and he made ready to go. Marriages were arranged for Gul-rang and Gul-chihra; the amīrs were addressed; Humāyūn was counselled and named to the succession. Bābar died on December 26th, 1530. 'Black fell the day,' says his daughter; 'we passed that ill-fated day each in a hidden corner.'

The question of Khalīfa's wish to supersede Humāyūn is of great interest. It is written of by Niẓāmu-d-dīn Aḥmad, in the *Ṭabaqāt*, who had the story he retails from his father, Muqīm, an old retainer of the Court. Abū'l-faẓl repeats the main statement, which is that Khalīfa had had thoughts of superseding Humāyūn by Muḥammad Mahdī Khwāja, the husband of Khānzāda Begam.[1]

A few of the many points involved in Niẓāmu-d-dīn's story find fitting entry here. Bābar must have been long conscious of the fact that he was not so strong as before he faced the Indian climate; he did not send for Humāyūn; he wished him to leave when he came unasked; he had 'Askarī in the full dignity of a commander near him; as he lay dying, he was fretfully anxious for Hindāl's coming; he and Khalīfa were friends of many years' testing; both knew the faults of Humāyūn; if Khalīfa had planned to set the latter aside, it is likely that the thought was not altogether absent from the mind of Bābar; it is not credible that Khalīfa should have regarded a supersession as practicable, if he had no acquaintance with the Emperor's doubts as to Humāyūn, and without knowing that these were shared by others than his master and himself, for the nomination would be made by Bābar and to his chiefs.

Muḥammad Mahdī Khwāja is one of those men about whose birth and descent particulars are looked for with the sure hope of success in the search. Yet nothing is said on the topic by Bābar or by Gul-badan. When he first appears on the scene (in the Persian version, and presumably also in the Elphinstone text), he is not introduced, as it is customary for Bābar to introduce, with some few words indicating family. This omission may be a result of forgetfulness bred of familiarity, or it may be, and most probably is, that he himself first met Muḥammad Mahdī at a date which falls in one of the gaps of his book.[2]

Niẓāmu-d-dīn's statements must have some corn of truth, and they imply that by birth, as well as by marriage and

---

[1] Neither of the sources thus describes Mahdī, but a somewhat full consideration of the several Mahdīs of the time allows no other than the husband of Khānzāda to be understood by the name Mahdī Khwāja of the two sources. *Cf.* Appendix, *s.n.* Muḥammad Mahdī.

[2] This omission, and perhaps some others, are straws pointing to the existence, at some time, of material which would fill the gaps.

military rank, Mahdī was a man who, without outrage, might be raised still higher. There are hints which make it seem probable that he was a Tīrmīzī sayyid and the son of a Tīmūrid mother. The suggestion of Tīrmīzī parentage is supported by the burial of Abū'l-ma'ālī *Tīrmīzī* in the place of interment of Mahdī and Khānzāda.[1]

It has suggested itself to me as possible that Khalīfa's plan of superseding Humāyūn was meant to apply only to Hindūstān, or at least to a part of Bābar's dominions. Abū-sa'īd had partitioned his lands amongst his sons; provinces so varied as Bābar's seem to demand division even more than his grandfather's had done. We look back to Bābar across Akbar's Indian Empire, and may not give sufficient weight to the fact that Dihlī and Āgra were not the centre or the desired heart of Bābar's. He wanted Farghāna and Samarqand and much more beyond the Oxus, and he had taken decisive steps towards securing his object through both his elder sons, and had given them charge and work of extension in those countries. Kābul was the true centre of his desired empire, and to force the Uzbegs back in widening circle was his persistent wish.

If Mahdī or any other competent man had ruled in Dihlī, by whatever tenure, this would not necessarily have

---

[1] It is singular that both Khalīfa and Mahdī disappear from prominent place with the death of Bābar. From Gul-badan it is known that the latter was living at the time of Hindāl's marriage with his sister Sulṭānam in 1537, because she names his gifts to the bridegroom. A good deal of search has failed to disclose other particulars of action or death of either man after Humāyūn's accession. Khalīfa's brother, Junaid (like Mahdī, a brother-in-law of Bābar), fought faithfully for Humāyūn till his recorded death. Khalīfa was older than Junaid, and the impression given by the early part of the Memoirs is that he was older than Bābar. The difficulty of the obvious interpretation of the silence about Khalīfa's later life is, that he withdrew support from Mahdī's promotion, and it is distinctly said of Humāyūn by Badayunī that he was made emperor by the concurrence of Khalīfa. So there would be no ground for a conspiracy of courtly silence about him. He was probably dead before the exile of the Tīmūrids from India in 1540, because his wife Sulṭānam was with the royal household, and made her pilgrimage shortly after the exodus to Sind.

ruined Humāyūn, or have taken from him the lands most coveted by Bābar. All Bābar's plans and orders were such as to keep Humāyūn beyond the Hindū-kush, and to take him across the Oxus. The dislike of the royal army to Hindūstān was a large factor in the question of centralizing government there, and so too would be the temptations to indolence afforded by its climate and customs, to which it was easy to foresee from Humāyūn's life in Sambhal that he would readily succumb.

Kābul was made an imperial domain by Bābar's written command to both elder sons, and his own words leave one in doubt as to his further intentions about it. To whom Hindūstān would have been given if Humāyūn had obeyed orders and had held fast in Badakhshān, there is nothing to show, but weight is due to the gist of the story of the supersession. Kāmrān declared that Kābul was given to his mother Gul-rukh, and Humāyūn gave it in fief to Kāmrān at his accession. There is mist over the scene from which only the accomplished facts emerge. Humāyūn came to India; he was Māham's son; she was there; Khalīfa let Mahdī fall; Humāyūn's personal charm reasserted itself over Bābar's anger, and he became Emperor of Hindūstān and all the imperial domains.

Child though Gul-badan was at her father's death, she must have been impressed by the events that preceded it: Alwar's death; her own accident at Sīkrī; her father's premonitions and dervish-moods; Humāyūn's sudden arrival and the anger it caused; his illness and the dread for his life; her father's awe-inspiring rite and its bewildering success; her sisters' marriages, which could not be joyful; the haunting suspicion of poison; the end and the blank,—all too much for so short a time in strange scenes and in a disabling climate.

Following the death came the forty days of mourning, and of good works and gifts at the tomb in the Garden of Rest at Āgra. Sīkrī furnished a part of the endowment for its readers and reciters, and Māham sent them food twice daily from her own estate. The tomb was put under the guardianship of a man whom our begam calls Khwāja Muḥammad ʿAlī ʿ*asas* (night-guard), and who may be he that 'never killed a sparrow,' and may be Māham's brother. If so, he will be heard of again under other and widely different circumstances in 1547. As is well known, Bābar's body was conveyed to Kābul, and there laid to rest in the spot chosen by himself.

Section II.—Under Humāyūn.

In Bābar's history the man holds the interest and lifts the eyes over his shortcomings to his excellence. No character demanding admiration attracts interest to Humāyūn, but yet his story is one which it needs a master-hand to unfold. A Tolstoi could depict his faults and merits; his qualities and defects rolled a tide of retribution over him and those bound to him as surely and visibly as it does over Anna Karénine and her associates. From the historic standpoint, Mr. Erskine has told the tale in a way to hold his readers, and it befits this humble introduction to build up only such framework as will support details, some of which concern the ladies of the time, and others of which may interest readers who are not Orientalists.

In order to realize how fully the fate of the ladies was involved in that of the Emperor, it must be remembered that his occupation of Hindūstān was unrooted, military and the sport of war. When we in Britain have to lament a reverse of arms, we do it in safe homes and we brace ourselves to what will come next, in the familiar surroundings of the daily tradesman, the usual postman, and the trivial comforts of the hearth. Even Colonials had a refuge under the flag at measurable distance from their outraged homes in 1899-1900. But when the Tīmūrids were defeated in 1539-40, and driven from Āgra and Dihlī and Lāhōr, there was no refuge open to all. Their head, Humāyūn, had none; a brother took his last. Like the Israelites, he and his followers then wandered in deserts and hungered and thirsted; dwelt in strange lands, pursued and attacked, exiled and humiliated. The course of events was less historic than biographical, was individual and not national. There were no nations behind Bābar and Humāyūn; there were only ruling families who came and went as they could or could not get the upper hand of other houses; and there was the dumb mass whom the earth nourished, and labour of whom fed, in luxury of life and strength of alien arms, whatever dynasty had just struck hardest.

An enumeration of the chief events of the downfall of Humāyūn and of his years of exile will give our required framework. He became Emperor in December, 1530. In the next year Kāmrān took possession of Lāhōr and the Panjāb, in addition to his grant of Kābul, and he was allowed to remain in possession of these wide and potential lands. In 1533 there were rebellions of the 'mīrzās.' By 1535 Gujrāt had been overrun, and in 1537 was lost. Years of indifference fostered the growth of Shīr Shāh *Afghān's* power, and there were campaigns against him in Bengal, which began well and ended ill. There was growing indignation against Humāyūn's character and private life, and this culminated in the attempt to set him aside for Hindāl in 1539. Through months of indolence and folly, he dropped oil on his own descending wheels, and practically abdicated the throne; finally, there were the crushing reverses of Chausa on June 27th, 1539, and of Kanauj on May 17th, 1540. Then came the flight of the Tīmūrids to Lāhōr, and their exodus from the lands that had been theirs east of the Indus.

Māham was spared the worst of these misfortunes; she died before Hindāl's marriage, which Jauhar places in 1537. Her son had certainly addicted himself to drugs before her death, but his worst lapses into sloth followed it, and it was after 1537 that the pace of his descent became rapid. Much can be learned from our princess of the reaction of outside events on the inner circle, and she gives details which could only be gathered in that circle. This is particularly so as to Hindāl's rebellion and the home conference about it, and about the murder in his name, but not by his act, of Humāyūn's favourite, Shaikh Bahlūl. Gul-badan, like the good sister she was, makes excuses for her brother, and those who have not her bias of affection, can add others and stronger. Hindāl was nineteen, a good and successful young general; he was supported by men of rank and age, some of whom had come from Gaur, and had seen Humāyūn's army perishing in that sink of fever and corruption, and Humāyūn buried within its walls. There was no ruler in Hindūstān; Shīr Shāh was between Humāyūn and the capital. The 'mīrzās' were lifting up their heads again, and a chief was needed. Hindāl was perhaps always the best of Bābar's sons in character, and certainly so when Humāyūn had become the changeling of opium. He had the Friday prayer (*khuṭba*) read in his own name; and on his behalf, Nūru-d-dīn Muḥammad, a son-in-law of Bābar and grandson of Sulṭān Ḥusain *Bāyqrā*, murdered Shaikh Bahlūl. The motive of the crime appears to have been desire to place the death as an impassable barrier between the royal brothers.

The news of Hindāl's rebellion stirred Humāyūn to move from Gaur. His march to Āgra was broken off tragically by the rout at Chausa, where he lost 8,000 of his best Tūrkī troops by sword or river. Here Ma'sūma was widowed, and here a terrible blank was made in the royal household by the loss of several women. Bega's (Ḥājī Begam) capture is known to all the histories, and so, too, is her return to Humāyūn. Shīr Shāh promised safety to all women found in the camp, and there is no reason to doubt that he did his best for them. But there had been fighting round their tents before his guards arrived, and some of Humāyūn's amīrs had perished in trying to defend them. It came about that there were losses of women and of children as to whose fate no word was ever heard again. Amongst them was 'Āyisha *Bāyqrā*, the wife of Qāsim Ḥusain Sulṭān Mīrzā. The next name in our begam's list takes us far back. It is that of Bachaka, a head-woman servant (*khalīfa*), and one such and so named had escaped from Samarqand with Bābar's mother in 1501. The one lost at Chausa had been a servant in Bābar's household, and may have been she of the memorable siege. Next are named two children, a foster-child and Bega's 'Aqīqa of six years old. Two of Humāyūn's wives of low degree also disappeared.

When Humāyūn had been rescued from the river by a lowly water-carrier, he made way to Āgra, and there had a conversation with Gul-badan about the loss of 'Aqīqa. The princess was then seventeen years old, and a comment of his, which she sets down, lets it be known that she is now a married woman. Humāyūn told her he did not recognise her at first, because when he went away with the army (1537) she wore the *tāq*, and now wears the *lachak*. The *tāq* is a cap, and the *lachak*,—a wife's coiffure—is a kerchief folded crossways, tied under the chin by two corners, and capable of much more elaboration and ornament than this simple description would lead one to suppose. This is Gul-badan's nearest approach to informing her readers of her marriage, and she never mentions her husband as such. He was her second cousin, Khiẓr Khwāja Khān, *Chaghatāi Mughal*, and of the line of the Great Khāns. His father was Aiman Khwāja, and his mother a cousin of Ḥaidar Mīrzā *Dughlāt*. One ancestor was that Yūnas whose fate as a chief of nomads was in such entertaining contrast to his taste as a lover of cities and books. Khiẓr had many other noteworthy kinsfolk, but to tell of them would lead too far afield. It is useful, however, to say that Gul-rang and Gul-chihra had married two of his uncles, and that his brother Yasīn (Ḥasan or Aīs)-daulat, the Fair Sulṭān, became the husband of Kāmrān's Ḥabība. He had two other brothers in India, namely, Mahdī and Mas'ūd. Their father and one at least of them came from Kāshghar to Āgra just after the death of Bābar.

Shortly after this interview Humāyūn took the field against Shīr Shāh, and Kāmrān, deserting his post, left Āgra and led off his 12,000 troopers towards Lāhōr. Under his escort went an immense convoy of women and helpless people, and he wished to take Gul-badan also. She was extremely unwilling to go and only partially resigned herself when she saw that it was Humāyūn's will. She bewailed herself as parting from those with whom she had grown up, and no uninitiated reader could guess that she was going with her father's son. She was a clever and attractive girl whose society was welcome to all her brothers, but in Kāmrān's wish to take her now there is something more. It is possible that he who liked her, thought of her safety; it is probable that, as he had attached two of her husband's brothers, Yasīn-daulat and Mahdī, and perhaps the third, Mas'ūd, he desired to have Khiẓr too. Gul-badan's departure from the home circle was perhaps her first adventure into the foreign world as a married woman. By going when she did and under the escort of Kāmrān's strong force, she was spared a terrible journey which her mother and the rest of the royal party made under care of Hindāl, with foes in front and behind, and at great peril.

There now followed that amazing battle at Kanauj, in which 40,000 men in armour fled, without a gun fired, before 10,000. Here again, as at Chausa, the deaths in the river were appalling, and here again the Emperor was saved by a lowly man. Again the remnant made its way to Āgra; but, says Ḥaidar, 'we made no tarry; broken and dispirited, in a state heart-rending to tell, we went on to Lāhōr.' Their road took them to Sīkrī, of which the memories and witness to Bābar's genius for living must have rubbed salt into the wounds of their spirit. Many ladies had remained in Āgra, and Humāyūn spoke to Hindāl of the difficulty of getting them safe to Lāhōr, and confessed that he had often regretted not killing 'Aqīqa with his own hand. Hindāl combated the suggestion, born of defeat, that a mother and sisters should be killed, and himself fought his way through country folk and Afghāns, and convoyed them safe to Lāhōr.

Here was a mighty gathering of Tīmūrids and their

following, and five months slipped by in uncertain counsels and fruitless talk. The four brothers met often to discuss plans, and it seems that the emptiness of this in practical result lay in what was in the mind of Kāmrān and made him object to every course proposed. He wished to make terms for himself with the daily approaching victor, and to keep Lāhōr and the Panjāb; but if this could not be, he meant to hold fast to Kābul and keep Humāyūn out of it. The fief of Kābul had been granted to him by Humāyūn; Humāyūn therefore could resume it. That he would now do so was Kāmrān's expectation; so, when Humāyūn proposed to go to Badakhshān, Kāmrān would not hear of it, because the road thither lay through Kābul, and once in that beloved city, it was highly improbable that Humāyūn would move further.

On October 30th, 1540, something decisive had to be done, for Shīr Shāh had crossed the Biah and might appear at any hour. 'It was like the Day of Resurrection,' says our princess; the confusion was extreme, and, like the simile, impossible for us to realize. It has been said that 200,000 souls left Lāhōr in flight on that day; an overtax of all resources of transport.

Happily for the fugitives, the Rāvī was fordable, but the Chanāb required boats and the Jehlam was in flood. Many episodes unfolded themselves in the *duāb* of the Rāvī and Chanāb. Ḥaidar Mīrzā took his departure for Kashmīr, hoping to secure in it a royal retreat; Hindāl and Yādgār-nāṣir deserted and went south for Multān; Humāyūn was urged to put further mischief out of Kāmrān's power by his death; he refused,—a refusal which would be upheld in the *ḥaram*, ever faithful to the injunctions of Bābar, and knowing these better than the real risks caused by Kāmrān's disloyalty. Penetrating everything was the irritation aroused by Kāmrān's opposition to the royal march for Kābul,—irritation which diffused itself and barely missed a sequel of bloodshed.

The depression and gloom of the men who were the responsible leaders of the fugitive mob must have been deep and painful; but what was in the minds of their dependents,—the ordinary troopers, the helpless women, the comfortless children, and the camp-followers?

There were many striking scenes in the lives of Bābar and Humāyūn, but none more dramatic than that in which the latter's flight through the Panjāb ended. A little west of the Jhelam, at Khushāb, the road runs through a ravine of an outlying spur of the Salt Range. Beyond this it forks, north-west for Kābul and south-west for Sind. Kāmrān asserted his intention to enter the defile first, perhaps with the object of closing the Kābul road. Humāyūn insisted on his right to take precedence, and blows threatened between their followers. Mediation was made by Abū'l-baqā, the man who had led Bābar to offer himself for his son in 1530. He directed Humāyūn's attention to the superior force of Kāmrān, and he told Kāmrān that it was the right of Humāyūn to take precedence. In the end Humāyūn marched first and took the southern road. At the fork of the ways each commander and many a man must have made or confirmed his choice between the brothers. And so the mighty caravan split itself, and followed Kāmrān and 'Askarī or Humāyūn.

With the Kābul section many women went to the safer asylum. They had no choice to make where the roads parted, but those of them who saw their litters turn southwards and themselves carried by a strange road, of which they knew that it took them from the old home in Kābul, must have had some bitter feelings about their destiny. I believe Gul-badan went with Kāmrān. She does not say so, but it comes out with tolerable clearness incidentally. Her mother, Dil-dār, had gone with Hindāl to Multān, and with her was Ḥamīda-bānū, Akbar's mother to be. Khānzāda seems to have gone with Humāyūn, for her niece mentions her later as an ambassador from him in Sind to Qandahār. No other writer speaks of this embassy, I think; but most tell of her other, made later from Kābul to Qandahār in the service of peace between Kāmrān and

Humāyūn, after the latter had returned from his Persian exile (1545).

Khiẓr is not mentioned as with Humāyūn in the desert wanderings, but he was in Qandahār with 'Askari in 1545. On the occasion of her reunion with Humāyūn in Kābul, in 1545, Gul-badan says that there had been a 'toil and moil of separation' lasting five years. The lustrum points to a farewell said at the Jhelam. One thing makes for her having gone with the royal party, and this is her lively account of what befell it; but she is equally lively about Persia; where she certainly did not go. She had excellent opportunity of hearing what went on in Sind because she met her mother again in 1543, after she had come to Kābul from Qandahār. She also met Ḥamida in 1545, and could hear from her not only about her wedding, concerning which she has such an excellent passage, but also about her visit to Persia. There was ample and easy opportunity for the two old companions to talk over the past and to refresh their memories when the book was being written in and after 1587 and when they were comfortably installed as the beloved and respected 'Beneficent Ladies' of Akbar. Moreover, Gul-badan has a note of acknowledgment to Khwāja Kīsīk for help derived from his writings, as to the early part of the royal wanderings. There is therefore nothing to contradict the probability that she continued under Kāmrān's protection from 1540, the date of her unwilling departure from Āgra, till 1545, when Humāyūn took Kābul.

During the lustrum in which she did not see Humāyūn, his adventures were too many and too remarkable for abbreviation in these pages. Mr. Erskine has told them with evident enjoyment, and Gul-badan supplements his narrative with some material he did not use; it may be interjected here that he had no knowledge of her book. For most of the period of the exile in Sind and Persia, Ḥamīda was a good authority, and more than once Gul-badan has prefaced a statement with 'Ḥamīda-bānū Begam says.' She was one in the cruel desert march to Umarkot; it will have been from her that the princess heard that

Akbar's birthplace was a beautiful spot where food was very cheap; she was one of the little band which fled from Quetta; she shared the qualified hospitality of the Persian king, and, it should be said, reproduced only a sense of good treatment by him; and she came back to Qandahār with his auxiliary army.

In Kābul Gul-badan did not want for old friends and kinswomen. She had her own home occupations and her children to look after; of these, though she names one only, Sa'ādat-yār, she may have had several; but there is no definite statement as to which of Khiẓr's children were also hers. She was not unkindly treated by Kāmrān, as were the other royal ladies whom he turned out of their usual homes and exploited in purse. Indeed, he wished to regard her as one of his own family and to distinguish between her and her mother; but of this she would not hear.

In 1543 she had again the society of Hindāl who, after losing Qandahār to Kāmrān, came as a prisoner upon parole to Kābul and his mother's house. The movements of Humāyūn were made known from Sind to Kābul with speed and completeness, and the news was acted on to Humāyūn's great detriment. There were domestic reasons why Shāh Ḥusain *Arghūn* should not be well disposed to Humāyūn, besides the substantial one of the latter's entry and long occupation of his country. Of the more intimate causes of ill-will one was inherited; Bābar had dispossessed the Arghūns from both Kābul and Qandahār, and not only so, but had given in marriage to his foster-brother Qāsim an Arghūn girl, Māh-chūchak, daughter of Muqīm Mīrzā. This was a great offence, because it was a misalliance in Arghūn eyes and because it was enforced and the bride was spoil of battle. The story of her anger and of her rebellion at her fate is delightfully told by Mr. Erskine, and to his pages readers may be safely referred for the sequel of my brief allusion to it.

When Qāsim *kūka* died, Māh-chūchak married her cousin, Shāh Ḥusain, and she was with him during Humāyūn's miserable stay in Sind.

Another cause of friction lay in the presence of a former wife of Ḥusain with Humāyūn's household. In 1524 Ḥusain had allied himself with Khalīfa's family by marrying his daughter Gul-barg. As the fact adds to the domestic complication, it may be mentioned that at the same time Ḥusain's stepdaughter, Nāhīd, the child of Qāsim and Māh-chūchak, married Khalīfa's son, Muḥibb-'alī. Ḥusain and Gul-barg (Rose-leaf) did not get on well, and she left him after what Mīr Ma'sūm calls two years of wedded life. She then, says the same author, went to India with *Jannat-āshyānī* (Humāyūn) 'previous to the *fitrat.*' This last word is frequently used of the rout at Chausa in 1539, but the next nearest catastrophe to which it would apply after 1524 is the death of Bābar, because Gul-barg is named by Gul-badan in Humāyūn's household shortly after his accession. She was with him in Sind in 1541 onwards, and so, too, was Sulṭānam,[1] who was perhaps her mother, and both were unlikely to make the best of Shāh Ḥusain to Humāyūn.

In 1545 Kābul heard that Humāyūn was on his way back from Persia with the Shāh's army behind him. A first result of this was to bring the little Akbar within reach of Khānzāda and to her charge. All the histories tell of his wintry journey from Qandahār taken with Bakhshī-bānū, the one being under three and the other about four. Their coming adds a touch of tenderness to the historic Khānzāda, who paces through the histories sad and wise and trusted. She kissed the baby feet and hands of Akbar, and declared they were the very hands and feet of Bābar, and that he was like him altogether. Her first marriage with Shaibānī had been made to save Bābar from captivity or death. She was divorced because suspected of leaning to his side when his interests conflicted with her husband's, and she had been restored to him (1511) when she was about thirty-

---

[1] The presence of Sulṭānam here, and a royal permission allowed to her to go to Makka and take her daughter also, gives the impression that Khalīfa is dead.

three years old.[1] To the reader's fancy she wears a mourning garb; she is mentioned with deference, and is a dignified figure in the turmoil of her day. Her third marriage,—she was doubly widowed at Merv,—takes an impersonal colour, as an alliance which her age, story and loss of her only son make seem rather one contracted to confer honour and afford her a safe home, than on any ground of personal affection. She bore Mahdī no child; she adopted his sister Sulṭānam at the age of two, and reared her to become the wife of Hindāl.

By March 21st Humāyūn was besieging Qandahār, and he then sent an envoy to Kābul, who would be a welcome guest as teller of the events since Humāyūn had left Quetta in 1543. This was Bairām Khān *Bahārlū*, and with him went Bāyazīd *bīyāt*. Bairām saw Akbar, and could take back to Ḥamīda news of his welfare; and also a number of princes who were kept in Kābul under Kāmrān's eye. These were Hindāl, Yādgār-nāṣir, some of the 'mīrzās,' Sulaimān, Ḥaram and Ibrāhīm.

Bairām spent six weeks waiting till Kāmrān should choose his course now that he knew his brother was the stronger; and when he left the city, he was accompanied by Khānzāda, charged to mollify Humāyūn and smooth the way for 'Askarī when the latter should submit. She went into Qandahār, but her presence did not bring about the immediate surrender, and the weary siege carried on its burden of suffering. Many of the amīrs of the defence began to slip away; the two Khiẓrs, *Hazāra* and *Chaghatāi*, dropped themselves over the wall. The first got away to the mountains with adventures which fit a Highland setting; the second sought Humāyūn and obtained forgiveness.

Qandahār was surrendered on September 3rd, and 'Askarī and his amīrs came out with swords hung round their

---

[1] The date of her return by Shāh Isma'īl to Bābar in 1511 falls in one of the long gaps (eleven years) of the Memoirs. This covers also, it is probable, Bābar's first association with Mahdī and the latter's marriage with Khānzāda.

necks, and some having winding-sheets in their hands. He was forgiven, and a feast with wine and talk and music sped the night away. While ʿAskarī was gay with the rest, someone laid before him his own letters to the Biluchī chiefs of whom Gul-badan tells, urging them to capture Humāyūn when he was in flight from Quetta. This was Humāyūn's revenge.

Meantime Kāmrān was in singular isolation in Kābul. He heard of the fall of Qandahār, of the move of the royal army for Kābul, of the death of the travel-worn Khānzāda, and of the escape of some of his princely *détenus*. He was depressed and irritable. He sent troops out to meet Humāyūn, but there was no fighting, and he fled by way of Ghaznī to Sind. Then came the end of the 'toil and moil' of separation, and Gul-badan met her brother again after five years, on November 15th, 1545. For awhile there was peace and festivity in Kābul. Ḥamīda followed the army in the spring; she had now a second child, a girl, born in Persia, and she took possession once more of her first-born. Humāyūn wished to see if Akbar, whom his mother had had to desert at Quetta when he was fourteen months old, would remember her now. He had him taken into a room in which a number of ladies had assembled and seated him on the *masnad*. The child recognized Ḥamīda, and made his way to her arms. Abū'l-faẓl, who tells the story, gives all the credit of the recognition to the boy; but to those not dazzled by the light in which Akbar lived for his historian, it seems extremely probable that the child had some help from the smile which he had known as one of the first happy things of life.

In the spring, too, Humāyūn set out on a campaign in Badakhshān. He sent word back to the governor of Kābul, Uncle Muḥammad ʿAli, that he was to strangle Yādgār-nāṣir, who had been tried and condemned to death for treachery. The khwāja declined the office. 'How should I kill the mīrzā, I who have never killed a sparrow?' This uncle (*ṭaghāī*) seems a mild man for his post. Another executioner was found, and the mīrzā 'was relieved of the pains of existence.'

Humāyūn took 'Askarī with him as a precautionary measure. Of the ladies, Māh-chūchak went, and in attendance, Bībī Fāṭima, the chief armed woman of his *ḥaram* and mother of Zuhra, whom Ḥamīda's brother was to marry and murder. Near Khishm Humāyūn fell alarmingly ill and lay unconscious for four days. He had nurses at hand whose excellence is attested by the annals, and it adds life to the scene to know that the long watch over the unconscious man was broken by his opening his eyes just when Māh-chūchak was dropping pomegranate-juice into his mouth. He recovered, but it was a perilous time for him and his supremacy, and had a bad sequel.

News of the illness went to Sind, and Kāmrān, reinforced by his father-in-law, Ḥusain, hurried up and seized Kābul. Winter was at its depth on the passes, and the amīrs with the royal force were anxious to get back to protect their families. They had premonitions that he would take the city again, and many slipped away in small parties and went to Kābul, where they found all their anticipations and dread justified. It does not seem right to stigmatize their leaving Humāyūn as traitorous; they had their own people to save, and this might be done by slight show of submission to Kāmrān. No one can consider Humāyūn a man who had claim to fidelity when the lives and honour of wives and children were in the balance. Indeed, to have left Kābul under the charge of Muḥammad 'Alī was to court disaster, and to make reasonable a good deal of independence of action in those whose unarmed people he could not protect.

Every fear of the amīrs was justified. On his northward march Kāmrān passed through Ghaznī, where Zahīd Beg was governor. He it was who when offered a Bengal appointment in 1538, had asked Humāyūn if he could not find another place to kill him in. He had not waited for a reply, but had left Bengal, and helped Hindāl to rebel in Āgra. Kāmrān now answered his question in Ghaznī, and after this murder hurried off towards Kābul. 'It was morning, and the Kābulīs were off their guard, and grass-cutters and water-carriers were going in and out as usual. Mīrzā Kāmrān went in with all these common people.' So speaks the princess. The gentle-hearted governor was at the *ḥamām*, and was brought before Kāmrān, without time given to dress, and there and then sabred. The list of other cruelties and murders is too terrible reading for these pages, and the ensuing siege was full of barbarous acts. Humāyūn crossed the passes as soon as it was practicable, and sat down to take the city. When Kāmrān saw at length that he could not hold it, he escaped through a hole fashioned in the wall, got through the trenches and away to the mountains. Some say Hindāl let him pass the royal lines; others that Ḥājī Muḥammad Khān *kūka* overtook him later (so destitute that he was being carried by a man), and that Kāmrān appealed to their milk-brotherhood and was allowed to go free. He then joined his hereditary foes, the Uzbegs.

In 1548 Humāyūn entered upon a campaign in Badakhshān which yielded interesting personal matters, such as this rivulet of the great stream of affairs can convey. He left Kābul on June 12th, and Ḥamīda bore him company with Akbar as far as Gul-bihār. As governor this time a soldier, and a man enraged against Kāmrān, was left in charge of Kābul. The campaign culminated in the capture of Tāliqān, which was made over on August 17th by Kāmrān, who was allowed to go to the refuge of all whose presence was undesired at home, Makka. Piety had no part in Kāmrān's intention to betake himself to the holy city, and when he had heard, with incredulous ears, that Humāyūn was meting out mercy without justice to the revolted amīrs he had captured, he took heart and himself asked forgiveness. It is almost incredible, and would be quite so if one did not know Humāyūn, that he was received with kettle-drums, trumpets, tears and pardon. Certainly Humāyūn never deprived himself of the luxury of tears and the loose rein on his feelings. So wonderful was the following scene that Mr. Erskine's words shall tell it: 'When Kāmrān approached the Emperor, who was sitting in state in the pavilion of public audience, he took a whip from the girdle of Muʿnim Khān, who stood by, and passing it round his neck, presented himself as a criminal. "Alas, alas!" exclaimed the Emperor, "there is no need of this; throw it away." The mīrzā made three obeisances, according to the usual etiquette of the Court, after which the Emperor gave him the formal embrace and commanded him to be seated. Kāmrān began to make excuses for his past conduct and to express his regret. "What is past is past," said the Emperor. "Thus far we have conformed to ceremony; let us now meet as brothers." They then rose and clasped each other to their breasts in the most affectionate manner, and both burst into tears, sobbing aloud, so as to affect all present. Humāyūn, on resuming his seat, desired his brother to sit next to him on the left, the place of honour, adding kindly in Tūrkī, the language of the family, "Sit close to me." A cup of sherbet was brought, of which the Emperor, having drunk one half, handed it to his brother, who drank the other. A grand entertainment followed, at which the four brothers (also Sulaimān), who now met for the first time after a long separation, sat on the same carpet and dined, or, to use the words of the historian, ate salt together. The festival was prolonged for two days in the midst of universal rejoicing. As Kāmrān, from the rapidity and hurried nature of his return, had left his tents behind him on the road, the Emperor ordered a set to be pitched close to his own, and, at his desire, consented to ʿAskarī's going to stay with him.'

For this historic feast Gul-badan has provided a *hors d'œuvre* in shape of a story of improper conduct in Sulaimān which, if it expressed derision, as her vague wording does not forbid to be read, was fully justified by both what had been and what was to come. It is a very funny little tale, and readers are commended to it.

To tears and professions were added lands and freedom. Kāmrān received Kūlāb, where Ḥaram Begam's father had once ruled for Bābar and Humāyūn. He was now dead, and his son, Chakr 'Alī, was left with Kāmrān there. The mīrza was not pleased with his fief. 'What!' he exclaimed to the bearer of the deed of grant, 'have I not been king of Kābul and Badakhshān? Kūlāb is a mere district of Badakhshān. How can I serve in it?' The bearer observed that he had heard Kāmrān was wise, and begged permission to remind him that the wonder was he had received anything at all. 'Askarī, too, was given a fief, and then, leaving them neighbours and at large, Humāyūn went back to Kābul in October, 1548.

A campaign was planned for 1549 against the Uzbegs and Balkh. This was done despite marked instability in the royal following. Instability or, in a plainer word, desertion, was an accident to which Humāyūn was peculiarly liable. One cause of it is more interesting than the common one of personal gain, because it is rooted in theological bias. Humāyūn's coquetry with Shiism in Persia is one of the most entertaining of the episodes of his sojourn there, and it had consequences in arousing distrust of him, which cropped up from time to time. Bābar himself had lost ground because of his tolerance to variety of faith. But to this, both in the father and still more in the son, were added, as causes of desertion, the flux and reflux of weak government which forbid men to know who will keep the upper hand and have power to oppress.

To return to the Balkh campaign: spring was waited for and there was delay for men. Spring came, and the minds of the ladies turned to thoughts of excursions out of town. They remarked more than once to Humāyūn that the *riwāj* would be coming up in the hills. This is a plant of subacid flavour which some say is like sorrel and some like rhubarb. It was, at least, a plant that people made excursions to eat, much as others go blackberrying. To these hints for change, the royal reply was that the army was going out; that it would pass by the Koh-i-dāman (which is renowned for its *riwāj*); and that the ladies should go too. Gul-badan must not be deprived of her story of the picnic, which illuminates the domestic ways of the court. The ladies went so far as to see the waterfall at Farza, and perhaps even to Istālif, twenty miles north of Kābul, and then returned.

There had been bad omens for the start and there followed plenty of bad news from the front to fix attention on them. Kāmrān broke his promise to come to Humāyūn's help. Gul-chihra's second husband, an Uzbeg prince, ran away when he came to know that the army was directed against his people. There was an extraordinary retreat without an enemy, and of which the cause seems to have been fear that, as Kāmrān was not there, he was oppressing Kābul. Humāyūn was left almost alone, and the Uzbegs attacked and killed many fugitives. His horse was wounded and the whole affair was a fiasco. After all, too, when Kābul was reached, there had been no sign of Kāmrān.

It was the expected that Kāmrān should not keep his word, but perhaps the unexpected was behind his conduct on the occasion of the Balkh campaign. Sulaimān and Ibrāhīm were with Humāyūn, and their presence might well have kept him away, for Gul-badan tells of an incident in which the three men had part and which did not make them good company for one another. It is a bit of scandal to which Ḥaram adds salt and vitality. It is repeated here because some little points do not quite stand clear in the begam's wording. While Kāmrān was in Kūlāb—*i.e.*, his last holding,—someone, who from her name of Tarkhān Begam must have been a woman of good birth, advised him to make love to Ḥaram Begam. Good, she said, would come of it. So Kāmrān sent a go-between with a letter and a kerchief to Ḥaram, who, furiously angry, at once summoned husband and son from wherever they were away from home, and told them of the advances made to her. She railed at Sulaimān, saying that it was clear he was thought a coward, and further observed that Kāmrān feared neither *her* nor her son. Much was packed in the pronoun here; there was ground to fear the energetic and resolute woman who had the army of Badakhshān at her disposal. She was a forceful person and had the go-between torn to pieces. Kāmrān was audacious, and his advances look the more so that Ḥaram's sister was his wife; but they may have been made rather to the charms of her army than to those of its commandante.

The events of 1550 sum up in Jauhar's words: 'Mīrzā Kāmrān wandered about the country with bad intentions.' In his course he surprised Humāyūn in the Qibchāq defile, and an engagement took place which was attended by great loss of life. It was witnessed by Kāmrān's wives and daughters from a commanding height. Bāyazīd mentions that the ladies wore turbans (*dastār-bastī*), a detail which may have been suggested by the great heat of the weather. Why the women were on the scene is perhaps explained by a similar record in the Memoirs which concerns a wife of Sulṭān Ḥusain *Bāyqrā*. Shahr-bānū, a daughter of Sulṭān Abū-sa'īd Mīrzā, was, with Ḥusain's other wives, present at a battle between her husband and her brother, Maḥmūd Mīrzā. She did not, as the other ladies did, leave her litter and mount a horse, so as to be ready for flight if necessary, but trusting to her brother, in the case of her husband's defeat, remained comfortably in her litter while the fight went on. This dispassionate composure so much offended Ḥusain that he divorced her. Perhaps Kāmrān's family, too, had prepared for whatever was to be their fate by protecting themselves against the sun and by being ready to mount.

In this encounter Humāyūn was badly wounded. Gulbadan was able to hear the details of the misadventure, because Khiẓr Khwāja was with her brother and, it may be said, fighting against his own, Yasīn-daulat. Khiẓr and Mīr Sayyid Bīrka *Tīrmīzī* helped to hold the wounded man up on an ambling pony when he could not sit his horse, and so they led him out of the fray, sustaining his courage as they went by tales of other princes who had come through plights as bad. The wound was on the head, and was like one of Bābar's in that it was given through a covering turban and this was uninjured. The pain was great and caused faintness. Humāyūn took off his quilted coat and gave it to a servant. The man finding its weight an encumbrance, left it lying; it was taken to Kāmrān, who posted off with it to Kābul, showed it as evidence of death, and once more took possession of the unfortunate city.

Jauhar has quaint stories of the destitution in which Humāyūn now was, with his camp equipage lost and deprived of all necessaries. He was helped along through the night, cold and weakened, and in the morning was placed in safety by the arrival of a body of reliable troopers under Ḥāji Muḥammad *kūka.* He warmed himself in the sun, washed his wound, said his prayer kneeling on a scarlet stool, and borrowed a coat from a servant to replace his own, which was blood-stained. Then came an old woman of the place and offered him a pair of silk trousers, that he might discard his blood-stained ones. He accepted, while saying they were not fit for a man's wear, and remitted her taxes for life. This was drawing well in anticipation of the time when his account in those regions would stand to his credit.

It is said that while he sat with his face still to the *qibla* one of his followers, Sultān Muḥammad *qarāwāl,* performed again for him the rite his father had observed, and expressed his willingness to die for him. Humāyūn spoke reassuring words and comforted his faithful sacrifice.

For nearly three months Kābul believed Humāyūn dead. These words cover much feeling, sad and joyful; but there is no one to tell the truth and say whether it was thought by some to offer better hope of peace that Humāyūn should be dead. There was always a large following of powerful officers ready to join Kāmrān, and one cannot suppose their changes in allegiance mere folly and fickleness. But no courtly author has told Kāmrān's side of the whole matter, nor his view of his own position.

With Kābul Akbar came again into his uncle's hands.

He was kept safe through all the vicissitudes of his father's career, and was well cared for both by Kāmrān and by ʿAskarī. It has been said that on one occasion Kāmrān exposed him on the battlements of Kābul to his father's guns, and this charge finds support from our princess. She however, it may be observed, makes no mention of the act attributed by some writers to Māham *anaga*, of interposing her own body to shield the child; indeed, she never once mentions this latterly influential woman. But this incident notwithstanding, it must be admitted that the boy was well treated. ʿAskarī's wife, who took charge of him after his capture at Quetta, is said to have been most kind to him. He was entrusted by Kāmrān to Khānzāda, itself an act of surety and kindness. Again and again he fell into his uncle's hands when Kāmrān was exasperated by foiled attempts to keep Kābul, and yet he survived. Kāmrān had a son; it would have surprised no one to learn that, as complement to his effort to oust Humāyūn from his higher place, he had killed Akbar to give his own son more chance. In this there is what fixes attention in the same way that it is fixed by Gul-badan's record of Kāmrān's anxiety to obtain from the elder ladies of his house sanction to have the *khuṭba* read in his name. It was in his power to have himself proclaimed ruler in Kābul, but he discussed his wish to be so proclaimed with the other members of the royal family before he did it, and the discussion was prolonged, and referred from Dil-dār to the greatest of the ladies, Khānzāda. In both these points there is something which, if better known, might mitigate the sweeping judgment usually passed upon Kāmrān as altogether wrong in all his doings.

Humāyūn spent some time in Ander-āb while his wound was healing and his army gathering, and here Ḥaram comes again upon the scene. Where Sulaimān and Ibrāhīm were, is not quite clear, but it was to Ḥaram a message went asking her for the army of Badakhshān. It was to come as quickly as possible, and fully equipped. It took the energetic woman only a few days to put some thousands of men in the field. It was she, says our princess, who did it all, took thought, and overlooked everything. Then she led the men to 'the pass,'—amongst so many possible, one cannot fix on which,—and having done her work, went home. It seems probable that Sulaimān and Ibrāhīm were already with Humāyūn, and that Ḥaram despatched a supplementary force. The battle in which it was to engage was that important fight at Ushtur-grām which Humāyūn tried hard to prevent by previous mediation, and which was forced on by Kāmrān's chief officer, Qarācha Khān.

There was much previous discussion as to terms of peace, but Kāmrān and Qarācha would have nothing less than Kābul. A second embassy offered alliance of the 'unique pearl of the *khilāfat*,' Akbar, with the mīrzā's 'dear daughter' (who may be 'Āyisha), and that Kābul should be theirs; and suggested that Humāyūn and Kāmrān should join forces and again attack Hindūstān. All came to nothing, because Qarācha cried, and enforced his cry, 'Our heads or Kābul.' The battle that followed was a complete success for the royal arms, and to add to its good results, Akbar, of whose safety there had been doubt, was brought to Humāyūn's camp. His father vowed charitable gifts for his restoration, and also that he would never part from him again.

A pleasant chance befell Humāyūn on the stricken field, for when he had claimed, as his share of booty, two driverless camels, he found in their loads his own books which he had lost at the Qibchāq defile. Many would be MSS. of the Persian poets; Bābar knew these well and often quotes the Gulistān; and Humāyūn was too much of a dilettante and verse-lover not to have made himself familiar with their round.

Happily the tale of the doings of Kāmrān is drawing to a close. He made a night attack, by which Hindāl lost his life, on the royal forces on November 20th, 1551; sued for help in vain from Sālim Shāh, the Emperor of Hindūstān; from Adam Ghakkar, and was surrendered by him to Humāyūn; was blinded by the insistence of the amīrs on August 17, 1553, and allowed to go to Makka. He was accompanied, as all the writers tell, by his Arghūn wife Māh-chūchak, and by her equal in compassion, a servant of Humāyūn, Chilma Beg. He made the *ḥaj* four times and he died on October 5th, 1557. Māh-chūchak survived him seven months. She only of his wives is commemorated as accompanying him to Makka, but I see no reason why others may not also be accepted as equally faithful. Her father opposed her going, and she roundly upheld her view of her duty and has been taken into the texture of history, but her co-wives may have gone unopposed and unpraised. How interesting Kāmrān might have made a book of Memoirs in which he set down his life from his own point of view, his motives, ambitions, opinions of right and wrong, and above all, if he had spoken his inner mind about the religious duties he was enabled to perform before death, through his defeat and mutilation! We do not know all the truth about him; certain crimes, of murder and of treachery after promise given, could never be palliated, but in the matter of possession of Kābul there may be much brought forward which would place him rather in the position of the defender of rights than their assailant. He had no courtly chronicler, and has borne the blame of much that could plausibly be traced back to Humāyūn's own defects and their outcome of opportunity.

To end the story of the faithful brothers;—ʿAskarī too received leave to go to Makka from Badakshān in 1551; he died between that city and Damascus in 1558. Both he and Kāmrān thus lived long enough to see their house triumph again in India and their weary thwartings of its elder branch set at naught by the firmer hands of Akbar's chiefs. Of ʿAskarī one clear characteristic only comes out: he was true to the blood-tie with his mother's son and own senior, Kāmrān.

A little return must now be made, in order to bring up the tale of home events to the date of those military. In 1551 the first marriage of the younger generation was arranged by the betrothal of Bakhshi-bānū to Ibrāhīm, son of Ḥaram. The Badakhshī trio had certainly deserved well of Humāyūn and, while doing the best they could to strengthen their own position, had given him efficient help. It is good to tell all that is known of Ḥaram. She seems to have had several daughters who played a part in public events as seals of alliance. When Humāyūn had passed a short time of repose in Kābul after his victory of Ushtur-grām, he sent to Ḥaram to ask Shāhzāda Khānam, one of these girls, in marriage for himself. His envoys were two persons whom Ḥaram did not consider worthy of their office. They were members of the royal household, and trusted members too, for one was Khwāja Jalālu-d-dīn Maḥmūd, *mīr sāmān*,[1] who, on Akbar's accession, was made commander of 2,500; and the other was Bībī Fāṭima, whom we know as having helped to nurse Humāyūn in his illness of 1546.

Ḥaram, the dominant partner in the command of Badakhshān, mother of a girl in whose veins was reputed to flow the blood of Alexander and of Tīmūr, daughter of a tribal chief, and conscious of intrinsic claim to deference, inquired of the two lowly messengers why no begam or lady (*āghācha*) had come to prefer the royal request. She must have known that Humāyūn could not mean to affront her; he had just given his daughter to her son and had testified gratitude for help in substantial ways to Sulaimān at the same time. She allowed herself to be mollified on condition that he himself should come to fetch his bride. The wedding does not seem to have taken place and the alliance was handed on to the next generation, in which, besides Ibrāhīm's, there was a betrothal of Muḥammad Hakīm to a daughter of Ḥaram.

While speaking of Ḥaram and the alliances of her family with the royal house, there may be named a high-handed act about another quasi-royal marriage. One of

---

[1] This title is sometimes rendered 'butler,' but this is misleading, and a word not linked in English with intoxicants would be better. Jalālu-d-dīn it was who led Humāyūn to give up the use of drugs, unfortunately late in life, by a gentle and forcible reproach.

Kāmrān's wives was Muhtarīma Khānam *Chaghatāi,* and on his death Sulaimān wished to marry her. Of her as co-wife, Ḥaram would not hear, and contrived to make her a daughter-in-law by marrying her to Ibrāhīm.

The death of Hindāl in the night attack of Kāmrān, on November 20th, 1551, was a heavy blow to Gul-badan. She writes of it with feeling, and casts light on the question of rank in the affections of a Musalmān wife. She asks why her son or her husband was not killed rather than her brother. Perhaps she spoke out of feeling born of the fact that no dead father's son can be replaced, and from the deeps of family affection. Dutiful and admirable as were many of the wives of this time, the tie between the husband and a wife can never be so close as it is where the husband's affection is never a divisible factor in the household. Gul-badan shows that Musalmānī affection centred on those of the same blood.

The royal ladies must have felt it hard when, after having mourned Humāyūn through Kāmrān for nearly three months, Hindāl was killed. This happened near Khiẓr Khwāja's fief of Jui-shāhī, which explains why the body was sent there for burial and entrusted to the khwāja. It was removed later to Kābul and laid at Bābar's feet. Hindāl was thirty-two years old, and left one daughter, Ruqaiya, who became the first wife of Akbar and survived him, a childless woman, to the age of eighty-four.

Unfortunately for her readers, our begam's book ends abruptly (just after she has mentioned the blinding of Kāmrān,) in the only MS. of which we have knowledge, *i.e.*, that belonging to the British Museum. The missing pages are a real loss. The narrative breaks off some three years before Akbar's accession, and for the future the best authority on our topics is silent. There is no occurrence of her own name in the histories until she goes to India in the first year of Akbar. Much of supreme importance happened to the royal family in the interval, and this makes regret the keener for the defective MS.

Set free from the burden of his brothers, Humāyūn

determined, in 1554, to try his fortune again in Hindūstān. He left Kābul on November 15th,—a date so near that of Bābar's start in 1525 that it looks as if both obeyed the same omen of the heavens,—and with Akbar dropped comfortably down the river from Jalālābād to Peshāwar. The course of his advance beyond the Indus can be followed in Mr. Erskine's pages, and need not be repeated here. He was proclaimed Emperor in Dihlī on July 23rd, 1555.

A little-known episode of the time is the visit to India and the court of Sīdī 'Alī *Reis*, a Turkish admiral of Sulaimān the Great, who by the exigencies of war and weather found himself obliged to travel with a few officers and fifty sailors from Sūrat to Lāhōr and thence across all the wide intervening lands to Turkey.[1] He was welcomed by Musalmāns for his master's sake, and he was offered appointments in India, all of which he refused. He was received with great honour by Shāh Ḥusain *Arghūn*, of whom he says that he had then reigned forty years, and had become so invalided during the last five that he could not sit his horse and used only boats for travel. Elsewhere it is said of Shāh Ḥusain that he was subject to fever of such kind that he could live only on the river, and that he used to spend his time in going up and down from one extremity to the other of his territory in search of ease and health. Probably this is a detail of the admiral's remark. He heard of Māh-chūchak (wife of Ḥusain), whom he calls Ḥaji Begam, as prisoner of 'Īsā *Tarkhān*, and of her return to Ḥusain. He heard, too, something which is not supported by other writers, namely, that she poisoned Ḥusain, and that he died in consequence ten days after she rejoined him. The improbability of this story is shown by the fact that later on she conveyed Ḥusain's body to Makka for interment, an act which would be incredible if the accusation of murder were true. Much that is interesting is told of the journey to the first place

---

[1] 'Travels and Adventures of Sīdī 'Alī Reis'; Vambéry; Luzac and Co., 1899.

where Sīdī ʿAli's route brought him into contact with Humāyūn's people, *i.e.*, Lāhōr. He arrived early in August, shortly after the Restoration (July 23rd), and there awaited royal orders, because the governor would not let him go on until the Emperor had seen him. When one tries to picture one's self without telegrams or newspapers, one judges that a kindly-disposed amīr would endeavour to forward everyone who could tell a tale for the entertainment of the court. Humāyūn sent for the admiral, and had him received, in the first half of October,[1] outside Dihlī by Bairām *Khān-i-khānān*, other great amīrs, 1,000 men, and 400 elephants. He dined with the *Khān-i-khānān*, and was then introduced to the presence.

As was natural, the Emperor wished to keep his guest at court permanently, if possible, and if not this, then long enough to 'calculate solar and lunar eclipses, their degree of latitude and exact date, and to help the court astrologers to study the sun's course and the points of the equator.' What fastened interest on the Ottoman was that he learned to write verses in Chaghatāi Tūrkī so well that Humāyūn called him a second ʿAlī Shīr *Nawaī*. He had a turn for chronograms, too, and at his first audience presented one of the taking of Dihlī, and made others subsequently which were admired. He was a clever man, and his literary aptitudes suited his royal host and the tone of the entourage. But he had other acquirements than those which ring well tho change of words and obtained him his sobriquet of 'book-man,' and these others he used to bring about an agreement between the Emperor and his own former host,

[1] M. Vambéry makes the Emperor urge, as a reason for keeping the admiral, that they were 'now close upon' the rains. But it was October, and, moreover, Humāyūn pointed out that the rivers were in flood and roads impassable. Perhaps this is a mistake of the admiral's, but still he saw the rivers, to his cost, in going to Dihlī. Those who may read the interesting little book, for which thanks are due to M. Vambéry, need to accept it in other places also with some caution—*e.g.*, p. 38, Sulṭān Maḥmūd *Bhakkarī* is called Ḥusain *Arghūn's* adopted brother, and, p. 40, his father. He was a *kūka*. Some of the mistakes may well be due to the difficulty of getting hold of a fact, and this especially on a journey. But *cf.* p. 43 *n.*

Sulṭān Maḥmūd *Bhakkarī*. An official paper was drawn up, to which Humāyūn, literally, set his fist, for he dipped his clenched hand in saffron and laid it on the deed. Maḥmud was much pleased, and both he and his vizier wrote their thanks to the mediator. This incident, and others too, gave occasion for other Tūrkī ghazels and higher praise. Sīdī 'Alī was constantly in the royal circle, and there were contests in verse-making and dilettante amusements which reveal the true and newly-risen Huma once more at ease in untranquillized India. The traveller had not much to coax court favour with in the way of gifts, and this plumed his poetic flights; when he was wearied by his detention, he carried two ghazels to the royal seal-bearer and let them plead for his departure. They were heard, and he got 'leave to go,' with gifts and passport.

His affairs were all in order for his start when there happened the fatal accident which ended Humāyūn's life. That Humāyūn should die violently was in keeping with the violent changes of his career; and that he met his death in a building of Shīr Shāh was a singular chance. His last hours of activity were filled by pleasant occupations; old friends had been seen who had just come back from Makka and would bring him news of both pilgrim brothers; letters had been read from home in Kābul; he had gone up to the roof of the Shīr Mandal, which he used as his library, and had shown himself to the crowd assembled below; then he had interested himself in the rising of Venus, with the object of fixing a propitious hour for a reception,—perhaps to include the farewell of the Turkish guest.

The Shīr Mandal is a two-storied building with flat roof in the middle of which rises a small cupola which looks like a shade from the sun. The roof is reached by two discontinuous, steep, and narrow flights of high and shallow granite steps, which are enclosed in walls and the upper one of which emerges through the roof. The Emperor on that Friday evening of January 24th, 1556, had started down the upper flight and was on its second step, when the *mu'azzin* raised the cry for prayer from the neighbouring mosque. Sīdī

ʿAli says, as though it were some individual habit of Humāyūn, that the latter had the custom of kneeling whenever he heard the cry; other writers say that he tried to seat himself. His foot became entangled, some say in his mantle (*postīn*), his staff slid along the smooth step, and he fell to the bottom of the flight with severe injuries to head and arm. It is professed that a letter went after the fall from him to Akbar, but this may be a part of the well-meaning deception in which the dangerous nature of the injuries was shrouded; it would seem more probable from the admiral's account of the episode, which is silent as to any recovery of consciousness, that the injuries to the head were too severe to allow of restoration to sense. Three days later Humāyūn died, on January 27th, and in the forty-eighth year of his age.

'We come from God, and to Him we return,' and 'There is no guard against fate,' are the quoted comments of the Turkish admiral. He counselled that the death should be concealed until Akbar's return to Dihlī, and brought forward experience drawn from his own country's similar circumstances. This was done and various fictions were composed. A man personated the dead Emperor in public audience, and there were rejoicings over his recovery from the fall. Sīdī ʿAlī took leave of the grandees, and convoyed the false news of Humāyūn's restoration to health in a friendly way along his route. By the time he reached Lāhōr he found that Akbar had been proclaimed, and his name read in the Friday prayers. Here, as before, the traveller had to wait for royal orders, because the governor had, or invented, useful orders for the crisis, that no one should pass to Kābul. Then he was sent to the presence in Kilānūr, where Akbar honoured his father's passport and let the harassed and home-sick man continue his journey, with money for expenses and a strong escort to Kābul.

Before bidding him good-bye on his still lengthy journey, it may be said that he and his four escorting begs and his sailors marched to Peshāwar through the night to escape that

Adam Ghakkar who had made over Kāmrān to Humāyūn; that they saw two rhinoceroses, an event which makes one wonder whether there still remained a part of the ancient lake of the plain of Peshāwar to serve as habitat for the huge and now vanished beasts; and that they crossed the many-memoried Khaibar.

In Kābul the admiral saw Humāyūn's two sons, Muḥammad Hakīm and Farrukh-fāl, who were born in the same month of 1553, one being the child of Māh-chūchak and the other of Khānish *āghā Khwārizmī*. This statement is a surprise, because Bāyazīd says that Farrukh died within a few days of birth. The admiral's information suggests an error in Bāyazīd's MS.

Sīdī ʿAlī found Kābul beautiful and speaks of its snowy girdle, its gardens and its running water. He traced pleasure and merriment and feasting everywhere, and even instituted comparison between it and Paradise to the disadvantage of the latter. But he had no time for 'frivolities,' and thought only of hurrying home. He saw Muʿnim Khān in the city, and being told by him that he could not cross the passes, observed that men had overcome mountains, and under the care of a local guide whose home was on the road, accomplished the feat with labour and safely. He took the road to Tāliqān and there saw our well-known friends, Sulaimān and Ibrāhīm, but he is silent as to Ḥaram. Here, too, he wrote and offered his ghazel, and was both welcomed and speeded. In Tāliqān we must leave him who has been a welcome new figure amongst familiar actors.

Section III.—Under Akbar.

Protected by the capable men who upheld Akbar, the royal ladies had not again to flee before foes or to suffer violent change of fortune. Humāyūn had planned their journey from Kābul to India. Akbar more than once in his first year of rule had to cancel the orders he had given to effect it. Three military affairs disturbed the plan,—the suppression of the revolt of Abū'l-maʿālī, the operations against Sikandar *Afghān*, and the encounter with Hīmū at Pānīpat. At length amīrs were named to escort the ladies from Kābul. The officers set out, but on their march received orders to act first against Sulaimān Mīrzā, who, on hearing of Humāyūn's death, had come over from Badakhshān to besiege Kābul. This was the first of a series of his attempts on the city, to which he laid fanciful claim as head of the house of Tīmūr after Humāyūn. The approach of the imperial troops broke up his siege, and his claim having been accommodated by reading his name once in the *khuṭba* at Kābul, he went home and left the ladies free to start.

They made their journey in time to arrive during the first quarter of 1557 near where lay the royal camp, at Mānkot, in the western Sewāliks. The Emperor came a stage from it to meet them, and was 'much comforted by the reunion.' With Ḥamīda-bānū Begam, to whom, as Empress-mother, the chief place must be assigned, were Gul-badan, Gul-chihra, Ḥājī, and Salīma Begams. There was also a large company of officers' wives.

Perhaps the ladies remained near the camp until it broke up and went to Lāhōr. It left that city on its march for Dihlī on December 7th, 1557; at Jalindhar it halted, and here, with pomp and amidst general interest, Bairām *Khān-i-khānān* married Salīma Sulṭān Begam, a grand daughter of Bābar. She was a half-niece of Humāyūn, and she had with Akbar cousinship of the 'four-anna' degree. Babar was their common ancestor, and their differing grandmothers diluted the cousinly relation.

This alliance had been arranged by Humāyūn, and the use of *sipurdan* by Abū'l-faẓl when writing of it, shows that what was now celebrated was a marriage, and not a betrothal. This point is mentioned here because some writers fix Salīma's age at this time as five, an estimate which is not supported by known facts of her life. The bride was probably a reward for the surpassing services done by Bairām for Humāyūn, the newest being those of the Restoration. Bairām was a man to whom seems due the largesse of the hand of a king's daughter; he out-topped his contemporaries by his full stature in capacity, culture, faithfulness, and character. Salīma,[1] though much his junior, was in other respects a fit wife for him. She was an educated woman; ranks amongst verse-makers so completely as to have a pen-name (*takhallas*), and stands out gently, by birth, character, and attainments.

Khiẓr Khwāja Khān had gone to Hindūstān with Humāyūn in 1554, and early in 1556 had been appointed by Akbar to the government of Lāhōr. He was left to carry on operations against Sikandar *Afghān* when Akbar was called away by Hīmū's movements, and he was defeated. The few words said about him give the impression that he was not a good soldier, and he is never again named in responsible command. The slight things recorded of him point to subsequent comfortable existence at court as the 'husband of the Emperor's aunt, Gul-badan Begam.' Once he made a gift of horses to Akbar; in 1563 he helped to nurse Akbar when the latter was wounded in Dihlī; and there is no record of his death. He was raised to high military rank, and at some time was *amīru-l-umarā'*, but the *Āīn-i-akbarī* does not place him in its list of *manṣabdārs*. He stands twelfth in the general list of the *Ṭabaqāt*, and amongst the chiefs of 5,000.

From her coming to India in 1557 to the time of her pilgrimage in 1574, our princess is not mentioned by the historians. The interval held much of deep interest to her and to others of her generation whose lives were slipping away under the safeguarding of Akbar. Some survivors of an older day, witnesses of Bairām's fidelity to Humāyūn, must have felt his downfall keenly. Ḥamīda can hardly have been ignorant of the intrigue which brought this about, because she was related to the chief actors in it,— Māham *anaga*, Adham Khān, and Shihābu-d-dīn Aḥmad

---

[1] The histories have a definite statement about her descent which yet presents difficulties when looked into. Its points are considered in the Appendix, *s.n.* Salīma.

Nishāpūrī. The last was governor of Dihlī, where she lived, and part of the scheme to separate Akbar from Bairām took him to Dihlī to see her, and thus under the eye of Shihāb. Ḥamīda must have had clear in memory the truly valid services done for her husband by Bairām during the Persian exile. The plot had its nucleus in a sayyid circle and in families religious by inheritance, and it was carried out at the point of the tongue. Muḥammad Bāqī Khān *kūka,* the *anaga's* elder son, does not appear as taking part in it. He served the Emperor till 1584, rose to be a chief of 3,000, and of his character nothing is known. His younger brother, Adham, although put to death in 1562, had become chief of 5,000. All that is said of him is bad, and he, like his mother, was fluent in detraction and did all in his power to poison the mind of Akbar against the worthiest of his amīrs.

Many comments have been made upon Māham *anaga,* both by the Persian writers and by their European commentators. Abū'l-faẓl calls her a cupola of chastity, and it is now possible to wipe from her reputation the stain suggested by Professor Blochmann when writing of the parentage of Adham. She was wife of Nadīm Khān *kūka,* a faithful servant of Humāyūn. This fragment of useful information was brought to light by Mr. Beveridge, who found it in a MS. of Colonel Hanna, which may yield other valuable matter on quasi-domestic points. Māham *anaga* may be granted the praise she deserves as a nurse who earned the affection of Akbar to the end of her life; she is entitled to such praise as belongs to a mother who screens a son's every fault and pushes his fortunes with all her influence. She must take the dispraise of not pushing her elder son's as she did Adham's. Bāyazīd *bīyāt* speaks of her as kind to him, and tells little stories which show her the centre of small affairs. I have not discerned in her any sign of talent. Whatever influence Akbar's affection gave her would be strengthened by her connection with his mother, and perhaps, too, with other women who were descended from Aḥmad *Jāmī.* Amongst these was Ḥājī

Begam, Humāyūn's widow and a person much regarded by the Emperor.

In the year following Bairām's death, Adham Khān, who, says the *Ṭabaqāt*, held a place higher than the other courtiers because he was his mother's son, was on duty in Mālwa against Bāz Bahādur *Sūr*. Incidents resulted which emphasize regret that for such as the actors in them Bairām had had to make way. Māham *anaga* was *de facto* prime minister; Mu'nim Khān had been made *Khān-i-khānān*, and it was looked for by his friend the *anaga* that he should become prime minister *de jure*. Bāz Bahādur was defeated and fled from Sārangpūr. Aping the Hindūs, he had ordered his servants to kill the women of his household in the event of his defeat. Several had been so killed, many had been wounded, when the sacrifice was interrupted by the imperialists under Adham. Badāyunī says that there followed slaughter by Adham and his colleague, Pīr Muḥammad Khān, of terrible extent, and his own eyes saw that these two regarded God's creation in mankind as leeks, cucumbers, and radishes,—a quaint turn of words which covers awful butchery. When remonstrated with in the name of the law, the murderers asked what was to be done with so many prisoners.

If the order for the death of the women of Bāz Bahādur's household had issued from a Rājpūt heart, there would have been no need for executioners while he was in flight. The victims were, however, not Rājpūtnīs, and they suffered only to gratify the vanity of a Moslim. Amongst those wounded was Rūp-matī, a dancing-girl renowned throughout Hindūstān for beauty, singing, and poetic gifts. Her name seems that of a Hindū. Her wounds, inflicted by Bāz Bahādur's order, were severe and she wished to die. Adham let her know that, if she would care for herself, he would send her to her master when she could travel. She took his promise as true, had her wounds dressed and recovered. When she claimed fulfilment of Adham's word, she was told to consider herself as his slave. He entered her room, raised her veil, and saw her dead by her own act.

Perhaps the point of deepest social degradation in this story is that Rūp-matī was, by men's decree, born to sin without blame, and yet she died because she loved one man. Her heart was single, and yet she was only the most charming, clever and beautiful of a crowd of dancing-girls, purchased slaves, to whom no man's loyalty and no mercy were thought due.

Adham Khān took much booty from Bāz Bahādur, and he disregarded the rule which required the choicest part to be sent to the Emperor; he also comported himself more like an independent ruler than a king's lieutenant. This angered Akbar, and he hurried off to Sārangpūr, out-distanced a messenger of Māham *anaga* whom she had sent with warnings, and took Adham by surprise. She herself came in next day and counselled surrender of the spoil. This and other matters having been adjusted, the Emperor started for his capital. No sooner was he gone than Adham, with his mother's connivance, regained possession of two of the most coveted of the captive women. News of this went after Akbar, who ordered them to be returned to the royal camp. When they came again within her power, the *anaga* had them murdered, so that they might not tell the tale of their abduction.

Having spent so many years under the influence of Māham *anaga*, it is to the credit of Akbar's humanity and mental force that there are not more than the recorded blots on his scutcheon; at nineteen he rebelled against his nurse, when she had set his feet on the primrose path to ruin of person and empire. He did not punish the murder of the captive girls, but he soon manifested his intention to depose his nurse and her son from power. Instead of appointing their friend Mu'nim prime minister, he summoned his foster-father, Shamsu-d-dīn Aḥmad *Ghaznavī* and gave him the post. Shamsu-d-dīn was an unlettered man, but he was staunch and had sons who were true to Jī-Jī *anaga's* nursling.

The next episode in which Māham *anaga* and her son appear, was one to shake the home fabric to its foundations, for Adham murdered Shamsu-d-dīn, bursting in upon him as he sat in business audience and unsuspicious. It was done on the night of May 16th, 1562. The incident is well known, how the murderer rushed to the *ḥaram* door and on the appearance of Akbar began to palliate his crime, but was struck down by a blow of the royal fist and then killed by royal order.[1]

It was the Emperor who told Māham *anaga* of her son's death: 'Māmā! we have killed Adham,' are the words put into his mouth by Bāyazīd. She fell ill from anger and grief; this blow shattered her heart's idol and her ambition for him and herself. Badāyunī says that she died after having presented the food of the fortieth day of mourning, and this points to her belief that the souls of the dead take final departure from earth on that day and after partaking of the food of their choice which the care of relations sets for them. Mother and son were buried in one spot, and Akbar placed his shoulder under his nurse's bier in sign of his sentiment to her.

Quite stirring news for discussion through some years, amongst the elder ladies of the royal family, would be the conduct of Māh-chūchak Begam in Kābul. She was the last recorded wife of Humāyūn, and was married in 1546, after the coming of Ḥamīda from Qandahār to Kābul. She was not a woman of birth,—one gathers a general impression that few royal wives married late in life were so,—and her title of begam was probably owed to her having borne a son, Muḥammad Hakīm. In 1554 Humāyūn had left her three-years-old boy as nominal governor of Kābul under charge of Muʿnim Khān, and in 1556 Akbar had confirmed the appointment. When Muʿnim went to court in 1561,

---

[1] Some writers put into Akbar's mouth, when he addressed Adham, an epithet which would imply baseness in his birth and opprobrium of his mother; but I am advised that from various considerations weight need not be given to the inference of the word, which, moreover, is not used by all the sources. The point is mentioned here because of the contradiction involved in the epithet with the statement of marriage with Nadīm *kūka*, and with the terms of respect employed towards the *anaga* by the Persian writer who uses the degrading epithet.

his son Ghanī became his *locum tenens*, but Ghanī had neither 'suavity nor sense,' and the begam shut him out of Kābul, one morning when he had gone to walk in the melon gardens. He went to India, and she took up the guidance of her boy's affairs. She chose three men to help her; two soon came by their deaths at her dictation, and the third became supreme. Akbar, and no doubt the ladies also, heard of these doings, and despatched Muʿnim Khān with men to put things straight. Māh-chūchak met Muʿnim at Jalālābād, utterly defeated him, and he fled to court. She then killed the last adviser of her trio and took another, whom she may have married, named Ḥaidar Qāsim *Kohbur*. These proceedings surprise one in Māh-chūchak, and bring her story down to the first half of 1564, when Abū'l-maʿālī appears upon her stage.

We cannot enter here into the previous history of Abū'l-maʿālī,—his rebellions, murders, imprisonment, pilgrimage, and reinvigorated return to wickedness. He now came to Kābul fresh from two assassinations in Hindūstān, a fugitive, and indited a letter to the ruling begam, with profession of affection and devotion to the memory of Humāyūn. She welcomed him, gave him her little daughter Fakhru-n-nisaʾ in marriage, and let him take the lead. Before long he stabbed Māh-chūchak with his own hand, murdered Ḥaidar Qāsim, and stirred revolt against himself which led to woeful slaughter within the walls of Kābul. Word of all this went from Muḥammad Hakīm to Sulaimān and Ḥaram, with a prayer for help. Ḥaram approving and accompanying, the army of Badakhshān marched over the passes, met Abū'l-maʿālī in the Ghurband valley, captured him, and sent him bound to the prince, who had him strangled. Both he and Adham Khān had justified Bairām's distrust, which had prompted him to wish their death early in Akbar's reign.

A little story of Ḥaram may be inserted here, somewhat after date. She had not been always on perfect terms with Sulaimān. Not only, a little earlier, had there been the discussion between them of his wish to take Muhtarīma to wife, which Ḥaram had frustrated by marrying the khanām to Sulaimān's son instead of to himself, but she had been angered extremely by the murder of one of her brothers by her husband and her son. She took the resolution of deserting Sulaimān and went over to Kābul, where then Mu'nim Khān was governor, and she had meant to carry on her complaints to Akbar. Mu'nim, however, who had been begged to mediate by Sulaimān, gave her good advice and pacified her, so that at last she consented to return to Badakhshān. He rode out to bid her farewell; she bade her camel kneel and dismounted; he got off his horse, and there was exchange of friendly greeting. She told him she regarded him as a brother and that for his sake she would never bring the army of Badakhshān against Kābul. It came several times later and with her approval, but Ḥaram could swear and break even 'awful oaths.' Bāyazīd *bīyāt* accompanied her to the Ghurband and was charmed by her suavity and agreeableness.

On the death of Abū'l-ma'ālī, Sulaimān sent home for a daughter and married her to Muḥammad Hakīm, partitioned out some of the lands of Kābul to his own people, and went home to Qila'-i-ẓafar. Irritation against the interlopers led to their expulsion by the Kābulīs, and this brought the Badakhshī forces again to Kābul, in 1564. Muḥammad Hakīm hurried to the Indus and complained to his big brother and Sulaimān was made to retreat.

In 1566 he and Ḥaram and their girls were again before the coveted Kābul, and on this occasion Ḥaram tried to supplement their failing military action by treachery. She got Sulaimān to lay an ambush for Muḥammad Hakīm, whom, with 'awful oaths' of amity, she had persuaded to have a meeting with her under profession of desire to adopt him now that her son Ibrāhīm was dead. The end of this affair was, in net result to the Badakhshīs, nothing; Ḥaram went home and Sulaimān followed. With them went the unfailing daughters, of whom Ḥaram seems to have had many, or who were betrothed and not

'entrusted,' so many recorded times. They had been near capture by the Kābulīs in the Four-walled Garden, but the commandant of the city recalled his men and let the girls go free, because he did not think it seemly to capture women.

This is not the place to follow Sulaimān's interesting fortunes to their close, under Akbar's protection, by death in Lāhōr in 1589. For our purpose, it is enough to say that he held Badakhshān so long as Ḥaram's watchful eye was on him, and lost it at her death. It was Muhtarīma's son, Shāh-rukh, his own grandson, who turned him out of his beloved Badakhshān, and in this, too, there may be Ḥaram's hand. Muhtarīma would not be likely to teach her boy dutiful conduct to Ḥaram or to Ḥaram's husband, for the two women were foes, and Ḥaram had tried to separate Muhtarīma from her son, and to expel her from Badakhshān to her parental home in Kāshghar. If Ḥaram had lived, her pride would have found content in two alliances of her grandson with daughters of the royal blood, —one a child of Muḥammad Hakīm, and the other of Akbar himself.

The ill-behaviour of Ḥamīda-bānū's brother, Khwāja Mu'aẓẓam, must have been a frequent annoyance to the inner circle of the elder ladies at court. From boyhood he had been fantastic and mischievous, and perhaps carried always the germ of the madness which overtook his last years. Bairām, the sensible, had exiled him, then had given him some countenance; on Bairām's fall he had received a fief, and, so far, had been favoured. But Akbar did not like him, and the murders he had committed were sufficient to warrant dislike. He was a true *parvenu*, assertive and relying on his sister to excuse his faults. Ḥamīda had been conscious before her marriage that her lowly birth was a point against her wedding with Humāyūn. The disparity in her case, as in other misalliances of the time, had raised unworthy people to power. Now, in 1564, Bībī Fāṭima lamented to Akbar that Khwāja Mu'aẓẓam had threatened to kill his wife Zuhra, who was her daughter. The Emperor consequently sent the khwāja word that he was coming to his house, and followed the message closely. As he entered, the khwāja stabbed Zuhra and then flung his knife, like a challenge, amongst the royal followers. Abū'l-fażl says that for punishment the murderer was flung into the river, but 'would not drown.' The more sensible Niẓāmu-d-dīn Aḥmad says he was beaten and then soused in the river. He died insane, in prison, at Gualīār. All the shortcomings and crimes of the man notwithstanding, Ḥamīda must have cherished some warmth of feeling for the tricksy boy who had lifted suspicion from her in the matter of the stolen rubies of the Persian episode.

In 1571 another old acquaintance comes to the front in the person of Nāhīd Begam, in whom our princess must have maintained interest for the sake of her father Qāsim, Bābar's foster-brother. Nāhīd, as has been said earlier, was the daughter of Qāsim and of Māh-chūchak *Arghūn*, who must not be confounded with Kāmrān's wife of the same name, one common amongst the Arghūn women of the time. She had married Muḥibb-'alī, son of Niẓāmu-d-dīn 'Alī *Khalīfa Barlās*, and who had risen to high military rank but now lived remote from soldiering and in reposeful retirement. Nāhīd's mother was now in her (third) widowhood for 'Īsā *Tarkhān Arghūn*, and she was not well regarded by her last husband's son, Muḥammad Bāqī *Tarkhān Arghūn*, the ruler of Tatta. Nāhīd, in 1571, went to see her mother, and perhaps conveyed to Bāqī the impression that her visit was something more than filial. He put Māh-chūchak in prison, and so behaved to Nāhīd that she hurried off to court and made bitter complaint of her own wrongs and of the rudeness shown to the royal attendants who had been with her in Sind. She told Akbar, too, that she had talked with Sulṭan Maḥmud *Bhakkarī*, that old retainer of Shāh Ḥusain who had kept the island-fort against Humāyūn in the forties, and for whom Sīdī 'Alī *Reis* had negotiated terms in 1555. Maḥmūd had suggested an attack on Tatta, and, supported by him,

Nāhīd pleaded for help from Akbar to act against Bāqī. She was very keen about her plan and persuaded the Emperor to give men and money.

Muḥibb-ʿalī was disturbed from his repose, and put at the head of the force. With him went Nāhīd and also a wife named Sāmīa and her son, Mujāhīd. For Nāhīd's ends the long war that followed was infructuous. An amusing episode of it was that Sāmīa, when things did not go as she wished, went into rebellion against Akbar, and actually held an entrenchment against the royal amīrs a day and a night. In the end, Muḥibb-ʿalī obtained a comfortable town appointment and nothing more is heard of the ladies. Probably they too accommodated themselves to the tolerant and forgiving atmosphere of Akbar's court.

Niẕāmu-d-dīn Aḥmad is somewhat more sober of diction than his fellow-penmen and so, when he says that the Gujrāt campaign of 1572 caused the royal ladies joy enough to last their lives, whole-hearted delight is pictured. This was the campaign which made beautiful Sīkrī the City of Victory (Fatḥ-pūr). Round one incident of the war womanly interest,—and surely compassion also,—will have centred. The veil of historic silence lifts for a brief moment, and shows Gul-rukh, Kāmrān's daughter, in flight with her son.

Gul-badan's long span of unchronicled life was probably spent in the peaceful occupation of a wife and mother, with variety from books, verse-making, festivities, and outside news. She must have found much to exercise her lively mind in Hindūstān. That she went about with the royal camp is shown by the record of the place assigned to her tent in the encampments. It was pitched next to Ḥamīda's, well within the great enclosure, and not far from the Emperor's own. Since she was a woman, she must have found food for observation in the doings and position of her sex under the conditions of their life in Hindūstān. How did *satī* look to her? What did she think of the *jūhar?* Both these Hindū customs were far different from those of her traditions in similar crises. She came of a tribe which boasts of the fidelity of its wives to the marriage tie. All the women of her house must have heard of the defiant act of Aīs-daulat, Bābar's grandmother, who had ordered her maids to stab a man to whom her captor had given her, and who then, for sole excuse, had observed that she was the wife of Yūnas Khān. Gul-badan had also in her own family history plenty of examples of the fate of captured girls, for many of her kinswomen had married foes of their tribe; and many too had become contented wives, well treated, and remaining in their foreign homes apparently without constraint.[1]

What Tīmūrid women saw amongst the Hindūs reveals another type of virtue and another standard of wedded life. Our princess must have heard something on the topic through her father's experience when she was a child. Wifehood and motherhood now gave her better insight into the problems which underlie social relations. She would hear that Rājpūtnīs died joyfully rather than be captured; that outmatched Rājpūts killed wives and children and went to certain death themselves,—a holocaust to honour. The early years of Akbar furnished plenty of such records.

How, one would like to know, did the Musalmānī regard the willing death by fire of the Hindū widow, in that exaltation which lifts thought above pain and terror and is admirable, whether in the martyr for faith or for wifely duty? Unfortunately, the barriers of language and habit must have kept Akbar's Rājpūt wives from charming the Musalmānī ladies by recital of the legends of their race. These Hindūs can never have been welcome inmates of the

---

1 I think, and the impression is gathered from the Memoirs, that although women and children were often murdered by victorious soldiers, wives were often returned to their husbands or families, and that enforced marriage was usually with the defeated leader's daughters. Perhaps the Muḥammadan law of divorce helped the wives. Injustice might easily be done under the rough-and-ready expectation that family ties would be set at naught by conquerors who were Muḥammadans. There was certainly diversity of action and of degree of mercy and chivalry.

palace to any of the Moslims; but, pagan as they were thought, their conduct as wives must have insinuated the thin edge of conviction that to no one form of faith is committed the nurture of the sense of duty.

One common thought Gul-badan and the rest could have shared with the Hindū ladies,—that of the duty of pilgrimage and of respect for holy places. When next history concerns itself with our begam, it is to tell of her setting out, in 1575, for Makka. The Emperor had been unwilling to part with her, and it may be, even, had delayed with the thought of accompanying her. His heart was now much set upon making the *ḥaj*, but he did no more than walk a short distance with a caravan from Āgra, dressed in the seamless wrapper of the Arabian ceremonies. Though debarred from leaving Hindūstān himself, he helped many others to fulfil this primary duty of their faith, and opened wide his purse for their expenses. Each year he named a leader of the caravan, and provided him with gifts and ample funds. Sulṭān Khwāja, Gul-badan's cicerone, took, amongst other presents, 12,000 dresses of honour. He did not bring her home again; this duty fell to Khwāja Yaḥyā (John). What circumstance extorted royal consent to Gul-badan's absence is not recorded; her advancing age,—she was past fifty,—and her dislike of the laxity in opinion and practice in matters of the Faith would add warmth to her request for leave to go.

Abū'l-faẓl has preserved the names of the chief ladies of the pilgrim party, but many others went with Gul-badan Begam, and for all the royal purse bore the cost. She was the lady of highest birth, and was probably a widow; next came Salīma Sulṭān Begam, widow of Bairām and wife of Akbar. It was not usual for a wife to make the pilgrimage, but Muḥammadan law stipulates that permission shall be granted to such wives as strongly desire to do so, and Salīma's seems a case in point. Next comes a woman whose presence reveals pleasant things. She was Sulṭānam, widow of Akbar's uncle, 'Askarī, and of her it is recorded in Akbar's babyhood that she cared for him when captured, with tender affection. It is probable that she had spent many years under the care and at the cost of the Emperor. Then come two step-nieces of Gul-badan, daughters of Kāmrān,—Ḥājī and Gul-ʿizār Begams. I do not know which child of his is veiled under the title of Ḥājī. She seems to be making her second *ḥaj*, and may well have gone on her first when her father was in Arabia. To these two the pilgrimage would have humanly pious significance, as a visitation to their father's tomb and to that of Māh-chūchak *Arghūn*, whom all his children must have held in reverence. Next comes a grand-daughter of Gul-badan herself, named Um-kūlsum (Mother of Plumpness), presumably after the daughter of her Prophet. Whether she was the child of Saʿādat-yār is not said, nor whether the last name on the list, Salīma Khānam, is that of a child of Gul-badan, as well as of Khiẓr Khwāja Khān. Here some of the inconveniences of polygamy show themselves to the seeker after family facts.

An old associate of our princess accompanied her in the person of Gul-nār *āghācha*, who had been of Bābar's household and was, I think, one of the two Circassians sent as a present to him by Shāh Ṭaḥmāsp in 1526. She was now well on her way through life and considerably older than Gul-badan Begam. Another of the party had also been of Bābar's household, Bībī Sarū-qad, or Sarū-i-sahī (Straight Cypress). She had been, too, in Humāyūn's service and later had married, with full *nisbat*, Muʿnim *Khān-i-khānān*. She was a widow, had been a singer and reciter, and was a 'reliable woman.' Like her in accomplishments were Bībī Safīya and Shāham *āghā*, both formerly of Humāyūn's household. Of the first and of Bībī Sarū-qad we have the happy little record that they sang in the moonlight on the road to Laghmān in 1549.

Fatḥpūr-sīkrī seems to have been the rallying-point of the caravan and October 15th, 1575, the day of departure from it. It started earlier than was usual, perhaps because the ladies could not travel fast. Caravans generally left Āgra in the tenth month—this left in the seventh—of the

Muḥammadan year. Akbar's second boy, Murād, was told off to escort the ladies to the coast. Sālim met them one stage out to give last greetings. At Gul-badan's request, Murād was excused from his long task of escort to Sūrat, and he went back to Āgra. One smiles to find that the princes were five and four years old. The real charge of the caravan was with several amīrs, one being Muḥammad Bāqī Khān *kūka*, and another Rūmī Khān of Aleppo, who may have been Bābar's artillery officer.

It is a real loss that there is no record of the journey from our begam's pen. It was to be adventurous; even perilous; and it was of great interest whether as sight-seeing travel or pious duty. Sūrat was the port of embarkation, but there are no details of the road taken to reach it. Father Rudolf Acquaviva passed between the same two terminal points in 1580, but the military movements of the interval may well have allowed him to travel where the ladies could not go. When they were first in Sūrat, it had been a royal possession for two years only, and even when the Father took the fairly direct route from it to Fatḥpūr-sīkrī, the Rājpūt peasantry was in arms against their new lord. The ladies were probably handed on from one garrisoned place to another as the immediate circumstances of conquest dictated. The main body of their *ḥaj* joined them by a tedious and weary route, first escorted through Goganda by the army which was on active service, and then passing on to Aḥmadābād, and, perhaps by water, to Sūrat.

The governor of the port, who was to have a good deal of trouble with this caravan, was Qulij Khān *Andijānī*, a sobriquet of pleasant sound in our begam's ears. He had inherited Tīmūrid service from many generations, and his father had been a grandee of Sulṭān Ḥusain *Bāyqrā*.

'There was peace with the isles of the Franks,' but it took the ladies a year to get to sea. The *Akbar-nāma* attributes some part of the delay to a foolish panic about the Firingīs which, after the ladies had embarked in their hired Turkish transport, the *Salīmī*, seized the other pilgrims who were to sail in the royal ship, the *Ilāhī*. The real ground appears to have been want of a pass. The Portuguese were then masters of the Indian waters, and no ship might dare to put to sea without toll paid and pass obtained. Alarm about the Portuguese was natural, for there were stories that the very pass was sometimes a letter of Bellerophon enjoining capture and death. Abū'l-faẓl says that, although the ladies embarked, they were unwilling to put out and desert their fellow-pilgrims. This may be mere broidery, or the one ship may have had a pass and the other not. Perhaps, too, as theirs was a hired transport, it was also one privileged to sail free. However this may be, Badāyunī makes the difficulty clear by saying that Khwāja Sulṭān's ships lay idle from want of the pass. He also, it may be added, quotes a legal opinion that at this time it was not lawful to make the *ḥaj* from India because, of the two practicable routes, one lay through the Shiah country of 'Irāq, and the other obliged a pass which bore the idolatrous stamp of the heads of the Virgin Mary and of Jesus Christ ('on whom be peace').

The *mīr ḥaj* sent word to the Emperor of his plight, who at once despatched orders to Qulij Khān, in Īdar, to go to Sūrat and arrange the difficulty. Qulij took with him a Cambayan, who was presumably a man versed in seafaring business,—hurried to Sūrat and overcame the difficulty.

It took the ladies a year to get to sea; they sailed on October 17th, 1576. Their port of debarkation is not mentioned; some pilgrims sailed by the Arabian, some by the Persian Gulf. They spent three and a half years in Arabia, and were able to make the *ḥaj* four times.

Some day perhaps a pious and enlightened Musalmān will set down the inner meaning he attaches to the rites of the pilgrimage. How interesting it would have been if our princess had told us what it was in her heart that carried her through the laborious duties of piety she accomplished during her long stay in her holy land! She might have given us an essential principle by which to interpret the religious meaning which devout women attach to the rites commanded on the pilgrimage.

The visitation duties are set down in Hughes' 'Dictionary of Islām,' where even their brief recital is attractive and adds to the wish of gauging the sentiment of believers in their efficacy. The acts prescribed are exhausting, not only to the body but also, one thinks, to the mind, because the very conception of the pilgrimage as a Divine ordinance keeps brain and heart tense, as all obedience does which sets the human will parallel to the Divine.

The mere recapitulation of the prescribed ceremonies is impressive: The halt six miles from the city to put on the seamless wrapper (*iḥrām*); the chanting of the pilgrim song; the prayer of intention and of supplication for grace to make the visitation duly; the contemplation, touch, and salutation of the mystic black stone; the sevenfold encompassment of the *ka'ba*, towards which from distant homes has been directed the prayer of the bygone years; the ascent of the Mount of Purity (*Ṣafā*), and prayer and confession of faith upon it; the race seven times repeated from its summit to that of the Mount of Marwa; the common worship in the Great Mosque, and the sermon preached to the assemblage of common believers; the various pilgrimages and prayers of the eighth and ninth days; and on the tenth the extraordinary pelting of devils, which is symbolized by the patriarchal rite of the stoning of the pillars of Mina. Later in the same day occurs the final act of the *ḥaj*, an animal sacrifice. Whether the ladies could pay a substitute to perform this is not said.

During these ten busy days the seamless wrapper is worn; after the sacrifice it is laid aside, and attention may be paid to the neglected toilette. The pilgrim stays three days longer in Makka—days of the 'drying of the blood of sacrifice,' 'three well-earned days of rest after the peripatetic performance of the last four.' Still, all is not finished; there should be more circuits of the *ka'ba*, another stoning at Mina, and a draught drunk from the sacred well. Our princess would certainly do everything which was due, and probably would go to Medina, and she would also make visitation to the tombs of many pious persons buried in the desirable soil of Arabia.

In 1579 Khwāja Yaḥyā was *mīr ḥaj*, a friend of Badāyunī, and the charitable man to whom Ḥusain the Patcher (*tukriya*) was indebted for decent burial. He was commissioned to escort the ladies home, and also to bring back curiosities and Arab servants,[1] who may perhaps have been wanted for the Arab *sarāī*, established near the mausoleum of Humāyūn, outside Dihlī.

The return journey was both adventurous and perilous. They were shipwrecked off Aden, and had to stay, some say seven, others twelve, months in that desolate spot, far less habitable then than now, with condensed water, a tide from the Suez Canal, occasional rain, and the British *rāj*. The governor did not behave well, and quitted the path of good manners, misconduct for which he was punished by his master, Sulṭān Murād of Turkey. One pleasant incident broke the gloom of the long delay. On a day of April, 1580, the rock-bound travellers saw a ship coming up from the south with the wind, and, wishing to know whose it was, sent a boat out to make inquiry. By a pleasant chance Bāyazīd[2] *bīyāt* with his wife and children were on board, and he shortened sail, though the wind was favourable, and gave and took news. Bāyazīd says that the persons who sent out the boat to him were Gul-badan Begam, Gul-ʿiẕār Begam, and Khwāja Yaḥyā. Perhaps

---

[1] The passage in the *Akbar-nāma* about these servants is in its author's later and difficult style. This led to mistake in my article of the *Calcutta Review*, April, 1898. I referred a difficulty the khwāja experienced to the ladies, whereas it was the servants who were unwilling to leave their Arabian domicile. Several other errors of that article are corrected in this book.

[2] His wife and a child died in Arabia; he wished to end his days on the sacred soil, and so sent home his other children. His wish also was to be laid beside his wife, and he tried her grave for several hours to see that it was neither too narrow nor too short. Happily for his readers, he did not stay in Arabia. His children were captured by the Portuguese, and he had to go back to their rescue. He sailed in 1582, but had long to wait in Mocha harbour for a wind, and this, with other delays, kept him eight months on board.

he was instrumental in getting them ships for return to India.

I do not know when the ladies succeeded in leaving Ạden, nor when they landed in Sūrat. Here they again waited long, and this delay is attributed partly to the rains and partly to the royal absence in Kābul. It was March, 1582, when they reached Fatḥpūr-sīkrī.

On the northward journey they visited the shrines of the Chishtī saints in Ajmīr, and there met Prince Sālim. Day after day there came an amīr with greetings from the Emperor, until he met the caravan at Khānwa. The night of reunion was kept awake by 'questions and entrancing stories; gifts were shown, and happiness brimmed over.' One item of home news would cloud the meeting: Bega Begam had died just too soon to welcome her old friends.

Arrived in Fatḥpūr-sīkrī, Gul-badan Begam would find much to ruffle her orthodoxy; for Father Rodolf Acquaviva was installed there and was giving Prince Murād lessons in the Christian faith. She would hear of the reverence shown by her nephew for the sacred things of an alien faith, and of his liking for the society of the pious and learned guest. Ḥamīda-bānū is named by the Father as protesting, with other ladies of the *ḥaram*, against the royal countenance of Christianity, and assuredly Gul-badan would swell the chorus of complaint, in which, too, Hindū wives would join the Moslim lamentation.[1] When the Father was leaving Fatḥpūr-sīkrī, he accepted only so much money as would pay his expenses back to Goa, but he asked a favour from Ḥamīda-bānū Begam. She had amongst her household slaves a Russian of Moscow and his Polish wife, with their two children. These four the Father begged to take with him to Goa. 'The begam, who was no friend to the Firingīs, was most unwilling to give up the slaves; but

[1] The whole account of Father Acquaviva's stay at the court is extremely interesting, and much of it may be read in Father Goldie's 'First Christian Mission to the Great Mughal' (Dublin: Gill and Co., 1897).

the Emperor would refuse nothing to the Father,' and the family was carried off to freedom.

The next thing known of our princess is that she wrote her *Humāyūn-nāma.* The book is its sole witness, for no one speaks of it. It is not literature, but a simple setting down of what she knew or had heard, for the help of the *Akbar-nāma.* This was not her only composition, for she followed the fashion of her day and wrote verses. Mīr Mahdī Shīrāzī has preserved in his *Tazkiratu-l-khwātīn* two lines of hers, in which her thought seems to be, 'No love, no fruit of life.'

> "*Har parī ki au bā 'ashaq khud yār nīst,*
> *Tū yaqīn mīdān ki hech az 'umr bar-khur-dār nīst.*"

Nine copies were made of Bāyazīd's *Humāyūn-nāma,* which was written in obedience to the royal command obeyed by Gul-badan Begam and also by Jauhar the Ewer-bearer. Of these two went to the Emperor's library; three to the princes Sālim, Murād, and Danyal; one to our begam; two to Abū'l-fazl; and one perhaps was kept by the author. This allotment brings out the little point that Gul-badan collected books. Badāyunī has a curious passage about himself which also discloses something 'bookish' of Salīma: 'On account of the book *Khirad-afza,* which had disappeared from the library, and concerning Salīma Sulṭān Begam's study of which the Emperor reminded me, an order was issued that my allowance should be stopped, and that they should demand the book of me.' He adds that Abū'l-fazl did not lay his refutation before the Emperor, and he does not clear up the awkward doubt as to what he had done with Salīma's desired book.

The remaining records of Gul-badan Begam's life are few and scanty. When she was seventy, her name is mentioned with that of Muḥammad-yār, a son of her daughter, who left the court in disgrace; again, she and Salīma join in intercession to Akbar for Prince Sālim; again, with Ḥamīda, she receives royal gifts of money and jewels. Her charities were large, and it is said of her that she added day unto day in the endeavour to please God, and this by succouring the poor and needy. When she was eighty years old, and in February, 1603, her departure was heralded by a few days of fever. Ḥamīda was with her to the end, and it may be that Ruqaiya, Hindāl's daughter, would also watch her last hours. As she lay with closed eyes, Ḥamīda-bānū spoke to her by the long-used name of affection, '*Jiu!*' (elder sister). There was no response. Then, 'Gul-badan!' The dying woman unclosed her eyes, quoted the verse, 'I die,—may you live!' and passed away.

Akbar helped to carry her bier some distance, and for her soul's repose made lavish gifts and did good works. He will have joined in the silent prayer for her soul before committal of her body to the earth, and if no son were there, he, as a near kinsman, may have answered the Imām's injunction to resignation: 'It is the will of God.'

So ends the long life of a good and clever woman, affectionate and dutiful in her home life, and brought so near us by her sincerity of speech and by her truth of feeling that she becomes a friend even across the bars of time and creed and death.

PART II.

GUL-BADAN BEGAM'S BOOK, THE 'HUMĀYŪN-NĀMA.'

IT is not generally known to English students of the (so-called) Mughal period of Indian history that Gul-badan Begam wrote a book. It was not known to Mr. Erskine, or he would have given fuller and more accurate accounts of the families of Bābar and Humāyūn. It escaped even Professor Blochmann's wider opportunities of acquaintance with Persian MSS. Until the begam's *Humāyūn-nāma* was catalogued by Dr. Rieu, it was a literary *parda-nishīn*, and since that time has been little better. Abū-'l-faẓl, for whose information it was written, does not mention it, but the *Akbar-nāma* is not without indication of its use.[1]

Bāyazīd's *Tārīkh-i-humāyūn* was reproduced several times on its completion. Gul-badan Begam's *Humāyūn-nāma* was written under the same royal order and for the same end. It would have been natural to reproduce it also, but no second example of it can be discovered by us in any of the accessible book-catalogues of Europe or India, and prolonged search, made by advertisement, private inquiry, and in person by my husband in India, has failed to disclose knowledge of its existence which may not conjecturally be traced to my own work upon it. Once hope arose that a second MS. was to reward the search, because a correspondent intimated that he possessed for sale a MS. which was inscribed as being the begam's. On examination this was found to be so, but the MS. was a copy of the *Kānūn-i-humāyūn* of Khwānd-amīr. It is now in the British Museum.

Hope was again aroused by a mention of Gul-badan's book in a recent work, the *Darbār-i-akbarī* of Shamsu-l-ulamā' 'Muḥammad Ḥusain *āzād*. Mr. Beveridge paid two visits to the author in Bombay, but could learn nothing from him. He appeared mentally alienated, denied all knowledge of the work, and that he had ever written of it. His reference may conjecturally be traced to my article in the *Calcutta Review* upon Gul-badan Begam's writings, and does not, unfortunately, appear to indicate access to a second MS.

The MS. from which I have translated belongs to the Hamilton Collection in the British Museum, and was bought in 1868 from the widow of Colonel George William Hamilton. It is classed by Dr. Rieu amongst the most remarkable of the 352 MSS. which were selected for purchase out of the 1,000 gathered in by Colonel Hamilton from Lucknow and Dihlī. It does not bear the vermilion

1 A passage about Bābar (*Bib. Ind.*, edit. I. 87) closely resembles the begam's on the same topic; and a divergence, noted by Mr. Erskine (Mems., 218 n.) as made from Bābar's narrative by Abū'l-faẓl, is made also by the begam.

stamp of the King of Oude, so the surmise is allowed that it came from Dihlī. It has been rebound (not recently, I believe), plainly, in red leather; and it is unadorned by frontispiece, margin, or rubric. Whether there has ever been a colophon cannot be said; the latter pages of the work are lost. The folio which now stands last is out of place, an error apparently made in the rebinding. Catch-words are frequently absent, and there are none on the last folio. There are blank fly-leaves, prefixed and suffixed, of paper unlike that of the MS..

The absence of a second MS., and, still more, the absence of mention of the work, seem to indicate that few copies ever existed.

Dr. Rieu's tentative estimate of the date of the British Museum MS. (seventeenth century) does not, I am counselled, preclude the possibility of transcription so late in the sixteenth century as 1587 (995 H.) onwards. It may be the first and even sole example.

Gul-badan Begam, as is natural, uses many Tūrkī words, and at least one Tūrkī phrase. Her scribe (who may be herself) does not always write these with accuracy; some run naturally from the pen as well-known words do; some are laboured in the writing, as though care had to be taken in the copying or original orthography.

Tūrkī was Gul-badan's native language; it was also her husband's; it would be the home speech of her married life. Persian was an accomplishment. These considerations awaken speculation: Did she compose in Persian? or in Tūrkī? That she read Tūrkī is clear from her upbringing and her references to her father's book. She has one almost verbal reproduction of a passage from it retained in Tūrkī.

The disadvantage of working from a single MS. is felt at every point, and nowhere more than when the MS. itself is under consideration.

TRANSLATION

OF THE

HUMĀYŪN-NĀMA OF GUL-BADAN BEGAM.

6

NOTE ON THE PERSIAN TITLES.

Of these there are two:

1. '*Humāyūn-nāma.* Written by Gul-badan Begam, daughter of Bābar Pādshāh.' This is on the first fly-leaf, which is of paper differing in colour and texture from that of the body of the MS., and identical with that of four blank sheets which are bound up at the end of the MS., perhaps to allow of writing in the missing portion of the work.

2. 'Accounts of Humāyūn Pādshāh. Put together by Gul-badan Begam, a daughter of Bābar Pādshāh and a paternal aunt of Akbar Pādshāh.' This stands on the first folio of the MS., which by the original paging is folio 10, and by the British Museum marking folio 2 (*a*).

(2*b* of the Persian text.)

IN the name of God, the Merciful, the Compassionate!

There had been an order[1] issued, 'Write down whatever you know of the doings of *Firdaus-makānī* and *Jannat-āshyānī*.'[2]

At the time when his Majesty *Firdaus-makānī* passed from this perishable world to the everlasting home, I, this lowly one, was eight[3] years old, so it may well be that I do not remember much. However, in obedience to the royal command, I set down whatever there is that I have heard and remember.

First of all, by way of invoking a blessing (on my work), and in pious commemoration, a chapter (*juzū*) is written about my royal father's deeds, although these are told in his memoirs.[4]

---

[1] Probably that mentioned by Abū'l-fazl, as issued for the gathering-in of material for the *Akbar-nāma*. (H. Beveridge, I. 29.) If so, the begam's book dates from about 1587 (995H.). There are indications of its use by Abū'l-fazl.

[2] Bābar's and Humāyūn's posthumous names, 'Dwelling' and 'Nesting in Paradise.' Several women, and notably Akbar's mother, have been named after death *Maryam-makānī*, 'Dwelling with Mary.' Bābar's half-sister, Shahr-bānū, is styled by A.F. *Bilqīs-makānī*,—Bilqīs being the Queen of Sheba. Many other examples might be quoted of the custom which, amongst some savage tribes, takes the extreme form of total suppression at death of the name borne in life, and towards which affection and reverence incline the most civilized peoples.

[3] Lunar years. Bābar died December 26th, 1530. The begam's dates and numerical statements must always be taken lightly.

[4] From this treasury Gul-badan's meagre historical sketch can be

From his Majesty *Ṣāḥib-qirānī*[1] down to my royal father there was not one of the bygone princes who laboured as he did. He became king in his twelfth[2] year, and the *khuṭba*[3] was read in his name on June 10th, 1494,[4] in Andijān, the capital of Farghāna. (3*a*)

For eleven full years his wars and struggles against the Chaghatāi and Tīmūrid and Uzbeg princes[5] in Māwarā'u-n-nahr (Transoxiana) were such that the tongue of the pen is too feeble and weak to recount them.

The toils and perils which in the ruling of kingdoms befell our prince, have been measured out to few, and of few have been recorded the manliness, courage and endurance which he showed in battle-fields and dangers. Twice he took Samarqand by force of the sword. The first time my royal father was twelve years old, the second nineteen, the third time he was nearly twenty-two.[6] For six months he was besieged[7] (in Samarqand), and neither Sulṭān Ḥusain Mīrzā *Bāyqrā*, his paternal uncle,[8] who

---

filled in. The *Tūzūk-i-bābarī* (Leyden and Erskine: Longman, Rees, etc., 1826.) will be referred to in these notes as the 'Memoirs' or 'Mems.'. Mr. W. Erskine's 'History of India under Bābar and Humāyūn' will be indicated by 'B. & H.'.

[1] *Lord of the fortunate conjunction, i.e.*, of Jupiter and Venus, a posthumous title of Tīmūr (1336-1405), from whom Bābar was fifth in descent.

[2] Bābar was born February 14th, 1483 (Muḥarram 6th, 888H.). He therefore became king of Farghāna (Khokand) when 11⅓ years old.

[3] The prayer and oration in which it is ordained that the name of the reigning sovereign should be recited. *Cf.* Dict. of Islām, Hughes, *s.v.*. The histories show that it was formerly so recited in India. The term 'Ruler of the Age' filled Victoria's place.

[4] Ramẓān 5th, 899H. [Text, 909H.].

[5] The first and second of this triad of foes were near and elder kinsmen; the third was the Shaibānī of the histories.

[6] Bābar occupied Samarqand three times. Twice he captured it, and the third time entered without a blow struck and amidst a popular welcome. The dates are respectively 1497, 1500, and 1511, and his age fifteen, seventeen, and twenty-nine.

[7] By Shaibānī, after the second occupation.

[8] *'ammū.* Ḥusain was of the fourth, and Bābar of the fifth degree of descent from their common ancestor, Tīmūr. Bābar's father was (*anglice*) Ḥusain's fourth cousin. As Ḥusain was of an elder generation, Bābar calls him 'uncle.' If *'ammū* were ever used to denote an uncle by marriage, it would have triple application here, since Ḥusain married in succession three paternal aunts of Bābar—Shahr-

AMĪR TĪMŪR (*ṢĀḤIB-QIRĀN*).

[*To face p.* 84.

(ruled) in Khurāsān, nor Sulṭān Maḥmūd Khān, his maternal uncle,[1] who ruled in Kāshghar, sent him help. When none came from any quarter, he grew desperate.[2]

At this difficult time, Shāhī Beg Khān[3] sent to say: 'If you would marry your sister Khānzāda Begam[4] to me, (3b) there might be peace and a lasting alliance between us.' At length it had to be done; he gave the begam to the khān, and came out himself (from Samarqand).[5] With 200 followers on foot, wearing long frocks on their shoulders and peasants' brogues on their feet, and carrying clubs in their hands,—in this plight, unarmed, and relying on God, he went towards the lands of Badakhshān (Badakhshānāt) and Kābul.[6]

Khusrau Shāh's[7] people and army were in Kunduz and the Badakhshānāt. He came and paid his respects to his Majesty,[8] my father, who, being as he was manly and kind and generous, did not in any way touch the question of retaliation, although Khusrau Shāh had committed such crimes as the martyrdom of Bayasanghar Mīrzā and the blinding of Sulṭān Mas'ūd Mīrzā, both of whom were sons of my royal father's paternal uncle. In addition to this, when in the early days of the forays,[9] his Majesty chanced

---

bānū, Latīf and Payanda. Ḥusain is the well-known Mæcenas of Herāt (1438-1506).

[1] *taghāi.* Sulṭān Maḥmūd Khān was full-brother of Qutluq-nigār, Bābar's mother, so that here *taghāi* is exactly equivalent to our 'maternal uncle.' Maḥmūd is 'the Khān' and the 'elder Khān' of the Memoirs, and also *Jānakī* or *Khānakī* and *Jāngī*. He was murdered by Shaibānī in 1508.

[2] He was eighteen.

[3] Abū'l-fatḥ Muḥammad Shāhbakht Khān *Uzbeg* (Shāhī Beg Khān and Shaibānī).

[4] For details of her life and that of all other women named in this book and some other contemporary works, see Appendix.

[5] Early in 907H. (July, 1501).

[6] Muḥarram, 910H. (June, 1504).

[7] A Qipchāq Tūrk, chief beg of Sulṭān Maḥmūd Mīrzā, the father of Bayasanghar and Mas'ūd. He was put to death by Shaibānī's Uzbegs in 910H. (1505).

[8] Brevet rank. Bābar was an exile from his own kingdom of Farghāna, and not yet master of Kābul.

[9] Tūrkī, *qazzāqī*, from *qazzāq* (Cossack), the name of the nomads whom the Russians term Kīrghiz. I think Gul-badan uses it to de-

to cross his country, he was watched and rudely driven out. Now he was pleased to command that Khusrau Shāh should take whatever his heart desired of his (own) jewels and golden vessels, and so he got leave to go to Khurāsān in kindness and safety, and took with him five or six strings of camels and five or six of baggage mules.[1] (4*a*)

His Majesty now set out for Kābul, which was occupied by Muḥammad Muqīm, a son of Ẕū'l-nūn *Arghūn*, and grandfather of Nāhīd Begam.[2] He had captured it after Ulugh Beg Mīrzā's[3] death from Mīrzā 'Abdu-r-razzāq, son of his Majesty's paternal uncle (Ulugh Beg).

His Majesty reached Kābul in safety. Muḥammad Muqīm kept command for a few days, and then by pact and agreement made over charge to the royal servants, and went off with goods and chattels to his father in Qandahār. This was in the last ten days of Rabī II., 910H.[4] Being now master of Kābul, his Majesty went to Bangash, took it at a blow, and returned to Kābul.

Her Highness, the khānam,[5] his Majesty's mother, had fever for six days, and then departed from this fleeting world to the eternal home. They laid her in the New Year's Garden. His Majesty paid 1,000 coined *misqāl* to his kinsmen, the owners of the garden, and laid her there.

At this time urgent letters arrived from Sulṭān Ḥusain Mīrzā, saying: (4*b*) 'I am planning a war against the Uzbegs. It would be excellent if you came too.' My royal father

---

scribe the time of her father's military incursions, made when he was trying to carve out a ruler's seat.

[1] The begam's brevity makes Bābar's capacity and forbearance seem alike remarkable. He had gathered a force, and safety was the condition of Khusrau's surrender (1504). Mr. Erskine writes (B. & H., I. 208.): 'Bābar, whose abhorrence of Khusrau was as deep as it was just, ordered his treasurer to send back the treasure, horses, and whatever had been presented to him, just as they were; although, says our author (Mīrzā Ḥaidar), the King had only one horse suitable for a person of his rank, and that was used by his mother.'

[2] Through his daughter Māh Chūchak.

[3] A son of Abū-sa'īd, known as *Kābulī*. He died 1502.

[4] October, 1504. Bābar was now twenty-three, and had acquired more territory than his lost Farghāna.

[5] Qutluq-nigār. She died June, 1505.

sought counsel of God. At length he set out to join the mīrzā. On the way news came that the mīrzā was dead. His Majesty's amīrs represented that, this being so, it was advisable to return to Kābul, but he replied: 'As we have come so far, we will carry our condolences to the princes.' In the end he went on towards Khurāsān.[1]

When the princes[2] heard of the royal visit, they one and all set out to give him honourable meeting, except Badī'u-z-zamān Mīrzā, who did not go because Barandūq Beg and Ẕū'l-nūn Beg—amīrs of Sulṭān Ḥusain Mīrzā—said, in effect, that as his Majesty was fifteen years younger than Badī'u-z-zamān Mīrzā, it was right that he should be the first to bow, and that they should then embrace one another. Qāsim Beg[3] rejoined: 'Younger he is by years, but by the *tūra*,[4] he has precedence because he has more than once taken Samarqand by force of the sword.' (5*a*) At length they agreed that his Majesty should bow on coming in, and that Badī'u-z-zamān should then advance to show him honour, and they should embrace. The mīrzā was not attending when his Majesty came in at the door; Qāsim Beg clutched my royal father's girdle and pulled it, and said to Barandūq Beg and Ẕū'l-nūn Beg: 'The agreement was that the mīrzā should come forward and that then they should embrace one another.' The prince then advanced in great agitation and they embraced.

As long as his Majesty was in Khurāsān, each one of the princes showed him hospitality, and feasts were arranged, and excursions to all the gardens and places of

---

[1] Bābar set out in June, 1506 (Muḥarram, 912H.). Ḥusain had died in May (Ẕū'l-ḥijja, 911H.), on his way northwards from Herāt, and at Bābā Ilāhī. Word reached Bābar when he had already made a great journey and had crossed the Saighan and Dandān-shikan passes to Kahmard. After receiving the news he marched some 800 miles to the mīrzās' camp on the Murgh-āb.

[2] Badī'u-z-zamān and Muḥammad Muẓaffar Ḥusain, sons of Sulṭān Ḥusain Mīrzā. The meeting was on November 6th, 1506 (Jumāda II. 8th, 912H.).

[3] Bābar's Prime Minister and (I believe) relation. He was of the Qūchīn tribe to which Bābar's grandmother, Aīs-daulat, belonged.

[4] The Rules of Chingīz Khān. These are referred to again on points of etiquette.

interest. They set forth to him the inconvenience of winter, and said: 'Wait till it is over, and we will fight the Uzbegs.' But they could not in any way settle about the war. Eighty years[1] long had Sulṭān Ḥusain Mīrzā kept Khurāsān safe and sound, but the mīrzās could not fill their father's place for six months. When his Majesty saw that they were careless[2] about his expenses and revenue, he went to Kābul on the pretext of seeing the places he had assigned to himself. (5*b*) Much snow had fallen that year. They took the wrong road. His Majesty and Qāsim Beg chose one[3] because of its shortness, but the amīrs had given other advice, and when this was not taken, they all left him without a thought for him. He and Qāsim Beg and his sons made a road in two or three days by removing the snow, and the people of the army followed. So they reached Ghūrband. Some Hazāra rebels having met his Majesty here, there was fighting; and cattle and sheep and goods without number belonging to the Hazāra fell into the hands of his people. Then they started for Kābul with their enormous booty.

At the skirts of Minār Hill they heard that Mīrzā Khān[4] and Mīrzā Muḥammad Ḥusain *Gūrkān*[5] had rebelled and

---

[1] A well-rounded number. Sulṭān Ḥusain was born 842H. (1438), and died 911H. (1506). Bābar calls the joint-kingship of his sons a strange arrangement and one never heard of, and quotes Sa'dī's well-known couplet as applicable—'Ten darvishes can sleep on one rug, but one climate cannot hold two kings.'

[2] While on the Murgh-āb, Bābar agreed to winter in Khurāsān, and he went with the joint-kings to Herāt in order to see the 'sights' of that renowned city. He certainly worked hard, for he names some fifty-two which he saw in twenty days. The invitation to winter was repeated, but neither quarters nor suitable conveniences (? revenues) were allotted. Bābar delicately says he could not explain his real motive for not remaining, and left under pressure of necessity on December 24th, 1506, after snow had fallen along a route which was a month's ordinary journey.

It was during this absence from Kābul that he married Māham, Humāyūn's mother.

[3] Through the Aimāq and Hazāra country, and south of his route to Herāt.

[4] Sulṭān Wais, a son of Bābar's paternal uncle, Maḥmūd, and his maternal aunt (*i.e.*, his mother's half-sister), Sulṭān Nigār Khānam.

[5] Father of Ḥaidar Mīrzā *Dughlāt*, author of the *Tārīkh-i-rashīdī*. He married Khūb-nigār, full-sister of Bābar's mother.

were holding Kābul. His Majesty sent a comforting and cheering letter (to his friends in the fort), and said: 'Be of good heart! I too am here. (6*a*) I will light a fire on the Hill of the Moon-faced Lady; do you light one on the Treasury, so that I may be sure you know of our coming. In the morning we will fall on the enemy, you from that side and we from this.' But he had fought and won before the people of the fort came out.

Mīrzā Khān hid himself in his mother's house; she was his Majesty's maternal aunt. Mīrzā Muḥammad Ḥusain was in his wife's house. She was his Majesty's younger maternal aunt. He flung himself down on a carpet, and in fear of his life cried to a servant, 'Fasten it up!' His Majesty's people heard of this. They took him out of the carpet and brought him to the presence. In the end, his Majesty forgave the mīrzās their offences, for the sake of his aunts. He used to go, in his old fashion, in and out of his aunts' houses,[1] and showed them more and more affection, so that no mist of trouble might dim their hearts. He assigned them places and holdings in the plain-country. (6*b*)

God the most High, having freed Kābul from the power of Mīrzā Khān, committed it to my royal father's care. He was then twenty-three years old[2] and had no child and greatly desired one. In his seventeenth year a girl[3] had been born to him by 'Āyisha Sulṭān Begam, a daughter of Sulṭān Aḥmad Mīrzā, but she had died in a month. The most high God blessed the taking of Kābul, for after it eighteen children were born. (1.) Of my Lady (*Akām*[4]) who was Māham Begam there were born his Majesty the Emperor

[1] Text, *khāna khālī khālahā'ī*. This I do not understand, as there were certainly no mothers' brothers present in Kābul now.

[2] He was twenty-three when he took Kābul from Muḥammad Muqīm *Arghūn* in 1504. Mīrza Khān's rebellion took place two years later.

[3] Fakhru-n-nisā', the Glory of Women. 'She was my first child, and I was just nineteen. In a month, or forty days, she went to the mercy of God.' (Mems. 90.)

[4] Written sometimes *Akām*, and sometimes *Akam*. The Tūrkī *Akā* is used as a title of respect from a junior to a senior. It has also the sense 'elder brother,' which makes application to a woman doubtful.

Humāyūn, and Bārbūl Mīrzā, and Mihr-jān (jahān) Begam, and Ishān-daulat Begam, and Fārūq Mīrzā.[1]

(2.) Ma'ṣūma Sulṭān Begam, daughter of Sulṭān Aḥmad Mīrzā, died in childbed. The mother's name they gave to the daughter.

(3.) Of Gul-rukh Begam were born Kāmrān Mīrzā, and 'Askarī Mīrzā, and Shāh-rukh Mīrzā, and Sulṭān Aḥmad Mīrzā, and Gul-'izār Begam.

(4.) Of Dil-dār Begam were born Gul-rang Begam, and Gul-chihra Begam, and Hindāl Mīrzā, and Gul-badan Begam, and Alwar Mīrzā.[2]

. In short, in taking Kābul he got a good omen. All his children were born there except two begams who were born in Khost, viz., Mihr-jān Begam, a daughter of Māham Begam, and Gul-rang, a daughter of Dil-dār Begam. (7*a*)

The blessed birth of the Emperor Humāyūn, the first-born son of his Majesty *Firdaus-makānī*, occurred in the night of Tuesday, Ẕū'l-qa'da 4th, 913H. (March 6th, 1508), in the citadel of Kābul, and when the sun was in the sign Pisces.

That same year his Majesty was pleased to order the amīrs and the rest of the world to style him emperor (*bādshāh*). For before the birth of the Emperor Humāyūn he had been named and styled Mīrzā Bābar. All kings' sons were called mīrzās. In the year of his Majesty Humāyūn's birth he styled himself *bādshāh*.

They found[3] the date of the birth in *Sulṭan Humāyūn Khān*, and also in *Shāh-(i)-fīroz-qadr*.[4]

After children had been born to him, news came that Shāh Ismā'īl had killed Shāhī Beg Khān.[5]

(*Cf.* Vambéry's 'Cagataische Sprach-studien.') Bābar uses the word (Mems. 208.), and Mr. Erskine suggests to read 'My Lady.'

[1] Born 1525; died 1527. His father never saw him.

[2] Gul-badan or her copyist does not balance accounts. She says eighteen, and names sixteen children. This may be a clerical error only.

[3] *i.e.*, by *abjad*. *Cf.* Steingass' Persian Dictionary, *s.v. abjad*.

[4] 'The king, victorious in might.'

[5] At Merv, December 2nd, 1510. *Cf.* B. & H., I. 302. On the removal of this formidable foe, Bābar again tried to regain his ancestral lands, but was still outmatched by the Uzbegs. Defeat by them led him to take a road of less resistance through Bajaur to Hindūstān.

His Majesty at this time entrusted Kābul to Nāṣir[1] Mīrzā, and set out[2] for Samarqand, taking with him his people and wives and children, who were Humāyūn Mīrzā, and Mihr-jahān Begam, and Bārbūl Mīrzā, and Maʿṣūma Begam, and Kāmrān Mīrzā. (*7b*)

With help from Shāh Ismāʿīl, he took Samarqand (October, 1511), and for eight (lunar) months the whole of Māwarā'u-n-nahr (Transoxiana) was in his power. Owing to want of co-operation in his brothers and to the opposition of the Mughals,[3] he was defeated at Kūl Malik by ʿUbaidu-l-lāh Khān. As he could not remain in those parts, he set out for Badakhshān and Kābul, and put out of his head further thought of Māwarā'u-n-nahr.

He had become master of Kābul in 910H. (1504). He had always desired to go into Hindūstān, and had not carried out his wish because of the feeble counsels of his amīrs and the non-agreement of his brothers. When at length these were gone,[4] and there remained no amīr such as could argue against it, he accomplished his desire.

Bajaur[5] he took in two or three hours and ordered a general massacre.

On the same day the father of Afghānī *āghācha*,[6] Malik Manṣūr Yūsufzai, came in and paid his respects. (*8a*) His Majesty took his daughter in marriage and then gave him leave to depart. He bestowed on him a horse and a suit of honour befitting a ruler, and said to him: 'Go and

---

[1] Bābar's half-brother, son of Umīd, an Andijānī.

[2] January, 1511 (Shawwāl, 916H.).

[3] For a more interesting cause of defeat, *cf.* B. & H., I. 321, *et seq.* 'Ubaidu-l-lāh was Shaibānī's nephew. Kūl (Lake) Malik is in Bokhārā. Bābar was again defeated by the Uzbegs in this same year (1511).

[4] *i.e.*, dead. Jahāngīr died in 1507 and Nāṣir in 1515, both from drinking. This passage resembles Bābar's own words. (Mems. 309.)

[5] Gul-badan is confusingly brief. Bajaur was attacked 925H. (1519) on the way to India, and its people put to the sword because they were 'rebels to followers of Islām' and addicted to infidel customs. (Mems. 246 *et seq.*.)

[6] The Afghān Lady. It is thus that Gul-badan always speaks of Bībī (Lady) Mubārika, the Yūsufzai wife of Bābar. Pavet de Courteille defines *āghācha* thus: 'Se dit des femmes par opposition à begam et khānam; dame.' I do not in Gul-badan's work trace any disrespect attaching to '*āghācha*,' such as is indicated by '*concubine*,' as which it is sometimes translated.

bring men and labourers, etc., to your native land and cultivate it.'

Qāsim Beg,[1] who was in Kābul, sent a letter saying: 'Another prince has been born. I have ventured to write as an omen of the conquest of Hind and of taking its throne. As for the rest, the Emperor is master, whatever is his pleasure'[2] (let it be done). In an auspicious hour his Majesty named him Mīrzā Hindāl.

Having subdued Bajaur, his Majesty went towards the Bhīra country, and on his arrival made peace without plundering. He took four *laks* of *shāhrukhīs*[3] and gave to his army, dividing them according to the number of his followers. He then set out for Kābul.[4]

Just now came a letter from Badakhshān saying: 'Mīrzā Khān is dead;[5] Mīrzā Sulaimān is young; the Uzbegs are near; take thought for this kingdom lest (which God forbid) Badakhshān should be lost.' (8*b*) Until there should be thought taken, Mīrzā Sulaimān's mother[6] had brought him (to the Emperor). Agreeably to this petition and their wish, the Emperor assigned to Mīrzā Sulaimān the lands and inheritance which had been his father's, and he gave Badakhshān to Mīrzā Humāyūn.

The mīrzā set out for his province. His Majesty and my Lady (*Akām*) followed and also went to Badakhshān, and there spent several days together. The mīrzā remained

---

1 Qāsim Beg *Qūchīn*, an ancient Beg of Andijān, and one of Bābar's best followers.

2 Qy., as to the child's name. His true name was Muḥ. Nāṣir, but he is only known as Hindāl. He was Gul-badan's full brother, and was given, before birth, to Māham Begam, who had lost all her children younger than Humāyūn. *Cf.* 24*a* n.

3 Estimated by Mr. Erskine at about £20,000 sterling.

4 End of February, 1519. In his winning fashion Bābar relates that he forbade the news of his return to be taken to Kābul, and that there was therefore no time to put his boys, Humāyūn and Kāmrān, on horseback, and that they were carried out in the arms of the nearest servants to offer their duty on his return, to a place between the fort gates and the citadel.

5 *Cir.* 926H. (1520). *Cf.* Mems. 286 n., and *Tār. Rash.*, Ney Elias and Ross, 373 n..

6 Sulṭān Nigār Khānam.

and my royal father and my Lady came back to Kābul[1] (926H.—1520).

After a time his Majesty set out for Qilāt and Qandahār.[2] He was victorious at once in Qilāt, and went on to Qandahār and kept its garrison shut up for a year and a half. Then, by the Divine favour and after great fighting and skirmishing, he captured it. Much gold fell into his hands, and he gave moneys and camels to his soldiers and the people of the army. Qandahār he bestowed on Mīrzā Kāmrān, and himself set off for Kābul.

His advance camp having been set up,[3] he crossed the hill of Yak Langa, and gloriously alighted in the valley of Dīh-i-ya'qūb on Friday, Ṣafar 1st, 932H. (November 17th, 1525), when the sun was in Sagittarius. (9*a*) He spent the following day there, and on the next set forth, march by march, for Hindūstān. In the seven or eight years since 925H. (1519)[4] the royal army had several times renewed the attempt on Hindūstān. Each time it used to conquer lands and districts, such as Bhīra, Bajaur, Sīālkūt, Dīpālpūr, Lāhōr, etc., up to the fifth time, when on Ṣafar 1st, 932H., his Majesty went, march by march, from his glorious encamping in Dīh-i-ya'qūb towards Hindūstān. He conquered Lāhōr and Sirhind, and every country that lay on his path.

On Friday, Rajab 8th, 932H. (April 20th, 1526), he

---

[1] Humāyūn was now thirteen years old. He was young to be sent so far as Badakhshān. That his parents went with him is one of Gulbadan's life-giving touches. *Akām* may now well have shown her boy to her father and her kinsfolk in Khost. (Memoirs of Bāyazīd, I.O. MS., 26*a*.)

[2] Held now by Shāh Beg *Arghūn*, father of Shāh Ḥusain, Humāyūn's later enemy in Sind. Firishta gives three years as the duration of the siege, Khāfī Khān four years, and Mīrzā Ḥaidar five years. The occurrence unfortunately coincides with one of the gaps in the Memoirs. This was Bābar's culminating attempt on Qandahār; his first being in 1505,—this one seems to have ended in 1522 (928H.).

[3] Gul-badan, by a sudden transition, passes over some three years, and, as it seems, using her father's Memoirs, enters on the account of his last and successful expedition to Hindūstān. Yak Langa is a hill between Kābul and Butkhāk, and on the road to Jalālābād.

[4] Text, 935H.; clearly a slip.

arrayed battle at Pānīpat[1] against Sulṭān Ibrāhīm, son of Sulṭān Sikandar, son of Bahlūl *Lodī*. By God's grace he was victorious, and Sulṭān Ibrāhīm was killed in the fight.

His victory was won purely by the Divine grace, for Sulṭān Ibrāhīm had a *lak* and 80,000 horse, and as many as 1,500 head of fierce elephants; (9*b*) while his Majesty's army with the traders and good and all (*badr* (?) *bad*, bad) was 12,000 persons and he had, at the outside, 6,000 or 7,000 serviceable men.

The treasures of five kings fell into his hands. He gave everything away. The amīrs of Hind represented that in Hindūstān it was thought disgraceful to expend the treasure of bygone kings, and that people rather added and added to it, while his Majesty, on the contrary, had given all away.[2]

Khwāja[3] Kilān[4] Beg asked leave several times to go to Kābul. He said: 'My constitution is not fitted for the climate of Hindūstān. If leave were given, I should tarry awhile in Kābul.' His Majesty was not at all, at all willing for him to go, but at last gave permission because he saw him so very urgent. He said: 'When you go, I shall send some of the valuable presents and curiosities of Hind which fell into our hands through the victory over

---

[1] 'A far-reaching, almost illimitable level tract, broken only by insignificant undulations. Here and there, where the shallow soil is moistened from some niggardly watercourse, grow sparse grasses and stunted thorn-bushes. But, for the most part, the eye falls only on the uniform yellowish-gray waste of sterile earth. Everywhere empty silence reigns, and it would almost seem as if this desert had been designed for the battlefield of nations.' (Emperor Akbar, F. v. Noer., trs. A.S.B. I. 74.)

Thrice in modern times a decisive battle has been fought out here: (1) by Bābar against Ibrāhīm and the Lodīs, 1526; (2) by Akbar against the Indian Afghāns in 1556; and (3) by Aḥmad Shāh Durrānī against the Marāthās in 1761.

[2] Bābar distributed the treasure on the 11th or 12th of May, 1526, and left himself so little that he was dubbed *qalandar*.

[3] M. Garçin de Tassy says, in his 'Mémoire sur la Religion Musalmane' (46 n.) that khwāja, like sayyid, is a title for a descendant of Muḥammad. Shaw's Tūrkī Dictionary states that khwāja is applied to the offspring of a sayyid by a woman of another family, also to their descendants. I find many instances where both titles are applied to the same man.

[4] One of Bābar's most admirable followers and friends, and perhaps a relation. He was one of seven brothers, sons of Maulānā Muḥammad *Ṣadru-d-dīn*, who spent their lives in Bābar's service.

Sultān Ibrāhīm, to my elder relations[1] and sisters and each person of the ḥaram. You take them. I shall write a list, and you will distribute them according to it. (10*a*) You will order a tent with a screen to be set up in the Garden of the Audience Hall for each begam,[2] and when a pleasant meeting-place has been arranged, the begams are to make the prostration of thanks for the complete victory which has been brought about.

'To each begam is to be delivered as follows: one special dancing-girl of the dancing-girls of Sulṭān Ibrāhīm, with one gold plate full of jewels—ruby and pearl, cornelian and diamond, emerald and turquoise, topaz and cat's-eye—and two small mother-o'-pearl trays full of *ashrafīs*, and on two other trays *shāhrukhīs*,[3] and all sorts of stuffs by nines—that is, four trays and one plate. Take a dancing-girl and another plate of jewels, and one each of *ashrafīs* and *shāhrukhīs*, and present, in accordance with my directions, to my elder relations the very plate of jewels and the self-same dancing-girl which I have given for them. I have made other gifts;[4] convey these afterwards. (10*b*) Let them divide and present jewels and *ashrafīs* and *shāhrukhīs* and stuffs to my sisters and children and the *ḥarams*[5] and kinsmen, and to the begams and āghās[6] and

---

[1] *walīyu-n-ni'matān*, lords of beneficence. Gul-badan's application of it is to 'benevolent ladies,' *i.e.*, the numerous aunts. It is a title of respect for seniors.

[2] I think each begam was to encamp with her own establishment and within her own enclosure (*sarāparda*), and not in hasty camp-fashion of community of quarters. This would exalt the assembly.

The *sarapārda* or enclosing canvas wall, run at optional distance round tents, was, it is stated in the *Ma'āsiru-r-raḥīmī*, invented by Bairam *Khān-i-khānān*, and if this is true, it must at this date have been a quite modern convenience.

[3] It is waste of time to try to estimate the amount of these money gifts, made as they were in coins of uncertain value and recorded, probably on hearsay, more than fifty years after bestowal. Mr. Erskine puts the *shāhrukhī* at from 10d. to 1s., Steingass, *s.v.ashrafī*, gives for its value about 16 *rupīs*, presumably of undegenerated rank.

[4] Qy., for the elder relations.

[5] Presumably of his kinsmen and of officers whose families were with Bābar's own in Kābul.

[6] This word seems to describe women who were heads of household departments and not merely the guardians of *ḥarams*.

nurses and foster-brethren and ladies, and to all who pray for me.' The gifts were made according to the list.

Three happy days they remained together in the Audience Hall Garden. They were uplifted by pride, and recited the *fātiḥa*[1] for the benediction and prosperity of his Majesty, and joyfully made the prostration of thanks.[2]

The Emperor sent by Khwāja Kilān a large *ashrafī*,[3] which weighed three imperial *sīr*, that is, fifteen *sīr* of Hind, for . . . 'Asas.[4] He said to the Khwāja: 'If 'Asas asks you, "What has the Emperor sent for me?" say, "One *ashrafī*,"' as there really was only one. 'Asas was amazed, and fretted about it for three days. His Majesty had ordered that a hole should be bored in the *ashrafī*, and that 'Asas should be blindfolded and the *ashrafī* hung round his neck, and that then he was to be sent into the *ḥaram*. The hole was bored and the *ashrafī* hung round his neck. He was quite helpless with surprise at its weight, and delighted and very, very happy. He took it in both hands, and wondered over it and said, 'No one shall get my *ashrafī*.' Each begam, too, gave (? him) ten or twelve *ashrafī*, so he had seventy or eighty. (11*a*)

After Khwāja Kilān Beg had started for Kābul, the Emperor made gifts in Agra to his Majesty Humāyūn and

---

[1] The first chapter of the Qurān.

[2] In this prostration the forehead touches the ground.

[3] Perhaps from the Lodī treasury. (*Cf.* J.A.S.B. Proceedings, 1883; Thomas, 423; Richardson's Ar. & Per. Dict., *s.v. sikka;* Memoirs of the Mughal Empire, Jonathan Scott, 3 and 3 n.)

[4] Lit. a night-guard. The words preceding 'Asas offer much difficulty. They may be read *ba 'ammū*,—to the paternal uncle of 'Asas. But the story is of 'Asas, the night-guard and not of his uncle. Perhaps *'ammū* is a clerical error for *'amah*, bewilderment, misleading, and this would suit the story well. Mr. Beveridge has suggested to me to read *'Umarī*, *i.e.*, an old servant of 'Umar Shaikh. This, too, would be appropriate, for the victim of the hoax is clearly an old man.

The title 'Asas is applied several times by Bābar. One 'Asas was a boon companion and partook of Bābar's vow before the battle of Khānwa. (Mems. 283 and 354; Firishta, Pers. Text, Briggs I. 449.) Gul-badan names one (20*b*) as entrusted with the care of Bābar's tomb,—Muḥ. 'Alī *'Asas*. I think he was brother to Māham Begam, and the governor of Kābul whom Kāmrān murdered in 1547.

to all the mīrzās and sulṭāns and amīrs. He sent letters in all directions, urgently saying, 'We shall take into full favour all who enter our service, and especially such as served our father and grandfather and ancestors. If such will come to us, they will receive fitting benefits. Whoever there may be of the families of *Ṣāḥib-qirān* and Chingīz Khān, let them turn towards our court. The most High has given us sovereignty in Hindūstān; let them come that we may see prosperity together.'

Seven[1] daughters of Sulṭān Abū-sa'īd came (to Hindūstān): Gūhar-shād Begam, and Fakhr-jahān Begam, and Khadīja Sulṭān Begam, and Badī'u-l-jamāl Begam, and Āq Begam, and Sulṭān Bakht Begam.

(Also) Zainab Sulṭān Khānam, daughter of his Majesty's maternal uncle, Sulṭān Maḥmūd Khān, and Muḥibb Sulṭān Khānam,[2] daughter of *Ilācha* Khān (Aḥmad), his Majesty's younger maternal uncle.

In short, all the begams and khānams went, ninety-six persons in all, and all received houses and lands and gifts to their heart's desire. (11*b*)

All through the four years that (my father) was in Āgra he used to go on Fridays to see his paternal aunts. One day it was extremely hot, and her Highness my lady (*Akām*) said, 'The wind is very hot, indeed; how would it be if you did not go this one Friday? The begams would not be vexed.' His Majesty said, 'Māham! it is astonishing that you should say such things! The daughters of Abū-sa'īd Sulṭān Mīrzā, who have been deprived of father and brothers! If I do not cheer them, how will it be done?'

To the architect, Khwāja Qāsim, his Majesty gave the following order: 'We command a piece of good service from you. It is this: whatever work, even if it be on a great scale, our paternal aunts may order done in their

---

[1] Six only named.
[2] Wife of Mīrzā Ḥaidar *Dughlāt*, the historian.

palace, give it precedence, and carry it out with might and main.'

He commanded buildings to be put up in Āgra on the other side of the river,[1] and a stone palace to be built for himself between the *ḥaram* and the garden. He also had one built in the audience court, with a reservoir in the middle and four chambers in the four towers. On the river's bank he had a *chaukandī*[2] built. (12*a*)

He ordered a tank made in Dholpūr, ten by ten,[3] out of a single mass of rock, and used to say, 'When it is finished, I will fill it with wine.' But as he had given up wine before the fight with Rānā Sangā, he filled it with lemonade.

A year after Sulṭān Ibrāhīm's death, the rānā[4] appeared from the Mandū (or Hindū) side with a countless host. Amīrs and rājas and rānās, every one of those who had come earlier and paid duty to his Majesty, now became an enemy and went and joined the rānā, until Kūl-jalālī and Sambhal and Rāprī—every *pargana*,—and rā'is and rājas and Afghāns became hostile. Nearly two *laks* of cavalry assembled.

At this time, Muḥammad Sharīf, the astrologer, said to the royal soldiers, 'It would be best for the Emperor not to fight, for the constellation *Sakkiz Yildoz* (Eight Stars) is opposite.' Amazing perturbation fell upon the royal army. They became exceedingly anxious and troubled,[5] and showed signs of cowardice. (12*b*) When his Majesty saw his army

---

[1] *i.e.*, opposite the fort.

[2] 'A building on the roof which has a door on each of the four sides.' Vullers, 602. Badāonī uses *ghurfa*, upper room, as an equivalent. *Cf.* Elliot's History of India, V. 347 and 503.

[3] About 20 feet by 20 feet. (Mems. 398 n..)

[4] This decisive battle was fought on March 16th, 1527, on the skirts of the hill of Sīkrī, at Khānwa. Akbar's *prænomen* of Fatḥipūr—the City of Victory—was given to Sīkrī in 1573 to commemorate the Gujrāt campaign.

[5] When the fight had been won, Bābar soundly rated Muḥammad Sharīf, gave him money, and dismissed him to the place from which he had emerged, apparently only to cause trouble. He had come to India with a royal kinsman from Kābul, and to Kābul in 1519 from Khost (Māham's home).

in this state, he thought over the whole position. As the enemy was close at hand, this device occurred to his blessed mind; he ordered the remnant of what remained over and above deserters and enemies, to gather together. One and all came—amīrs and khāns and sulṭāns; plebeian and noble, low and high. Then he addressed them, and said: 'Do you not know that there lies a journey of some months between us and the land of our birth and our familiar city? If our side is defeated, (God preserve us from that day! God forbid it!) where are we? where is our birthplace? where our city? We have to do with strangers and foreigners. It is in every way best for each man to set resolutely before himself the two alternatives: if we win, we are avengers of the cause of God; if we lose, we die martyrs. In either fate is our salvation; each is a step and upward stage in greatness.'

To this they all agreed. They swore by the divorce of their wives and on the Holy Book; they recited the *fātiḥa*, and said, 'O King! God willing, we will not spare ourselves in sacrifice and devotion, so long as there are breath and life in our bodies.'[1] (13*a*)

Two days before the battle his Majesty renounced wine, and, indeed, he forswore all forbidden things. Following his example, 400 young men of name, who had given proof of manliness and one-mindedness and friendship, also renounced these things when he did. His Majesty broke up all forbidden utensils,—vessels of gold and of silver, goblets and flasks, etc.; and he gave them to the poor and needy.

He also sent abroad *firmāns* with the announcement: 'We exempt (you) from all dues and octroi and tithe on corn, and from all illegal imposts, so that no one, trader or

---

[1] Mr. Erskine thus gives Bābar's words: 'Every man dies. God only survives unchangeable. He who comes to life's feast must drink the parting cup of death. How much better to die with honour than to live with infamy!'

Perhaps, as Gul-badan says, Bābar touched also the thought of home, and this would be recorded by the woman.

other, may be hampered in his comings and goings, but all may move unmolested and free from interference.'

In the night[1] before the battle word was brought that Qāsim Ḥusain Sulṭān,—a grandson of Sulṭān Ḥusain Mīrzā through a daughter, 'Āyisha Sulṭān Begam,—had come to within ten *kōs* (of the royal camp) on his way from Khurāsān. (13*b*)

This news delighted his Majesty greatly. He asked, 'How many men are with him?' When he heard 'thirty or forty,' he at once sent off 1,000 troopers, all armed and equipped, at midnight, so that they might march in again with Qāsim Ḥusain Sulṭān, and in this way the enemy and outsiders be let know that reinforcements had come in good time. Everyone who heard the plan thought it a good one.

Next morning, which was March 16th, 1527 (Jumāda II. [13th], 933H.), his Majesty arrayed battle against Rānā Sangā on the skirts of the hill of Sīkrī, where now Fatḥpūr has been built[2] and peopled. By the Divine grace he was victorious and became an avenger of the cause of God.[3]

A year later my lady (*akām*), who was Māham Begam, came from Kābul to Hindūstān. I, this insignificant one, came with her in advance of my sisters, and paid my duty to my royal father. When my lady reached Kūl(-jalālī—*i.e.*, 'Alighar), his Majesty had sent two litters with three horsemen. (14*a*) She went on post-haste from Kūl to Āgra. His Majesty had intended to go as far as Kūl-jalālī to meet her. At evening-prayer time some one came and said to him: 'I have just passed her Highness on the road, four miles out.' My royal father did not wait for a horse to be

---

1 Bābar says that Qāsim had come earlier and with 500 men. Muḥ. Sharīf, the 'rascally fellow' and 'evil-minded wretch,' was with him. (Mems., 352.)

2 How beautifully built may, in small part, be seen by visiting the Oriental section of the South Kensington Museum and there examining the architectural reproductions, the drawings of Mr. W. B. Carpenter, the photographs, etc. The South Kensington Museum and the British Museum furnish numerous illustrations for Gul-badan Begam's MS., and add to it the charm of life and reality.

3 *Ghāzī*. Bābar now assumed this title, because he had vanquished non-Muḥammadans.

saddled but set out on foot. He met her near the house of Māham's *nanacha*.[1] She wished to alight, but he would not wait, and fell into her train and walked to his own house.[2]

At the time of her meeting his Majesty, she desired me to come on by daylight and pay my respects to him.

. . . [3]nine troopers, with two sets of nine horses and the two extra litters which the Emperor had sent, and one litter which had been brought from Kābul, and about a hundred of my lady's Mughal servants, mounted on fine (*tipūchāq*) horses,[4] all elegance and beauty.[5]

My royal father's Khalīfa[6] with his wife Sulṭānam[7] came as far as Naugrām[8] to meet (us). My *māmās*[9] had made me alight at the Little Garden, and having spread a small carpet, seated me on it. They instructed me to rise when Khalīfa came in, and to embrace him. When he came, I rose and embraced him. Then his wife Sulṭānam came in

---

[1] *dar pesh khāna nanacha Māham.* This might read 'in the advance camp.' Māham's *nanacha* appears thrice in the MS. : here and at 18*b* and 26*a*. She is clearly of the innermost circle. The word may be rendered 'dear little mother,' and is one of close affection.

[2] *Cf.* Mems., 423.

[3] *tūqūz.* The Tūrks made kings' gifts by nines and attached superstitious reverence to the number.

[4] A *tipūchāq* horse, according to Shaw, is long-necked like a Tūrkmān horse, and it seems also to be one with speed, beauty, and specially-trained paces. Vambéry says, 'ein fettes, gutes Pferd.'

[5] The above passage is inserted without break in the text and suggests transcription from an imperfect MS. It may be an enumeration of the items of the cortége which followed Māham with Gul-badan.

[6] Sayyid or Khwāja Niẓāmu-d-dīn 'Alī *Barlās* and Bābar's *vazīr*. His brother, Junaid *Barlās*, married Shahr-bānū, a half-sister of Bābar.

[7] Clearly an intimate. There were close relations, as has been said, between this *Barlās* family and Bābar. *Cf.* Biographical Appendix, *s.n.* Sulṭānam.

[8] Some four miles from Āgra and on the east of the Jamna. The royal palace was not yet built on the western bank. *Cf.* Rājpūtāna Gazetteer, III. 274.

[9] Steingass translates 'mother,' 'matron,' and 'old women.' One *māmā* is named later, 'Fakhru-n-nisā', my māmā.' (26*a*) She was the mother of Nadīm Khwāja *kūka*. She is several times mentioned, and it appears from a MS. belonging to Colonel Hanna which Mr. Beveridge has examined, that she was mother-in-law of the celebrated Māham *anaga* who was Nadīm's wife.

too. (14*b*) I, not knowing, wished to get up, but Khalīfa raised objections, and said: 'She is your old serving-woman. There is no need to rise for her. Your father has exalted this old servant (? himself) by giving such an order[1] about him. So be it! what power have slaves?'

From Khalīfa I accepted 6,000 *shāhrukhīs* and five horses, and Sulṭānam gave me 3,000 and three horses. Then she said: 'A hasty meal (*mā ḥaẓarī*) is ready. If you will eat you will honour your servants.' I consented. There was a raised platform in a pleasant spot, and a pavilion of red cloth with lining of Gujrātī brocade, and six canopies of cloth and brocade, each of a (differing) colour, and a square enclosure[2] of cloth with painted poles.

I sat in Khalīfa's quarters. The meal drew out to almost fifty roast sheep,[3] and bread and sherbet and much fruit. Having at length eaten my breakfast, I got into my litter and went and paid my duty to my royal father. (15*a*)

I fell at his feet; he asked me many questions, and took me for a time in his arms, and then this insignificant person felt such happiness that greater could not be imagined.

When we had been in Āgra three months, the Emperor went to Dholpūr. Her Highness Māham Begam and this lowly person also went. A tank had been made there, ten (*gaz*) by ten, out of one piece (of rock). From Dholpūr his Majesty went on to Sīkrī. He ordered a great platform made in the middle of the tank, and when it was ready, he used to go and sit on it, or to row about. This platform still exists.

They also made a *chaukandī* in the Sīkrī garden, and my

---

[1] (?) as that she should rise to greet him.

[2] Text, *chahār chūqa-i-sarāparda*. *Cf. Notices et Extraits*, Quatremère, XIV. 498.

[3] The 'fifty' sheep will not reduce by any reading I can suggest. *Cf. anglice* 'heaps of,' 'hundreds of,' etc. Perhaps the flock is a product of childish weariness recalled half a century later. Possibly one should read *panj āhār*, five foods, *i.e.*, courses, dishes. Gul-badan is now between five and six. Her doubt as to the reception due to Sulṭānam rings true, and Khalīfa's words suggest a little play-acting to please the small traveller; he treated her like a grown-up, and she tried to act one.

royal father put up in it a *tūr-khāna*,[1] where he used to sit and write his book.[2]

I and Afghānī *āghācha* were sitting in the front of the lower storey when my lady went to prayers. I said to Afghānī *āghācha* : 'Pull my hand.' She pulled, and my hand came out. My strength went and I cried. (15*b*) Then they brought the bone-setter and when he had bound up my hand, the Emperor went to Āgra.

After his arrival, word was brought that the begams were on the way from Kābul. My royal father went as far as Naugrām to give honourable reception to my dearest lady (*aka-jānam*),[3] who was my oldest paternal aunt and my royal father's eldest sister. All the begams who had come with her, paid their duty to the Emperor in her quarters. They were very happy and made the prostration of thanks, and then set off for Āgra. The Emperor gave houses to all the begams.

A few days later he made an excursion to the Gold-scattering Garden (*Bāgh-i-zar-afshān*). There was a place in it for ablution before prayers. When he saw it, he said : 'My heart is bowed down by ruling and reigning; I will retire to this garden. As for attendance, Ṭāhir the ewer-bearer will amply suffice. I will make over the kingdom to Humāyūn.' On this my lady (*akām*) and all his children broke down, and said with tears : 'God keep you in His own peace upon the throne many, many years, and may all your children after you reach a good old age!' (16*a*)

A few days later Alwar Mīrzā fell ill. His illness led to an affection of the bowels, which grew worse and worse in spite of all that the doctors could do, and at last he passed from this transitory world to the eternal home. His Majesty was very sad and sorry, and Alwar's mother, Dil-dār Begam, was wild with grief for the child, who was a

---

[1] "Perhaps a space enclosed by a low railing." (Mems., 202 n..) Possibly and suitably, a mosquito-room (*ṭaur*, net). *Cf.* Khwāndamīr, B.M. Or. 1,762, and Add. 30,774, ff. 25-114.

[2] The *Tūzūk-i-bābarī*.

[3] Khānzāda Begam.

rarity of the world and unique of the age. As her lamentation passed due bounds, his Majesty said to my lady and the begams: 'Come, let us make an excursion to Dholpūr.' He himself went comfortably and pleasantly by water, and the begams also begged to go by boat.

Just then there came a letter from Maulānā Muḥammad Farghārī (Parghālī) in Dihlī, saying: 'Humāyūn Mīrzā is ill and in an extraordinary state. Her Highness the begam should come at once to Dihlī, for the mīrzā is much prostrated.'[1] (16b)

My lady was very much upset on hearing this news, and started for Dihlī, like one athirst who is far from the waters. They met in Mathura. To her experienced eye he seemed ten times weaker and more alarmingly ill than she had heard he was. From Mathura the two, mother and son, like Jesus and Mary, set out for Āgra. When they arrived, this insignificant one went with her own sisters to visit that royal angel of goodness.

He was then growing weaker and weaker. Every time he came to his senses, his pearl-dropping tongue asked for us, and said: 'Sisters, you are welcome! Come, and let us embrace one another. I have not embraced you.' It might be three times that he raised his head and that his jewel-dropping tongue let fall these uplifting words.

When his Majesty came and saw how it was, his light-revealing countenance at once became sad and pitiful, and he began more and more to show signs of dread. (17a) On this my lady said: 'Do not be troubled about my son. You are a king; what griefs have you? You have other sons. I sorrow because I have only this one.'[2] His Majesty rejoined: 'Māham! although I have other sons, I love none as I love your Humāyūn. I crave that this

---

[1] *Cf. Bābar-nāma*, Ilminsky, 502 *et seq.*, and P. de Courteille, II. 457 *et seq.*, where is one of the supplementary fragments included in Kehr's *Bābar-nāma* (*Tūzūk*) and possibly taken from the Bukhārā MS. (*Cf.* Notes on the Tūrkī texts of the *Bābar-nāma*, A. S. Beveridge. Journal of the Royal Asiatic Society, July, 1900.)

[2] All Māham's other children died in childhood.

BĀBAR IN PRAYER, DEVOTING HIMSELF FOR HIS SON.

[*To face p.* 105.

cherished child may have his heart's desire and live long, and I desire the kingdom for him and not for the others, because he has not his equal in distinction.'

During Humāyūn's illness[1] his Majesty walked round him and turned his face (in intercession) to his Reverence, Murtaẓa 'Alī Karīmu-l-lāh. He kept up that going-round from the Wednesday and made intercession from the Tuesday, in anxiety and deep dejection. The weather was extremely hot and his heart and liver burned. While going round he prayed, saying in effect: 'O God! if a life may be exchanged for a life, I who am Bābar, I give my life and my being for Humāyūn.'[2]

That very day he fell ill, and Humāyūn poured water on his head, and came out and gave audience. (17*b*) Because of his illness, they carried my royal father within, and he kept his bed for two or three months.

As he grew worse, a messenger was sent to summon his Majesty Humāyūn, who had gone towards Kalinjar. He came post-haste, and on paying his duty to the Emperor, noticed that he was very feeble. Filled with compassion, he began to break down, and kept saying to the attendants: 'How has he come to such a lamentable pass all at once?' He sent for the doctors, and said to them: 'I left him well. What has happened all at once?' They said this and that in reply.

---

[1] The account of Bābar's self-surrender which follows is somewhat puzzling to translate, but the sense is clear and the important statements are in accordance with other sources.

[2] One of Kehr's (Ilminsky's) 'fragments' (which, if it be not Bābar's own, it is not improbable was added to the *Tūzūk* by Jahāngīr) tells this story in Bābar's person. After rejection of the suggestion to sacrifice for Humāyūn's life the great diamond (? the *Koh-i-nūr*), the narrative continues (P. de C., II. 460.): 'J'entrai dans la chambre où il se tenait, et je tournai trois fois autour de lui, en commençant par la tête et en disant, "J'assume sur moi tout ce que tu souffres." En même instant je me sentis tout alourdi, tandis que lui se trouvait léger et dispos. Il se leva en pleine santé, et moi je m'affaissai, accablé de malaise.'

Faith in the rite of circumambulation still prevails in Persia. Bābar, it is clear, believed his devotion to have borne fruit. (*Cf.* Hughes, Dict. of Islām, *s.v.* Intercession. For Karīmu-l-lāh, see Badāyunī, *Bib. Ind.* Text, III. 191.).

The whole time my royal father kept repeating: 'Where is Hindāl? What is he doing?' Just at this time some-one came in and said: 'Mīr Bardī Beg, the son of Mīr Khurd Beg,[1] conveys his obeisance.' My royal father, full of agitation, sent for him at once and asked: 'Where is Hindāl? When will he come? What trouble waiting gives!' (18*a*) Mīr Bardī said: 'The fortunate prince has reached Dihlī; he will wait on you to-day or to-morrow.' On this my royal father said to Mīr Bardī Beg: 'Ill-fated little fellow! I have heard that they married your sister in Kābul, and you in Lāhōr.[2] It is because of the wedding festivities that you have (not)[3] sooner brought my son, and so my weary waiting has been very long.' He asked: 'How tall has Hindāl Mīrzā grown?' and 'What is he like?' As Mīr Bardī was wearing one of the mīrzā's dresses, he showed it and said: 'This is a robe of the prince which he bestowed on his servant.' His Majesty called him nearer and said: 'Let me see how tall and how big Hindāl has grown.'[4] He kept repeating, 'Alas! a thousand times alas! that I do not see Hindāl,' and asking everyone who came in: 'When will Hindāl come?'

During his illness, he laid a command on my lady, and said: 'Marriages ought to be arranged for Gul-rang Begam and Gul-chihra Begam. (18*b*) When the royal aunt, my elder sister,[5] honours me with a visit, tell her that I say it has occurred to me to give Gul-rang to Isān-tīmūr Sulṭān and Gul-chihra to Tūkhta-būghā Sulṭān.'[6]

---

1 Hindāl's guardian from birth (1519-1530). He had previously been Bābar's *bakāwal* (house-steward). One of his sons, Khwāja Ṭāhir Muḥammad, served under Humāyūn and Akbar, and was *mīr farāghaṭ* (master of comfort). He may be the Mīr Bardī (qy. a child's sobriquet, Master Full-of-fun) of this episode. Ṭāhir's son, Bāqī, was a sewer, *i.e.*, table-decker (*sufra-chī*).

2 Hindāl, with whom doubtless Mīr Bardī and his father were travelling, was on his way from Badakhshān to the court.

3 The text has no negative.

4 Hindāl was now about eleven years old, so Mīr Bardī must also have been a boy.

5 Khānzāda Begam—*aka-jānam*—dearest lady.

6 Isān (Ishān, or Yussun) was the ninth, and Tūkhta-būghā the tenth, son of Aḥmad Khān, Bābar's maternal uncle. They were uncles of Gul-badan's own husband, Khiẓr Khwāja.

Dearest lady, the smiling one,[1] came, and they said to her: 'The Emperor spoke in this manner, and it has occurred to him in such a way. It now remains to know your pleasure. Let it be as you wish.' She said the same and, 'God grant blessing and peace! His idea is very good.' My *chīcha*[2] herself and Badīʿu-l-jamāl Begam and Āq Begam, both of whom were paternal aunts of his Majesty, were conducted into the hall. Having raised an estrade[3] and spread carpets and chosen a propitious hour, Māham's *nanacha* made both *sulṭāns* bow the knee[4] in order to exalt them to the rank of sons-in-law.

Meantime his Majesty's disorder of the bowels increased. The Emperor Humāyūn broke down again when he saw his father's condition worsen, and called the doctors, and said to them: 'Think it well over and find some remedy.' (19*a*) Having consulted together, they said: 'Small is our

---

[1] *tabassum kunān.*

[2] This Tūrkī word presents great difficulty.

Vambéry has *jīcha*, Kirghiz, mother, and *chīcha*, aunt (inferentially maternal); Shaw, *chīchā*, Qāzzāq, mother. P. de Courteille, Dict., *chīcha*, an elder sister. The word has in Samarqand the meaning 'maternal aunt.'

It occurs again in the text (23*a*), and is used for Gul-badan's sisters, the brides of this page (19*a*); so that it may be right (spite of the singular number) to read 'my elder sisters themselves'—*i.e.*, the brides. But it might be 'my mother.'

The word occurs at least once in the Memoirs. (Ilm., 446; Ers., 387.) It is preceded by one which Ilminsky writes *yanka*, and Erskine *Bikeh* (*Bega*). The letters of both words might be identical and the points only decisive. Shaw says *yangā* is an elder brother's wife; Vambéry, *belle-sœur, Schwagerin*; and Erskine (208 n..), bridesmaid, by which, I believe, is meant one who leads the bride to the bridegroom—an exactly appropriate use here, since Ḥabība *yangā* brings her daughter Maʿṣūma to marry Bābar. (N.B.—Shaw writes *yangā* and *chīchā*, where Vambéry and others have a final 'round *hā*.')

But if the *chīcha* of Mems., 387, is to be read 'elder sister,' Bābar can apply it only to Khānzāda Begam (elsewhere called by him *aulugh īgāchī* (Ilm., 116.); and this would, I believe, make the reading of *Bikeh* (*Bega*) difficult, since Khānzāda could not be called anything less than *Khānam*. The same objection would apply to the reading of *chīcha* as mother or as maternal aunt. This inclines one to read *yanka*, and not *bikeh*, at Mems., 387; and the Zainab of the sentence may be grand-daughter (*nabīra*), through the female line, of the *belle-sœur, or bridesmaid*, of Khānzāda Begam. But nothing is clear as to the relationship.

[3] Text, *ṣufā dāda*. Perhaps, content was given to all, but *ṣuffa*, estrade, fits better with the following *basāṭ*.

[4] *Zānū zanā'īnda*, literally, 'striking the knee.' Mems., 204 n..

luck, for our remedies are of no avail. We hope that God, the most Holy, will soon give one from His invisible treasures.'

When they felt his Majesty's pulse, they came to the opinion that there were symptoms of the same poison as that given him by Sulṭān Ibrāhīm's mother. It was in this way: that ill-fated demon (the mother) gave a *tōla* of poison to one of her maids, and said: 'Take this and give it to Aḥmad the taster and tell him to put it in some way or other into the special dishes prepared for the Emperor.' And she promised him large rewards. The ill-fated demon did this although his Majesty used to call her "mother," and had assigned her place and lands with every favour, and had been kindly pleased to say: 'Consider me as in the place of Sulṭān Ibrāhīm.'[1] But as ignorance prevails amongst those people, she did not regard his kindnesses. The (fitting) hemistich is well known:

> 'Everything reverts to its original type,
> (Whether pure gold, or silver, or tin).'[2]

To cut short the story: the cook (Heaven having made him blind and deaf,) spread the poison which had been brought and given to him, on the Emperor's bread only, and so little was eaten. But the symptoms of this illness were like that one's, seeing that day by day he lost strength and became more and more emaciated. (19*b*) Every day the disorder increased and his blessed countenance changed.

Next day[3] he called his chiefs together and spoke after this wise: 'For years it has been in my heart to make over my throne to Humāyūn Mīrzā and to retire to the Gold-scattering Garden. By the Divine grace I have obtained all things but the fulfilment of this wish in health of body. Now, when illness has laid me low, I charge you all to acknowledge Humāyūn in my stead. Fail not in loyalty

---

[1] Her son, who died fighting Bābar at Pānīpat.

[2] Pers. and Hind. Proverbs, T. Roebuck, Calcutta, 1824, p. 124, and Mems., 13.

[3] (?) after Humāyūn's arrival.

to him. Be of one heart and one mind with him. I hope to God that Humāyūn also will bear himself well towards men.

'Moreover, Humāyūn, I commit to God's keeping you and your brothers and all my kinsfolk and your people and my people; and all of these I confide to you.'

At these words hearers and onlookers wept and lamented. His own blessed eyes also filled with tears.

When his family and the people within the *ḥaram* heard of these occurrences, they were stupefied and overwhelmed, and cried and lamented.

Three days later he passed from this transitory world to the eternal home. The death took place on Monday, December 26th, 1530 (Jumāda I. 5th, 937H.). (20*a*)

They brought out our paternal aunt[1] and our mothers[2] on the pretence that the doctors were coming to look. All rose. They took all the begams and my mothers to the Great House.[3]

Black fell the day for children and kinsfolk and all. They bewailed and lamented; voices were uplifted in weeping; there was utter dejection. Each passed that ill-fated day in a hidden corner.

The death was kept concealed. After a time Araish Khān,—he was an *amīr* of Hind,—said: 'It is not well to keep the death secret, because when such misfortunes befall kings in Hindūstān, it is the custom of the *bāzār* people to rob and steal; God forbid that the Mughals not knowing, they should come and loot the houses and dwelling-places. It would be best to dress someone in red, and to set him on an elephant, and to let him proclaim that the Emperor Bābar has become a dervish and has given his throne to the Emperor Humāyūn.' This his Majesty Humāyūn ordered to be done. People were at once re-assured by the proclamation, and all offered prayers for

---

1 Khānzāda Begam.
2 Bābar's wives.
3 Perhaps 'palace,' and the sense may be that they did not go to their separate residences but remained nearer to the dead.

his welfare. On Friday, December 29th, 1530 (Jumāda I. 9th, 937H.), the Emperor Humāyūn mounted the throne, and everyone said: 'May all the world be blessed under his rule.' (20*b*)

After that he came to visit his mothers and sisters and his own people, and he made inquiry after their health and offered sympathy, and spoke with kindness and commiseration. He was pleased to order: 'Let each keep the office, and service, and lands, and residence which he has had, and let him serve in the old way.'

On the same day Hindāl Mīrzā, having come from Kābul, paid his homage to the Emperor, who received him with kindness, and was very happy, and bestowed on him many things from the treasures left by their father.

After my royal father's death, there were the good works and consecrated days of the first assembly[1] at his tomb.[2] His Majesty named Muḥammad 'Alī *'asas*[3] its guardian, and ordered the appointment of sixty good reciters of the whole Qurān and readers with good voices, so that the congregational prayers might be said five times daily and the whole Qurān recited, and prayer offered for the soul of the royal dweller in Paradise (*Firdaus-makānī*). (21*a*) The whole of Sīkrī—now known as Fatḥpūr—together with five *laks* charged on Bayāna, was given as an endowment to the

---

[1] *ma'rka.* Raverty (Afghān Dict..) gives as the first meaning of this word 'a party of ambassadors, or persons sent to make peace between two tribes'; and, secondly, as 'the business of making peace, or an arrangement between two tribes.' Lane and other writers render it 'battle-field' and 'battle,' etc. Steingass adds 'hubbub, turmoil' (modern colloquial). Gul-badan uses it for the common social assemblies she names, and here for the gathering of relations at a tomb.

[2] Bābar's body was laid first in the Rām or Arām Bāgh (Garden of Rest), on the opposite side of the river from the present *Tāj-maḥāll.* Later it was taken to Kābul. Mr. Erskine (B. & M., I. 517 *et seq.*.) quotes a charming passage from Burns' 'Travels in Bokhārā' (II. 121 *et seq.*), which describes Bābar's self-chosen resting-place. He follows this by an eloquent estimate of Bābar's character which makes clear his regret in bidding farewell to the great and vivid personality he has so admirably set before his readers.

[3] *i.e.*, of the night-guard. I believe he was the brother of Māham Begam.

tomb, for the support of the men of learning (*'ulamā*) and the reciters who were attached to it.

My lady made an allowance of food twice daily: in the morning an ox and two sheep and five goats, and at afternoon prayer-time five goats. She gave this from her own estate during the two and a half years that she remained in the prison of this world.

During my lady's life I used to see his Majesty in her residence. When she fell into bad health, she said to me: 'It will be very hard that when I am gone, the Emperor Bābar's daughters should see their brother in Bībī Gul-barg's[1] house.' Just as though her words were in the royal heart and mind, his Majesty used always, so long as he was in Hindūstān, to come to our house. He used to visit us and showed us kindness and affection and favour without stint. He used to come to the house of this insignificant one, and there would come Ma'ṣūma Sulṭān Begam, and Gul-rang Begam, and Gul-chihra Begam,[2] etc. —all the married ladies—and pay their duty to him. (21*b*)

In short, after the death of my royal father and my lady, his Majesty, in the fulness of his affection, showed this broken one such favour, and spoke with such boundless compassion to this helpless one, that she did not know she was orphaned and headless.[3]

During the ten[4] years after the death of his Majesty *Firdaus-makānī* that his Majesty *Jannat-āshyānī* was in Hind, the people dwelt in repose and safety, and obedience and loyalty.[5]

Six months after the death of his Majesty *Firdaus-*

---

[1] *Cf. post.* 29*b*, and 'Biographical Appendix,' *s.n.*.

[2] These three were her half and full sisters respectively.

[3] Gul-badan was about eight at her father's death. At three she had been adopted by Māham Begam.

[4] Really about nine.

[5] This rose-coloured picture accords neither with the facts nor with the narrative of Gul-badan. It may be that some limiting word has slipped out; *e.g.*, 'in Āgra,' or 'the people of the country,' in opposition to the dispossessed Afghāns, conquerors of earlier date, or Bābar's people, *i.e.*, household.

makānī, Biban[1] and Bāyazīd advanced from the direction of Gaur. On the news of this, his Majesty at once left Āgra and moved to meet them. He defeated them, and then went to Chanāda (Chunār),[2] took it, and thence returned to Āgra.

My lady, who was Māham Begam, had a great longing and desire to see a son of Humāyūn. Wherever there was a good-looking and nice girl, she used to bring her into his service. Maywa-jān, a daughter of Khadang (? Khazang), the chamberlain (*yasāwal*),[3] was in my employ. One day (after) the death of his Majesty *Firdaus-makānī*,[4] my lady said: 'Humāyūn, Maywa-jān is not bad. Why do you not take her into your service?' So, at her word, Humāyūn married and took her that very night. (22*a*)

Three days later Bega Begam[5] came from Kābul. She became in the family way. In due time[6] she had a daughter, whom they named 'Aqīqa. Maywa-jān said to Lady (*Aka*) Māham Begam, 'I am in the family way, too.' Then my lady got ready two sets of weapons, and said: 'Whichever of you bears a son, I will give him good arms.' Then she packed up the arms, and got ready gold and silver walnuts. She procured also the (special) arms of a Mughal commander, and was very happy, and

---

1 Text, Bibban. Biban and Bāyazīd were two distinguished Afghān chiefs and supporters of the fallen Lodī dynasty. The defeat named here occurred at Daura, on the Gumtī, 1531 (937H.).

All who love the story of an adventurous life, chequered through character of individuals in a marked degree, should fill out Gul-badan's brief narrative from Mr. Erskine's life of Humāyūn.

2 1532 (938H.). Taken from Shīr Shāh late in 1532 (939H.).

3 An attendant on a man of rank, who carries a gold or silver staff (Johnson, Pers. Dict., *s.v.*.); chamberlain in the service of Khāns of Tūrkistān (Zenker, *s.v.*.) Gul-badan's use of the word (81*b*) would allow a more extended sense.

4 Text has also *dar hayāt khud*. This is not the only instance of a similar redundant expression.

5 Bega had had one son, Al-amān. She is known in the later histories as Ḥājī Begam, but she made her pilgrimage in 972H.. She was captured at Chausa in 1539 (946H.) by Shīr Shāh; and most writers give her at this date the brevet title of Ḥājī. It is probable that *Bega* was not her personal name. It is the title of a lady of rank, and answers to *beg*.

6 Text, *b'ad az yak sāl*, which, read literally, spoils the story.

kept saying: 'Perhaps one of them will have a son.' She kept watch till Bega Begam's 'Aqīqa was born. Then she kept an eye on Maywa-jān. Ten months went by. The eleventh also passed. Maywa-jān said: 'My maternal aunt was in Mīrzā Ulugh Beg's[1] *ḥaram.* She had a son in the twelfth month; perhaps I am like her.' So they sewed tents and filled pillows.[2] But in the end everyone knew she was a fraud.

His Majesty who had gone towards Chanāda (Chunār), returned safe and sound.

My lady who was Māham Begam, gave a great feast. (22*b*) They lit up the bāzārs.[3] Before that time people used to illuminate the bāzārs (only). Then she gave orders to the better class and to the soldiers also to decorate their places and make their quarters beautiful, and after this illumination became general in India.

. . . a jewelled throne,[4] ascended by four steps, and above it gold-embroidered hangings, and laid on it a cushion and pillows embroidered in gold.

The covering of the pavilions and of the large audience tent was, inside, European brocade, and outside, Portuguese cloth. The tent-poles were gilded; that was very ornamental.

(My lady) had prepared a tent-lining and a *kannat*[5] and *sar-i-kannat* of Gujrātī cloth-of-gold, and a ewer for rose-water, and candlesticks, and drinking-vessels, and rose-water sprinklers,—all of jewelled gold.

With all her stores of plenishing, she made an excellent and splendid feast.

---

1 This will be Bābar's paternal uncle, known as *Kābulī*.

2 *i.e.*, made all preparations. Perhaps *khirgāhā dokhta* is not 'sewed tents,' but 'pitched tents.' *Cf. zamīn-doz.*

3 I am very doubtful as to the meaning of the following paragraph. It can hardly be true that India waited for Māham to instruct it in the art of illumination or decoration. I have conjecturally read that, whereas formerly only *bāzārs* were made to look festive, she had other houses adorned.

4 Here follows a list of arrangements, plenishing and gifts for the feast. There are here and at p. 123 *ff.* many difficult words in it.

5 Ar., a pent over a doorway, a veil, an umbrella. Perhaps *qanāt*, a screen, an enclosure for tents, the tent walls.

. . . twelve strings of camels, and twelve of mules, and seventy *tipūchāq* horses, and one hundred baggage horses. She gave special robes of honour to 7,000 persons. The festivities lasted several days.[1]

At this time came news that Muḥammad-zamān Mīrzā[2] had killed the father of Ḥājī Muḥammad Khān *kūkī*,[3] and was meditating rebellion. (23*a*) His Majesty sent to summon them[4] to the presence, and having laid hands on them, imprisoned them in Bayāna, in charge of Uncle Yādgār. Uncle Yādgār's men sided with Muḥammad-zamān Mīrzā, and let him escape (1533—940H.). At this time it was ordered that Sulṯān Muḥammad Mīrzā[5] and Nai[6] (Walī) Khūb Sulṯān Mīrzā should both be blinded. Nai Khūb Sulṯān lost his sight, but the man who had the blinding of Muḥammad Sulṯān did not injure his eyes.[7] Muḥammad-zamān Mīrzā and Muḥammad Sulṯān Mīrzā,

---

1 The feast here credited to Māham Begam may be that of the first anniversary of Humāyūn's accession. Of this Gul-badan gives an account, minus such details as are set down here, at 24*a et seq.*.

At the 'accession feast,' held December 19th, 1531, and thus not quite a year after the accession, it is said by Niẓāmu-d-dīn Aḥmad that 12,000 robes were bestowed, 2,000 of these being 'special.' For details as to *khil'at*, *cf.* Memoirs, 274 n..

Lists are dull reading, unless each item calls up an image. It is easy to add splendour and beauty to Gul-badan's few poor words by looking at actual things of the kinds she names, as may be done in the Oriental Section of the South Kensington Museum. The links between Persia and India in her day and earlier and later were many and close. Many Persians born and bred in Persia or by descent formed part of the Mughal court. Persian art and manufacture were at their highest development, experts say, in the fourteenth and fifteenth centuries. The uncritical eye doubts if the products of those centuries, as exhibited in the examples England possesses, can be excelled for splendour and satisfying charm. With such things the personages of our begam's book surrounded themselves.

2 Son of Badī'u-z-zamān Mīrzā, and grandson of Sulṯān Ḥusain Mīrzā *Bāyqrā*, and husband of Ma'ṣūma, a daughter of Bābar. He was drowned in the Ganges at the rout of Chausa.

3 *Cf.* B. & H., II., *s.n.*.

4 *Sic;* apparently the names of his fellow-rebels are omitted. They occur below.

5 Grandson, through a daughter, of Sulṯān Ḥusain Mīrzā *Bāyqrā*, and thus, a cousin of Muḥammad-zamān.

6 Called both Nai and Walī in the histories.

7 See Mr. Erskine's interesting note on blinding. (B. & H., II. 14 n.).

with his sons, Ulugh Mīrzā and Shāh Mīrzā, made their escape a few days later.

There was perpetual disturbance from these people during the years we were in Hind.

When his Majesty returned from the campaign against Biban and Bāyazīd, he was in Āgra[1] for about a year. He said to my lady: 'I am sad at heart in these days. If you approved, I would go with you to Gualīār.'[2] Her Highness my lady, and my mother (*ājam*),[3] and my sisters Ma'ṣūma[4] Sulṭān Begam, whom we used to call Elder sister[5] Moon, and Gul-rang Begam, whom we used to call Elder sister Rose,—we all were in Gualīār in attendance on the beneficent ladies.[6]

As Gul-chihra Begam was in Oude, and her husband, Tūkhtā-būghā Sulṭān, went to the mercy of God, her attendants wrote to his Majesty from Oude and said: 'Tūkhtā-būghā Sulṭān is dead. (23*b*) What is the order about the begam?' His Majesty said to Mīr Zāycha:[7] 'Go and bring the begam to Āgra. We also are going there.'

At this time her Highness my lady said: 'If you approve, I will send for Bega Begam and 'Aqīqa, so that they also may see Gualīār.' She despatched Naukār[8] and Khwāja Kabīr, who brought them from Āgra.

---

[1] 'Occupied in dreamy speculations of false sciences' *i.e.*, astrology. (B. & H., II. 14.) The date is 1534 (941H.).

[2] The histories tell us that the Gualīār expedition was a military demonstration against Bahādur Shāh of Gujrāt. Khwānd-amīr fixes its date as Sha'bān 939H. (February, 1533).

[3] Taken as it is written, this name might be charmingly translated as 'Ma desirée,' but considered with other words in this text after which the enclitic *am* (my) is incorrectly written, it seems that prosaic 'my mother,' Tūrkī, *achām*, is safer. In favour, however, of reading *ājam*, desire, is the wording on 25*b* (No. 48 of the guest-list), *ājam wālida-i-mā*, our mother. *Ājam* occurs also at 29*b*.

[4] Her husband, Muḥammad-zamān, is the rebel of this name just spoken of.

[5] *Chīcha;* which I have rendered 'elder sister' to suit the actual relationship between Gul-badan and her two sisters. *Cf.* 18*b* n..

[6] The aunts, presumably.

[7] The Chief Astrologer.

[8] Bābar names this man as being sent from India in charge of gifts to Kābul (Mems., 337.), and Gul-badan names him again (67*b*) as guardian of the begams' doorway in the citadel of Kābul.

They let two months slip by in one another's company in Guāliār, and then set out for Āgra, which they reached in February, 1534 (Sha'bān, 940 H.).[1]

In April (Shawwāl) my lady was attacked by a disorder of the bowels. On the 27th of the same month (13th Shawwāl) she passed from this transitory life to the eternal home.

The stamp of orphanhood was set anew on my royal father's children, and especially on me, for whom she herself had cared. I felt lonely and helpless and in great affliction. Day and night I wept and mourned and grieved. His Majesty came several times to comfort me, and showed me sympathy and kindness. I was two years old when her Highness my lady took me into her own house and cared for me, and I was ten when she departed from this life. (24*a*) I remained one year more in her house.[2] When I was eleven, and his Majesty went to Dholpūr, I

---

[1] This date cannot be right. The following are approximately correct for this time: Visit to Guāliār undertaken, Sha'bān, 939H. (February, 1533). Return to Āgra and Māham's illness, Shawwāl (April). Death of Māham, 13th Shawwāl (May 8, 1533). Forty days of mourning carries on the time to late in Ẕū'l-qa'da (June). Start for Dihlī, beginning of Ẕū'l-hijja,—after June 24. The building of Dīnpanā was begun Muḥarram, 940H. (July, 1533).

[2] Māham had also adopted Hindāl. Bābar details the circumstances, but the abbreviation, as it seems, of the Persian text, has led to an error. (Mems., 250.) Those children of Bābar who died young, were not born in 'this year' (925H.), as will be seen in the fuller rendering of Ilminsky, 281, and of P. de C., II. 44: 'Après Humāyūn (b. 913H.) j'eus encore plusieurs enfants, nés de la même mère que lui, mais qui ne vécurent pas.'

We know from Gul-badan that these were Bārbūl, Mihr-jahān, and Īshān-daulat.

'Hindāl n'était pas encore venu dans le monde. Comme j'étais dans ces parages [Kehrāj, in Mandesh, and on his way to India], il m'arriva une lettre de Māham, dans laquelle elle me disait, "Sera-ce un fils ou une fille? Prononcez vous-même sur la part que me réserve la fortune; à moi de mettre l'enfant dans le monde [Erskine, 'I will regard the child as mine'] et de l'élever." Le vendredi, 26 du mois, toujours à ce même campement, j'adjugeai Hindāl à Māham [before birth], et je lui écrivis à ce sujet une lettre qui lui fut portée à Kābul par Yūsuf 'Alī *rikāb-dār* [courier] quoique Hindāl ne fût pas encore né.'

A passage now follows which, as is noted by P. de C., is neither in the Persian version of the Memoirs nor in the English translation:

'Pour bien comprendre tout ce qui à été dit plus haut, il faut savoir que jusqu'à cette époque, de tout les enfants nés de la même mère

accompanied my mother.[1] This will have been before he went to Guālīār and began to build.[2]

At the end of the mourning for my lady, his Majesty went to Dihlī[3] and began to build the fort of Dīn-panā.[4] He then returned to Āgra.

Dearest lady[5] (Khānzāda Begam) said to his Majesty: 'When will you make Mīrzā Hindāl's marriage feast?' His

---

que Humāyūn, soit un fils [*i.e.*, Bārbūl], cadet par rapport à lui, l'ainé par rapport à mes autres enfants et trois filles, dont l'une etait Mihrjān, il n'y en avait pas un qui ne fût mort en bas-âge. Je souhaitais vivement de lui voir naître un frère ou une sœur. [*i.e.*, a child of Māham. There were other children of other wives.]

'Précisément à cette époque Dil-dār *āghācha* se trouvait enceinte. Je ne cessais de répéter, "Plût à Dieu que l'enfant qui va naître, sortît du même sein que Humāyūn!" A quoi ma mère [*sic.* Tūrkī text, Ilminsky, 271, *ḥazrat wālida*] me répondait, "Si Dil-dār *āghācha* met au monde un fils, ne pourrais-je pas le prendre et m'en charger?" "Rien de mieux," faisais-je à mon tour.

'D'ordinaire les femmes ont la manière suivante de consulter le sort, quand elles veulent savoir si elles auront un fils ou une fille. Elles prennent deux morceaux de papier; sur l'un elles écrivent, 'Alī ou Ḥasan, sur l'autre Fāṭima; puis elles les placent dans deux boules de limon qu'elles mettent dans une coupe d'eau. Celles des deux qui s'ouvre la première, leur sert à prognostiquer l'avenir; si elle renferme le nom d'un garçon, il y aura un garçon; si c'est celui d'une fille, il y aura une fille, disent-elles. On employa cette méthode; ce fut un enfant mâle qui en sortit. En recevant cette bonne nouvelle, j'écrivis aussitôt pour en faire part à ma mère [*sic*]. Quelques jours plus tard, effectivement Dieu me donna un garçon. Trois jours après sa naissance et avant de l'annoncer, on enleva l'enfant, bon gré, mal gré, à sa mère et on l'apporta chez moi où on le garda. Lorsque j'en donnai avis à ma mère [*sic*], celle-ci apprenant qu'elle avait obtenu l'objet de ses vœux, donna au jeune prince le nom de Hindāl, qui était pour nous de bon augure. Par cet arrangement cet enfant fût pour moi [? nous] à la fois un frère cadet (for Humāyūn) et un fils (for Māham and himself).

The words *ḥazrat wālida* cannot mean the mother of Bābar She had been dead some fourteen years. They may be equivalent to *Sulṭān-wālida*—*i.e.*, the mother of the heir-apparent. Certainly it was Māham who adopted Hindāl. This initial misconception as to the identity of *Ḥazrat wālida* runs through the whole translation of this most interesting passage. According to Gul-badan, Fārūq (born in 932H.) was Māham's son. Bābar names the birth. (Mems., 343.)

[1] *i.e.*, returned to her own mother's charge *i.e.*, Dil-dār's.

[2] An obscure passage. Humāyūn was building about this time. (Elliot, V. 126.)

[3] Beginning of Ẕū'l-ḥijja, 939H. (June—July, 1533).

[4] *Humāyūn-nāma*, Khwānd-amīr. (Elliot, V. 125.)

[5] *Cf.* 15*b* n.,

Majesty replied: '*B'ismu-l-lāh.*' When Mīrzā Hindāl was married, my lady (Māham) was living, but there was delay in arranging the feast. (Khānzāda Begam) said: 'The things for the Mystic Feast are also ready. Let us first celebrate this, and afterwards Mīrzā Hindāl's.' His Majesty said: 'Let whatever my royal aunt wishes be done.' She replied: 'May God bless it and make it good.'

DESCRIPTION OF THE HOUSE OF FEASTING WHICH WAS SET UP ON THE RIVER'S BANK, AND WHICH WAS CALLED THE MYSTIC[1] HOUSE:

First there was a large octagonal room with an octagonal tank in the centre, and again, in the middle of the reservoir, an octagonal platform on which were spread Persian (*wilāyatī*) carpets. (24*b*) Young men and pretty girls and elegant women and musicians and sweet-voiced reciters were ordered to sit in the tank.[2]

The jewelled throne which my lady had given for the feast was placed in the fore-court of the house, and a gold-embroidered divan[3] was laid in front of it, (on which) his Majesty and dearest lady sat together.

On her right sat her paternal aunts, the daughters of Sulṭān Abū-sa'īd Mīrzā:

1.[4] Fakhr-jahān Begam.
2. Badī'u-l-jamāl Begam.
3. Āq[5] Begam.
4. Sulṭān Bakht Begam.

---

[1] *Tilism;* Greek, τέλεσμα, talisman. Perhaps an epithet drifted from astrological phraseology. This feast commemorated the accession of Humāyūn. *Cf. Humāyūn-nāma*, trs. Sada-sūkh La'l (B.M. Add. 30,774, p. 76.): 'talismanic palace,' which may be the building named by Gul-badan. *Cf.* 'samite, mystic,' of Tennyson. Khwānd-amīr speaks at length of this feast in his *Humāyūn-nāma*, and calls the building in which it was held *'imārat-i-ṭilism*.

[2] The sequel to this order follows later.

[3] *tūshak*, (?) *anglice*, squab.

[4] Translator's numbering. For details as to each woman *cf.* Appendix *s.n.*.

[5] This epithet,—the Fair,—is given to several persons, not all women; and in some instances the true name is also known—*e.g.*, Yasīn-daulat Sulṭān, Kāmrān's son-in-law, and Salīqa, daughter of Sulṭān Aḥmad Mīrzā.

5. Gūhar-shād Begam.

6. Khadīja Sulṭān Begam.

Upon another cushion sat our paternal aunts, the sisters of his Majesty, *Firdaus-makānī:*

7. Shahr-bānū Begam.

8. Yādgār Sulṭān Begam.

(N.B.—Other guests of the right follow).

9. 'Āyisha Sulṭān Begam, daughter of Sulṭān Ḥusain Mīrzā.

10. Ulugh Begam, daughter of Zainab Sulṭān Begam, a paternal aunt of his Majesty.

11. 'Āyisha Sulṭān Begam.

12. Sulṭānī Begam, daughter of Sulṭān Aḥmad Mīrzā, paternal (great-) uncle of his Majesty[1] and mother of Kilān Khān Begam. (25*a*)

13. Bega Sulṭān Begam, daughter of Sulṭān Khalīl Mīrzā, paternal (grand-)uncle of his Majesty.

14. Māham Begam.[2]

15. Begī Begam, daughter of Ulugh Beg Mīrzā *Kābulī*, paternal (grand-)uncle of his Majesty.

16. Khānzāda Begam, daughter of Sulṭān Mas'ūd Mīrzā; on her mother's side, grand-daughter of Payanda Muḥammad Sulṭān Begam, paternal (grand-)aunt of his Majesty.

17. Shāh Khānam, daughter of Badī'u-l-jamāl Begam (No. 2.).

18. Khānam Begam, daughter of Āq Begam (No. 3.).

19. Zainab Sulṭān Khānam, daughter of Sulṭān Maḥmūd Khān, eldest maternal (grand-)uncle of his Majesty.

20. Muḥibb Sulṭān Khānam, daughter of Sulṭān Aḥmad Khān,—known as Ilācha Khān, the younger maternal uncle of the elder[3] Emperor (Bābar).

---

[1] The words used of Sulṭānī do not grammatically apply to 'Āyisha, but I believe she is also a daughter of Sulṭān Aḥmad Mīrzā and is Bābar's first wife, who left him under the influence of an elder sister, perhaps Salīqa Sulṭān (Āq Begam). Salīqa married a son of Sulṭān Maḥmūd Mīrzā, and may have acted under the evil impulses of the family quarrels which did so much to embitter, if also to stimulate, Bābar's early ambitions.

[2] This is not 'my lady,' whose death has been already recorded.

[3] *kilān;* perhaps, great.

21. Khānish, sister of Mīrzā Ḥaidar and daughter of (a) maternal (great-)aunt of his Majesty.

22. Bega Kilān Begam.[1]

23. Kīchak Begam.

24. Shāh Begam, mother of Dil-shād Begam, and daughter of Fakhr-jahān Begam (No. 1.), paternal (great-) aunt of his Majesty.

25. Kīchakna Begam.

26. Apāq (Āfāq) Begam, daughter of Sulṭān Bakht Begam (No. 4.).

27. Mihr-līq (? Mihr-bānū) Begam, paternal aunt of his Majesty.

28. Shād Begam, grand-daughter of Sulṭān Husain Mīrzā, and daughter of a paternal aunt of his Majesty (? No. 22.).

29. Mihr-angez Begam, daughter of Muẓaffar (Ḥusain) Mīrzā, and grandchild of Sulṭān Ḥusain Mīrzā. (25b) They had great friendship for one another (? Shād and Mihr-angez), and they used to wear men's clothes and were adorned by varied accomplishments, such as the making of thumb-rings[2] and arrows, playing polo, and shooting

---

[1] Probably the daughter of Sulṭān Maḥmūd Mīrzā and mother of Shād Begam (No. 28.) by a son, Ḥaidar, of Sulṭān Ḥusain Mīrzā.

[2] Text *zih-gīrī tarāshī*, which might be experimentally rendered carving thumb-rings, a gentle art of the day. But if *wa* be inserted, each word would represent a separate accomplishment of the well-bred in knightly arts. These would be congenial to a lady who played polo (*chaugān*). *Cf.* Bābar's account of Ḥaidar's accomplishments (Ilminsky, 14, Mems., 13, P. de C., 22.), and Ḥaidar's own recital in his prologue to the *Tārīkh-i-rashīdī*.

I suggest to take *tārashī* (a word not used by Bābar or Ḥaidar) as equivalent to the fletchery (*auq*), or the 'making arrow-heads' (*paikān*), of Bābar.

Another possible reading has been suggested to me by Mr. Beveridge —(*a*)*z hikīrī tarāshī*, 'by cutting arrows.' *Hikrī* is a Hindī name for cultivated reeds grown on low marshy grounds. (Wilson's Glossary, *s.v.*, and Platt's Hindustānī Dict..) There is nothing improbable in Gul-badan's use of a Hindī word. Arrows were fashioned from these reeds and men-at-arms practised the art. Gujrāt reeds were exported for arrows to Persia. The omission of the *alif* of *az* is not infrequent in the MS..

A few words on the *zih-gīr* find fit insertion here. It is a thumb-ring worn on the right hand as a protection against the fret of the bow-string both in drawing and release. Persians, like the Japanese and Mongols and Chinese, drew with the thumb. The *zih-gīr* is of eccentric

with the bow and arrow. They also played many musical instruments.

30. Gul Begam.
31. Fauq Begam.
32. Khān (? Jān) Begam.
33. Āfroz-bānū Begam.
34. Āgha Begam.
35. Fīroza Begam.
36. Barlās Begam.

There were other begams, very many, adding up altogether to ninety-six stipendiaries. There were also some others.

After the Mystic Feast (938 H.) came Mīrzā Hindāl's wedding-feast (Jauhar, 944 H.). Some of the begams already named went away,[1] and (of those) some had sat at the right hand in that assembly (*i.e.*, the Mystic Feast).[2]

Of our begams :

37. Āgha (*Āghā,—passim, āgha*), Sulṭān *āghācha*, mother of Yādgār Sulṭān Begam.
38. *Ātūn māmā.*
39. Salīma.
40. Sakīna.
41. Bībī Ḥabība.

---

thickness and unequal width, elongating on one side into a tongue. This elongation lies along the inner side of the thumb, and points towards the thumb-tip. In drawing, the thumb crooks round the string which pulls against the *zih-gīr*. The arrow is released by straightening the thumb, and the string then flies over the hard surface of the ring. The *zih-gīr* is of jade, crystal, ivory, brass, gold, etc.. Some are chased and carved, and some are jewelled. In December, 1898, a remarkable one was offered for sale at an auction in Edinburgh of Lord Dalhousie's collections and the jewels of his daughter, Lady S. G. Brown (Connemara). It is cut from a single emerald, and inscribed: '*Jihat zihgīr shāh-i-shāhān Nādir ṣāḥib-qirān bar taskhīr-i-hind az jawāhar-khāna intikhāb shud*' ('Selected for a thumb-ring for the king of kings and lord of happy conjunction Nādir, from the jewel-room on the conquest of Hind').

An interesting account of Persian archery is included in the 'Book of Archery,' G. Agar Hansard (Lond., 1840.). It, however, calls the *zih-gīr*, *safn*. *Safn* is the rough skin of a fish or lizard which is used to smooth the arrow-shafts. (*Cf.* Lane's Ar. Dict..)

[1] *Ba wilāyatī.* (?) to Kabul and other outside places.

[2] Perhaps this is an explanation of the paucity of right-hand wedding-guests.

42. Ḥanīfa Bega.

And the others who had sat[1] at the Emperor's left on embroidered divans.

43. Ma'ṣūma Sulṭān Begam.
44. Gul-rang Begam.
45. Gul-chihra Begam.
46. This insignificant one, the broken Gul-badan.
47. 'Aqīqa Sulṭān Begam.
48. Ājam, our mother, who was Dil-dār Begam.[2]
49. Gul-barg Begam.
50. Bega Begam. (26*a*)
51. Māham's *nanacha*.
52. Sulṭānam, the wife of Amīr (Niẓāmu-d-dīn) *Khalīfa*.
53. Alūsh Begam.
54. Nāhīd Begam.
55. Khurshīd *kūka*, and the children of my royal father's foster-brothers.
56. Afghānī *āghācha*.
57.[3] Gul-nār *āghācha*.
58. Nāz-gul *āghācha*.
59. Makhdūma *āgha*, the wife of Hindū Beg.
60. Faṭīma Sulṭān *anaga*, the mother of Raushan *kūka*.
61. Fakhru-n-nisā' *anaga*, the mother of Nadīm *kūka*.
62. The wife of Muḥammadī *kūka*.
63. The wife of Mu'yid Beg.
64. The *kūkas* of his Majesty: Khurshīd *kūka*.
65. Sharīfu-n-nisā' *kūka*.
66. Fatḥ *kūka*.
67. Rabī'a Sulṭān *kūka*.

---

[1] (?) At the Mystic Feast. Its left-hand guests have not been specified. There are no repetitions of names, although the list seems to give the guests at both feasts. Perhaps down to and including No. 36 the names are of begams who were at the first feast, and then went away. Then come 'our begams' of the right, whose home was near Humāyūn, and who were at both feasts.

[2] *Cf.* 23*b* n..

[3] Nos. 57 and 58 are, perhaps, the two Circassians whom Shah Ṭahmāsp sent as a gift to Bābar (Mems., 347.). Gul-nār is named in Abū 'l-fazl's list of pilgrims who went with Gul-badan to Makka in 983H., and as being of Bābar's household. They (Nos. 57 and 58) are named also by Firishta.

68. Māh-liqā *kūka*.
69. Our nurses (*anaga*).
70. Our *kūkas*.
71. The begams' people and the wives of the amīrs.

Those who were on the right.

73. Salīma Bega.
74. Bībī Neka.
75. Khānam *āgha*, daughter of Khwāja 'Abdu-l-lāh *Marwārīd*.
76. Nigār *āgha*, mother of Mughal Beg.
77. Nār Sulṭān *āgha*.
78. Āgha *kūka*, wife of Mu'nim Khān.
79. Daughter of Mīr Shāh Ḥusain, (illegible) Bega.
80. Kīsak Māham.
81. Kābulī Māham.
82. Begī *āgha*.
83. Khānam *āgha*.
84. Sa'ādat Sulṭān *āgha*.
85. Bībī Daulat-bakht.
86. Naṣīb *āgha*.
87. (Illegible) Kābulī.

Other begas and āghas, the wives of the amīrs, sat on this hand, and all were present at the marriage feast. (26*b*)

This was the fashion of the Mystic House: (there was) a large octagonal room in which they gave the feast, over against this a small room, also octagonal. In both every sort of profusion and splendour appeared. In the large octagonal hall was set the jewelled throne, and above and below it were spread out hangings (*adṣaqahāī*) embroidered with gold, and wonderful strings of pearls (*shadhīhā*) hung, each 1½ yards (*gaz*) in length. At the end of each string (*larī*) were two glass globes. There had been made and hung some thirty or forty strings.

In the small room, in an alcove, were set a gilded bedstead and *pān*-dishes,[1] and water-vessels and jewelled drinking-vessels, and utensils of pure gold and silver.

---

[1] This word excites curiosity as to the time when Gul-badan's people learned to eat *pān*.

Facing west (was) the audience hall; facing east, the garden; on the third side and facing south, the large octagon; and on the side facing north, the small one. In these three houses were three upper rooms. One they named the House of Dominion,[1] and in it were nine military appurtenances, such as a jewelled scimitar and gilded armour, a broad dagger and a curved dagger, and a quiver, all gilt, and a gold-embroidered overmantle.[2] (27*a*)

In the second room, called the House of Good Fortune, an oratory had been arranged, and books placed, and gilded pen-cases,[3] and splendid portfolios,[4] and entertaining picture-books written in beautiful character.[5]

In the third room, which they called the House of Pleasure, were set out a gilded bedstead and a coffer of sandal-wood, and all imaginable pillows. Then in front were spread specially choice coverlets,[6] and before these table-cloths, all of gold brocade. Various fruits and beverages had been got ready, and everything for merriment and comfort and pleasure.

On the feast-day of the Mystic House, his Majesty ordered all the mīrzās and begams to bring gifts,[7] and everyone did so. He said: 'Divide the gifts into three heaps.' They made three trays of *ashrafīs* and six of *shāhrukhīs*. One of *ashrafīs* and two of *shāhrukhīs* he

---

[1] As to this threefold classification, Elliot and Dowson, V., 119, may be consulted.

[2] Six articles only are separately named, but the *qūr* (translated armour) may be taken in the sense given to it in the *Āīn* (Blochmann, 109.), and include four weapons, which makes the total the mystic nine. *Cf. Āīn, l.c.*, and plates. (N.B.—The numbering of the weapons [*l.c.* p. 110.] does not agree with that of the plates. Plate X. should be consulted.)

[3] *qalam-dān.* Several such are to be seen at the S. K. M. They are boxes damascened or painted with pictures, about 10 inches by 3 inches, and contain writing implements. 'Gilded' does not seem an appropriate epithet. Perhaps the dictionaries define imperfectly.

[4] *juz-dān.* Perhaps the beautiful book-covers of the day. Those having flaps might be called portfolios.

[5] *muraqqa'.*

[6] *nihālcha.* Placed, I presume, over carpets.

[7] *sāchaq.* This word appears to have a special meaning of wedding-gifts, but Gul-badan uses it elsewhere more widely.

gave to Hindū Beg and said: 'This is the share of Dominion; give it to the mīrzās and chiefs and vazīrs and soldiers.' (27*b*)

He gave in the same way to Mullā Muḥammad Farghārī (Parghālī) and said: 'This is the share of Good Fortune. Give it to those who are eminent and respectable, and to theologians and religious men, to ascetics and graybeards, and dervishes and devotees, and the poor and the needy.'

Concerning one tray of *ashrafīs* and two of *shāhrukhīs* he said: 'This is the portion of Pleasure. This is mine. Bring it forward.' They did so. He said: 'What need is there to count?' First he himself vouchsafed his blessed hand and said: 'Let them take to the begams on one small tray *ashrafīs* and on another *shāhrukhīs*. Let each person take her hands full.' What was left, that is two trays of *shāhrukhīs*,—which may have been 10,000,—and all the *ashrafīs*, —about 2,000—he gave in largesse, and scattered[1] first before the *walī 'u-n-ni'matān* (beneficent seniors), and then to those present at the entertainment. No one received less than 100 or 150, and those in the tank especially received very much. (28*a*) His Majesty was pleased to say: 'Dearest lady! if you approved, they might put water in the tank.' She replied: 'Very good,' and went herself and sat at the top of the steps. People were taking no notice, when all at once (?) the tap was turned and water came. (28*a*) The young people got very much excited. His Majesty said: 'There is no harm; each of you will eat a pellet of anise[2] and a bit of comfit[3] and come out of there.' Upon this, everyone who would eat the comfit came out quickly. The water was as high as their ankles. To end the story, everyone ate the comfit and all came out.

Then the viands of the feast were set forth, and robes of

---

[1] *niṣār.* Again a word which, like *sāchaq*, would seem to fit the marriage feast better than the accession.

[2] *shīt.* The text has no points and would yield *seb*, apple; but anise is the better remedy against cold.

[3] *ma'jūn*, any medical confection, but commonly an intoxicant. Here it may be some preventive of chill.

honour were put on,[1] and gifts bestowed, and head-to-foot dresses given to the comfit-eaters and others.

On the margin of the tank was a room (*tālār*)[2] fitted with talc windows, and young people sat in the room and players made music. Also a woman's bāzār[3] had been arranged, and boats had been decorated. In one boat was made (?) the semblance of six people (*kasī*) and six alcoves (*kanj*); in (another) an upper room, and below it a garden with amaranthus and cockscombs and larkspurs[4] and tulips. In one place there were eight boats, so that there were eight pieces.[5]

In short, everyone was astonished and amazed who beheld what gift of contrivance the great God had bestowed on the blessed mind of his Majesty. (28*b*)

The Description of Mīrzā Hindāl's (Marriage) Feast is as follows:[6]

Sulṭānam Begam (*i.e.*, the bride) was a sister of Mahdī Khwāja.[7] My father's brother-in law (*yazna*) had no child except Ja'far Khwāja, and there was no child (?) of Khānzāda Begam).[8] Dearest lady had taken care of Sulṭānam

---

[1] It was now that 12,000 *khil'ats* are said to have been distributed. In this passage Gul-badan twice uses the expression *sar u-pāī*. Perhaps one might say that the 'young people' were given new clothes from head to foot, and so shake off the fetters of the rigid *khi'lat*, *sar-u-pāī*, and 'honorary dresses.'

[2] The dictionaries I have seen, explain *tālār* as a saloon built of wood and supported on four columns, and this is appropriate here. Le Strange and Haggard (Vazīr of Lonkurān) say, 'Alcove or chamber in which a ruler sits to give public audience and hear suitors.' It is raised above the level of the (*e.g.*) courtyard, so that petitioners are below the *hakīm*. Approaching this meaning is the 'throne' of the dictionaries.

[3] *Cf.* *Āīn*, Blochmann, 276; *Khushroz*, or Day of Fancy Bāzārs.

[4] *nā-firmān*, stubborn, (?) because they will break and not bend. Balfour (Cyclopædia) and Forbes (Hind. Dict.) give larkspur; Fallon, poppy. An account of the boats, etc., may be read in B.M. MS. Add. 30,774, where is a translation by Sir H. Elliott's *munshī* from Khwānd-amīr.

[5] *parcha*. Perhaps flower-gardens; perhaps Fr. *pièce*. *Cf. Un appartement de deux, trois pièces.*

[6] Jauhar's date for this is 944H. (1537).

[7] Many difficulties gather round this name. *Cf.* Appendix *s.n.* Mahdī Khwāja.

[8] The copyist has perhaps omitted one *āka-janām*.

as though she were her child. Sulṭānam was two years old when Khānzāda Begam took charge of her. She (Khānzāda) loved her very much, and thought of her as a brother's child of her own. She made a most entertaining and splendid feast.

A *kūshka*[1] and hangings (*adṣaqa*)[2] and five divans and five pillows for the head (*yīstūq*), and one large pillow and two round ones (*galūla*); and girdles (*qūshqa*) and veils (*naqāb*), together with a tent[3] . . . . with three gold-embroidered cushions and head-to-foot dresses for a prince, with collar and bordering of gold embroidery, and bath-wrappers (*fauṭa*) and napkins (*rūpāk*) and embroidered towels (*rūmāl*) and an embroidered mantle (*qūrposh*) to be worn over the armour.

For Sulṭānam Begam: nine jackets (*nīm-tana*)[4] with garniture of jewelled balls,[5] one of ruby, one of cornelian,

---

[1] M. Quatremère uses this word twice with perhaps two meanings. (Notices et Extraits, XIV. 324, 325 and 406-8.) At p. 408 he translates it *kiosques*, and it seems to be a building. At pp. 324 and 406 he leaves it untranslated. (Here it may have the sense given by Gul-badan.) It is named amongst items prepared for ambassadors at a post-house. These are: '*kat*, trône; *bastar*, estrade; . . . *kushka; jinlik; sandalī*, siége,' etc. Gul-badan might intend to name a canopy or screen for a sleeping-place in a large room or a movable kiosk with sleeping comforts.

[2] *Cf.* 22*b*.

[3] A word follows *tent* which I cannot make out. It resembles *j-(ḥ,ch)-l-gh* (no vowels).

[4] *nīm-tana, i.e.*, demi-corps. Like many of Gul-badan's words, this is marked by Steingass as 'modern colloquial.' Apropos of this, Dr. Fritz Rosen says in the preface of his Modern Persian Colloquial Grammar, that the Persian of Irān differs 'in every respect' from the Persian of India. The Persian of Gul-badan allows one to feel at home with the vazīr of Lonkurān, and with Dr. Rosen's own book. Perhaps the difference he indicates is between the literary and colloquial. Gul-badan's Persian, however, is presumably that of contemporary Irān, and her teachers were probably Persian born. Dr. Rosen's remark appears to require some restriction.

[5] *tukma* (*dār*), usually translated *buttons;* but the button is so associated with the button-hole as to suggest a fastening. A dressmaker might say 'ball-trimming.' Globular buttons were and are placed round the neck and hem of a boddice. The vazīr of Lonkurān ordered a jacket with garniture of twenty-four gold buttons, smaller than a hen's and larger than a pigeon's. Vests trimmed with 'buttons' (Mems.) are repeatedly named by Bābar as gifts.

one of emerald, one of turquoise, one of topaz, and one of cat's-eye.

Again: of necklaces, nine; and one embroidered collar and bordering, and four short jackets[1] with ball-trimming (*tukma-dār*), and one pair of ruby earrings and another of pearls, three fans,[2] and one royal umbrella.

One *dirakht*[3] and two *khuṭb*[3] and other furniture and effects, and household goods and chattels and workshops[4] of all sorts. (29*a*) Khānzāda Begam gave everything she had collected, and she arranged a feast such as had not been made for any other child of my royal father. She planned it all and carried it all out.

. . . nine *tipūchāq* horses, with jewelled and gold-embroidered saddles and bridles; and gold and silver vessels and slaves,[5] Tūrkī and Circassian and Arūs (? Rūs) and Abyssinian,—of each (race) a royal gift of nine.

What my royal father's brother-in-law[6] (Mahdī Khwāja) gave to the mīrzā was a set of nine *tipūchāq* horses, with jewelled and gold-embroidered saddles and bridles; and

---

[1] *chār qartījī;* a suggested rendering only. Johnson gives *kartī* (*qartī*) as a short boddice reaching to the hips, and the *qar* recurs in other words, having the sense of a body garment; *e.g.*, *qarṭaq*, a short-sleeved jacket; *qarza*, a woman's vest.

[2] *pankha.*

[3] I find no help as to these words in the dictionaries. My only suggestion as to their possible meaning is too slightly based to be of value. It is this: In the South Kensington Museum, Oriental Section, I have seen tall lamp-stands so shaped that they recall the *Quṭb* pillar outside Dihlī. That such stands would be a part of good household furnishing the South Kensington Museum allows us to suppose. We have our 'tall lamps,' our 'pillar lamps,' and also our 'branched candlesticks,' which may be a term parallel to *dirakht*, a tree.

[4] *kār-khānahā.* These may be the kitchen and its plenishing; the goldsmith's, with his tools, furnaces, and appliances; the perfumer's, etc.. *Cf.* *Aīn*, Blochmann, and *Tār. Rash.*, E. & R., 470.

[5] *ghulāmān*, which I have rendered slaves, because they were a gift. But I know no warrant for such servitude as is thus implied.

[6] *yazna*, which is explained by Vambéry and Steingass as 'husband of the king's sister.' Niẓāmu-d-dīn Aḥmad styles Mahdī Khwāja *damād*, which Meninsky and Steingass explain as 'husband of the king's sister' and 'son-in-law.' I do not find *yazna* rendered son-in-law by any of the dictionaries. To read *yazna* 'brother-in-law of the king' agrees with the detailed statement of Mahdī's relation to Bābar made by Bāyazīd *bīyāt*. *Cf.* Appendix, *s.n.* Khānzāda.

gold and silver vessels, and two other sets of nine horses, baggage animals, with velvet saddles and bridles; and brocade and Portuguese cloth, and Tūrkī and Ḥabshī and Hindī slaves,—in all, three sets of nine; and three head of elephants.

In his Majesty's leisure after the feast came news that the vazīr of Sulṭān Bahādur, Khurāsān Khān by name, had attacked Bayāna. His Majesty despatched Mīrzā 'Askarī, with several amīrs, Mīr Faqr-'ali Beg and Mīr Tardī Beg, etc.. These went to Bayāna and fought and defeated Khurāsān Khān.[1] (29*b*) The Emperor set out for Gujrāt shortly afterwards, in prosperity and safety. It was on the 15th of the revered Rajab 941H.[2] that he quite decided to go himself to Gujrāt. He set up his advance camp in the Gold-scattering Garden, and there spent a month while the forces were gathering in.

On court days, which were Sundays and Tuesdays, he used to go to the other side of the river. During his stay in the garden, *ājam* (Dil-dār Begam) and my sisters and the ladies (*ḥaramān*) were often in his company. Of all the tents, Ma'ṣūma Sulṭān Begam's was at the top of the row. Next came Gul-rang Begam's, and *ājam's* was in the same place. Then the tent of my mother,[3] Gul-barg Begam and of Bega Begam[4] and the others.

They set up the offices (*kār-khānahā*) and got them into

---

[1] Mīrzā Muqīm, Khurāsān Khān.

[2] January 29th, 1535. Abū'l-faẓl gives Jumāda I., 941H. (November, 1534) as the time for collecting the troops. Perhaps the begam's date is that of departure, a day liable to postponement when Humāyūn was in pleasant quarters.

[3] It may be that the copyist has transferred the words 'my mother' from a quite usual place,—preceding or following the *ājam* of the previous sentence. They are inappropriate to Gul-barg Begam; at least, I have never seen them used to describe a brother's wife, and such I believe this Gul-barg to be. We know of a 'Bībī Gul-barg,' mentioned somewhat condescendingly (21*a*) by Māham Begam; I incline to take Gul-barg there and here as Khalīfa's daughter, and the former wife of Mīr Shāh Ḥusain *Arghūn*. *Cf.* Appendix, *s.n.* Gul-barg.

[4] This is, I think, Humāyūn's wife and the mother of 'Aqīqa. The object of Gul-badan's enumeration of the tents seems to be desire to show that Bābar's daughters and widow had places of honour higher than Humāyūn's family.

order. When they had put up the pavilions (*khaima*) and tents (*khar-gāh*) and the audience tent (*bār-gāh*), the Emperor came to see the camp and the splendid set-out, and visited the begams and his sisters. As he had dismounted somewhat near Ma'ṣūma Sulṭān Begam's (tent), he honoured her with a visit. All of us, the begams and my sisters, were in his society. (30*a*) When he went to any begam's or sister's quarters, all the begams and all his sisters used to go with him. Next day he came to the tent[1] of this lowly person, and the entertainment lasted till the third watch[2] of the night. Many begams were there, and his sisters, and ladies of rank (*begahā*) and of position (*āghāhā*), and other ladies (*āghāchahā*), and musicians and reciters. After the third watch his Majesty was pleased to command repose. His sisters and the begams made resting-places (*takīa*) in his presence.[3]

Bega Begam woke (us) up, and said: 'It is time for prayers.'[4] His Majesty ordered water for ablution[5] made ready where he was, and so the begam knew that he was awake. She began a complaint, and said to him: 'For several days now you have been paying visits in this garden, and on no one day have you been to our[6] house. Thorns have not been planted in the way to it. We hope you will deign to visit our quarters also, and to have a party and a sociable gathering there, too. How long will you think it right to show all these disfavours to us helpless ones? We too have hearts. Three times you have honoured other places by visits, and you have run day and night into one in amusement and conversation.' (30*b*)

When she had finished, his Majesty said nothing, and

---

1 *khāna*, lit., house.

2 *pahr*. Gul-badan names the Hindūstānī division of time into watches on which her father had commented as being a novelty to himself. (Mems., 331.)

3 It seems, as again later on, that they fell asleep where they were seated, on mattresses and provided with pillows.

4 The early morning prayers, about which the opinion is expressed that prayer is better than sleep.

5 *wazū'*, ablution before prayers. *Cf.* Hughes, Dict. of Islām.

6 From what follows, Gul-barg would seem to be the fellow-sufferer.

went to prayers. At the first watch of the day he came out and sent for his sisters and the begams, and for Dil-dār Begam, and Afghānī *āghācha,* and Gul-nār *āghācha,* and Meywa-jān and Āghā-jān, and the nurses (*anagahā*). We all went, and he said not a word, so everyone knew he was angry. Then after a little he began: 'Bībī, what ill-treatment at my hands did you complain of this morning?' and: 'That was not the place to make a complaint. You all (*shumā*) know that I have been to the quarters of the elder relations (*walī'u-n-ni'matān*) of you all (*shumāyān*). It is a necessity laid on me to make them happy. Nevertheless, I am ashamed before them because I see them so rarely. It has long been in my mind to ask from you all a signed declaration (*sijlī*), and it is as well that you have brought me to the speaking-point. I am an opium-eater. If there should be delay in my comings and goings, do not be angry with me. Rather, write me a letter, and say: "Whether it please you to come or whether it please you not to come, we are content and are thankful to you."'

Gul-barg Begam wrote to this effect at once, and he settled it with her.[1] Bega Begam insisted a little, saying: 'The excuse looked worse than the fault.[2] (31*a*) We complained in order that your Majesty might lift up our heads by your favour. Your Majesty has carried the matter to this point! What remedy have we? You are Emperor.' She wrote a letter and gave it to him, and he made it up[3] with her also.

On February 18th, 1534 (Sha'bān 14th, 941 H.), he set out from the Gold-scattering Garden and marched for Gujrāt, to fall upon Sulṭān Bahādur. They confronted one another at Manhasūr (Mandsūr); a battle was fought, and Sulṭān Bahādur, on his defeat, fled to Champānīr. Then

---

[1] *ba Gul-barg Begam daryāftand.*

[2] A familiar proverb. *Cf.* Steingass, 840, *s.v.* 'azr.

[3] *daryāftand.* Gul-badan frequently uses this word as meaning to embrace and to greet, a sense not mentioned by Johnson or Steingass. The *ba* of the earlier instance (note 1.) induced me to give it the notion of coming to an understanding. *Cf.* 16*b*.

his Majesty resolved to pursue him. Sulṭān Bahādur left Champānīr and went towards Aḥmadābād.[1] His Majesty took the country of Aḥmadābād also, and portioned out the whole of Gujrāt to his men. Aḥmadābād he bestowed on Mīrzā 'Askarī,[2] Bahrūch on Qāsim Ḥusain Sulṭān,[3] and Patan on Yādgār-nāṣir Mīrzā.[4]

He himself, with a small following, went from Champānīr to visit Kanbāyat[5] (Cambay). A few days later there came a woman with news, and said: 'Why are you sitting here? The men of Kanbāyat have gathered, and will fall upon you unless your Majesty rides off.' The royal amīrs attacked the rabble,[6] and got them into their hands and cut them in pieces. (31*b*)

His Majesty then went to Baroda, and from there towards Champānīr.[7] We had settled down, when there

---

1 Taking his treasure with him, Sulṭān Bahādur fled before Humāyūn to Champānīr, Aḥmadābād, Cambay and Diu.

2 Humāyūn's half-brother.

3 Grandson, through a daughter, of Sulṭān Ḥusain Mīrzā *Bāyqrā;* on his father's side an Uzbeg.

4 Humāyūn's first cousin, the son of Bābar's half-brother Nāṣir. He was a posthumous child. Mr. Beveridge has drawn my attention to the fact,—of which there are other examples,—that he is called Yādgār, a souvenir, of Nāṣir, his father.

5 This excursion preceded the allotment of fiefs. Gul-badan's way of putting the pursuit of Bahādur is borne out by some other writers. This was Humāyūn's first sight of the sea, and the spectacle seems to have been more in her mind than was Bahādur. Akbar's first sight of the sea is also commemorated in the histories.

6 Abū'l-faẓl calls them Bhils and Gawārs. (H.B. I. 309.) They were rude tribesmen acting in Bahādur's interests. Maternal affection saved the small royal camp. The 'woman' had a son a slave in it, and she purchased his freedom by revealing the designs of her fellow-tribesmen. Although Cambay had not furnished the assailants, it paid in fire and pillage for the attack. It lay near, was an enemy's town, and such an incident as the onslaught of the Bhils would not allow of fine distinction of race and person.

7 Behind this dull statement is a stirring episode. Humāyūn took Champānīr after a four months' blockade, by night escalade of a rock so nearly perpendicular that seventy or eighty iron spikes had to be driven in to allow ascent. Thirty-nine men climbed up. Bairām Khān was the fortieth, Humāyūn the forty-first of the three hundred who mounted. Such a Bābar-like episode makes regret the keener that Humāyūn's life was ruined and stained by his slavery to a drug. The loot of Champānīr was enormous; it had been regarded as impregnable, and was full of treasure. It was taken in 1536 (943 H.).

SHĪR SHĀH *AFGHĀN.*

[*To face p.* 133.

was a tumult, and Mīrzā 'Askarī's people left Aḥmadābād and came to the Emperor. They represented to him that Mīrzā 'Askarī[1] and Yādgār-nāṣir Mīrzā had conspired, and wished to go to Āgra. On hearing this, he himself was forced to go; he left the important affairs of Gujrāt [(?) its pacification], and turned away and went to Āgra. Here he spent as much as a year.[2]

He then went to Chanāda (Chunār), and took it,[3] and also Benares. Shīr Khān was in Charkanda,[4] and made an offer of service, saying: 'I am your old servant. Give me a place with a fixed boundary in which I may establish myself.'

His Majesty was considering this, when the king of Gaur Bangāla[5] came wounded and a fugitive. For this reason he gave no attention (to Shīr Khān), but marched towards Gaur Bangāla. Shīr Khān knew that his Majesty had gone there, and went himself also with a large detachment of horse, and joined his son (Jilāl Khān), who was in Gaur with his servant Khawāṣ Khān. Shīr Khān sent them out, and said: 'Go and fortify Garhī.'[6] (32*a*)

Both came and occupied Garhī. His Majesty had written to Jahāngīr Beg: 'Advance a stage, and go up

---

Humāyūn now relapsed into an evil mood of feasting and indolence. He remained near Champānīr, and affairs entered on a recurrent phase. There was complete relaxation of discipline.

Gul-badan's 'we had settled down' (*nishista budīm*) allows the inference that she and other ladies had joined the camp. A later instance will be found of the inopportune presence of women and children with the army. But it may mean merely 'we were comfortably awaiting events' in Āgra.

[1] He was thinking of having the *khuṭba* read in his own name in Āgra. Such an aspiration in Humāyūn's brothers was encouraged by his own abdications of sovereignty.

[2] A fatal year which allowed Shīr Khān to gather force. Gul-badan's recital of the historical events of this time has no value.

[3] Shīr Khān.

[4] Jhārkand.

[5] Sayyid Maḥmūd Shāh. He had been defeated by Shīr Khān. (*Cf.* Erskine's notes on Stewart's Jauhar, B. M. Add. 26,608, p. 12.)

[6] 'The gate of Bengal,' a pass between it and Bihār, and which has a hill on one hand and the Ganges on the other. It is the Teria garhī or Tilia gulley of our maps.

to Garhī.' There was fighting, and Jahāngīr Beg was wounded and many men were slain.

When the Emperor had spent three or four days in Kohlgānū (Colgong), it became advisable for him to march on and halt near Garhī. He marched forward, and when he came near Garhī, Shīr Khān and Khawāṣ Khān fled by night, and he entered Garhī next day. Thence he went to Gaur Bangāla, and took it.

He was nine months in the far-away country of Gaur, and named it Jannatābād.[1]

He was comfortably and safely in Gaur, when news came that some of the amīrs had deserted and joined Mīrzā Hindāl.[2]

Khusrau Beg[3] (*kūkaltāsh*) and Zahīd Beg[4] and Sayyīd Amīr[5] paid their respects to the mīrzā, and said: 'The Emperor has gone comfortably far away, and the mīrzās, Muḥammad Sulṭān Mīrzā and his sons, Ulugh Mīrzā and Shāh Mīrzā, have again raised their heads,[6] and continually keep showing themselves in company.' (32*b*)

Just at this time the asylum of shaikhs, the servitor (*bandagī*) Shaikh Bahlūl, hid[7] armour and horse-accoutre-

---

[1] City of Paradise. The demoralizing effects of life in Gaur were felt under Akbar. Humāyūn, with his empire crumbling around him, was now (as Jauhar testifies) 'so much devoted to pleasure and sensual enjoyment that, after the first month, he was never seen, as he was always shut up in a private apartment of the palace.' Naturally, Gul-badan's next item of narrative is of rebellion,—this time by her own brother, Hindāl.

[2] He was only nineteen, and the crown may well have seemed at anyone's service. The date is 1538 (945H.). Humāyūn in Gaur was cut off from his capital by Shīr Khān.

[3] Bābar first names him in 1507-8 as coming from Harāt. There are two men named Khusrau *kūkaltāsh* by Bābar, but they were not contemporaries. One died in 1502-3, before the other came upon the scene.

[4] Husband of the sister of Bega Begam, Humāyūn's wife. He was put to death by Mīrzā Kāmrān at Ghaznī in 1547.

[5] Sayyid Nūru-d-dīn Mīrzā, the father of Salīma Sulṭān Begam, and the husband of a daughter of Bābar. *Cf.* App. *s.n.* Gul-rang.

[6] Hindāl had recently defeated them. (Erskine, II. 89 *et seq.*.) For causes of Hindāl's rebellion, and for Bega Begam's part in it, see Erskine's Jauhar, *l.c.*, p. 13.

[7] Some words seem to be omitted, *e.g.*, 'was accused of.' Gul-badan

ments and military stores in an underground place, and would have loaded them on carts and sent them to Shīr Khān and the mīrzās.[1] Mīrzā Hindāl would not believe it, so Mīrzā Nūru-d-dīn Muḥammad was sent to inquire into the matter. He found the armour and accoutrements, and had *Bandagī* Shaikh Bahlūl killed.[2] The Emperor, on hearing news of it, set out for Āgra.

He was coming by that side of the Ganges (*i.e.*, the left bank) opposite Mungīr, when his amīrs represented: 'You are a great king! Return by the way you came, lest Shīr Khān should say: "Forsaking his road of advance, he took another of retreat."'[3] The Emperor returned to Mungīr, and brought many of his people and his family by boat up the river as far as Ḥajīpūr-Patna.

When he went (to Bengal) he had left Qāsim (Ḥusain Sulṭān Uzbeg) there. Now came news of Shīr Khān's approach. Whenever there was fighting, the royal troops won.

Just now Bābā Beg (*Jalāīr*) came from Jaunpūr and Mīrak Beg from Chanāda (Chunār), and Mughal Beg from Oude. (33*a*) As these three amīrs joined the Emperor, corn became dear.

Then,—such was God's will,—they had halted without precaution, when Shīr Khān came and fell upon them. The army was defeated, and many kinsmen and followers remained in captivity. His Majesty's own blessed hand was wounded. Three days he remained in Chunār, and then came to Arāīl.[4]

---

cannot have believed the accusation. Perhaps, however, her long friendship with Nūru-d-dīn's daughter Salīma would make her pen discreet in blaming his murder of the shaikh.

[1] The rebels mentioned on p. 23*b*.

[2] For the probable facts, *cf.* B. & H., II. 162 *et seq.*.

[3] It was Mu'yid Beg *Duladai Barlās* who urged this foolish point of honour, and who thus led to the disaster at Chausa. He was a cruel man as well as one ignorant in military matters. He was a favourite of Humāyūn, but the Emperor's followers rejoiced when he died.

[4] Gul-badan's brevity (natural enough even if she were more historic in method) is somewhat misleading. Mr. Erskine allows one to follow

When his Majesty reached the river's bank, he stopped, bewildered as to the crossing, and said: 'How to cross without boats!' Then came the rāja (Bīrbahān) with five or six horsemen and led him through a ford. For four or five days his people were without food or drink. At last the rāja started a bāzār, so that the people of the army lived some days in comfort and repose. The horses also were rested. Many men who were on foot bought fresh mounts. In short, the rāja rendered fitting and dutiful services. Later on his Majesty gave him leave to go, and at the hour of mid-day prayer came himself, safely and comfortably, to the bank of the Jamna. The army crossed at a ford they had found. A few days later they came to Karra, where corn and grass were plentiful, because it was his Majesty's own country. (33*b*)

When his people were rested, he went on to Kalpī, and then marched on to Āgra.

Before his arrival in Āgra, he heard news that Shīr Khān was coming (from) the direction of Chausa. Great anxiety fell upon his people.

Of many who were in that rout (at Chausa) there was never heard, in any way soever, news or sign. Amongst them were 'Āyisha Sulṭān Begam, daughter of Sulṭān Ḥusain Mīrzā[1] (*Bāyqrā*); and Bachaka, who was a *khalīfa* of my royal father;[2] and Bega-jān *kūka;* and 'Aqīqa Begam;[3] and Chānd Bībī, who was seven months with

---

the misadventures which culminated in the defeat. This—the rout at Chausa—occurred near to where the Sōn falls into the Ganges and at Chūpat Ghat, on June 27th, 1539 (Ṣafar 9th, 946H.). The statement of Humāyūn's visit to Chunār, I do not find elsewhere. Chunār was then held by royalists. The Araīl named is presumably that near Allāhābād.

[1] Wife of Qāsim Ḥusain Sulṭān *Uzbeg*, whose timely arrival gave Bābar so much satisfaction. (13*a*) Qāsim had been Governor of Patna (32*b*), but, from the circumstance of his wife's being at Chausa, would seem to have left it with Humāyūn.

[2] A Bachaka, who was a *khalīfa* of Bābar's household, escaped with him from Samarqand in 1501 (907H.), some thirty-eight years before the Chausa episode. *Khalīfa*, as applied to a woman, denotes a servant or slave who exercises surveillance over other women-servants, and has charge of rooms,—an upper maid-servant.

[3] Bega Begam's daughter, who will have been about eight years old.

child, and Shād Bībī, all three[1] (*sic*) of whom were of his Majesty's *ḥaram*. Of these several people, he never heard even a word, as to whether they were drowned or what became of them. In spite of all possible inquiry and search, what had become of them was never found out.

His own illness[2] dragged on for forty days, and he then grew better.

At this time, when Khusrau Beg (*kūkultāsh*), and Diwāna Beg, and Zahīd Beg, and Sayyid Amīr, had come on in advance of his Majesty, news again arrived that the mīrzās, Muḥammad Sulṭān Mīrzā and his sons, had come to Kanauj. (34*a*)

After Shaikh Bahlūl's murder, Mīrzā Hindāl went to Dihlī. He took with him Mīr Faqr-ʿalī and other well-wishers to frustrate and disperse the mīrzās. The mīrzās fled, and came into the Kanauj quarter. Mīr Faqr-ʿalī brought Mīrzā Yādgār-nāṣir to Dihlī. As there was neither friendliness nor confidence between Mīrzā Hindāl and Mīrzā Yādgār-nāṣir, Mīrzā Hindāl, when Mīr Faqr-ʿalī made this mistake, sat down out of sheer annoyance and besieged Dihlī.[3]

When Mīrzā Kāmrān heard these things, there arose in him also a desire of sovereignty. With 12,000 fully equipped horsemen he went to Dihlī. Mīr Faqr-ʿalī and Mīrzā Yādgār-nāṣir closed the city gates on his approach. Two or three days later, Mīr Faqr-ʿalī, having made an agreement, went and saw Mīzrā Kāmrān. He represented: 'The news heard of his Majesty and Shīr Khān may be so and so.[4] Mīrzā Yādgār-nāṣir, from thought of his own interest, does not wait on you. The advisable course at this crisis is, that you should lay hands on Mīrzā Hindāl,

---

[1] Perhaps the copyist has omitted a name; perhaps, as a child of Humāyūn, 'Aqīqa is 'of the *ḥaram*.'

[2] From his wound or from distress of mind. The 'forty days' suggest the ceremonial term of mourning.

[3] The whole of the above paragraph it would be safest to hide with Hindāl under his sister's charitable cloak. For a historical account of the time, see B. & H., II., Book IV., Cap. IV.

[4] Clearly the ill news of the rout at Chausa.

go to Āgra, and not think of establishing yourself in Dihlī.' (34b)

Mīrzā Kāmrān gave heed to Mīr Faqr-ʿalī's words, and bestowed on him a head-to-foot dress. He then seized Mīrzā Hindāl and came to Āgra. He visited the tomb of *Firdaus-makānī*,[1] saw his mother and sisters, and halted in the Rose-scattering[2] Garden.

At this time Nūr Beg brought word of his Majesty's coming.[3] As Mīrzā Hindāl was excluded from the presence because of the murder of Shaikh Bahlūl, he went to Alwar.[4]

A few days after his Majesty's arrival, Mīrzā Kāmrān came from the Rose-scattering Garden and paid his respects to him. We paid our respects on the evening of the day he came. He took notice of this insignificant one, and was kindly pleased to say: 'I did not know you at first, because when I led the army (whose footprints are victorious[5]) to Gaur Bangāla, you wore the high cap (*ṭāq*), and now when I saw the muslin coif[6] I did not recognise you. And oh, my Gul-badan, I used very often to think of you, and was sometimes sorry, and said: "I do wish I had brought her!" But at the time of the disaster (*fiṭrat*) I was thankful I had not, and I said: (35a) "Thank God I did not bring Gul-badan!" For although ʿAqīqa[7] was young, I have been

---

[1] Bābar's remains then had not been conveyed to Kābul in 1539.

[2] (?) Gold-scattering. Mr. Erskine calls it so, and it is likely to be that already mentioned by Gul-badan more than once.

[3] Retreating from Chausa.

[4] His own *jāgīr*.

[5] *ẓafr-aẓar*. This, after Chausa, can only be a precative of Gul-badan's.

[6] This change appears to indicate that Gul-badan, who is about eighteen or nineteen years old, has been married. The Persian has *lachaq qaṣāba*, without conjunction. Steingass and Johnson describe the *lachaq* as a square mantle worn by women, doubled into a triangle, but here the description given in the *Burhān-i-qāṭiʿ* is more àpropos, *i.e.*, a square of stuff folded cornerwise and put upon the head so that the corners tie under the chin. It is often (*l.c.*) elaborately embroidered in gold. *Qaṣāba* appears to have the same meaning as *lachaq*.

[7] *Cf.* p. 33b.

consumed by a hundred thousand regrets and cares, and have said: "Why did I take her with the army?"'

A few days later he came to see my mother. He had with him the Holy Book. He commanded the attendants to retire[1] for awhile, and they rose and there was privacy. Then he said to *ājam* (Dil-dār Begam) and this insignificant one, and to Afghānī *āghācha*, and Gul-nār *āghācha*, and Nār-gul *āghācha*, and my nurse (*anaga*): 'Hindāl is my strength[2] and my spear;[3] the desirable light of my eyes, the might of my arm, the desired, the beloved. May what I do be right! What shall I say to Mīrzā Muḥammad Hindāl about the affair of my[4] Shaikh Bahlūl? What was to be has been! Now there is no anger in my heart against Hindāl. If you do not believe it' . . . He had lifted up the Holy Book when her Highness my mother, Dil-dār Begam, and this poor thing snatched it from his hand. All cried, 'May what you do be right! Why do you say such things?'

Then again he spoke: 'How would it be, Gul-badan, if you went yourself and fetched your brother, Muḥammad Hindāl Mīrzā?' (35*b*) Her Highness, my mother, said: 'This girlie (*dukhtarak*) is young. She has never made a journey (alone). If you approved, I would go.' His Majesty said: 'If I give you this trouble, it is because it is clearly incumbent on fathers and mothers to feel for their children. If you would honour him with a visit, it would be a healing-balm applied for us all.'

Then he sent Mīr Abū'l-baqā[5] with her Highness my mother, to fetch Mīrzā Hindāl. At once on hearing this

---

[1] *kināra kardand.* This metaphor recalls the arrangement of carpets in Persian rooms, with the carpet proper in the centre, an upper end (*sar-andāz*) and borders (*kināra*). 'Go aside' might be a good rendering.

[2] *qūl*, Mongolian,—main body of an army. [3] Ar. *qanāt.*

[4] Here and in the apostrophe to Gul-badan I have allowed the *man* to indicate the affection Humāyūn had for his half-sister and for the revered shaikh. It might be, however (as at 'Now there is no anger,' *cf.* text), the simple first person.

[5] B. & H., II., *s.n.*.

news: 'She has come to see me!' Muḥammad Hindāl Mīrzā made his mother happy by giving her honourable meeting. He came with her from Alwar, and paid his duty to his Majesty.[1] About Shaikh Bahlūl he said: 'He used to send arms and military appurtenances to Shīr Khān. When this was ascertained, I killed the shaikh on account of it.'

To put it briefly: in a short time came news that Shīr Khān had come near Lakhnau.

In those days his Majesty had a certain servant, a water-carrier. (36*a*) As he had been parted from his horse in the river at Chausa and this servant betook himself to his help and got him safe and sound out of the current, his Majesty now seated him on the throne. The name of that menial person we did not hear, some said Niẓām, some said Sambal. But to cut the story short, his Majesty made the water-carrier servant sit on the throne, and ordered all the amīrs to make obeisance to him. The servant gave everyone what he wished, and made appointments. For as much as two days the Emperor gave royal power to that menial. Mīrzā Hindāl was not present at his court;[2] he had taken leave, and had again gone to Alwar with the intention of getting arms ready. Neither did Mīrzā Kāmrān appear. He was ill, and sent to say to his Majesty: 'Gifts and favours of some other kind ought to be the servant's reward. What propriety is there in setting him on the throne? At a time when Shīr Khān is near, what kind of affair is this to engage your Majesty?'

In those days Mīrzā Kāmrān's illness increased amazingly. He became weak and so thin that his face was not in the least his own, and there was no hope of his life. (36*b*)

---

[1] Hindāl was received in the presence of Kāmrān and other kinsmen. Humāyūn said to Kāmrān: 'You know who is to blame! Why did Hindāl rebel?' Kāmrān passed on the question to Hindāl himself, who, with profound shame, pleaded that being young he had listened to bad advice, and begged forgiveness. (Erskine's notes on Stewart's Jauhar, B. M. Add. 26,608.)

[2] Lit., in that assembly.

By the Divine mercy he grew better. He suspected that the Emperor's mothers,[1] by his Majesty's advice, had given him poison. His Majesty came to hear of this, and instantly went to see the mīrzā and swore that he had never had such a thought, nor given such an order to any one. Nevertheless, Mīrzā Kāmrān's heart was not purged. Afterwards he got worse, day after day, and he lost power of speech.

When news came that Shīr Khān had left Lakhnau, the Emperor marched towards Kanauj, and left Mīrzā Kāmrān in Āgra to act for him. In a few days the mīrzā heard that he had made a bridge of boats and crossed the Ganges. On this, he himself marched out of Āgra towards Lāhōr.[2]

We had settled down[3] when he sent[4] a *farmān* like a king's, and said: 'You[5] are commanded to go with me to Lāhōr.' He must have said[6] to his Majesty about me something of this sort: 'I am very ill and very miserable and lonely, and I have no one[7] to sympathize with me. (37*a*) If you will order Gul-badan Begam to go with me to Lāhōr, it will be a real favour and kindness.' For his sake his Majesty will have said: 'She shall go.' Two or three days after the Emperor had gone towards Lakhnau, the mīrzā sent a *farmān*,[8] in royal style, to the effect: 'Most assuredly you will come with me.' Then my mother must have said: 'She has never travelled apart from us.' He replied:[9] 'If she has not travelled alone, do you also go with her.' He sent as many as 500 troopers and trusty grooms, and both his foster-father and his foster-brother, and said (to my mother): 'If she may not go with me (to

---

[1] *i.e.*, Bābar's widows. [2] A treacherous defection.
[3] The royal family, after the Emperor's and the mīrzā's departure.
[4] Perhaps from his first halting-place outside the city.
[5] Clearly Gul-badan. [6] Before either brother left Āgra.
[7] *i.e.*, of his kinsfolk, and especially of his women kinsfolk.
[8] This, I think, is the one already named.
[9] *īshān farmudand.* This seems to mean Humāyūn, and to refer the following speech back to the earliest discussion of the project of Gul-badan's journey at the time Humāyūn was still in Āgra. The whole episode is confused in narrative.

Lāhōr), come all of you one stage.' When one stage was reached, he began to declare, on his oath: 'I will not let you go.' Then he took me by main force, with a hundred weepings and complaints and laments, away from my mothers, and my own mother and my sisters, and my father's people, and my brothers, and parted us who had all grown up together from infancy.[1]

I saw that the Emperor's command also was in the affair. I was helpless. (37*b*) I wrote a suppliant letter, saying: 'I never expected your Majesty to cut off this insignificant one from your service, and to give her to Mīrzā Kāmrān.' To this humble note he sent a compassionate answer (*salām-nāma*), to this effect: 'I had no heart to part with you, but the mīrzā persisted, and was miserable, and begged very hard, and I was obliged to trust you to him. For just now there is important work[2] on hand. God willing, I will send for you when it is settled.'

When the mīrzā was starting, many people, amīrs and traders and so on, made preparation with the intention of letting their wives and families march under his escort to Lāhōr. When we reached (the city) news came of a battle on the Ganges, and that defeat had befallen the royal army.[3]

At least there was this limit to misfortune,—his Majesty and his brothers came safely through the peril.[4] Our other relations[5] came from Āgra by way of Alwar to Lāhōr. (38*a*)

---

[1] It must be remembered that Gul-badan's husband, Khiẓr Khwāja, was a brother of Āq Sulṭan (Yasīn-daulat), Kāmrān's son-in-law, and Kāmrān may have had other motives than affection for desiring her presence, *e.g.*, the attraction of her husband's contingent.

[2] The opposition of Shīr Khān, soon to be closed at Kanauj. Gul-badan's enforced departure with Kāmrān saved her a painful and hazardous flight.

[3] May 17th, 1540 (Muḥarram 10th, 947H.). Mīrzā Ḥaidar gives an admirable account of it as 'the battle of the Ganges.' Gul-badan's full brother, Hindāl, led the van at Kanauj, and defeated Shīr Khān's son, Jalāl. Hindāl was a successful general. 'Askarī, Kāmrān's full brother, was defeated by Khawās Khān.

[4] As at Chausa, so at Kanauj, Humāyūn was nearly drowned. Here he was saved by Shamsu-d-dīn Muḥammad of Ghaznī, whose wife, under the sobriquet of Jī-jī *anaga*, became a nurse of Akbar.

[5] They were convoyed by Hindāl. See *infra*.

Just now the Emperor said to Mīrzā Hindāl: "'Aqīqa Begam disappeared in that first interregnum (*fitrat*[1]), and I repented extremely, and said: "Why did I not kill her in my own presence?" Now, again, it is difficult to convey women with us.' Mīrzā Hindāl answered: 'What it would be to your Majesty to kill a mother and a sister, speaks for itself! So long as there is life in me, I will fight in their service. I have hope in the most high God, that,—poor fellow as I am,—I may pour out my life's blood for my mother and my sisters.'

Then the Emperor set out for Fatḥipūr (Sīkrī) with Mīrzā 'Askarī and Yādgār-nāṣir Mīrza and the amīrs who had come safely off the battlefield.[2]

Mīrzā Hindāl sent on before him[3] her Highness his mother, who was Dil-dār Begam, and his own sister, Gulchihra Begam, and Afghānī *āghācha*, and Gul-nār *āghācha*, and Nār-gul *āghācha*, and the amīrs' wives and families, etc.. He was marching along when the Gawārs pursued him in great numbers. (38*b*) Some of his troopers charged and defeated them. An arrow struck his horse.[4] There was much fighting and confusion. Having saved the helpless women from the bond of the Gawārs, he sent on (to Lāhōr) his mother and sister, and many of the amīrs' people, etc., and went to Alwar. Here he got together tents and pavilions and numerous requisites, and then started for Lāhōr. He arrived in a few days,

---

[1] *i.e.*, battle of Chausa. *Fitna* would read more easily here. Perhaps behind *fitrat* is the notion of relaxation in effort, or of an interval between two periods of good fortune.

[2] Amongst them was Ḥaidar Mīrzā, who describes the fugitives as 'broken and dispirited, and in a state heartrending to tell.' Sīkrī must have rubbed salt into their wounds, since it recalls Bābar's triumph. Their halting-place there was his garden, a token of his genius for living.

[3] The known enemy, Shīr Khān, was in the rear. With Hindāl's marriage-feast fresh in mind, one may give a thought to Sulṭānam. She was probably of this party, since her husband's contingent was with Humāyūn, and he was not on his *jāgīr* of Alwar.

[4] *Asp-i-mubārik*, (?) the horse which had the happiness to bear him. Perhaps *asp* is a mistake for some word to which 'blessed' would be a more fit adjective.

and brought what was wanted for the princes and the amīrs.

His Majesty alighted in Khwāja Ghāzī's garden near Bībī Ḥāj-tāj.[1] Every day there was news of Shīr Khān; and during the three months that the Emperor was in Lāhōr word was brought day after day: 'Shīr Khān has advanced four miles,' 'six miles,' till he was near Sirhind.

One of the amīrs was named Muẓaffar Beg. He was a Tūrkmān. The Emperor sent him with Qāzī 'Abdu-l-lāh to Shīr Khān to say: 'What justice is there in this? I have left you the whole of Hindūstān. Leave Lāhōr alone, and let Sirhind, where you are, be a boundary between you and me." (39a) But that unjust man, fearless of God, did not consent, and answered: 'I have left you Kābul. You should go there.'

Muẓaffar Beg marched at once, and sent on an express to say: 'A move must be made.' As soon as this message came, his Majesty set off. It was like the Day of Resurrection. People left their decorated places and furniture just as they were, but took with them whatever money they had. There was thankfulness to God, because mercifully a ford was found across the Lāhōr water (Rāvī) where everyone crossed. His Majesty halted a few days on the river's bank. Then an ambassador came from Shīr Khān. The Emperor had decided to see him next morning, when Mīrzā Kāmrān made a petition, saying: 'To-morrow there

---

[1] Abū'l-faẓl says that Hindāl's quarters were in Khwāja Ghāzī's garden, and Humāyūn's in Khwāja Dost *munshī's*.

Bībī Ḥaj, Bībī Tāj, Bībī Nūr, Bībī Ḥūr, Bībī Gūhar, and Bībī Shābaz are said to have been daughters of 'Aqīl, brother of 'Alī (Muḥammad's son-in law). They were famous for piety and asceticism. After the murder of Imām Ḥusain at Kerbela, these ladies left Syria for India in obedience to a secret intimation. They alighted outside Lāhōr at the place named by Gul-badan and where their shrine now is. They converted many of the townspeople to their faith, and thus angered the, presumably Hindū, governor. He sent his son to command their departure, but the son fell under their influence, and remained near them. This still more angered his father, who went out against them and their followers with an armed force. The ladies prayed that their honour might be preserved, and they not be seen by strange men. Immediately the earth opened and swallowed them. (*Khazīna'u-l-aṣfiyā*, II. 407.)

will be an entertainment, and Shīr Khān's envoy will be present. If I may sit on a corner of your Majesty's carpet, so that there may be distinction between me and my brothers, it will be a cause of my exaltation.'[1]

Ḥamīda-bānū Begam says it was his Majesty who wrote and sent the following verse to the mīrzā.[2] I had heard that he sent it to Shīr Khān by the envoy. This is the verse:

> 'Although one's image be shown in the mirror,
> It remains always apart from one's self.' (39*b*)
> 'It is wonderful to see one's self in another form:
> This marvel will be the work of God.'

When Shīr Khān's ambassador arrived he paid his respects.

The Emperor's blessed heart was cast down. He fell asleep in a sad mood, and saw in a dream a venerable man, dressed in green from head to foot and carrying a staff, who said: 'Be of good cheer; do not grieve;' and gave his staff into the royal hand. 'The most high God will give you a son who shall be named Jalālu-d-dīn Muḥammad Akbar.' The Emperor asked: 'What is your honourable name?' He answered: 'The Terrible Elephant,[3] Aḥmad of Jām;' and added: 'Your son will be of my lineage.'[4]

---

[1] For an account of Kāmrān's odious and fruitless treachery see B. & H., II. 200 *et seq.*. The meaning of his message to Humāyūn is not clear to me. Perhaps he wished to show the envoy that he was not on the level of Hindāl and 'Askarī, but able to claim recognition as a ruler and as Humāyūn's equal. Perhaps it was a hint to Humāyūn that he must recognise Kāmrān's equality in the lands in which the latter had been supreme while he himself ruled in Dihlī.

At this time Humāyūn was strongly advised to put Kāmrān to death. He refused, but later on and after a dreary waste of good nature, his filial piety had to yield to the common-sense of his victimized followers and allow the blinding.

[2] At the time when the verse was written Ḥamīda was not married. The discussion in 1587 (*circa*) of a 'point' between the ladies is a living touch to the old MS.. Which was likely to be right,—Ḥamīda who might later have heard the story from her husband, or Gul-badan who was in Lāhōr? Gul-badan puts the difference of opinion gently but does not surrender, and leaves her readers to draw their own inferences.

[3] *Zinda-fīl.*

[4] Humāyūn was of the lineage of Aḥmad of Jām through his mother Māham. (A. N., *Bib. Ind.*, ed. I. 121.) To give force to the prophecy,

In those days Bībī Gūnwar[1] was with child. Everyone said: 'A son will be born.' In that same garden of Dost *munshī* and in the month of Jumāda'u-l-awwal, a daughter was born whom they named Bakhshī-bānū.

At this time his Majesty appointed Mīrzā Ḥaidar to take Kashmīr. Meantime, news was brought that Shīr Khān was there. A wonderful confusion followed, and the Emperor decided to march off next morning. (40*a*)

While the brothers were in Lāhōr, they conferred and took counsel and asked advice, but they did not settle on any single thing. At last the news was: 'Shīr Khān is here.' Then, as there was no help for it, they marched off at the first watch of the day (9 a.m.).

The Emperor's wish was to go to Kashmīr, where he had sent Mīrzā Ḥaidar *Kāshgharī*; but news of the mīrzā's success had not yet come, and people counselled: 'If your Majesty were to go to Kashmīr, and the country was not conquered at once, it would—with Shīr Khān in Lāhōr—be a very difficult time.'

Khwāja Kilān Beg[2] was in Sīālkōt, and disposed to serve his Majesty. With him was Mū'yid Beg, who wrote: 'The khwāja greatly wishes to serve you and would come, but he has Mīrzā Kāmrān to consider. If your Majesty would come quickly, his help would be made easy in an excellent way.' The Emperor at once took arms and equipment, and set out to go to the khwāja, and joined company with him and brought him along.[3]

---

however, the coming child's mother had to be of the same descent, since Humāyūn's claim to rank as of the saint's lineage required no prophetic announcement. Indeed this story seems to cast doubt on that claim. Akbar's mother, Ḥamīda, was of the line of Aḥmad of Jām. So, too, was Bega (Ḥājī) Begam. Another of the same family was Bābū or Bānū *āghā*, wife of Shihābu-d-dīn Aḥmad of Nishāpūr.

1 To give value to Aḥmad's prophecy, Bībī Gūnwar ought also to have traced back to him. She does not seem to have been a woman of rank. The girl now born was at least the third child of Humāyūn, there having been Al-amān and 'Aqīqa, children of Bega Begam and now both dead.

2 The well-known old servant of Bābar and now one of Kāmrān's chief amīrs.

3 The begam's story here does not agree with that of Mr. Erskine's authorities. Mū'yid Beg is the ill-adviser of the march from Bengal to Chausa.

The Emperor was pleased to say: 'With my brothers' concurrence, I shall go to Badakhshān. (40*b*) Let Kābul remain the fief of Mīrzā Kāmrān.' But Mīrzā Kāmrān would not consent to (his Majesty's) going to Kābul,[1] and said: 'In his lifetime the Emperor *Firdaus-makānī* gave Kābul to my mother (Gulrukh Begam). It is not right (for you) to go to Kābul.'

Then said his Majesty: 'As for Kābul, his Majesty *Firdaus-makānī* often used to say, "My Kābul I will give to no one; far from it! Let none of my sons covet it. There God gave me all my children, and many victories followed its capture." Moreover, this expression of opinion is recorded many times in his *Wāqi'a-nāma*. What was the good of my showing kindness to the mīrzā from civility and brotherliness, if he now keep on talking in this way!'

Let his Majesty talk as he would, pacifying and conciliating, the mīrzā resisted more and more. When he saw that there was a large following with Mīrzā Kāmrān, and that the mīrzā was in no way willing for him to go to Kābul, he had no resource but to move towards Bhakkar and Multān. Having arrived in Multān, he halted one day. (41*a*) A small quantity of corn was obtained in the fort and having divided that little amongst his men, he marched on till he came to the bank of a river which was seven rivers in one.[2] He stood distracted. There were no boats, and he had a large camp with him. Then there came word that Khawāṣ Khān,[3] with several amīrs, was coming up behind.

There was a Balūchī named Bakhshū (*sic*) who had forts

---

[1] Kāmrān may well have feared that Humāyūn would get no further than Kābul on his way to Badakhshān.

[2] *i.e.*, the Indus. The begam's 'seven' is interesting. *Cf.* 'Sketch of the Hindūstānī Language,' C. J. Lyall, p.1 n.. '*Hindo* represents an earlier *Hindau*, being the modern Persian for the ancient Hendava, *i.e.*, a dweller in the country of the *sapta hindū* (Sk. *sapta sindhu*), or "seven rivers," now called, with the omission of two (probably the Saraswati and Drishadwati or Ghaggar) the Panj-āb.'

[3] A follower of Shīr Khān.

and many men. His Majesty sent him a banner and kettledrums, and a horse, and a head-to-foot suit, and asked for boats and also for corn. After a time Bakhshū *Balūchī* got together and sent about a hundred boats, full of corn too, for the royal service,—a proper attention which pleased the Emperor very much. He divided the corn amongst his people, and crossed the water[1] safe and sound. May mercy be shown to Bakhshū for his dutiful service!

After a weary journey, they reached Bhakkar at last. The fort is in the middle of the river and very strong. The governor, Sulṭān Maḥmūd (*Bhakkarī*),[2] had fortified himself in it. (41*b*) The Emperor alighted safe and well over against the fort, near which was a garden[3] made by Mīrzā Shāh Ḥusain *Samandar*.[4]

At length his Majesty sent Mīr Samandar to Shāh Ḥusain Mīrzā with this message: 'We have come into your territory under compulsion. May your country be blessed to you! We shall not take possession of it. Would to Heaven you would yourself come and pay us your respects, and do us the service which is our due! We intend to go to Gujrāt, and should leave you your own country.' By tricks and wiles, Shāh Ḥusain kept his Majesty as much as five months in Samandar; then he sent a person to wait on him, and to say: 'I am arranging my daughter's wedding-feast, and I send (someone) to wait on you. I shall come (later).' His Majesty believed him, and waited still three months. Sometimes there was corn to be had, sometimes not. The soldiers killed and ate their horses and camels. Then his Majesty sent again, by

---

[1] The Gāra, near Uch.

[2] Foster-brother of Shāh Ḥusain *Arghūn*, and the man for whom Sīdī 'Alī *Reis* negotiated terms with Humāyūn in 1555.

[3] A delightful garden, the Chār-bāgh of Rūhrī (Lūhrī), on the left bank of the Indus. Shāh Ḥusain felt no anxiety as to military operations after hearing that Humāyūn had camped here. *Chār-bāgh* seems to denote a royal and private garden.

[4] 'A place in Hindūstān from which aloes are brought.' (Steingass, *s.v.*.) *Cf.* *Samandūrī*, aloe-wood, of the *Āīn*. (Blochmann 80.) Samandar seems an equivalent for Sind.

Shaikh 'Abdu-l-ghafūr,[1] to ask: 'How much longer will you be? What prevents you from coming? (42a) Things have come to such a pass that there is inconvenience, and many of my men are deserting.' The reply was: 'My daughter[2] is promised to Mīrzā Kāmrān, and a meeting with me is impossible. I could not wait on you.'

As at this time Mīrzā Muḥammad Hindāl crossed the river, some said he might be going to Qandahār.[3] On hearing this his Majesty sent several people after him to make inquiry and to say: 'It is reported that you plan going to Qandahār.' When questioned, the mīrzā said: 'People have given a wrong impression.' On this the Emperor came[4] to see her Highness my mother.

The mīrzā's *ḥaram* and all his people paid their respects to his Majesty at this meeting. Concerning Ḥamīda-bānū Begam, his Majesty asked: 'Who is this?' They said: 'The daughter of Mīr Bābā Dost.' Khwāja Mu'aẓẓam[5] was standing opposite his Majesty, who said: 'This boy will be one of my kinsmen (too?).'[6] Of Ḥamīda-bānū he said: 'She, too, is related to me.' (42b)

In those days Ḥamīda-bānū Begam was often in the mīrzā's residence (*maḥall*). Another day when his Majesty came to see her Highness my mother, he remarked: 'Mīr

---

[1] Humāyūn's treasurer (*mīr-i-māl*) whose official functions must now have been of the least pressing.

[2] The admirable Māh-chūchak who insisted upon accompanying the blinded Kāmrān to Makka. As her peer in compassion may be commemorated Chilma Beg *kūka*. (B. & H., II., 418.)

[3] He encamped at Pāt (text, Paṭr), about twenty miles west of the Indus and about forty miles north of Sehwān. Pāt is in the *sarkār* of Sīwīstān, a little to the east of the highroad to Hyderābād, and not far north of Meānī, the scene of Napier's victory of 1843. I am indebted to Major-General Malcolm R. Haig for the information that Pāt is 'now a ruin, having been destroyed in the latter part of the eighteenth century when two Kalhora chiefs of Sind called in the Afghāns to quell domestic troubles.'

[4] Leaving his troops to prosecute the siege of Bhakkar, and passing through Dārbila where was his cousin, Yādgār-nāṣir. From the wording it might be supposed that Gul-badan was with her mother in Pāt, but I believe she was in Kābul at this time.

[5] *Cf.* Appendix, *s.n.* Ḥamīda-bānū.

[6] (?) interrogative, but the preceding verb is *guftand*, and not *pursīdand*.

Bābā Dost is related to us. It is fitting that you should give me his daughter in marriage.' Mīrzā Hindāl kept on making objections, and said: 'I look on this girl as a sister and child of my own. Your Majesty is a king. Heaven forbid there should not be a proper alimony, and that so a cause of annoyance should arise.'[1]

His Majesty got angry, and rose and went away. Then my mother wrote and sent a letter, saying: 'The girl's mother has even before this been using persuasion.[2] It is astonishing that you should go away in anger over a few words.' He wrote in reply: 'Your story is very welcome to me. Whatever persuasion you may use, by my head and eyes, I will agree to it. As for what they have written about alimony, please Heaven, what they ask will be done. My waiting eye is on the road.' My mother fetched his Majesty, and on that day she gave a party. When it was over, he went to his own quarters. (43*a*) On another day he came to my mother, and said: 'Send someone to call Ḥamīdā-bānū Begam here.' When she sent, the begam did not come, but said: 'If it is to pay my respects, I was exalted by paying my respects the other day. Why should I come again?' Another time his Majesty sent Subḥān Qulī, and said: 'Go to Mīrzā Hindāl, and tell him to send the begam.' The mīrzā said: 'Whatever I may say, she

---

1 This looks like a side-glance at the wasted fortunes of royalty. No kingdom! No revenues! Whence then the dowry? It is clear from the sequel that the important point was being pressed.

Jauhar says that Ḥamīda had been already asked in marriage, but not betrothed or perhaps promised. Her objections to marry Humāyūn seem personal, and may indicate preference for another and dislike for him. She is said to have been fourteen years old and Humāyūn was thirty-three, an opium-eater, and much married already. Her objections, whatever their true basis, must have been strong or they could hardly have survived, for Gul-badan to record, through the many years of prosperity and proud motherhood which her husband's renewed sovereignty in India and her son's distinction secured to her.

Behind Gul-badan's story of the wooing of Ḥamīda there were doubtless many talks over 'old times' when the royal authoress was freshening her memory for her literary task, begun (it seems probable) when she was about sixty-five and Ḥamīda some few years younger.

2 *Mādar-i-dukhtar az īn ham peshtar nāz mīkanad.* Perhaps, 'caressed the idea.'

will not go. Go yourself and tell her.' When Subḥān Qulī went and spoke, the begam replied: 'To see kings once is lawful; a second time it is forbidden. I shall not come.' On this Subḥān Qulī went and represented what she had said. His Majesty remarked: 'If she is not a consort (*nā maḥram*), we will make her a consort (*maḥram*).'

To cut the story short: For forty days the begam resisted and discussed and disagreed. At last her highness my mother, Dil-dār Begam, advised her, saying: 'After all you will marry someone. Better than a king, who is there?' The begam said: 'Oh yes, I shall marry someone; but he shall be a man whose collar my hand can touch, and not one whose skirt it does not reach.' Then my mother again gave her much advice. (43*b*)

At last, after forty days (discussion), at mid-day on Monday (fault) Jumīdu-l-awwal (*sic*) 948H. (September, 1541), and in Pātr (*sic*), his Majesty took the astrolabe into his own blessed hand and, having chosen a propitious hour, summoned Mīr Abū'l-baqā and ordered him to make fast the marriage bond. He gave the mīr two laks of ready money for the dower[1] (*nikāḥāna*), and having stayed three days after the wedding in Pātr, he set out and went by boat to Bhakkar.

He spent a month at Bhakkar and he sent Mīr Abū'l-baqā to Sulṭān *Bhakkarī*. The mīr fell ill while away, and went to the mercy of God.[2]

His Majesty then gave Mīrzā Hindāl leave to go to Qandahār, and he dismissed Mīrzā Yādgār-nāṣir to his own place, Lār. He himself went towards Seāwān[3] (Sehwān),

---

[1] Perhaps the ladies romance a little here. Humāyūn was certainly at a loss for money now and later.

[2] This is not a historic account of the death. He was sent to Yādgār-nāṣir and was shot while crossing the river on his return to Rūhrī by adherents of Shāh Ḥusain. His death caused great grief to Humāyūn. (B. & H., II., 222.)

[3] At the end of September, 1541. Ḥindāl's leave is a sisterly gloss on his acceptance of an invitation to Qandahār given by its governor, Qarācha Khān.

which is six or seven days' journey from Tatta.[1] Sehwān has a strong fort, in which was Mīr 'Alīka, a servant of his Majesty the Emperor.[2] There were several cannon, so no one could possibly go near. Some of the royal soldiers made trenches, and got near and gave him ('Alīka) advice, and said: (44a) 'Disloyalty is not well at such a time,' but Mīr 'Alīka did not agree with them. Then they made a mine and cast down a tower, but they could not take the fort. Corn became dear and many men deserted. The Emperor spent six or seven months there.

Mīrzā Shāh Ḥusain treacherously laid hands on the royal soldiers in all directions, and made them over to his people, and said: 'Take them and throw them into the salt sea.' Three[3] or four hundred would be gathered into one place and flung into boats and thrown into the sea, till as many as 10,000 were cast forth.

[4]As after this there were few men even with the Emperor, (? Shāh Ḥusain) filled several boats with cannon and muskets, and came from Tatta against him. Sehwān is near the river. (? Mīr 'Alīka) hindered the coming of the royal boats and provisions, and sent to say: '(?) I am maintaining my loyalty. March off quickly.' Having no remedy, the Emperor turned to Bhakkar.

When he came near and before he could reach it, Mīr (Shāh) Ḥusain *Samandar* had sent word to Mīrzā Yādgār-nāṣir: (44b) 'If the Emperor, when he is retreating, should

---

1 Semblance of relevance can be given to this statement only by reference to other writers. Humāyūn had intended to go to Tatta at this time, and was diverted from the journey by a slight success of arms. He then besieged Sehwān.

2 Certainly not so, for 'Alīka was an Arghūn and follower of Shāh Ḥusain. Perhaps Gul-badan wrote or intended to convey that 'Alīka had served Bābar as once all the Arghūns had done. Perhaps she has confused the import of the story that Mīr 'Alīka when sent by Shāh Ḥusain to take command of Sehwān, actually passed through Humāyūn's lines and the bāzār without recognition as an enemy.

3 Text, thirty—*sīṣad*. No wonder Humāyūn's force vanished! He is said to have left Hindūstān, *i.e.*, Lāhor, with a following of 200,000. This presumably included Kāmrān's party, and was made up of soldiers and women, children, traders, servants, etc.. At this time Humāyūn had lost both Hindāl's and Yādgār-nāṣir's troops.

4 The narrative becomes much confused here.

come near Bhakkar,[1] do not let him in. Bhakkar may remain your holding. I am with you; I will give you my own daughter.' The mīrzā believed him and did not allow the Emperor to enter the fort, but wished to make him go on, either by force or fraud.

His Majesty sent a messenger to say: 'Bābā,[2] you are as a son to me. I left you in my stead, so that you might help me in case of need. What you are doing is done by the evil counsel of your servants. Those faithless servants will be faithless to you also.' Whatever his Majesty urged had no effect.[3] Then he said: 'Very well! I shall go to Rāja Māldeo.[4] I have bestowed this country on you, but Shāh Ḥusain will not let you keep it. You will remember my words.' Having said this to the mīrzā, the Emperor marched away by way of Jīsalmīr, towards Māldeo. He reached Fort Dilāwar (Dirāwal), on the rāja's frontier, a few days later. (45*a*) He stayed there two days. Neither corn nor grass was to be had. He then went to Jīsalmīr, and on his approach the rāja sent out troops to occupy the road, and there was fighting. The Emperor and some others went aside off the road. Several men were wounded: Alūsh[5] Beg, brother of Shāhaṃ *Jalāīr* and Pīr Muḥammad the equerry, and Raushang the wardrobe-keeper, and some others.[6] At length the royal troops won and the infidels fled into the fort. That day the Emperor travelled 60 *kos* (*cir.* 120 miles), and then halted on the bank of a reservoir.

Next he came into Sītalmīr, where he was harassed all day till he reached Pahlūdī, a *pargana* of Māldeo. The

---

[1] The mīrzā was at Rūhrī and had not possession of the fort. *Cf.* B. & H., II., 226, for a good account of his treachery and credulity.

[2] (?) 'My dear boy'—the Persian word of endearment. The relative position and ages of Humāyūn and Yādgār-nāṣir make 'father' inappropriate.

[3] In this extremity Humāyūn turned his thoughts towards Makka.

[4] Rāja of Jūdpūr (Mārwār), who had proffered help.

[5] Var., Lūsh and Tarsh,—all three names of such disagreeable import as to suggest that they are either nicknames or were bestowed to ward off evil influences. Perhaps *ūlūs* should be read. *Cf.* App. *s.n.*.

[6] Muqīm *Harāwī*, father of Niẓāmu-d-dīn Aḥmad, took part in this engagement.

rāja was in Jodhpūr, and sent armour and a camel's-load of *ashrafīs*, and greatly comforted his Majesty by saying: 'You are welcome! I give you Bīkanīr.' The Emperor halted with an easy mind, and despatched *Atka* Khān (Shamsu-d-dīn *Ghaznavī*) to Māldeo, and said: 'What will his answer be?'[1]

In the downfall and desolation in Hind, Mullā Surkh, the librarian, had gone to Māldeo, and had entered his service. (45*b*) He now wrote: 'Beware, a thousand times beware of advancing. March at once from wherever you are, for Māldeo intends to make you prisoner. Put no trust in his words. There came here an envoy from Shīr Khān who brought a letter to say: "By whatever means you know and can use, capture that king. If you will do this, I will give you Nagōr and Alwar and whatever place you ask for."' *Atka* Khān also said when he came: 'This is no time for standing.' So at afternoon prayer-time the Emperor marched off. When he was mounting, they captured two spies and brought them bound before him. He was questioning them when suddenly they got their hands free, and one snatched a sword from the belt of Muḥammad *Gird-bāz*[2] and struck him with it, and then wounded Bāqī *Gualīārī*. The other at once unsheathed[3] a dagger and faced the bystanders, wounded several and killed the Emperor's riding-horse. They did much mischief before they were killed. (46*a*) Just then there was a cry, 'Māldeo is here!' The Emperor had no horse fit for Ḥamīda-bānū Begam. He may have asked for one for her from Tardī Beg,[4] who apparently did not give it. He then said: 'Let the camel of Jauhar, the ewer-bearer, be got ready for me. I will ride it, and the begam may have

---

[1] Presumably to *Atka* Khān's message from Humāyūn.

[2] (?) *gird-bāzū*, strong-limbed.

[3] Doubtful translation; *az mayān yak kashīda*.

[4] This excellent officer is frequently a scapegoat. Our begam, however, imputes her blame tentatively. For estimate of his character see B. & H., I. and II., *s.n.*. Jauhar brings Raushan Beg into a similar story of this terrible journey.

my horse.' It would seem that Nadīm[1] Beg heard that his Majesty was giving his horse to the begam and thinking of riding a camel, for he mounted his own mother on a camel and gave her horse to the Emperor.

His Majesty took a guide from this place, and mounted and rode for 'Umrkōt. It was extremely hot; horses and (other) quadrupeds[2] kept sinking to the knees in the sand, and Māldeo was behind. On they went, thirsty and hungry. Many, women and men, were on foot. (46*b*)

On the approach of Māldeo's troops, the Emperor said to Īshān(Īsān)-tīmūr Sulṭān and to Mu'nim Khān[3] and a number of others: 'You all come slowly, and watch the enemy till we have gone on a few miles.' They waited; it grew night, and they missed their way.

All through that night the Emperor went on, and at dawn a watering-place was found. For three days the horses had not drunk. He had dismounted when a man ran in, shouting: 'The Hindūs are coming up in numbers, mounted on horses and camels.' Then the Emperor dismissed Shaikh 'Alī Beg (*Jalāīr*), and Raushan *kūka* and Nadīm *kūka*, and Mīr Payanda Muḥammad, brother of Muḥammad Walī, and many others.

They recited the *fātiḥa*, and his Majesty said: 'Go, fight the infidels!' He thought: 'Īshān-tīmūr Sultān, and Mu'nīm Khān,[4] and Mīrzā Yādgār,[5] and the rest whom we left behind, have been killed or captured by these people who have now come to attack us.' He mounted and left the camp with a few followers.

Of the band which his Majesty had sent out to fight after reciting the *fātiḥa*, Shaikh 'Alī Beg struck the Rājpūt captain with an arrow, and cast him from his horse. (47*a*)

---

[1] The husband of Māham *anaga*, Akbar's celebrated nurse. (R.A.S.J., January, 1899, art. Māham *anaga*, H. Beveridge.) His mother was Fakhru-n-nisā'. *Cf.* Gul-badan, 26*a* and 71*a*.

[2] Perhaps ponies only. Text, *chārwā*.

[3] Gul-chihra's husband.

[4] The well-known *Khān-i-khānān* of Akbar's reign.

[5] Perhaps 'Uncle Yādgār' (*ṭaghāī*), the father of Bega Begam. Yādgār-nāṣir was not here, but still in Sind.

Several more (of the royal troop) hit others with arrows; the infidels turned to flee, and the fight was won. They brought in several prisoners alive. Then the camp went slowly, slowly on; but his Majesty was far ahead. Those who had recited the *fātiḥa* came up with the camp.

There was a mace-bearer named Bihbūd. They sent him galloping after the Emperor, to say: 'Let your Majesty go slowly. By Heaven's grace, a victory has been vouchsafed, and the infidels have fled.' Bihbūd himself was taken to the presence, and conveyed the good news.[1]

His Majesty dismounted, and a little water even (*ham*)[2] was found, but he was anxious about the amīrs, and said: 'What has happened to them?' Then horsemen appeared in the distance, and again there was a cry: 'God forbid! Māldeo!'[3] His Majesty sent a man for information, who came running back and said: 'Īshān-tīmūr Sulṭān, and Mīrzā Yādgār, and Mu'nim Khān are all coming, safe and sound.' They had missed their way. Their return rejoiced the Emperor, who rendered thanks to God.

Next morning they marched on. For three days they found no water. (47*b*) On the fourth, they came to some very deep wells, the water of which was extraordinarily red. The Emperor halted and alighted near one of the wells; Tardī Beg Khān was at another; at a third, Mīrzā Yādgār, and Mu'nim Khān, and Nadīm *kūka;* and at the fourth, Īshān-tīmūr Sulṭān, and Khwāja Ghāzī, and Raushan *kūka*.

As each bucket came out of the wells into reach, people flung themselves on it; the ropes broke, and five or six persons fell into the wells with the buckets. Many perished from thirst. When the Emperor saw men flinging themselves into the wells from thirst, he let anyone drink from

---

[1] And also, tied to his girths, two heads of foes which he flung at Humāyūn's feet.

[2] to brim of the cup of joy.

[3] These cries remind one that even now Humāyūn must have had with him a huge contingent of helpless beings, women and children and non-combatants.

his own water-bottle. When everyone had drunk his fill, they marched on again at afternoon prayer-time.

After a day and a night they reached a large tank. The horses and camels went into the water and drank so much that many died. There had not been many horses, but there were mules and camels. (48*a*) Beyond this place water was found at every stage on the way to 'Umrkōt,[1] which is a beautiful place with many tanks.

The rānā[2] gave the Emperor an honourable reception, and took him into the fort, and assigned him excellent quarters. He gave places outside to the amīrs' people. Many things were very cheap indeed; four goats could be had for one *rupī*. The rānā made many gifts of kids and so on, and paid such fitting service that what tongue could set it forth?

Several days were spent in peace and comfort.

The treasury was empty. Tardī Beg Khān had a great deal of money, and the Emperor having asked him for a considerable loan, he lent 80,000 *ashrafīs* at the rate of two in ten.[3] His Majesty portioned out this money to the army. He bestowed sword-belts and *cap-à-pie* dresses on the rānā and his sons. Many people bought fresh horses here.

Mīr Shāh Ḥusain had killed the rānā's father. For this, amongst other reasons, the rānā collected 2,000 or 3,000 good soldiers and set out with the Emperor for Bhakkar.[4] (48*b*)

In 'Umrkōt he left many people, and his family and relations, and also Khwāja Mu'aẓẓam to have charge of the *ḥaram*. Ḥamīda-bānū Begam was with child. Three days after his Majesty's departure, and in the early morning of Sunday, the fourth day of the revered Rajab, 949H.,[5]

---

[1] The little desert town must indeed have seemed a haven after the terrible journey, and not least so to the young wife who some two months later became the mother of Akbar. Humāyūn reached 'Umrkōt on August 22nd, 1542 (Jumāda I. 10th, 949H.).

[2] Text, *passim*, *ra'nā*. The 'Umrkōt rānā's name was Parsād.

[3] (?) 20 per cent. *Cf.* Mems., 138.

[4] After a stay of seven weeks in 'Umrkōt.

[5] October 15th, 1542.

there was born his imperial Majesty, the world's refuge and conqueror, Jalālu-d-dīn Muḥammad Akbar *Ghāzī*. The moon was in Leo. It was of very good omen that the birth was in a fixed Sign, and the astrologers said a child so born would be fortunate and long-lived. The Emperor was some thirty miles away when Tardī Muḥammad Khān took the news to him. He was highly delighted, and by way of reward and largesse (*niṣār*) for the tidings he forgave all soever of Tardī Muḥammad Khān's past offences. He gave the child the name he had heard in his dream at Lāhōr, the Emperor Jalālu-d-dīn Muḥammad Akbar.

On leaving this place, the Emperor went towards Bhakkar with as many as 10,000 men who had gathered round him, people of the rānā and of the outlying tribes and Sūdmas (Sodhas) and Samīchas. (49*a*) They reached the district of Jūn, where there was one of Shāh Ḥusain's servants with some troopers. He fled.[1] Here there was the Mirror Garden, a very pleasant and enjoyable place where the Emperor alighted. He assigned its villages (? of Jūn) in *jāgīr* to his followers.

It is a six days' journey from Jūn to Tatta. The Emperor was as much as six[2] months in Jūn, and brought his family and people and the whole 'Umrkōt party there.[3] The Emperor Jalālu-d-dīn Muḥammad Akbar was six months old when they took him to Jūn. The party which had come from various places with the royal family and the *ḥaram* now broke up. As for the rānā, he marched off at midnight for his own country, on account of a coolness[4] caused by some talk between him and Tardī Muḥammad Khān.[5] All the Sūdmas and Samīchas went off by agree-

---

1 *Cf.* B. & H., II., 256, for stories of the taking of Jūn.

2 Other writers say nine.

3 Ḥamīda and her baby were good travellers. They left 'Umrkōt when the child was under five weeks old (November 20th), and joined Humāyūn early in December (1542).

4 *shukr-rangī*. I do not find this word in dictionaries, and translate tentatively on the analogy of *shukr-āb*, a tiff.

5 Other writers give Khwāja Ghāzī as the second in the quarrel.

INCIDENTS FOLLOWING THE BIRTH OF AKBAR.

At the top, on the right, are Hamīda-bānū and the child ; on the left, the news is announced with sound of castanets and tambourines.

In the middle, the hour of birth is being communicated to the astrologers.

At the foot, the news is being given to Humāyūn by Tardī Beg, and is welcomed by music and dancing.

[*To face p.* 158.

ment with him, and the Emperor was left alone, as before, with his own people.

He sent brave Shaikh 'Alī Beg (*Jalāīr*) and Muẓaffar Beg *Turkmān* towards the large district of Jājkā (Ḥāj-kān). (49*b*) Mīrzā Shāh Ḥusain sent a force to attack him, and there was a famous fight. At last Muẓaffar Beg was routed and fled, and Shaikh 'Alī Beg (*Jalāīr*) was killed and perished with all his men.[1]

A squabble arose between Khālid Beg[2] and Tarsh Beg, a brother of Shāham Khān *Jalāīr* and his Majesty turned all his favour to Tarsh Beg. So Khālid Beg deserted and went with all his men to Mīr Shāh Ḥusain. Then the Emperor ordered Khālid Beg's mother, Sulṭānam, to prison and this made Gul-barg[3] Begam angry. Then he forgave Sulṭanam and gave her leave to go to the blessed Makka with Gul-barg Begam. Soon after this Tarsh Beg also deserted. The Emperor cursed him, and said: 'For his sake, I dealt harshly with Khālid Beg, who on this account left the circle of the faithful for the circle of the disloyal. Tarsh Beg will die young.' So it was! Fifteen days later, a servant killed him with a knife as he lay sleeping in a boat. When the Emperor heard of it he grew sad and thoughtful. (50*a*) Shāh Ḥusain Mīrzā brought boats up the river to near Jūn, and his men and the Emperor's often fought on board, and many were killed on both sides. Day by day there were desertions to Shāh Ḥusain. In one of these fights was killed Mullā Tāju-d-dīn whom his Majesty held in the greatest favour as a pearl of knowledge.

There was a squabble between Tardī Muḥammad Khān and Mu'nīm Khān. Mu'nīm Khān consequently deserted.

---

[1] A stubborn fight, and fateful for Humāyūn. It occurred in November, 1543.

[2] Son of Niẓāmu-d-dīn 'Alī *Khalīfa Barlās* and of Sulṭānam who appears to be Gul-badan's former hostess (14*a*).

[3] Daughter of Khalīfa, and as such sister or half-sister of Khālid, and daughter or stepdaughter of Sulṭānam. She is, I believe, the Gul-barg of earlier episodes and a wife of Humāyūn.

Very few amīrs remained; amongst them were Tardī Muḥammad Khān and Mīrzā Yādgār and Mīrzā Payanda Muḥammad and Muḥammad Walī and Nadīm *kūka* and Raushan *kūka* and Khadang[1] the chamberlain. Then there was word brought: 'Bairām Khān has reached Jājkā (Ḥāj-kān) on his way from Gujrāt.' The Emperor was delighted, and ordered Khadang and others to give him honourable meeting.

Meantime Shāh Ḥusain Mīrzā had heard of Bairām Khān's coming and sent to capture him. Bairām Khān rashly went into a hollow, and there they fell upon him. (50*b*) Khadang the chamberlain was killed. Bairām Khān and the rest escaped, and the khān came and paid his respects to the Emperor.

At this time letters arrived (addressed to) Mīrzā Hindāl for his Majesty from Qarācha Khān, saying: 'You have been long near Bhakkar, and during the whole time Shāh Ḥusain Mīrzā has given no sign of good-will but the reverse. By Heaven's grace, an easy way is open, and it is best for the Emperor to come here (to Qandahār). This is really advisable. If he will not come, come you yourself without fail.' As his Majesty's coming was delayed, Qarācha Khān went out and met Mīrzā Hindāl, and made over the town to him (in the autumn of 1541).

Mīrzā 'Askarī was in Ghaznīn, and to him Mīrzā Kāmrān wrote: 'Qarācha Khān has given over Qandahār to Mīrzā Hindāl. Qandahār must be considered.' His idea was to take it from Mīrzā Hindāl.

On hearing of these things, his Majesty came to his aunt Khānzāda Begam,[2] and said with great urgency: 'Pray do

---

1 Probably the father of Maywa-jān. Bairām arrived April 12th, 1543 (Muḥarram 7th, 950H.).

2 From this it would seem that Khānzāda was in Sind with Humāyūn. No other writer, I believe, mentions this or the embassy on which she is now sent. The Uzbegs and Turkmāns do not appear àpropos here. If, as Gul-badan says,—and her authority is good,—Khānzāda now went to Qandahār, she will have gone on to Kābul, possibly with Hindāl after he surrendered the town to Kāmrān. Of Mahdī Khwāja, Khānzāda's husband, I find no mention made by any

NAUTCH IN CELEBRATION OF AKBAR'S BIRTH.

[*To page p.* 160.

me the honour of going to Qandahār and advising Mīrzā Hindāl and Mīrzā Kāmrān. (51*a*) Tell them that the Uzbegs and the Turkmāns are near them, and that the best plan is to be friends amongst themselves. If Mīrzā Kāmrān will agree to carry out what I have written to him, I will do what his heart desires.'

Mīrzā Kāmrān came to Qandahār four days after the begam's arrival.[1] Day after day he urged: 'Read the *khuṭba* in my name'; and again and again Mīrzā Hindāl said: 'In his life-time his Majesty *Firdaus-makānī* gave his throne to the Emperor Humāyūn and named him his successor. We all agreed to this, and up till now have read the *khuṭba* in his name. There is no way of changing the *khuṭba*.'[2] Mīrzā Kāmrān wrote to her Highness, Dil-dār Begam:[3] 'I have come from Kābul with you in mind. It is strange that you should not once have come to see me. (51*b*) Be a mother to me as you are to Mīrzā Hindāl.' At last Dil-dār Begam went to see him, and he said: 'Now I shall not let you go till you send for Mīrzā Hindāl.' Dil-dār Begam said: 'Khānzāda Begam is your elder kinswoman, and oldest and highest of you all. Ask her the truth about the *khuṭba*.' So then he spoke to *Āka*. Her Highness Khānzāda Begam answered: 'If you ask me! well! as his Majesty *Firdaus-makānī* decided it and gave his throne to the Emperor Humāyūn, and as you, all of you, have read the *khuṭba* in his name till now, so now regard him as your superior and remain in obedience to him.'

To cut the matter short, Mīrzā Kāmrān besieged Qandahār and kept on insisting about the *khuṭba* for four

---

historian after Bābar's death,—a singular fact and matched by the similar disappearance of the great Khalīfa. Abū'l-faẓl names his tomb. *Cf.* App. *s.n.* Khānzāda.

[1] She had a weary journey from Jūn to Qandahār, and Kāmrān had another, but less toilsome, from Kābul. Kāmrān kept Hindāl besieged, but there seems to have been a good deal of communication between besiegers and beleaguered.

[2] Our memory is better than the begam's, and we remember that Hindāl found no difficulty in changing the *khuṭba* to his own name in Dihlī.

[3] She would be probably with her son Hindāl in the fort.

months. At last he settled it in this way: 'Very well! the Emperor is now far away. Read the *khuṭba* in my name and when he comes back, read it in his.' As the siege had drawn out to great length, and people had gradually come to cruel straits, there was no help for it; the *khuṭba* was read. (52*a*) He gave Qandahār to Mīrzā 'Askarī and promised Ghaznīn to Mīrzā Hindāl. When they reached Ghaznīn, he assigned the Lamghānāt and the mountain passes (Tangayhā)[1] to the mīrzā, and all those promises were false.[2]

Mīrzā Hindāl went off to Badakhshān, and settled down in Khost and Andar-āb. Mīrzā Kāmrān said to Dil-dār Begam: 'Go and fetch him.' When she arrived, the mīrzā said: 'I have withdrawn myself from the turmoil of soldiering, and even[3] Khost is a hermitage. I have quite settled down.' The begam answered: 'If you intend to lead the darvish-life, even[3] Kābul is a hermitage. Live where your family and kinsfolk are. That is the better plan.' Then she made him come, and for awhile he lived as a darvish in Kābul.

About this time, Mīr Shāh Ḥusain sent to the Emperor to say: 'The course favouring fortune is for you to march for Qandahār. That is the better plan.' His Majesty was willing, and replied: 'Horses and camels are scarce in my camp; give me some to travel with to Qandahār.' (52*b*) Shāh Ḥusain Mīrza agreed, and said: 'There are a thousand camels on the other side of the river, which I will send to you as soon as you have crossed.'

[If words by Khwāja Kasak (? Kīsīk), kinsman of Khwāja Ghāzī, are recorded about the journey from Bhakkar and Sind, they are copied from the writings of the said Khwāja Kasak.[4]]

---

1 (?) The *Tangī* of Rudyard Kipling.

2 The *Tārīkh-i-badāyunī* states that Ghaznīn was given to Hindāl and then taken away, and Mr. Erskine comments on this as probably untrue. (B. & H., II. 265 n..) Gul-badan here supports 'Abdu-l-qadīr.

3 'as good as any other place' is perhaps the import of the *ham*.

4 We surmise that this is a gloss of Gul-badan, who has copied from a diary or writings of Khwāja Kasak. This name may be the Tūrkī *kīsīk*, a guard, a sentinel. No Persian word seems appropriate.

HYMN OF PRAISE FOR AKBAR'S BIRTH.

Of especial interest are the faces of the open-mouthed singers. Hamīda-bānū is probably the featureless person on the estrade.

[*To face p.* 162.

At length the Emperor went on board boats, with kinsfolk and family, army and the rest, and travelled for three days on the great river. At the frontier of Shāh Ḥusain Mīrzā's territory is a village called Nuāsī.[1] Here they halted, and his Majesty sent Sulṭān Qulī, the head-camel-driver, to fetch the camels. Sulṭān Qulī brought a thousand, all of which his Majesty gave to his amīrs, and soldiers, and others, ordering them to be apportioned.

The camels were such that one might say they had not known city, or load, or man for seven, or rather seventy, generations. As horses were few, many people took camels to ride on, and what were left were assigned for the baggage. Every camel which was mounted, at once flung its rider to the ground, and took its way to the jungle. (53*a*) Every pack-camel, when it heard the sound of horses' feet, jumped and bounded and tossed off its load, and went off and away to the jungle. If a load was fixed so fast that, jump as it would, it could not get it off, it carried it away and ran with it into the jungle. This was the way the Emperor started for Qandahār. Some 200 camels must have gone off like this.

Shāh Ḥusain Mīrzā's head-camel-driver Maḥmūd was in Sīwī (Sībī), and when the Emperor came near, he strengthened the citadel and retired into it. His Majesty came prosperously to within twelve miles' distance. Then word was brought that Mīr Allāh-dost and Bābā Jūjūk[2] had arrived in Sīwī from Kābul two days earlier, and were going on to (visit) Shāh Ḥusain Mīrzā. By them Mīrzā Kāmrān had sent a dress of honour, and *tipūchāq* horses, and much fruit, and they were to ask for Mīrzā Shāh Ḥusain's daughter.[3]

The Emperor said to Khwāja Ghāzī: 'As there is the

---

[1] Runāī, B. & H., II. 262. The text is clear.

[2] Both these names may be sobriquets. Abu'l-faẓl names Shaikh 'Abdu-l-wahab as Allāh-dost's companion. (A. N., *Bib. Ind.* ed. I. 189 *et seq.*.)

Jūjūk is perhaps the Tūrkī 'sweet-savoured,' and an epithet of 'Abdu-l-wahab, a lawyer with persuasive tongue.

[3] The daughter has already been named as promised.

tie of father and son[1] between you and Allāh-dost, write and ask him in what way Mīrzā Kāmrān stands towards me, and what he will do if I go into his neighbourhood.' (53*b*) He also gave this order to Khwāja Kasak: 'Go to Sīwī, and ask Mīr Allāh-dost whether he thinks it advisable for me to come to Kābul.' The khwāja set out, and the Emperor said: 'We will not march till you have returned.'

When the khwāja came near Sīwī, Maḥmūd, the head-camel-driver, caught him, and asked: 'Why are you here?' 'To buy horses and camels,' he answered. Maḥmūd ordered: 'Feel under his arm and search his cap. Heaven forbid that he should have brought a letter to win over Allāh-dost and Bābā Jūjūk.' They searched, and brought out the letter from under his arm. He had no chance to twist it into a fold.[2] Maḥmūd took it and read it, and, not letting the khwāja go, forthwith conveyed Allāh-dost and Bābā Jūjūk into the fort, and with various roughnesses made them swear: 'We had no knowledge of his coming here.' (54*a*) (?) He has taken the initiative;[3] and 'Khwāja Ghāzī is related to us and he was with Mīrzā Kāmrān,[4] and this is why he has written.' Maḥmūd decided to send all three to Shāh Ḥusain, and Mīr Allāh-dost and Bābā Jūjūk spent the whole night smoothing him down and entreating him, and in the end they were set free.

Mīr Allāh-dost sent 3,000[5] pomegranates and 100 quinces for his Majesty's use, and wrote no letter, because he was afraid it might fall into the wrong hands. By word of mouth he sent to say: 'If a letter should come from Mīrzā Askarī or the amīrs, it would not be bad to go to Kābul;

---

1 Probably a spiritual relationship; that of religious teacher and disciple.

2 (?) to toss it secretly into a corner.

3 *sabq khwānda ast.* Perhaps Kasak as a pupil 'has said his lessons to us,' *i.e.*, to Allāh-dost.

4 He had been Kāmrān's *dīwān* up to the time when the royal family left Lāhōr, and he joined Humāyūn when the brothers parted for Sind and for Kābul.

5 Text, *sīṣad*, but perhaps only 300 should be read.

but if not, it will be clear to your Majesty that nothing is to be gained by going. You have few followers. What, then, will happen?'

Kasak came and reported this. The Emperor was stupefied and bewildered, and said: 'What is to be done? Where am I to go?' They all consulted together. (54*b*) Tardī Muḥammad Khān and Bairām Khān gave it as their opinion that it was impossible to decide to go anywhere but to the north and Shal-mastān,[1] the frontier of Qandahār. 'There are many Afghans in those parts,' they said, 'whom we shall draw over to our side. Mīrzā 'Askarī's people, too, will join us.'

Having settled it in this way, they recited the *fātiḥa* and went, march by march, for Qandahār. Near Shal-mastān they halted in a village named Ranī (? Ralī), but as it had snowed and rained, and was extremely cold, they determined to go on to Shal-mastān. At afternoon prayer-time an Uzbeg youth, mounted on a sorry and tired-out pony, came in, and cried out: 'Mount, your Majesty! I will explain on the way; time presses. There is no time to talk.'[2] The Emperor mounted the very hour the alarm was given, and went off.

He went two arrows' flight, and then sent Khwāja Mu'aẓẓam and Bairām Khān to fetch Ḥamīda-bānū Begam. (55*a*) They went and mounted her, but there was not a chink of time in which to take the Emperor Jalālu-d-dīn Muḥammad Akbar. Just when the begam left the camp to join his Majesty, Mīrzā 'Askarī came up with 2,000 troopers. There was an outcry, and when he heard it, he entered the camp[3] and asked: 'Where is the Emperor?' People said: 'He went hunting long ago.' So the mīrzā knew that his Majesty had gone away just as he himself

---

[1] Approximately Quetta. The route seems to have been over the Bolan.

[2] The youth was Chupī Bahādūr, a former servant of Humāyūn. Gul-badan's story differs in some details from that told by other writers.

[3] Late in 950H. (1543). The little Akbar reached Qandahār on December 15th, 1543.

came in. Then he took possession of the Emperor Jalālu-d-dīn Muḥammad Akbar, and gave him in charge to his wife Sulṭānam,[1] who showed him much kindness and affection. He made all the royal followers march, saying: 'Go to Qandahār.'

His Majesty, when he left, took the road to the mountains. He went eight miles, and then travelled as fast as possible.[2] (55*b*) He had with him Bairām Khān, Khwāja Mu'aẕẕam, Khwāja Nīāzī, Nadīm *kūka*[3] and Raushan *kūka*, and Ḥājī Muḥammad Khān, and Bābā-dost the paymaster, and Mīrzā Qulī Beg *chūlī*,[4] and Ḥaidar Muḥammad the master of the horse, and Shaikh Yūsuf *chūlī*, and Ibrāhīm the chamberlain, and Ḥasan 'Alī, the chamberlain, and Ya'qūb the keeper of the armoury, and 'Ambar the superintendent and the royal agent (*mulk-mukhtār*), and Sambal captain of a thousand, and Khwāja Kasak.[5]

Khwāja Ghāzī says:[6] 'I also was in attendance.' This company went with the Emperor, and Ḥamīda-bānū Begam says,[6] 'There were as many as thirty people,' and that of women there was, besides herself, the wife of Ḥasan 'Alī, the chamberlain.

The prayer before sleep had passed before they reached the foot of the mountains. The snow lay deep, so there was no road to go up by. Their minds were full of anxiety lest that unjust creature, Mīrzā 'Askarī, should follow them. At last they found a way up, and climbed it in some sort of fashion. They were all night in the snow, and (at first) there was neither wood for fire nor food to eat.

---

[1] I believe she was in Qandahār, and that she received the child on his arrival there.

[2] Perhaps he rode four kos, and then, having waited for Ḥamīda, hurried on.

[3] His wife, Māham *anaga*, remained behind with Akbar. With Akbar was also *Atka* Khān (Shamsu-d-dīn Muḥammad) and his wife, Jī-jī *anaga*.

[4] Humāyun's sobriquet for those who went to Persia with him; from *chūl*, a desert. Others in this list might claim it.

[5] Niẕāmu-d-dīn Aḥmad puts the number of the party at twenty-two.

[6] The tense used suggests conference and talking over. Jauhar says that Khwāja Ghāzī joined Humāyūn in Persia from Makkạ. This looks like a contradiction of Jauhar.

They grew very hungry and feeble. (56*a*) The Emperor gave orders to kill a horse. There was no cooking-pot, so they boiled some of the flesh in a helmet, and some they roasted. They made fires on all four sides, and with his own blessed hand the Emperor roasted some meat which he ate. He used to say: 'My very head was frozen by the intense cold.'

Morning came at last, and he pointed to another mountain, and said: 'There are people on that; there will be many Bilūchīs there; and there we must go.' On they went, and reached the place in two days. They saw a few houses near them, and a few savage Bilūchīs whose speech is the tongue of the ghouls of the waste.

The Emperor halted on the skirt of the mountain. There were about thirty people with him. The Bilūchīs saw him, and collected and came near. He had settled comfortably in his tent, so they knew from far off that he was halting. They said to one another: 'If we seize these people and take them to Mīrzā 'Askarī, he will certainly give us their arms, and many gifts besides.' (56*b*)

Ḥasan 'Alī, the chamberlain, had a Bilūchī wife who understood what the ghouls of the waste were saying, and who made it known that they meant mischief. Early in the morning the Emperor thought of marching on, but they said: 'Our chief is not here. When he comes, you shall go.' Besides this, the time had become unsuitable, and so the whole night was spent there in strict watchfulness.

Part of the night had gone when the chief arrived. He waited on the Emperor, and said: 'A *farmān* has come from Mīrzā Kāmrān and Mīrzā 'Askarī, in which it is written: "It is reported that the Emperor may visit your dwellings. If he does, beware!—a thousand times beware!—of letting him go. Seize him and bring him to us. You can keep his goods and horses. Take him to Qandahār." As I had not seen your Majesty, I at first had this evil thought, but now I will sacrifice my life and the lives of my family, I have five or six sons, for your Majesty's head, or rather for one hair of it. (57*a*) Go where you wish. God protect you! Mīrzā 'Askarī may do what he likes.' The Emperor gave him a ruby and a pearl and some other things.

At dawn he marched to honour Fort Bābā Ḥājī[1] by a visit. He reached it in two days. It belongs to the Garmsīr,[2] and lies on the river (Halmand). There are many sayyids there, and they waited on the Emperor and showed him hospitality.

Next morning Khwāja 'Alāwalu-d-dīn (Jalālu-d-dīn) Maḥmūd,[3] having left Mīrzā 'Askarī, came with an offering of a string of mules, and one of horses and tents, etc., whatever he had. Once more the royal heart was at ease. Ḥājī Muḥammad Khān *kūkī*[4] brought thirty or forty troopers and offered a string of mules.

Being helpless because of the disunion of his brothers[5] and the desertion of his amīrs, it now seemed best to the Emperor,—with reliance on the Causer of causes,—to decide upon going to Khurāsān.[6] (57*b*)

After many stages and a journey of many days, he came to parts adjacent to Khurāsān. When Shāh Ṭahmās (*sic*) heard that he had reached the Halmand, he remained sunk in wonder and thought, and said: 'The Emperor Humāyūn has come to our frontier by the perfidious revolution of the firmament,—the firmament unpropitious and crooked of gait! The Lord, whose existence is necessary, has led him here!'

He sent all sorts of people to give honourable reception,

---

[1] Fort of the Pilgrim Father.

[2] *i.e.*, a warm climate, a winter habitation in low ground, and cultivated fields.

[3] He was a revenue-collector of the mīrzā.

[4] Son of Bābā Qūshka, an intimate of Bābar.

[5] Kāmrān was master of Kābul and Ghaznī, Qandahār, Khutlān and Badakhshān. 'Askarī was attached to his full-brother's fortunes, and Hindāl was a prisoner in Kābul. Shīr Shāh ruled Bābar's Indian Empire, and Shāh Ḥusain was in Sind. Certainly there seemed no 'crack' to hold Humāyūn. The date is December, 1543.

[6] *i.e.*, on his way to Persia proper. Humāyūn's messenger to the Shāh was Chupī Bahādur. (55*a* and n..)

nobles and grandees, low and high, great and small. All came to the Halmand to meet the Emperor.[1]

The Shāh sent all his brothers to meet his Majesty,—Bahrām Mīrzā, and Alqās Mīrzā, and Sām Mīrzā. All came and embraced him, and escorted him with full honour and respect. As they drew near (the Shāh) his brothers sent him word, and he also came riding to meet the Emperor. They embraced. (58*a*) The friendship and concord of those two high-placed pāshas was as close as two nut-kernels in one shell.[2] Great unanimity and good feeling ensued, so that during his Majesty's stay in that country, the Shāh often went to his quarters, and on days when he did not, the Emperor went to his.

In Khurāsān[3] his Majesty visited all the gardens and the flower-gardens, and the splendid buildings put up by Sulṭān Ḥusain Mīrzā, and the grand structures of olden days.

There was hunting eight times while he was in 'Irāq, and each time trouble was taken for him also. Ḥamīda-bānū Begam used to enjoy the sight from a distance in either a camel or a horse litter. Shāhzāda Sulṭānam,[4] the Shāh's sister, used to ride on horseback, and take her stand

---

[1] He had crossed the river without receiving invitation or permission, because of Kāmrān's threatened approach. The incidents of Humāyūn's visit to Persia are very entertaining. (B. & H., II. 275 *et seq.*.)

[2] A figure of speech too compact to leave room for the facts. The intercourse of the pāshas was dramatic with human passion and foible. Much of the story would be distasteful to Gul-badan's family pride and vexatious to her orthodoxy.

[3] Not only in Khurāsān but on and off the route to Ṭahmāsp's summer quarters where the pāshas met, did Humāyūn visit noteworthy places. He saw Harāt as his father had done, and later his devious journey took him to Jām, where he saw the shrine of his own and of Ḥamīda's ancestor, the Terrible Elephant, Aḥmad. He visited the tomb of the Founder of the Ṣafī dynasty at Ardabīl, and the date of his visit (1544) makes it probable that he trod that 'Holy Carpet' of Ardabīl which had been woven in 1540 for the shrine and which now attracts our respectful admiration in the Oriental Section of the Victoria and Albert Museum (S. K. M.).

[4] This lady afforded Humāyūn vital assistance in Persia, and even pleaded for his life when it was in the balance. She was highly esteemed by Ṭahmāsp, and had influence in state affairs.

behind her brother. His Majesty said (to Ḥamīda-bānū): 'There was a woman riding behind the Shāh at the hunt. She stood with her reins held by a white-bearded man. People told me it was Shāhzāda Sulṭānam, the Shāh's sister.' (58*b*) In short, the Shāh showed the Emperor much hospitality and courtesy, and laid a charge (on his sister) to show motherly and sisterly hospitality and sympathy (to Ḥamīda-bānū Begam).[1]

One day, when Shāhzāda Sulṭānam had entertained the begam, the Shāh said to her: 'When (next) you offer hospitality, let it be arranged outside the city.' It was on a beautiful plain, rather more than four miles out, that they pitched tents (*khaima*) and folding-tents (*khirga*) and an audience-tent (*bārgā*), and also set up *chatr*[2] and *ṭāq*.[3]

In Khurāsān and those parts they use enclosing screens (*sarāparda*), but they do not put them at the back. The Emperor set up an all-round screen after the Hindū fashion (*hindūāna*). Having pitched the tents, the Shāh's people put coloured chicks (*cheghhā*) all round. His kinswomen and his paternal aunt were there, and his sisters and the ladies of his *ḥaram*, and the wives of the khāns and sulṭāns and amīrs, about 1,000 women in all splendour and adornment.

That day Shāhzāda Sulṭānam asked Ḥamīda-bānū Begam: (59*a*) 'Are such *chatr* and *ṭāq* met with in Hindūstan?' The begam answered: 'They say two *dāng*[4] with respect to Khurāsān, and four *dāng* with respect to Hin-

---

1 An obscure passage in the text, and conjectural only in translation. The Persian words I have rendered 'motherly and sisterly' are *mādarāna wa khwāharāna*. On this same page occurs *hindūāna*; at 43*b*, *nikāḥāna*, and at 62*a*, *pādshāhāna*.

2 (?) umbrella-shaped tents.

3 round-topped tents or balconies, or arched erections.

4 or *dānak*. Hazarding a guess, the meaning 'quarter of the world' seems fittest to select from the several of *dāng* or *dānak*. Others conceivably applicable are 'a small grain' (*anglice*, peppercorn in this connection), and the sixth of anything (*anglice*, the colloquial 'fraction'). Doubtless my difficulty is none to those experienced in colloquial Persian.

Hamīda's ready use of a colloquial phrase to express that the reputedly greater contains the less is neat and diplomatic.

dūstān. When a thing is found in two *dāng*, it is clear it will be found better in four.'

Shāh Sulṭānam said also, in reply to her own paternal aunt, and in confirmation of the begam's words: 'Aunt, it is strange that you ask, "Where are two *dāng?* where are four *dāng?*" It is clear anything would be found better and more wonderful (in four than in two).'

They passed the whole day very well in sociable festivity. At the time of eating, all the amīrs' wives stood and served, and the Shāh's ladies placed[1] food before Shāhzāda Sulṭānam.

Moreover, they were hospitable[2] with all sorts of stuffs, embroidered and others, to Ḥamīda-bānū Begam, as was incumbent and fitting. The Shāh went on in advance[3] and was in his Majesty's quarters till the prayer before sleep. (59*b*) When he heard that Ḥamīda-bānū Begam had arrived, he rose from the presence and went home. To such a height of pleasantness and kindness was he amiable!

Raushan *kūka*, spite of his former fidelity and services, was now faithless, in that foreign and perilous country, about some valuable rubies. These used to be kept in the Emperor's amulet-case (*ṭumār*[4]), and of this he and the begam knew and no one else. If he went away anywhere, he used to give the amulet-case into her charge. One day she was going to wash her head, so she bundled the case up in a handkerchief, and put it on the Emperor's bed. Raushan *kūka* thought this a good chance to steal five rubies. Then he agreed with Khwāja Ghāzī, and trusted them to him, meaning by-and-by to barter them away.

When the begam came back from washing her head, the Emperor gave her the amulet-case, and she at once knew

---

[1] *māndand*, used transitively; also at 4*a*.

[2] *mihmānī kardand.* (?) In the way of gifts, or perhaps by lavish decoration.

[3] *i.e.*, from the place of entertainment to the town.

[4] Also *ṭūmār*, an amulet-case of gold or silver suspended on the neck.

from its lightness in her hand that it had lost weight, and said so. (60*a*) The Emperor asked: 'How is this? Except you and me, no one knows about them. What can have happened? Who has taken them?' He was astonished.

The begam said to her brother, Khwāja Mu'azzam: 'So and so has happened. If at this pinch you will act the brother to me and will make inquiry in some way quietly, you will save me from what one may call disgrace. Otherwise, as long as I live, I shall be ashamed in the royal presence.'

Khwāja Mu'azzam said: 'One thing occurs to me! I, who am so closely connected with his Majesty, have not the means to buy even a poor pony,[1] but Khwāja Ghāzī and Raushan *kūka*[2] have each bought themselves a *tipūchāq* horse. They have not paid the money for them yet. This purchase is not without a ray of hope.'

The begam answered: 'O brother! now is the time for brotherliness! That transaction must certainly be looked into.' Khwāja Mu'azzam answered: 'O elder moon-sister![3] tell no one about it. Heaven willing, I have hope that the right will be righted.' (60*b*)

He went out, and inquired at the house of the horse-dealers: 'For what price did you sell those horses? When is the money promised? What security has been given for the payment?' The dealers answered: 'Both men promised us rubies, and took the horses.'

From them he went to the khwāja's servant, and said: 'Where is the khwāja's wallet, with his honorary dress and his clothes?[4] Where does he keep it?' The servant answered: 'My khwāja has no wallet and no clothes. He has one high cap which, when he goes to sleep, he

---

[1] Text, *tātū*.

[2] Jauhar states that amongst other disaffected persons these two men, and a third, Sulṭān Muḥammad, the spearman (*nazabāz*), had just returned from Makka, and were of Kāmrān's party. Gul-badan makes it seem probable that Jauhar's statements apply only to Sulṭān Muḥammad. (*Cf.* list of companions of Humāyūn on his journey, 55*b*.)

[3] *māh chīcham*. *Cf.* 18*b* n..

[4] *nūrī wa parī*.

puts under his head or his arm.' Khwāja Mu'azzam saw the meaning of this, and made up his mind for certain that the rubies were with Khwāja Ghāzī, and were kept in his high cap. He came and represented to his Majesty: 'I have found trace of those rubies in Khwāja Ghāzī's high cap. In some way I will steal them from him. (61*a*) If he should come to your Majesty and seek redress against me, let your Majesty say nothing to me.' The Emperor listened, and smiled.

Khwāja Mu'azzam then repeatedly played off tricks and little jokes and pleasantries on Khwāja Ghāzī, who came and set it forth to the Emperor. 'I am a lowly man,' said he, '(? but) I have a name and a position. What does the boy Khwāja Mu'azzam mean by playing off these tricks and jokes, and making fun of me in this foreign land, and insulting me?' His Majesty said: 'On whom does he not? He is young. It often comes into his head to do terrifying and ill-bred things. Do not take it to heart. He is only a boy.'

Another day, when Khwāja Ghāzī was seated in the reception-room, Khwāja Mu'azzam, pretending an accident, filched his cap from his head. Then he took out the matchless rubies, and laid them before his Majesty and Ḥamīda-bānū Begam. His Majesty smiled, and the begam was delighted, and said, 'Bravo!' and 'Mercy be upon you.' (61*b*)

Khwāja Ghāzī and Raushan *kūka*, in shame at their deed, made secret communications to the Shah, and carried their talk so far that his heart was troubled. His Majesty saw that the Shāh's intimacy and confidence were not what they had been, and at once sent some of whatever rubies and other jewels[1] he possessed as a gift to him, who then said: 'Khwāja Ghāzī and Raushan *kūka* are in fault; they turned my heart from you, and truly I used to regard you

[1] It was now that Humāyūn gave to the Shāh the 'diamond which had been obtained from Sulṭān Ibrāhīm's treasury,' *i.e.*, the *Koh-i-nūr*. (*Asiatic Quarterly Review*, April, 1899, art. 'Bābar's Diamond,' H. Beveridge.)

as a brother.' Then the two sovereigns again became of one mind, and made clean heart to one another.

The two wrong-doers were excluded from the presence, and were made over to the Shāh, who, when opportunity occurred, got possession of those rubies,[1] and, as to the men, ordered: 'Let them be kept in custody.'[2]

His Majesty's time in 'Irāq was (now) spent happily. In various ways the Shāh showed good feeling, and every day sent presents of rare and strange things. (62*a*)

At length the Shāh despatched his own son and khāns and sulṯans and amīrs with his Majesty to help him, together with good arms and tents, folding and audience tents; and *chatr* and *ṯāq* and *shamiāna*, excellently wrought, and all sorts of the things necessary and fit for a king, from the mattress-warehouse and the treasury and the workshops and kitchen and buttery. In a propitious hour those two mighty sovereigns bade one another farewell, and his Majesty left that country for Qandahār.[3]

At the time of his departure, he asked pardon from the Shāh for the offence of those two faithless ones (Khwāja Ghāzī and Raushan *kūka*), and, having himself forgiven them, took them with him to Qandahār.

When Mīrzā 'Askarī heard (1545) that he was on his way from Khurāsān and approaching Qandahār, he sent the Emperor Jalālu-d-dīn Muḥammad Akbar to Mīrzā Kāmrān in Kābul, who gave him into the care of Dearest Lady, Khānzāda Begam, and our paternal aunt. (62*b*) He was two and a half years old when she received him into her charge. She was very fond of him, and used to kiss his hands and feet, and say: 'They are the very hands and feet of my brother the Emperor Bābar, and he is like him altogether.'[4]

---

[1] (?) those already bartered away.

[2] They were, it would seem, let down by tent-ropes into the celebrated underground prison of Sulaimān's *Diwān*. (Jauhar, Stewart, 72.)

[3] Humāyūn again indulged his love of travel and sights, and delayed so long in Persian territory that the Shāh, coming unexpectedly upon him, angrily turned him off without ceremony.

[4] The child was just over three. It was now that he and Bakhshībānū travelled together to Kābul in the snow.

When Mīrzā Kāmrān was sure that the Emperor was approaching Qandahār, he went to Dearest Lady and cried, and was very humble, and said with countless pains:[1] 'Go you (May your journey be safe!) to Qandahār to the Emperor and make peace between us.'

When she left (Kābul) she made over the Emperor Akbar to Mīrzā Kāmrān, who gave him into the care of (Muḥtarīma) Khānam. Then she travelled as fast as possible to Qandahār. The Emperor besieged Mīrzā Kāmrān[2] and Mīrzā 'Askarī for forty days in the city, and he sent Bairām Khān on an embassy to Mīrzā Kāmrān.[3] (63*a*) Mīrzā 'Askarī grew dejected and humble, admitted his offences, and came out and paid his duty to the Emperor, who then took possession of Qandahār (September 4th, 1545). He bestowed it upon the son of the Shāh, who in a few days fell ill and died.[4] When Bairām Khān[5] arrived, it was given into his charge.

The Emperor left Ḥamīda-bānū Begam in Qandahār and set out after Mīrzā Kāmrān. Dearest Lady, Khānzāda Begam, went with him, and at Qabal-chak[6] she had three days of fever. The doctors' remedies were of no avail, and on the fourth day of her illness she passed to the mercy of God. At first she was buried at Qabal-chak, but three months later her body was brought to Kābul and laid in the burial-place of my royal father.[7]

During several years that Mīrzā Kāmrān was in Kābul,

---

1 of persuasion.

2 The context shows that this is wrong, and so do the histories.

3 Bairām saw Akbar in Kābul, and also Hindāl, Sulaimān, Ḥaram, Ibrāhīm and Yādgār-nāṣir, all under surveillance. The embassy reached Kābul before Khānzādā left, and she travelled with Bairām on his return to Humāyūn.

4 He was an infant.

5 The begam's chronology is faulty here. Bairām had returned before the capitulation.

6 For location of this place *cf. Akbarnāma* H. B., I. 477 n.. It seems to have been in the mountain district of Tīrī, between the basins of the Halmand and the Arghand-āb.

7 Khānzāda, Mahdī (her husband) and Abū'l-ma'ālī are buried in the same spot.

he had never made a hostile raid,[1] and now, all at once, when he heard of his Majesty's approach, desire to break forth (? hunt) seized him, and he went into the Hazāra country.[2] (63*b*)

Mīrzā Hindāl, who had chosen the darvish's corner (in Kābul), now heard of the Emperor's return from 'Irāq and Khurāsān, and of his success in Qandahār. He saw his chance, and sent for Mīrzā Yādgār-nāṣir, and said: 'The Emperor has come to Qandahār, and has been victorious. Mīrzā Kāmrān sent Khānzāda Begam to sue for peace, but the Emperor did not agree to his sort of peace. The Emperor sent Bairām Khān as his envoy, and Mīrzā Kāmrān did not agree to what he proposed. Now the Emperor has given Qandahār to Bairām Khān and has set out for Kābul. Come now, let us, you and I, plan and agree together, and scheme how to betake ourselves to his Majesty.' Mīrzā Yādgār-nāṣir agreed, and the two made their plan and compact. Mīrzā Hindāl said: 'You make up your mind to run away and when Mīrzā Kāmrān hears of it, he will certainly say to me: "Mīrzā Yādgār-nāṣir has gone off; go and persuade him to come back with you." (64*a*) You go slowly, slowly on till I come. Then we will go as quickly as we can and pay our respects to the Emperor.'

Having so settled it, Mīrzā Yādgār-nāṣir ran away. The news went to Mīrzā Kāmrān, who came back at once to Kābul and sent for Mīrzā Hindāl and said: 'Go and persuade Mīrzā Yādgār-nāṣir to come back.' Mīrzā Hindāl mounted at once, and joined Mīrzā Yādgār-nāṣir with all speed. Then they travelled post-haste for five or six days, when they were honoured by paying their duty to the Emperor.

---

[1] *tākht raftan.* I do not know what the begam wishes to say. Kāmrān had made hostile raids to Badakhshān and against the Hazāras. One might read 'hunting expedition.'

[2] He had a Hazāra wife. Perhaps the passage about Kāmrān's hostile raid or hunting is merely an introduction to Hindāl's plan of scape. (*Cf.* B. & H., II. 314, 315, for this story.)

They advised the Khimār[1] Pass as the best route. On Ramẓān 9th, 951H. (the third week of October, 1545), his Majesty ordered a halt in that pass. News of this went to Mīrzā Kāmrān on the same day and disturbed him greatly. He had his tents taken out very quickly and encamped in front of the Guzar-gāh.[2] (64b)

On the 11th of the same month, the Emperor ordered a halt in the valley of (?) Tīpa, and Mīrzā Kāmrān[3] also came and drew up opposite to fight. Then all his amīrs deserted and were exalted by kissing the royal feet. Even Bāpūs[4] who was one of his well-known officers, deserted him with all his following and was exalted by kissing the royal feet. The mīrzā was left solitary and alone. 'No one remains near me,' he thought, so he threw down and destroyed the door and the wall of the house of Bāpūs[5] which was near, and went softly, softly past the New Year's Garden and the tomb of Gul-rukh Begam,[6] dismissed his 12,000 troopers, and went off.

When it was dark, he went on in the same direction to Bābā Dashtī,[7] and halted near a piece of water, and sent back Dostī *kūka* and Jūkī *kūka* to fetch his eldest daughter Ḥabība, and his son Ibrāhīm Sulṭān Mīrzā, and Hazāra Begam[8] who was the brother's child of Khiẓr Khān (Hazāra), and Māh Begam[9] who was sister of Ḥaram (Khurram) Begam, and Māh-afroz, mother of Ḥājī Begam,[10] and Bāqī *kūka*.[11] (65a) This party went with the mīrzā,

---

[1] (?) *himār*, the Ass's Pass.

[2] (?) The Ferry Garden, or perhaps Bābar's burial-place.

[3] Not in person, I believe. His troops were under Qāsim *Barlās*.

[4] Governor (*ātalīq*) of Yasīn-daulat (Āq Sulṭān), the betrothed husband of Ḥabība.

[5] Mr. Erskine says that Kāmrān escaped by a breach opened in a wall. He went by way of Bīnī-ḥiṣār to Ghaznī, where 'Askarī still was.

[6] (?) His mother.

[7] The Desert Father; perhaps a shrine in a lonely spot. (*Cf.* Khwāja Khiẓr, *infra*, 70b.)

[8] A wife.

[9] Probably a wife.

[10] Brevet rank at this time. She made one pilgrimage in 983H. (1576). She may, however, have gone earlier with her blinded father, but not so early as 1545.

[11] (?) The elder brother of Adham and son of Māham *anaga*. Mahām *anaga* would be in Kābul now.

who planned to go to Tatta and Bhakkar. In Khiẓr Khān Hazāra's country, which lies on the way to Bhakkar, he married Ḥabība Begam to Āq Sulṯān and entrusted her to him, while he himself went on.

The victorious Emperor dismounted in triumph in the Bālā-i-ḥisār when five hours of the night of Ramẓān 12th had passed,—prosperously and with safety and good luck.[1] All those followers of Mīrzā Kāmrān who had been promoted to the royal service, entered Kābul with drums beating (November, 1545).

On the 12th of the same month, her Highness my mother, Dil-dār Begam, and Gul-chihra Begam, and this lowly person paid our duty to the Emperor. For five years we had been shut out and cut off from this pleasure, so now when we were freed from the moil and pain of separation, we were lifted up by our happiness in meeting this Lord of beneficence again. Merely to look at him eased the sorrow-stricken heart and purged the blear-eyed vision. (65*b*) Again and again we joyfully made the prostration of thanks. There were many festive gatherings, and people sat from evening to dawn, and players and singers made continuous music. Many amusing games, full of fun, were played. Amongst them was this: Twelve players had each twenty cards and twenty *shāhrukhīs*. Whoever lost, lost those twenty *shāhrukhīs*, which would make five *misqāls*.[2] Each player gave the winner his twenty *shāhrukhīs* to add to his own.[3]

To widows and orphans, and kinsfolk of men who had

---

[1] The hour was probably fixed by astrological counsel. Abū'l-faẓl, who may follow the begam's statement, says that the entry took place on the 12th; other writers name the 10th. The only reason for dwelling on the point is the agreement of Abū'l-faẓl and Gul-badan.

[2] One *shāhrukhī* was about ten pence. Four *shāhrukhīs* made one *misqāl*.

[3] Mr. Erskine says that the earliest mention of cards as made known to him by an Oriental writer is when Bābar sends some to Shāh Ḥusain *Arghūn* who was 'very fond' of them, by Mīr 'Alī, the armour-bearer, in 933H. (1526-27). No doubt such an easy means of speeding the hours was known to the ladies of Bābar's family as early as to anyone else, and Gul-badan is perhaps merely describing a new game.

been wounded and killed at Chausa and Kanauj, or Bhakkar, or who were in the royal service during those intermissions,[1] he gave pension, and rations, and water, and land, and servants. In the days of his Majesty's good fortune, great tranquillity and happiness befell soldiers and peasants. They lived without care, and put up many an ardent prayer for his long life. (66*a*)

A few days later he sent persons to bring Ḥamīda-bānū Begam from Qandahār. When she arrived, they celebrated the feast of the circumcision of the Emperor Jalālu-d-dīn Muḥammad Akbar. Preparations were made, and after the New Year[2] they kept splendid festivity for seventeen days. People dressed in green,[3] and thirty or forty girls were ordered to wear green and come out to the hills. On the first day of the New Year they went out to the Hill of the Seven Brothers and there passed many days in ease and enjoyment and happiness. The Emperor Muḥammad Akbar was five years old when they made the circumcision feast in Kābul. They gave it in that same large Audience Hall Garden.[4] They decorated all the bāzārs. Mīrzā Hindāl and Mīrzā Yādgār-nāṣir, and the sulṯāns and amīrs, decorated their quarters beautifully, and in Bega Begam's garden the begams and ladies made theirs quite wonderful in a new fashion.

All the sulṯāns and amīrs brought gifts to the Audience Hall Garden. (66*b*) There were many elegant festivities and grand entertainments, and costly *khi'lats* and head-to-

---

[1] Text, *faṯrathā*. The begam writes this word sometimes with a *tā* and sometimes with a *to'e*.

[2] *i.e.*, Persian era. Niz̤āmu-d-dīn Aḥmad places the date of entry into Kābul by Humāyūn on Ramz̤ān 10th, 953H., and says Akbar was then four years, two months and five days old. 'Some place the event in the year 952H., but God knows the truth.' It is strange that there should be doubt about a historical event occurring not more than fifty years before this resigned statement was made. Abū'l-faz̤l gives Ramz̤ān 12th, 952H. (November 17th, 1545), as the date of entry, which would fix the feast for March, 1546, when Akbar was three years and five months old. (Born October 15th, 1542.)

[3] Probably in honour of the spring season.

[4] This is the garden where the ladies rejoiced after the victory at Pānīpat. (10*b*) Hence, perhaps, the use of the word 'same.'

foot[1] dresses were bestowed. Peasants and preachers, the pious, the poor and the needy, noble and plebeian, low and high,—everybody lived in peace and comfort, passing the days in amusement and the nights in talk.

Then the Emperor went to Fort Victory (Qila'-i-ẓafar).[2] In it was Mīrzā Sulaimān, who came out to fight but could not stand face to face with his Majesty and so decided to run away. The Emperor then entered the fort safe and sound. Then he went to Kishm, where, after a little while, an illness attacked his blessed frame and he slept day and night.[3] When he came to his senses, he sent Mun'im Khān's brother, Faẓā'il Beg, to Kābul, and said: 'Go! comfort and reassure the people of Kābul. Set them at ease in various ways.[4] Let them not quarrel. Say: "It began ill, but has ended well."' (67*a*)

When Faẓā'il Beg had gone, he (Humāyūn) went one day nearer Kābul.[5]

False news having been sent to Mīrzā Kāmrān in Bhakkar, he set out post-haste for Kābul. In Ghaznī he killed Zāhid Beg[6] and then came on. It was morning; the Kābulīs were off their guard; the gates had been opened in the old way, and water-carriers and grass-cuts were going in and out, and the mīrzā passed into the fort with all

---

[1] Perhaps there is expressed here a difference of degree of honour in the *khi'lat* and *sar-u-pāī*.

[2] Sulaimān had not made submission to Humāyūn,—hence this expedition to Badakhshān.

[3] He is said to have been insensible for four days. He was nursed by Māh-chūchak and Bībī Fāṭima, an armed woman (*ordū-begī*) of the *ḥaram*. She was, it would seem, mother of Zuhra *āghā*, the wife of Khwāja Mu'aẓẓam, and to save whose life Akbar nearly lost his own. (Elliot, V. 292; B. & H., II. 330 *et seq.*.)

[4] (?) As to his health, and their own safety from Kāmrān's return, and the continuance of the situation as he had left it. The illness and convalescence lasted at least two months. He fell ill in Shāhdān, between Khishm and Qila'-i-ẓafar, and Qarācha Khān, his vazīr, behaved with decision and good sense, so that Humāyūn's authority was upheld.

[5] Doubtful translation. Humāyūn is elsewhere said to have gone to Qila'-i-ẓafar to recruit, and Faẓā'il to have arrived in Kābul a few hours after the first news there of the illness. Perhaps one of these occurrences is behind this obscure statement.

[6] Husband of Bega Begam's sister.

these common people. He at once killed Uncle Muḥammad Alī[1] who was in the hot bath. He alighted at the college of Mullā ʿAbdu-l-khāliq.

When the Emperor was starting for Qilaʿ-i-ẓafar, he placed Naukār[2] at the door of the *ḥaram*. Mīrzā Kāmrān must have asked: 'Who is in the Bālā-i-ḥiṣār?' and some-one must have said: 'It is Naukār.' Naukār heard of this and at once put on a woman's dress and went out. The mīrzā's people laid hands on the doorkeeper of the fort, and took him to Mīrzā Kāmrān, who ordered him to be imprisoned. (67*b*) The mīrzā's people went into the Bālā-i-ḥiṣār, and plundered and destroyed innumerable things belonging to the *ḥaram*, and they made settlement[3] for them in Mīrzā Kāmrān's court (*sarkār*). He put the great begams into Mīrzā ʿAskarī's house and there he shut up a room with bricks and plaster and (?) dung-cakes, and they used to give the ladies water and food from over the four walls.[4]

In what was once Mīrzā Yādgār-nāṣir's house he put Khwāja Muʿaẓẓam[5] and ordered his own wives and family to stay in the palace where the royal *ḥaram* and the begams once lived. He behaved very ill indeed to the wives and families of the officers who had left him for the Emperor, ransacking and plundering all their houses and putting each family into somebody's custody.[6]

When the Emperor heard that Mīrzā Kāmrān had come from Bhakkar and was acting in this way, he returned from Qilaʿ-i-ẓafar and Andar-āb safe and sound to Kābul. Qilaʿ-i-ẓafar he gave to Mīrzā Sulaimān. (68*a*)

---

[1] Brother of Māham Begam.

[2] Probably the servant sent with gifts by Bābar from Āgra to Kābul. The name looks like that of an Abyssinian. Is it 'new in work,' and a sobriquet given in youth and retained?

[3] *ẓabṭ wa rabṭ*. Is this an indication of Gul-badan's opinion that Kāmrān profited by the robbery of his relations? His cruelties at this time make theft look innocent. (B. & H., II. 336 *et seq.*.)

[4] The translation of this passage is doubtful.

[5] An undue honour, perhaps prompted by the khwāja's disgrace with Humāyūn.

[6] Probably for the exploitation so often named in the histories.

When he came near to Kābul, Mīrzā Kāmrān sent for her Highness my mother and for me from the house,[1] and gave my mother orders to reside in the armourer's house. To me he said: 'This is your house as well as mine. You stay here.' 'Why,' I asked, 'should I stay here? I will stay with my mother.' He then went on: 'Moreover, write to Khiẓr Khwāja Khān and tell him to come and join me and to keep an easy mind, for just as Mīrzā 'Askarī and Mīrzā Hindāl are my brothers, so is he. Now is the time to help.' I answered: 'Khiẓr Khwāja Khān has no way of recognising a letter[2] from me. I have never written to him myself. He writes to me when he is away, by the tongue of his sons. Write yourself what is in your mind.' At last he sent Mahdī Sulṯān[3] and Shīr 'Alī to fetch the khān. From the first I had said to the khān: 'Your brothers may be with Mīrzā Kāmrān, (but) God forbid that you should have the thought of going to him and joining them. (68*b*) Beware, a thousand times beware of thinking of separating yourself from the Emperor.' Praise be to God! the khān kept to what I said.

When the Emperor heard that Mīrzā Kāmrān had sent Mahdī Sulṯān[3] and Shīr 'Alī to fetch Khiẓr Khwāja Khān, he himself despatched Qambar Beg, the son of Mīrzā Ḥājī, to the khān, who was then in his own *jāgīr*, and said: 'Beware, a thousand times beware! Let there be no joining Mīrzā Kāmrān. Come and wait on me.' The result of this auspicious message was that the khān set out at once for court, and came to the 'Uqābain (Hill of the two eagles) and paid his respects.

When the Emperor passed Minār Hill, Mīrzā Kāmrān sent forward all his well-ordered soldiers under Shīr

---

[1] Presumably the brick and mud quarters of the ladies.

[2] *Suād na dārad ki khaṭ-i-marā shinasad.* I understand that he had not seen her handwriting, and would not know whether a letter purporting to be hers was a forgery. Gul-badan names one son only, Sa'ādat-yār, as being her own. She is now about twenty-five

[3] Brother of Khiẓr and of Yasīn-daulat (Āq Sulṯān).

Afkan,[1] the father of Shīroya, so that they might go out and fight. We saw from above[2] how he went out with his drums beating, out beyond Bābā Dashtī, and we said, 'God forbid you should fight,' and we wept. (69*a*) When he reached the Afghāns' village (*Dih-i-Afghānān*), the two vanguards came face to face. The royal advance-guard at once drove off the mīrzā's[3] and, having taken many prisoners, brought them to the Emperor. He ordered the Mughals to be cut to pieces.[4] Many of the mīrzā's men who had gone out to fight were captured and some of them were killed and some were kept prisoners. Amongst them was Jūkī Khān, one of Mīrzā Kāmrān's amīrs.

In triumph and glory and to the sound of music, the Emperor entered the 'Uqābain, with Mīrzā Hindāl in attendance and a splendid cavalcade. He set up for himself tents and pavilions and an audience hall.[5] He gave Mīrzā Hindāl charge of the Mastān bridge,[6] and stationed the amīrs one after another. For seven months he kept up the blockade.[7] (69*b*)

It happened one day that Mīrzā Kāmrān went from his own quarters to the roof (? of the citadel), and that someone fired a gun from the 'Uqābain. He ran and took himself off. Then he gave this order about the Emperor Akbar: 'Bring him and put him in front.'[8] Someone let his august Majesty (Humāyūn) know that Mīrzā Muḥammad Akbar was being kept on the front, so he forbade the guns to be fired and after that none were aimed at the

---

[1] Son of Quch Beg, an amīr who lost his life in trying to protect Bega Begam at Chausa.

[2] From the citadel where the ladies were.

[3] The begam underrates Humāyūn's victory. The struggle was fierce, renewed and stubborn.

[4] Doubtful translation.

[5] I think she merely wishes to say that Humāyūn camped out on the 'Uqābain, and did not take up quarters under a roof.

[6] Under it flows the stream which issues from the defile of Dih-i-ya'qūb. *Cf. Āīn*, Jarrett, I. 404.

[7] Of the Bālā-i-ḥiṣār, the actual citadel.

[8] Gul-badan's narrative does not support the story that Māham *anaga* exposed herself to save Akbar. This person,—who later on became so important,—is nowhere named by the begam as in charge of Akbar. Her husband, Nadīm *kūka*, is so named.

Bālā-i-ḥiṣār. Mīrzā Kāmrān's men used to fire from the town upon the Emperor on the 'Uqābain. The royal soldiers put Mīrzā 'Askarī to stand right in front and made fun of him.

Mīrzā Kāmrān's men also used to make sallies from the fort, and on both sides many were killed. The royal troops were often the victors and then the others had not courage to come out. For the sake of his wives and children and the begams and the household, etc., the Emperor did not have the cannon fired nor did he place the large houses in difficulty. (70*a*)

When the long siege was ended, they (*i.e.*, the ladies) sent Khwāja Dost Khāwand *madārchī*[1] to his Majesty to say: 'For God's sake, do whatever Mīrzā Kāmrān asks, and save the servants of God from molestation.'[2]

The Emperor sent for their use from outside nine sheep, seven flasks of rose-water, one of lemonade, and seven sets of nine dress-lengths[3] and some made-up jackets.[3] He wrote:[4] 'For their sakes, I could not use force against the citadel, lest I should give an advantage to their enemies.'[5]

During the siege Jahān Sulṭān Begam who was two years old, died. His Majesty wrote: 'Some time or other, if we had used force against the citadel, Mīrzā Muḥammad Akbar would have disappeared.'

To finish the story: There were always people in the Bālā-i-ḥiṣār from evening prayer till dawn, and there was a continuous uproar. The night Mīrzā Kāmrān went away,[6] prayer-time passed and indeed bedtime came, and there was no noise at all. (70*b*)

There was a steep stair by which people came up from

---

[1] Follower of the Musalmān saint Madār.

[2] This message seems one from the imprisoned ladies. The khwāja to whom it was entrusted may now, as in the earlier siege of Kābul, have been Kāmrān's envoy to Humāyun.

[3] *pārcha* and *nīmcha dokhta*. There seems between these words an apposition which I render by the Englishwoman's colloquial terms.

[4] Presumably to some kinsman or official to whom the gifts were consigned.

[5] *i.e.*, by injuring the royal household.

[6] April 27th, 1547 (Rabī' I. 7th, 954H.).

below. When all the city was asleep, there suddenly sounded (on the stair) a clashing and clinking of armour, so that we said to one another: 'What a noise!' Perhaps a thousand people were standing in front (of the fort). We were afraid, but all at once, without warning, off they went. Qarācha Khān's son Bahādur brought us word that the mīrzā had fled.[1]

Having thrown a rope, they (or he) brought up Khwāja Mu'azzam by way of the wall.[2]

Our people and the begam's people and the rest who were outside, took away the door which had kept us fastened in. Bega Begam urged: 'Let us go to our own houses.' I said: 'Have a little patience. We should have to go by the lane and perhaps too someone will come from the Emperor.' At that moment 'Ambar Nāẓir came and said: 'This is the royal order: "They are not to leave that place till I come."' In a little while the Emperor came and embraced Dil-dār Begam and me, and then Bega Begam and Ḥamīda-bānū Begam, and said: 'Come quickly out of this place. (71*a*) God preserve His friends from such a house, and let such be the portion of His foes.' He said to Nāẓir: 'Guard one side,' and to Tardī Beg Khān: 'Guard the other, and let the begams pass out.' All came out, and we spent the evening of that day with the Emperor in perfect content till night became morning. We embraced Māh-chūchak Begam and Khānīsh *āghā* and those of the *ḥaram* who had been with the Emperor on the campaign.

In Badakhshān Māh-chūchak had a daughter born. On the same night the Emperor had this dream: 'Fakhru-n-nisā', my *māmā*,[3] and Daulat-bakht came in by the door,

---

[1] Niẓāmu-d-dīn Aḥmad says that Kāmrān escaped by a hole fashioned for the purpose in the wall 'on Khiẓr Khwāja's' side. This suggests that Gul-badan's husband connived at the evasion, unless one remembers that Khiẓr Khwāja is a place outside Kābul.

[2] I do not understand this sentence. Either the followers of Kāmrān drew the khwāja up into the fort-precincts to take him with them, he having displeased Humāyūn and being nearly connected with him, or the ladies had him drawn up. He was, it seems, not a prisoner. (67*b*)

[3] Fakhru-n-nisā', the mother of Nadīm *kūka*, would seem from this to have been Humāyūn's own attendant in childhood.

and brought something or other, and then left me alone.' Consider it as he might, he could only ask: 'What does this dream mean?' Then it occurred to him that, as a daughter had just been born, he would call her after the two, and taking *nisā'* from one, and *bakht* from the other, would run them together into *Bakht-nisā'*.

Māh-chūchak had four daughters[1] and two sons,—Bakht-nisā' Begam, and Sakīna-bānū Begam, and Amīna-bānū Begam, and Muḥammad Hakīm Mīrzā, and Farrukh-fāl Mīrzā. (71*b*) She was with child when the Emperor went to Hindūstān (1554), and bore a son, in Kābul, whom they named Farrukh-fāl Mīrzā. A little later Khānish *āghā* had a son whom they named Ibrāhīm Sulṭān Mīrzā.

The Emperor spent a full year and a half in Kābul, prosperously and happily, and in comfort and sociability.[2]

After taking flight from Kābul, Mīrzā Kāmrān went to Badakhshān, and there stayed in Tāliqān. One day the Emperor was in the Inner Garden,[3] and when he rose at dawn for prayers, news came that many of the amīrs who formerly were with the mīrzā, had gone to him again. Amongst them were Qarācha Khān and Muṣāḥib Khān, and Mubāriz Khān and Bāpūs.[4] Many wretches fled by night and went to join the mīrzā in Badakhshān.

In a propitious hour the Emperor also started for Badakhshān. He besieged the mīrzā in Tāliqān, and after a time made him agree to submit and become obedient (72*a*) when he waited on the Emperor, who bestowed Kulāb on him, and gave Qila'-i-ẓafar to Mīrzā Sulaimān, Qandahār (*sic*; (?) Kunduz) to Mīrzā Hindāl, and Tāliqān to Mīrzā 'Askarī.

---

1 Gul-badan does not name Fakhru-n-nisā' who became the wife of Shāh 'Abū'l-ma'ālī and of Khwāja Ḥasan *Naqshbandī*. Perhaps she is Bakht-nisa'.

2 From 1547; but a term of one and a half years does not quite fit the facts. Humāyūn started for the north on June 12th, 1548. (B & H., II. 352.)

3 *ōrta-bāgh*.

4 Perhaps it may be taken as an indication of the degradation of 'home life' that Qarācha and Bāpūs again joined Kāmrān, although the latter had exposed Qarācha's son and a wife of Bāpūs on the battlements, with the utmost dishonour, and had killed three of the latter's children and flung their bodies from the ramparts.

One day at Kishm[1] they had set up[2] the tents and there was an assembly of the brothers, his Majesty the Emperor Humāyūn, and Mīrzā Kāmrān, and Mīrzā 'Askārī, and Mīrzā Hindāl, and Mīrzā Sulaimān.[3]

His Majesty enjoined certain regulations[4] which are fixed for interviews with kings, and said: 'Bring ewer and basin so that we may wash our hands and eat together.' He washed his hands and Mīrzā Kāmrān washed his. By years Mīrzā Sulaimān (b. 920H.) had precedence of Mīrzā 'Askarī (b. 922H.) and Mīrzā Hindāl (b. 925H.). So, to show him respect, the two brothers set the ewer and basin first before him.

After washing his hands Mīrzā Sulaimān did something improper with his nose. Mīrzā 'Askarī and Mīrzā Hindāl were much put out, and said: 'What rusticity is this? (72*b*) First of all, what right have we to wash our hands in his Majesty's presence? but when he bestows the favour and gives the order, we cannot change it. What sense is there in these nose-wagging performances?' Then the two mīrzās went and washed their hands outside and came back and sat down. Mīrzā Sulaimān was very much ashamed. They all ate at one tablecloth.

At this gathering his Majesty graciously remembered this lowly person, and said to his brothers: 'Gul-badan Begam used to say in Lahor: "I wish I could see all my brothers together!" As we have been seated together since early morning, her words have occurred to my mind. If it be the will of the most high God, may our assembly be kept in His own place! He knows without shadow that it lies not in my heart's depths to seek any Musalmān's ill;

---

1 Abū'l-fazl says the meeting was at Ishkāmish, and this seems to agree with the movements of Humāyūn better than Kishm.

2 *khirgā dokhta būdand.* Certain tents are termed *dokhta*, sewed. They seem to have been large, and were laced together, whence, perhaps, *dokhta*.

For an interesting account of this historic family gathering see B. & H., II. 358 *et seq.*.

3 'Brother' by courtesy and custom; *anglice*, 'cousin.'

4 *Tūrā*, the Institutes of Chingīz Khān of which the begam makes other mention.

how then, should I seek the hurt of my brothers? May God grant to you all the same divine and beneficent guidance, so that our agreement and concord may endure!' (73*a*)

There was wonderful cheerfulness and happiness because many officers and their followers met their relations again, for they too had been sundered because of their masters' quarrels. Nay! one might rather say they had thirsted for one another's blood. Now they passed their time in complete happiness.

On his return from Badakhshān the Emperor spent a year and a half in Kābul and then resolved to go to Balkh. He took up his quarters in the Heart-expanding Garden,[1] and his own residence was over against the lower part of the garden, and the begams were in Qulī Beg's house because it was close by.

The begams said to the Emperor over and over again: 'Oh, how the *rīwāj*[2] will be coming up!' He replied:

---

[1] *i.e.*, moved out of the city as a preliminary to marching.

[2] The following account of this plant is taken from Conolly's Travels, I., 213 n.. It is translated by him from the *Makhāzinu-l-adwiya* (Treasury of Medicines). '*Rībās, rīvās, rīwāj* or *jigarī* (so named from a person of Nishāpūr who first discovered it) is a shrub two or three feet high, in appearance like beet (*salq*). In the middle are one or two short stems of little thickness; the leaves, which separate lengthwise like those of a lettuce, are downy and green, but towards the root, of a violet or whitish colour. The heart is white, delicate, juicy, acidulous and slightly astringent. Altogether the stalk is the size of a man's arm and when the plant is large every leaf has the size of a man's hand. Ārd-shīr was named *Rāwand-dast* (rhubarb-hand) from the length of his hands. The root is called *rāwand* (rhubarb). The top is like the claw of a fowl. The flower is red, and the taste is subacid with a little sweetness. The seed is formed at the top of a long slender stalk which springs up annually in the centre of the plant. It grows where snow lies and in mountainous countries. The best grows in Persia. It is medicinally attenuating and astringent, gives tone to the stomach, and improves the appetite. A collyrium of the juice strĕngthens the eye and prevents opacity, and a poultice of it with barley-meal is a useful application to sores and boils. The juice of the *rīvās* is harsher than that of unripe grapes.' For mention of the name *rīwāj* see *Tabaqāt-i-akbarī*, Lucknow lith. ed., 215; *Tūzūk-i-jahāngīrī*, 47. Vullers, *s.v.*, etc.. Mr. Erskine writes (Mems., 138 n..): 'It is described as somewhat like beetroot, but much larger, red and white in colour, with large leaves that rise little from the ground. It is a pleasant mixture of sweet and acid. It may be the rhubarb, *rāwand*.'

'When I join the army, I shall travel by the Koh-dāman, so that you may come out and see the *rīwāj* growing.' It was at afternoon prayer-time that he rode out[1] (of Kābul) to the garden. Qulī Beg's house where the begams were, was close by and overlooked it, and his Majesty pulled up as he passed, and all the begams saw him, and rose and made the *kōrnish.* (73*b*) Directly they had made this salutation, he beckoned with his own blessed hand, to say: 'Come.'[2]

Fakhru-n-nisā' *māmā* and Afghānī *āghācha* went on a little ahead. There was a stream in the lower part of the garden which Afghānī *āghācha* could not cross, and she fell off her horse. For this reason there was an hour's delay.[3] At last we set out with his Majesty. Māh-chūchak Begam not knowing, her horse went up a little.[4] His Majesty was very much annoyed about this. The garden was on a height and the walls were not yet made. Some vexation now showed itself in his blessed countenance and he was pleased to say: 'All of you go on, and I will follow when I have taken some opium and got over my annoyance.' He joined us when we had, as he ordered, gone on a little. The look of vexation was entirely laid aside and he came with a happy and beautiful look in his face.

It was a moonlight night. (83*a*) We talked and told stories,[5] and Mīr (fault) and Khānish *āghācha* and Ẕarīf the reciter and Sarū-sahī and Shāham *āghā* sang softly, softly.

Up to the time of our reaching Laghmān, neither the

---

[1] Presumably from Kābul, and on the day of starting for Balkh *viâ* the Koh-dāman.

[2] The ladies seem to have been waiting for this signal to start.

[3] Probably to allow for the coming of a less unpropitious hour. This expedition to Balkh ended in a way calculated to attract notice to ill-omens such as the begam's misadventures would seem.

[4] *andak buland raft.* Perhaps the horse reared, the begam not knowing how to manage it; but the later and otherwise irrelevant sentence about the unfinished wall suggests that the begam went too high up the hill. The party is now on its way to see the *rīwāj* growing, and Humāyūn's temper is tried by the various contretemps of the ladies' cavalcade.

[5] A folio of the MS. is, I believe, misplaced, and folio 83 should come in here. In the MS. volume this is the last folio.

royal tents nor the pavilions of the *begams* had arrived, but the *mihr-amez*[1] tent had come. We all, his Majesty and all of us, and Ḥamīda-bānū Begam sat in that tent till three hours past midnight and then we went to sleep where we were, in company with that altar of truth (Humāyūn).

Early next morning he wished to go and see the *rīwāj* on the Kōh. The begams' horses were in the village, so the starting-time passed before they came up. The Emperor ordered that the horses of everyone who was outside should be brought. When they came he gave the order: 'Mount.'

Bega Begam and Māh-chūchak Begam were still putting on their head-to-foot dresses, and I said to the Emperor: 'If you think well, I will go and fetch them.' 'Go,' he answered, 'and bring them quickly.' I said to the begams and to Māh-chūchak Begam and the rest of the ladies: 'I have become the slave of his Majesty's wishes. What trouble waiting gives!' I was gathering them all together and bringing them when he came to meet me and said: 'Gul-badan! the proper hour for starting has gone by. (83*b*) It would be hot the whole way. God willing, we will go after offering the afternoon prayer.' He seated himself in a tent with Ḥamīda-bānū Begam.[2] After afternoon prayers, there was the interval between two prayers before the horses arrived. In this interval he went away.[3]

Everywhere in the Dāman-i-kōh the *rīwāj* had put up its leaves. We went to the skirts of the hills and when it was evening, we walked about. Tents and pavilions were pitched on the spot and there his Majesty came and stayed. Here too we passed the nights together in sociable talk, and were all in company of that altar of truth.

In the morning at prayer-time, he went away to a

---

[1] Perhaps a tent of Humāyūn's invention, in the name of which *mihr* means *sun*. *Cf.* 'another of his (Humāyūn's) inventions was a tent which had twelve divisions, corresponding to the signs of the Zodiac. Every sign had a lattice through which the lights of the stars of dominion shone.' (*Akbar-nāma*, H. Beveridge I. 361.)

[2] Perhaps, a tent of Hamīda having come, he seated himself in it.

[3] (?) the start was made to see the *rīwāj*.

distance (*bīrūn*), and from there wrote separate letters to Bega Begam and to Ḥamīda-bānū Begam and to Māh-chūchak Begam and to me and to all the begams,[1] saying: 'Becoming spokeswoman of your own fault, write apologizing for the trouble you have given. God willing, I shall say farewell and go to join the army either at Farẓa or Istālīf, and if not we shall travel apart.' (74*a*)

Then everyone wrote to apologize for having given trouble, and sent the letter for his holy and elevating service.

In the end his Majesty and all the begams mounted and rode by Lamghān to Bihzādī. At night each one went to her own quarters, and in the morning they ate (? alone), and at mid-day prayer-time rode to Farẓa.

Ḥamīda-bānū Begam sent nine sheep to the quarters of each one of us. Bībī Daulat-bakht had come one day earlier to Farẓa and had got ready plenty of provisions and milk and curds and syrup and sherbet and so on. We spent that evening in amusement. In the early morning (we went) above Farẓa to where there is a beautiful waterfall. Then his Majesty went to Istālīf and passed three days, and then in 958H.[2] marched towards Balkh.

When he crossed the pass, he sent *farmāns* to summon Mīrzā Kāmrān and Mīrzā Sulaimān and Mīrzā 'Askarī, and said: 'We are on the march to fight the Uzbegs; now is the time for union and brotherliness. You ought to come as quickly as possible.' Mīrzā Sulaimān and Mīrzā 'Askarī came and joined him. (74*b*) Then march by march they came to Balkh.

In Balkh was Pīr Muḥammad Khān,[3] and on the first

---

[1] Humāyūn's comprehensive displeasure looks like a fit of temper directed against every and any one. It is possible, however, that a page which might describe other untoward matters besides unpunctuality, has been altogether lost. The sentence which now continues the story, places all the ladies, deprived of their evening of talk and amusement, in chastened solitude.

[2] B. & H., II. 368, has 956H. (1549), and other differences of detail.

[3] Son of Jānī Beg, and uncle of the famous 'Abdu-l-lāh Khān *Uzbeg*. He ruled till 974H. (1566-67).

day his men sallied out and drew up in battle array. The royal army carried off the victory, and Pīr Muḥammad's men tasted defeat and returned to the city. By the next morning the khān had come to think: 'The Chaghatāī are strong; I cannot fight them. It would be better to get out and away.' Just then the royal officers joined in representing that the camp had become filthy, and that it would be well to move to a desert place (*dasht*). His Majesty ordered them to do so.

No sooner were hands laid on the baggage and pack-saddles, than others raised a clamour and some cried out: 'We are not strong enough.' Since such was the Divine will, the royal army took the road without cause from a foe, without reason or motive.[1] The news of their march reached the Uzbegs and amazed them. Try as the royal officers would, they produced not a scrap of effect. It could not be hindered: the royal army ran away. (75*a*)

The Emperor waited a little, and when he saw that no one was left, he too had to go. Mīrzā 'Āskarī and Mīrzā Hindāl, not having heard of the confusion, rode up to the camp. They found no one and saw that the Uzbegs had gone in pursuit, so they too took the road and made for Kunduz. After riding a little way, his Majesty stopped and said: 'My brothers are not here yet: how can I go on?' He asked the officers and attendants whether anyone would bring him news of the princes. No one answered or went. Later on word came from the Mīrzā's people in Kunduz that they had heard of the disaster and did not know where the princes had gone. This letter upset the Emperor very much. Khiẓr Khwāja Khān said: 'If you approve, I will bring news.' 'God's mercy on you!' rejoined his Majesty. 'May they have gone to Kunduz!' (75*b*)

Two days afterwards the khwāja, to the Emperor's great

---

[1] From other sources we learn that the royalists were anxious on two grounds; (1) as to the threatened arrival of an overwhelming Uzbeg force from Bukhārā, and (2) lest Kāmrān should again take Kābul and have their families at his mercy. The last was perhaps the dominant motive for the flight without a pursuer.

delight, brought word that Mīrzā Hindāl had arrived at Kunduz safe and sound. His Majesty gave Mīrzā Sulaimān leave to go to his own place, Qila'-i-ẓafar, and came himself to Kābul (1550, 957H.).

While Mīrzā Kāmrān was in Kūlāb, a woman named Tarkhān[1] Bega, who was a thorough cheat, showed him the way by saying: 'Make a declaration of love to Ḥaram Begam.[2] Good will come of it.' Acting on these words of an ill-judging adviser, he actually sent a letter and a kerchief[3] to Ḥaram Begam by the hand of Begī *āghā*. This woman laid the letter and the kerchief before the begam and then set forth the mīrzā's devotion and passion. Ḥaram Begam said: 'Keep that letter and that kerchief now and bring them again when the mīrzās come home.' Begī *āghā* then wept, and moaned, and coaxed, and said: 'Mīrzā Kāmrān has sent you this letter and this kerchief; he has loved you a long time, and you have no pity for him.' (76*a*) Ḥaram Begam began to show her disgust and violent anger, and at once sent off for her husband, Mīrzā Sulaimān, and her son, Mīrzā Ibrāhīm. She said to them: 'Mīrzā Kāmrān must have come to think you are cowards, since he sends me a letter like this. Have I deserved to be written to in this way? He is as your elder brother, and I am to him as a younger brother's wife.[4] Send off a letter for me about it and rebuke him. As for this wretch of a woman, tear her piece by piece. Let her be a warning to others that no man may cast the evil eye of sinful thought upon another man's womanfolk. What does such a man deserve who, the son of a mother, yet does such monstrous things, and who fears neither me[5] nor my son?'

---

[1] This title indicates rank. A 'Tarkhān Begam' was wife of Sulṭān Aḥmad Mīrzā. (Mems., 22.)

[2] or Khurram. One of her sisters was a wife of Kāmrān.

[3] What fascination may lurk in an embroidered kerchief can be guessed by inspecting the dainty examples in the South Kensington Oriental Section.

[4] *kīlin*. Both here and at 77*b* this word seems to have wider meaning than is given by the Turkī and Persian dictionaries.

[5] The begam's martial character spices this story, since her husband

Instantly hands were laid on Begī *āghā* Bībī, condemned of fate to die, and she was torn in pieces. In consequence of this affair, Mīrzā Sulaimān and Mīrzā Ibrāhīm were displeased with Mīrzā Kāmrān, or rather they became his enemies. (76*b*) They wrote to the Emperor that Mīrzā Kāmrān wished to thwart him and that this could not be better seen than in his failure to go to Balkh with him.

After this the mīrzā, in Kūlāb,[1] could not find, in his terror-stricken thoughts, any better remedy than to become a darvish. He sent his son, Abū'l-qāsim (Ibrāhīm) to Mīrzā 'Askarī, and betook himself to Tāliqān with his daughter 'Āyisha (Sulṭān Begam), and said to his wife (Muḥtarīma Khānam): 'Do you and your daughter follow me later. I will send for you to whatever place I settle on: Till then go and stay in Khost and Andar-āb.' The khānam was related to the Uzbeg khāns, and some of her kinsfolk let the Uzbegs[2] know: 'If you want booty, there are goods and men and women servants; take these, and let the lady go free, for if 'Āyisha Sulṭān Khānam's[3] nephew hears to-morrow (that she has been hurt), he will certainly be very angry with you.' By a hundred plans and wiles, and with a hundred anxieties, and without her goods, she got free from the Uzbeg bondage, and reached Khost and Andar-āb. Here she stayed.

When Mīrzā Kāmrān heard of the royal disaster in Balkh, he said: 'The Emperor is not so friendly to me as he was.' (77*a*) So he left Kūlāb, and went hither and thither.

At this time (1550) his Majesty came out from Kābul. When he reached the Qibchāq defile, he incautiously halted in a low-lying place, and Mīrzā Kāmrān, coming from higher ground, armed and equipped, poured down foes upon him.

---

did not dare even to make war without her consent. Perhaps Kāmrān's devotion extended to the armed force she disposed of. It was clearly in Tarkhān Bega's eye.

1 In Kūlāb were the kinsfolk of his wife, Māh Begam, sister of Haram Begam, daughter of Sulṭān Wais *Qibchāq*, and sister of Chakr 'Alī Khān.

2 *i.e.*, across whose country she had to travel.

3 (?) Mughal Khānam.

Since such was the Divine will, a barbarian,—inwardly blind, an ill-fated oppressor and ill-omened tyrant,—inflicted a wound on the Emperor. The blow reached his blessed head, and all his forehead and his dear eyes were stained with blood.

It was just like it was in the Mughal war when the blessed head of his Majesty *Firdaus-makānī*, the Emperor Bābar, was wounded by a Mughal, and his high cap and the turban wrapped round it were not cut, but his blessed head was badly hurt. His Majesty Humāyūn used to say with surprise: 'I wondered at it, for cap and cloth were whole, and yet the head was cut.'[1] The very same thing happened now to his own head.

After the rout in the Qibchāq defile, his Majesty went to Badakhshān, and Mīrzā Hindal, and Mīrzā Sulaimān, and Mīrzā Ibrāhīm came and waited on him. (77*b*) He went[2] to Kābul and the mīrzās were in attendance, friendly and united and at peace together, when Mīrzā Kāmrān approached. His Majesty sent a message to Ḥaram Begam: 'Ask my *kīlīn*[3] to send me the army of Badakhshān as quickly as possible and ready for service.' In a few days, —a very short time,—the begam had given horses and arms to some thousands of men. She herself superintended and took thought and she came with the troops as far as the pass. From here she sent them forward, and while she went back they went on and joined the Emperor.

---

[1] 'Tambol let fall a heavy sword-blow on my head. It is a singular fact that, though not a thread of my cap of mail was injured, yet my head was severely wounded.' (Mems., 266. Also 111.)

[2] Niẓāmu-d-dīn Aḥmad, 'after forty days.'

[3] *Cf.* 77*a* n.. This story bears out Ḥaram's military reputation. Kāmrān's power of attraction and Humāyūn's present risk can be gauged by the fact that even after the defeat at Chārīkārān some 1,500 horse were with the former, and many amīrs again went over to him.

It was now that the remarkable compact which effected Kāmrān's downfall was made between Humāyūn and his amīrs. (B. & H., II. 338.) These swore fidelity by whatever oath would bind them and then, at the instance of Ḥājī Muḥammad Khān *kūka*, Humāyūn bound himself to,—do as he was told. The compact was effective. The amīrs were the long-suffering victims of Humāyūn's folly and their present turning was, he admitted, justifiable.

Either at Chārīkārān or Qarā-bāgh there was fighting with Mīrzā Kāmrān and his Majesty's army was successful. The mīrzā fled to the mountain passes (*tangayhā*) and Lamghānāt.[1]

Āq Sulṭān (Yasīn-daulat) who was the mīrzā's son-in-law, said in effect to him (*gufta bāshad*): 'You are continually thwarting the Emperor. What is the meaning of it? It is not what should be. (78*a*) Either make your submission and obeisance to the Emperor or give me leave to go, so that men may distinguish between us.' Mīrzā Kāmrān said fiercely: 'Have my affairs come to such a pass that *you* offer me advice?' Āq Sulṭān also spoke angrily, 'If I stay with you, my position will be unlawful,' and left him at once, and went with his wife (Ḥabība) to Bhakkar. The mīrzā wrote to Mīrzā Shāh Ḥusain, and said: 'Āq Sulṭān has displeased me and has gone away. If he comes to Bhakkar, do not let his wife be with him. Part them and tell him to go where he likes.' Shāh Ḥusain Mīrzā at once, on receiving the letter, deprived Ḥabība Sulṭān Begam of the company of Āq Sulṭān and let him depart for the blessed Makka.[2]

In the fight at Chārīkārān, Qarācha Khān[3] and many of Mīrzā Kāmrān's well-known officers were killed.

'Āyisha Sulṭān Begam[4] and Daulat-bakht *āghācha* were in flight for Qandahār, and were captured at the Khimār Pass, and brought in by the Emperor's people. Mīrzā Kāmrān went to the Afghāns,[5] and stayed amongst them. (78*b*)

From time to time his Majesty used to visit the orange-gardens. That year also, according to his old habit, he went to the mountain passes (*tangayhā*) to see the oranges. Mīrzā Hindāl was in attendance, and of the ladies (*ḥaramān*),

---

1 Niẓāmu-d-dīn Aḥmad, 'mountains of Mandrūd.' B. & H., II. 393, 'by the Pass of Bādpaj towards the Afghān country.'

2 Kāmrān was the son-in-law of Mīr Shāh Ḥusain *Arghūn*, and was therefore able to secure this interference with Āq Sulṭān's domestic affairs.

3 *Cf.* Elliot, V. 233.

4 Kāmrān's daughter.

5 *i.e.*, Lamghān.

there went Bega Begam, Ḥamīda-bānū Begam, Māh-chūchak Begam and many others. I could not go because my son, Sa'ādat-yār, was ill at the time. One day his Majesty, attended by Mīrzā Hindāl, was hunting near the mountain passes. They had very good sport. The Emperor went towards where the mīrzā was hunting and had made a very good bag. Following the rules of Chingīz Khān, the mīrzā proffered his game to the Emperor, for it is a rule of Chingīz Khān that inferiors should so act towards their superiors. In short, he gave the Emperor all his game. Then it occurred to him: 'There is still my sisters' portion. (79*a*) They shall not complain again. I will hunt once more and get them a share.' Again he busied himself in hunting, and had taken one head of game, and was returning, when someone sent by Mīrzā Kāmrān blocked the road, and shot an arrow at the unwitting mīrzā which struck his blessed shoulder. Acting on the thought 'God forbid my sisters and womenfolk should be upset by news of this,' he wrote off at once to say: 'Ill begun has ended well![1] Do not be anxious, for I am getting better.' To finish the story: as it was hot, his Majesty went back to Kābul, and in the course of a year the arrow-wound got better.

A year later word was brought that Mīrzā Kāmrān had collected troops and was preparing for war. His Majesty also, taking military appurtenances, set out for the mountain passes (*tangayhā*) with Mīrzā Hindāl. He went safe and well, and made his honouring halt in the passes. Hour by hour, and all the time, spies kept bringing news: 'Mīrzā Kāmrān has decided that an attack must be made to-night.' (79*b*) Mīrzā Hindāl went to the Emperor and submitted his advice: 'Let your Majesty stay on this high ground, and let my brother (nephew) Jalālu-d-dīn Muḥammad Akbar *pādshāh* stay with you, so that careful watch may be kept on this height.' Then he called up his own men, and encouraged and cheered them one by one, and said: 'Put

---

[1] Repetition of a proverb already quoted.

earlier services in one scale and the service of this night in the other. God willing! whatever claim you can make, you shall be exalted to its degree.'[1] One by one he allotted their posts, and then called for his own cuirass and surtout, and high cap and helmet.

His wardrobe-keeper had lifted up the wallet when someone sneezed,[2] and he set it down for a while. Because of this delay, the mīrzā sent to hurry him. Then the things were brought quickly, and he asked: 'Why were you so long?' The man replied: 'I had lifted the wallet when someone sneezed, and I therefore put it down. So there was a delay.' (80*a*)

The mīrzā replied: 'You were wrong. (You should have) said rather: "May there be a blessed martyrdom."' Then he went on: 'Friends all! be my witness that I abjure all forbidden things and all indecorous acts.' Those present recited the *fātḥiha* and prayed: 'May there be benediction.' He said: 'Bring my vest and cuirass and surtout.' He put them on and went out to the trenches to encourage and solace his men. Just then his *ṭabaqchī*,[3] hearing his voice, cried: 'They are attacking me.' The mīrzā, hearing this, dismounted and said: 'Friends, it is far from brave to give no help when my servant is at the point of the sword.' He himself went down into the trench but not one of his followers dismounted. Twice he sallied from the trenches, and in this endeavour became a martyr.

I do not know what pitiless oppressor slew that harmless youth[4] with his tyrant sword! Would to Heaven that

---

[1] Perhaps the notion of this sentence is, 'To-night's service will equal or outweigh previous services, and the lower to-night's scale is forced, the greater will be my largesse.'

[2] It is hardly necessary to say that sneezing is by many nations regarded as an omen of other things than catarrh.

[3] Clerk of the scullery who has charge of plates and dishes, utensils which are often of value by material and by workmanship.

[4] Hindāl was killed on Ẕī'l-qa'dā 21st, 958H. (November 20th, 1551). He was born before March 4th, 1519 (Mems., 258.), and was therefore in his thirty-third year.

Gul-badan always speaks of her brother with affection, and her story

merciless sword had touched my heart and eyes, or Sa ādat-yār, my son's, or Khiẓr Khwāja Khān's! Alas! a hundred regrets! Alas! a thousand times alas! (80*b*)

HEMISTICH.

O well-a-day! O well-a-day! O well-a-day!
My sun is sunk behind a cloud.

All may be said in a word: Mīrzā Hindāl gave his life freely for his sovereign.

Mīr Bābā Dost lifted him up and carried him to his quarters. He told no one, and fetched servants and placed them at the entrance and gave orders: 'Tell everyone who asks, that the mīrzā is badly wounded and that the Emperor forbids anyone to enter.'

Then he went and said to his Majesty: 'Mīrzā Hindāl is wounded.' The Emperor called for a horse; 'I will go and see him.' Mīr 'Abdu-l-ḥaī said: 'He is badly hurt. It is not desirable that you should go.' He understood, and however much he tried,[1] he could not help it, he broke down.

Jūī-shāhī[2] was Khiẓr Khwāja Khān's *jāgīr*. The Emperor sent for him and said: 'Take Mīrzā Hindāl to Jūī-shāhī and care for his burial.' The khān took the camel's bridle,[3] and when he was going away with weeping and lament and voice uplifted in grief, (81*a*) his Majesty heard of the mourning and sent him word: 'We must have patience! This sorrow touches my heart more closely than yours, but I do not give way because I think of our bloodthirsty, tyrannical foe. With him at hand, there is no help but patience.' Then the khān with a hundred regrets, miserable and stricken, conveyed the body to Jūī-shāhī, and there laid and left it.

If that slayer of a brother, that stranger's friend, the

---

shows that she mourned his loss many years. Her book lets us see a group of living and feeling men and women.

[1] *ḥafẓ kardand.* Perhaps as a matter of etiquette which demands composure in public.

[2] Text, Jūsāhī, the modern Jalālābād, on the road to Kābul.

[3] *i.e.*, that of the camel which bore the corpse.

monster, Mīrzā Kāmrān had not come that night, this calamity would not have descended from the heavens.

His Majesty sent letters to his sisters in Kābul, and the city at once became like one house of mourning. Doors and walls wept and bewailed the death of the happy, martyred mīrzā.

Gul-chihra Begam had gone to Qarā Khān's house. When she came back, it was like the day of resurrection.[1] Through weeping and sorrow she fell quite ill and went out of her mind.

It was by Mīrzā Kāmrān's evil fate that Mīrza Hindāl became a martyr. From that time forth we never heard that his affairs prospered. On the contrary, they waned day by day and came to naught and perished. (81*b*) He set his face to evil in such fashion that fortune never befriended him again nor gave him happiness. It was as though Mīrzā Hindāl had been the life, or rather the light-giving eye of Mīrzā Kāmrān, for after that same defeat he fled straight away to Salīm Shāh, the son of Shīr Khān. Salīm Shāh gave him a thousand *rupīs*.[2] Then the mīrzā told in what position he was, and asked help. Salīm Shāh said nothing openly in reply, but in private he remarked: 'How can a man be helped who killed his own brother, Mīrzā Hindāl? It is best to destroy him and bring him to naught.' Mīrzā Kāmrān heard of this opinion and one night, without even consulting his people, he resolved on flight and got away, and his own men had not even a word of it. They stayed behind and when news of the flight reached Salīm Shāh, he imprisoned many of them.

Mīrzā Kāmrān had gone as far as Bhīra and Khūsh-āb when Adam Ghakkar, by plot and stratagems, captured him and brought him to the Emperor. (82*a*)

To be brief, all the assembled khāns and sulṭāns, and high and low, and plebeian and noble, and soldiers and the

---

1 Khwānd-amīr compares a hustle of people to the day of resurrection.

2 A scornful measure of Kāmrān's fall. The date is the end both of 1552 and of 959H..

rest who all bore the mark of Mīrzā Kāmrān's hand, with one voice represented to his Majesty: 'Brotherly custom has nothing to do with ruling and reigning. If you wish to act as a brother, abandon the throne. If you wish to be king, put aside brotherly sentiment. What kind of wound was it that befell your blessed head in the Qibchāq defile through this same Mīrzā Kāmrān? He it was whose traitorous and crafty conspiracy with the Afghāns killed Mīrzā Hindāl. Many a Chaghatāī has perished through him; women and children have been made captive and lost honour. It is impossible that our wives and children should suffer in the future the thrall and torture of captivity. (82*b*) With the fear of hell before our eyes[1] (we say that) our lives, our goods, our wives, our children are all a sacrifice for a single hair of your Majesty's head. This is no brother! This is your Majesty's foe!'

To make an end of words, one and all urgently set forth: 'It is well to lower the head of the breacher of a kingdom.'

His Majesty answered: 'Though my head inclines to your words, my heart does not.' All cried out: 'What has been set before your Majesty is the really advisable course.' At last the Emperor said: 'If you all counsel this and agree to it, gather together and attest it in writing.' All the amīrs both of the right and left assembled. They wrote down and gave in that same line (*miṣra'*): 'It is well to lower the head of the breacher of the kingdom.' Even his Majesty was compelled to agree.

When he drew near to Rohtās, the Emperor gave an order to Sayyid Muḥammad: 'Blind Mīrzā Kāmrān in both eyes.' The sayyid went at once and did so.

After the blinding, his Majesty the Emperor[2] . . . .

END OF THE MS.

---

[1] *bar jahannum*, which I take as an oath. *Cf. bar ḥaq.*

[2] Here in the MS. volume follows folio 83, which I have conjectured should follow folio 73*b*, and have placed there.

APPENDIX A.

Biographical Notices of the Women mentioned by Bābar, Gul-badan, and Ḥaidar.[1]

I. Āfāq (Āpāq) Begam.

Princess of the Universe ; Ar. *āfāq*, four quarters, universe, etc..

She is mentioned, without clue to her parentage, by Bābar, as a wife of Sulṭān Ḥusain Mīrzā *Bāyqrā*. He mentions her again, with others of the mīrzā's widows, as seen in Harāt in 912H. (1506-7), and here his wording, both in the Turkī and the Persian texts, allows the inference that she is a daughter of Sulṭān Abū-sa'īd *Mīrān-shāhī*. Mr. Erskine translates the passage thus : 'Pāyanda Sulṭān Begam, my father's sister, Khadīja Begam and the other (Turkī, *yena;* Pers., *dīgar*) daughters of Sulṭān Abū-sa'īd Mīrzā.'

When greeting the ladies, Bābar gave Āfāq precedence over Khadīja, and notes the fact. Khadīja was not a woman of birth.

Ḥusain *Bāyqrā* married three daughters of Abū-sa'īd, Shahr-bānū, Pāyanda, and Āfāq. The last bore him no child, but she reared and educated nine children of his by her own foster-sister, Bābā *āghācha*.

Early in 932H. (1525) she went from Harāt to Kābul and was received by Bābar (before his departure for India in November, 1525) with all possible respect and kindness. He gives the impression that

---

[1] This Appendix makes no pretence at completeness. It contains the gatherings in of work on Gul-badan Begam's *Humāyūn-nāma*.

she was an affectionate and devoted woman, and says that her tender care of her husband in illness surpassed that of all the other ladies of the *ḥaram*.

News of her death reached Bābar when he was besieging Chandīrī in 934H. (January, 1528).

Mems., 182, 183, 204.

II. Āfāq Begam. (No. 26.)[1]

She was a daughter of Sulṭān-bakht Begam; her father's name has not yet come to my knowledge; she was a grand-daughter of Sulṭān Abū-sa'īd Mīrzā.

Bābar mentions the arrival of a daughter of Sulṭān-bakht Begam in Āgra in 935H. (October, 1528), and Gul-badan supplies the name Āfāq by naming an Āfāq of this parentage as at the Mystic Feast in 938H. (1531).

Gul-badan. Persian text, 25*b*.
Mems., 387.

(*Afghānī āghācha*, the Afghān lady. See Mubārika Bībī.)

III. Afroz-bānū Begam. (No. 33.)

Pers. *afroz*, dazzling, illuminating, and *bānū*, (?) a form of *bān* (*vān*), which in composition means holding, possessing. Also a prince or chief.

Nothing is said to identify her. She was at the Mystic Feast (1531).

Gul-badan, 25*b*.

IV. Āghā Begam. (No. 34.)

Turkī, *āghā*, a title of honour, and Ar. *sulṭān*, sway, pre-eminence. Steingass classes the word *āghā* as Persian. It may be *āka*, lady. The dictionaries do not apply it to women.

Mentioned as at the Mystic Feast in 1531. She may be *Bāyqrā* (*infra*).

Gul-badan, 25*b*.

---

[1] Numbers so entered are those of Gul-badan's guest-list, 24*b* *et seq.*.

V. Āghā Begam *Bāyqrā.*

She was a daughter of Sulṭān Ḥusain Mīrzā *Bāyqrā* and of Pāyanda Sulṭān Begam *Mīrān-shāhī.* Her descent being so high through both parents, her name *Āghā* rises above its frequent application to wives of less degree. Here it may have the meaning of *chief* or *great.* She married her cousin Murād who was a son of Rābi'a-sulṭān Begam (Bedka). The *Ḥabību-s-siyār,* 327 *et seq.* (lith. ed.), states that she died before she reached maturity, but this does not agree with Bābar's statements. The *Ḥabīb* places her death earlier than 912H. (1506).

Mems., 181.
Ḥabību-s-siyār, lith. ed., 327 *et seq.*.

VI. Aghā *kūka.* (No. 78.)

Wife of Mun'im Khān ; at Hindal's Feast (1537).

Gul-badan, 26*a.*

VII. Āghā-sulṭān *āghācha.* (No. 37.)

(?) The lady of chief honour.

She was a wife of 'Umar Shaikh Mīrzā (died 1494), and mother of Yādgār Sulṭān Begam (Bābar's half-sister). She was present at Hindāl's marriage feast (1537), and probably at the Mystic Feast, in 1531. She is classed amongst 'our begams.'

Gul-badan, 25*b.*
Mems., 10, 14.

VIII. Āghā-sulṭān Sulṭanam *Dughlāt.*

She was a daughter of Muḥammad Ḥaidar Mīrzā *Dughlāt,* and therefore aunt of the author of the *Tārīkh-i-rashīdī.* She married 'Abdu-l-qadūs Beg *Dughlāt* in Kāshghar, after 877H. (1472-73). Her husband was alive in 900H. (1494-95), and was governor of Khost for Sulṭān Maḥmūd Mīrzā *Mīrān-shāhī.*

Mems., 27.
Tār. Rash., E. and R., 95, 103.

IX. Āī Begam *Mīrān-shāhī.*

Turkī, *āī*, moon. Her name is not mentioned in the Memoirs, but is so by Ilminsky (Mems., 30; Ilminsky, 34, line 7 from foot).

She was the fourth daughter of Sulṭān Maḥmūd Mīrzā *Mīrānshāhī* and Khānzāda *Termizī* II.; and wife of Jahāngīr Mīrzā, half-brother of Bābar. She was betrothed in 901H. (1495-96), married in 910H. (1504-5), bore one daughter, and was widowed not later than 914H. (1508-9).

Mems., 30, 128.
Pavet de Courteille, I. 57, 262.

X. Āka Begam *Bāyqrā.*

Āka is clearly a title; her personal name I have not found. Her sister who is styled *Bedka*, appears to be named Rābi'a-sulṭān.

Daughter of Manṣūr Mīrzā *Bāyqrā* and Fīroza Begam *Mīrān-shāhī*, full and elder sister of Sulṭān Ḥusain Mīrzā. Bābar states (Mems., 176, 177) that she married (his uncle) Sulṭān Aḥmad Mīrza, and had a son, Kīchak Mīrzā (the young or small prince). But he does not mention her, either as Āka or otherwise, amongst Aḥmad's wives (Mems., 22), and he says that Aḥmad had two sons who died young. Kīchak, however, lived to change his military occupations for literature.

It is singular that a marriage of the oldest *Mīrān-shāhī* of his generation with the oldest *Bāyqrā* girl should not have been entered in Aḥmad's biographical notice.

Mems., 22, 23, 176, 177.

(Ālūsh—Anūsh—Begam, Ūlūs, *q.v.*.)

XI. Amīna Begam *Mīrān-shāhī.*

Ara., *amīn*, faithful.

Daughter of Humāyūn and Māh-chūchak.

Gul-badan, 71*a*.

XII. Āq Begam *Bāyqrā*.

Turkī, *āq*, fair. The word is frequently a sobriquet and the bearer's personal name is occasionally known; *e.g.*, Yasīn-daulat, Āq Sulṭān; Salīqa Begam, Āq Begam. But frequently the personal name is not traceable.

Daughter of Sulṭān Ḥusain Mīrzā *Bāyqrā* and Pāyanda Sulṭān Begam *Mīrān-shāhī*; first cousin of Bābar; wife of Muḥammad Qāsim *Arlāt*.[1] She had one daughter, known as the Black-eyed (*qarā-gūz*) Begam.

Mems., 181.

XIII. Āq Begam *Mīrān-shāhī*. (No. 3.)

Āq Begam was a daughter of Abū-sa'īd *Mīrān-shāhī* and Khadīja. She was one of the several paternal aunts of Bābar who went to India at his invitation. She reached Āgra in October, 1528 (Ṣafar, 935H.), and was met by her nephew. She was present at the double wedding of Gul-rang and Gul-chihra in 1530 (937H.), and was probably at Bābar's death-bed. She was at the Mystic Feast on December 19th, 1531 (Jumāda I. 9th, 938H.).

Gul-badan, 11*a*, 18*b*, 20*a*, 24*b*.
Mems., 179, 182, 387.

XIV. Aq Begam *Mīrān-shāhī*.

Third daughter of Sulṭān Maḥmūd Mīrzā *Mīrān-shāhī* and Khanzāda Begam *Termizī*; and first cousin of Bābar. The Memoirs do not mention her marriage or (as usual alternative) early death. She was full sister of a wife of Bābar, Zainab.

Mems., 30.

(Aq Begam, Salīqa, *q.v.*.)

---

[1] Muḥammad Qāsim was a Tīmūrid through his grandmother, Bega Begam, the sister of 'Abdu-l-qāsim Bābar *qalandar*, King of Khurāsān (died 1457).

XV. ʽAqīqa (ʽAfīfa) Begam *Mīrān-shāhī.* (No. 47.)

Her name may be ʽAqīqa, a cornelian, etc., or ʽAfīfa, a chaste, modest woman. Our begam's MS. allows both readings. I have used the first but the second seems the more appropriate in sense.

She was a daughter of Humāyūn and Bega and second child of both parents. She was born in Āgra in 1531. It is only from her aunt Gul-badan that anything is known of her. She went to Guāliār with her mother in (?) 1534; she was at Hindāl's feast in 1537, and she was lost at Chausa on June 27th, 1539.

Gul-badan, 22*a*, 23*b*, 25, 33*b*, 34*b*.

XVI. *Ātūn māmā.* (No. 38.)

An *ātūn* is a teacher of reading, writing, and embroidery, etc. *Māmā* seems to be the title of old women-servants.

Bābar mentions an *ātūn* in 1501. He met her at Pashāghar whither she had come on foot from Samarqand and where she again joined her old mistress, Bābar's mother, Qutluq-nigār Khānam. She had been left behind in the city after Shaibānī's capture of it because there was no horse for her to ride.

Gul-badan mentions an *ātūn māmā* as at Hindāl's wedding feast, and as *māmā* seems to be used for old servants, it is possible that she is the woman mentioned by Bābar.

Gul-badan, 26*a*.
Mems., 99.

XVII. ʽĀyisha-sulṭān Begam *Bāyqrā.* (No. 9.)

Ar. ʽ*aish*, joy, and *sulṭān*, sway, pre-eminence. *Cf.* App. *s.n.* Daulat.

Daughter of Sulṭān Ḥusain Mīrzā *Bāyqrā* and Zobaida *āghācha* of the Shaibān sulṭāns. ʽĀyisha married, (1) Qāsim Sulṭān *Uzbeg*, a Shaibān sulṭān, and by him became the mother of Qāsim Ḥusain Sulṭan *Uzbeg*, an amīr of Bābar and Humāyūn; (2) by *yanga-lik* (*cf.* App. *s.n.* Jāmal), Būran Sulṭān, a kinsman of Qāsim Sulṭān, and by whom she had ʿAbdu-l-lāh Sulṭān *Uzbeg* who entered Bābar's service. ʿĀyisha was at the Mystic Feast in 1531, and she was lost at Chausa in 1539 (946H.).

Khwānd-amīr gives 929H. (1522-23) as a date at which ʿĀyisha was in Qāsim Sulṭān's *ḥaram*, but this does not agree with Bābar's narrative. His entry that ʿAbdu-l-lāh was in his service and although young, acquitting himself respectably, cannot at latest have been made after 1530. From 1522 to 1530 is all too short for widowhood, remarriage, birth of ʿAbdu-l-lāh, and his growth to respectable military service.

Gul-badan, 24*b*, 33*b*.
Mems., 182.
Ḥabību-s-siyār, lith. ed., 327 *et seq.*.

XVIII. ʿĀyisha-sulṭān Begam *Mīrān-shāhī*. (? No. 11.)

Third daughter of Sulṭān Aḥmad Mīrzā *Mīrān-shāhī* and Qūtūq (Katak) Begam. She was a first cousin of Bābar, and his first wife. They were betrothed in Samarqand when he was five years old, 894H.(1488-89), and married in Shaʿbān, 905H. (March, 1500), at Khojand during the 'troubles' *i.e.*, conflict with Khusrau Shāh and Aḥmad Tambol. Bābar says that at first he had no small affection for ʿĀyisha and that it declined. She was the mother of his first child, Fakhru-n-nisāʿ (born 907H., 1501). She left Bābar before the overthrow (*wirānī*) of Tāshkand by Shaibānī in 909H. (1503), being influenced by the 'machinations' of her elder sister, probably Salīqa, who was married to one of those many kinsmen who tried to overthrow the boy-king of Farghāna.

Gul-badan mentions an ʿĀyisha Sulṭān Begam (No. 11) as being at the Mystic Feast, without describing her. The following entry (No. 12) is that of Sulṭānī, a daughter of Sulṭān Aḥmad Mīrzā, and described as being such. It seems likely that Gul-badan meant this note as to parentage to apply to both begams (Nos. 11 and 12). (*Cf.* App. *s.n.* Sulṭānan.)

Gul-badan, 6*b*, 24*b*.
Mems., 22, 78, 90.

XIX. Āyisha-sulṭān Begam *Mīrān-shāhī.*

Daughter of Kāmrān Mīrzā.

Firishta (lith. ed., 241) and Khāfī Khān (I. 122) say that Kāmrān left one son and three daughters.

The son is called Ibrāhīm by Gul-badan, and in the early part of the *Akbar-nāma.* (*Bib. Ind.*, ed., I. 226.) Later the A. N. and other sources call him Abū'l-qāsim, which may be a hyonymic (*kunyat*).

As to the three girls, Firishta, without naming them, gives the information that:

No. 1 married (*a*) Ibrāhīm Ḥusain Mīrzā (*Bāyqrā*).
No. 2 ,, (*b*) Mīrzā ʿAbdu-r-raḥman *Mughal.*
No. 3 ,, (*c*) Fakhru-d-dīn *Mashhadī* who died in 986H. or 987H. (No. 88 of Blochmann's list. *Āīn-i-akbarī*, p. 406).

Khāfī Khān's information coincides with Firishta's verbally as to No. 3, and actually as to No. 1 and No. 2. For Ibrāhīm can be described as a son of a 'paternal uncle,' if these words are used in the wide sense given to them by contemporary writers. So, too, can 'Abdu-r-raḥman, if he be No. 183 of Blochmann's list—a Dughlāt Mughal and cousin of Mīrzā Ḥaidar.

If we take the girls' names from other sources we can (conjecturally in part) fill up the table.

1. Gul-rukh is known in history as the wife of Ibrāhīm Ḥusain Mīrzā *Bāyqrā.*

2. Kāmrān's eldest daughter, Ḥābība, was forcibly parted from her husband, Āq Sulṭan, in about 1551-52, and this would allow re-marriage to (*b*) or (*c*). Āq Sulṭān went to Makka from Sind 1551-52 (*cir.*), and his name disappears thenceforth.

3. 'Āyisha may also have married (*b*) or (*c*).

In the list of the pilgrims of 983H. (A. N. *Bib. Ind.*

ed., III. 145) are included 'Ḥājī and Gul-'izār, *farzand-ān* of Mīrzā Kāmrān.'[1] We have already the three names required by Firishta and Khāfī Khān, *i.e.*, Gul-rukh, Ḥabība and 'Āyisha. Gul-'izār is 'superfluous.' Perhaps *farzandān* may be read 'offspring,' and she may be a granddaughter. Or Ḥabība or 'Āyisha may have predeceased Kāmrān, and for this reason three girls only be specified by historians who wrote of the time of his death.

Which one of the daughters was the Ḥājī Begam of 983H. is not clear.[2] It would seem that this was her second pilgrimage, since she is enrolled as Ḥājī before starting. Kāmrān's daughters may have gone—one or all—to Makka after his blinding and during the four years of his life there. Of the three, Gul-rukh is the only one of whom it is on record that she was widowed in 983H., and therefore quite free to make the *Ḥaj*. Ibrāhīm Ḥusain died in 981H. (1573).

Ḥājī Begam was visited by Akbar and she died in 991H. (1583).

Gul-badan, 77*a*, 78*a*.
Akbar-nāma, III. 145, 373, 375.

XX. 'Āyisha-sulṭān Khānam and Khātīm, Mughal Khānam, *Chaghatāī Mughal.*

Daughter of Sulṭān Maḥmūd Khān. In 909H. (1503) she, together with other ladies of her father's household, was captured by Shaibānī and was married by him. She bore him a son, Muḥammād-raḥīm Sulṭān. She wrote Turkī verses, and her name

[1] Mr. Beveridge tells me that a MS. *Akbar-nāma* belonging to the R.A.S. has *wa* (and) before *farzandān*, but it does not seem practicable to read this.

[2] Professor Blochmann (*Āīn*, p. 465, No. 187) has (by a slip of reference numbering) confused Ḥājī Begam, daughter of Kāmrān, with Ḥājī Begam, Bega Begam, widow of Humāyūn. The latter died in 989H. before Gul-badan's party returned. Bega Begam went to Makka in 972H..

appears in the biography of poetesses by Fakhrī *amīrī*. Mīrzā Ḥaidar says that some of her children and of two other Mughal khānams (Daulat and Qūt-līq) who were forcibly married at the same time, were living and reigning in Transoxiana at the time of his writing the *Tārīkh-i-rashīdī*. She is, I think, the 'Āyisha named by Gul-badan on 76*b*.

Tār. Rash., 160, 192, 193.
Gul-badan, 76*b*.
Jawāhiru-l-'ajāib. Fakhrī *amīrī* (Bodleian MS.).

XXI. Bābū *āghā* (*Māmā āghā*).

Professor Blochmann writes the name *Bābū;* but *Bābā*, darling, or *Bānū*, lady, would seem more appropriate for a Persian woman.

She was the wife of Shihābu-d-dīn Aḥmad Khān *Nishāpūrī*, and was related to Ḥamīda-bānū Begam *Jāmī*, Akbar's mother. Abū'l-faẓl calls her Māmā *āghā*. He says that she was a good woman, and that on her death Akbar went to her house and offered condolence because of her relationship to his mother.

Shihābu-d-dīn was *damād* of Māham *anaga*, and as *damād* is presumably used here in its more common sense of 'son-in-law,' Bābū *āghā* would seem to be a daughter of Māham *anaga*.

Akbar-nāma, Bib. Ind. ed., III. 716.
Āīn-i-akbarī, Blochmann, 333.

XXII. Bachaka *Khalīfa*.

Gul-badan, Bachaka; Mems., Bachaka; Ilminsky, Bīchkā. Vambéry (*Chaghatäische Sprachstudien*) has an appropriate word, *bechek*, Chok. (? Kokand), *zierrath; ornament*. The name is presumably Chaghatāī Turkī, as the bearer of it was an old family servant of a Farghāna household.

Bachaka was a head woman-servant (*khalīfa*) of Bābar's household, and was one of two women who escaped with his mother and him from Samarqand in 1501. There was a Bachaka whom Gul-badan calls a '*khalīfa* of my royal father,' lost at Chausa in 1539, and the two references may well be to the same woman.

Mems., 98.
Gul-badan, 33*b*.
Ilminsky, 116.

XXIII. Badī'u-l-jamāl Khānam *Chaghatāī Mughal.*

The khānam of rare beauty; Ar. *badī'*, astonishing, rare; *jamāl*, beauty.

Daughter of Sa'īd Khān *Chaghatāī Mughal*, ruler of Kāshghar; and first cousin, once removed, of Bābar. She married Bāush Sulṭān of the Uzbeg Kazāks. On her father's death, her brother Rashīd insisted upon her divorce, and then gave her in marriage to Muḥammadī *Barlās* whom Ḥaidar Mīrzā styles 'a peasant.'

Tār. Rash., E. & R., 453.

XXIV. Badī'u-l-jamāl Begam *Mīrān-shāhī.* (No. 2.)

She was a daughter of Sulṭān Abū-sa'īd Mīrzā *Mīrān-shāhī.* She went to India during Bābar's life; was at the double wedding of his daughters, and at the Mystic Feast in 1531.

Mems., 387.
Gul-badan, 11*a*, 18*b*, 24*b*.

XXV. Bairām (Maryam) Sulṭān.

Ilminsky calls her Bairam; Khwānd-amīr, Maryam. The Mems. give her no name.

She was the elder daughter of Sulṭān Ḥusain Mīrzā *Bāyqrā* and Mīnglī-bī *āghācha Uzbeg.* She married Sayyid 'Abdu-l-lāh Mīrzā of Andikhūd (a Tīmūrid through his mother). She bore a son, Sayyid Birka, who served Bābar.

Ilminsky, 209.
Mems., 181.
Ḥabību-s-siyār, 327 *et seq.*.

XXVI. Bakhshī-bānū Begam.

Princess Good-fortune. Pers. *bakhsh*, fortune, and *bānū* (*vān*), possessing.

She was a daughter of Humāyūn and of Gūnwar Bībī, and was born in Jumāda I., 947H. (September, 1540), the year of the Tīmūrid exodus from India. She fell into the hands of her uncle ʻAskarī with her father's camp and the baby Akbar in 1543. In 1545 she was sent with Akbar in the depth of winter from Qandahār to Kābul. In 957H. (1550), and when ten years old, she was betrothed by her father to Ibrāhīm, son of Sulaimān and Ḥaram. Ibrāhīm (b. 1534) was six years older than Bakhshī-bānū, and he was killed in 1560, leaving her a widow of twenty. In the same year she was given in marriage by Akbar to Mīrzā Sharafu-d-dīn Ḥusain *Aḥrārī*.

Gul-badan, 39*b*.
Akbar-nāma, *s.n.*.

XXVII. Bakhtu-n-nisāʼ Begam.

Felicity of womanhood; Pers. *bakht*, felicity, fortune, and *nisāʼ*, woman.

She was a daughter of Humāyūn and Māh-chūchak, and was born in 957H. (1550). Gul-badan says that she received her name in accordance with Humāyūn's interpretation of a dream. There is, however, ground for thinking that she and Fakhru-n-nisāʼ, both mentioned in the histories as daughters of Māh-chūchak, are one and the same person. Gul-badan enumerates three daughters of Māh-chūchak, and says that there were four. It is her habit to state, in such matters, one more than she names. She mentions Bakht, but not Fakhr.

Of Bakhtu-n-nisāʼ it is recorded in the histories that she came from Kābul to India with her son Diwālī, after the death of Mīrzā Muḥammad Hakīm, her brother (993H.—1584-85), and that she was concerned in a reconciliation effected by Salīma-sulṭān Begam between Akbar and Salīm.

Of Fakhru-n-nisā it is recorded that she married Shāh Abū'l-ma'ālī *Termizī* and Khwāja Ḥasan *Naqshbandī*.

Gul-badan, 71*a*.
Khāfī Khān (*Bib. Ind.* ed.), I. 226.
Badāyunī, Lowe, 72.
Akbar-nāma, *s.n.*.
Aīn-i-akbarī, Blochmann, 322.

XXVIII. Bakht-sulṭān Begam *Mīrān-shāhī*. (No. 4.)

Daughter of Sulṭān Abū-sa'īd Mīrzā *Mīrān-shāhī* and mother of Āfāq (No. 26). She went to India shortly after its conquest by Bābar, and was at the Mystic Feast.

Mems., 387.
Gul-badan, 11*a*, 24*b*, 25*b*.

XXIX. Barlās Begam. (No. 36.)

There is no clue given by which to identify this lady. Others who were, like herself, at the Mystic Feast might, by tribal descent, be styled *Barlās*.

Gul-badan, 25*b*.

(Bedka, Rabī'a, *q.v.*.)

XXX. Bega *āghā*.

Bega is perhaps not a personal name. It appears to be a feminine of *beg*, but its application is not always to the daughters of *begs*, as may be seen by the instances here given. For a confusion of *bega* and *yanga cf.* App. *s.n.* Zainab.

A messenger of Mīrzā Kāmrān to Ḥaram Begam.

Gul-badan, 75*b*.

XXXI. Bega Begam *Bāyqrā*.

Daughter of Sulṭān Ḥusain Mīrzā *Bāyqrā* and Pāyanda-sulṭān Begam *Mīrān-shāhī*; full sister of Ḥaidar *Bāyqrā*; first cousin of Bābar; wife of Bābar

Mīrzā of Ḥājī Tarkhān who was her first cousin and the son of Rabīʿa-sulṭān (Bedka) *Bāyqrā*.

Khwānd-amīr says that she married 'Khwāja Māulānā.' This may be a second marriage or a confusion with Kīchak, her sister.

Mems., 177, 181.
Ḥabību-s-siyār, 327 *et seq.*.

XXXII. Bega Begam and Bībī.

The Emperor Jahāngīr, when in his Memoirs enumerating the gardens of Kābul, mentions one which belonged to Bega Begam, a widow of his father's grandfather, *i.e.*, Bābar. Which of Bābar's wives is indicated by this title cannot be said with certainty.

Jauhar has a story of Kāmrān's want of consideration for 'Bega Begam,' in which the points useful here are that on the day in 1545 when Humāyūn took Kābul from Kāmrān, he asked for food from Bega Begam, and he said of her that she was the very person who had brought Bābar's bones and laid them in Kābul.

These two references of Jahāngīr and Jauhar are probably to the same lady. Of Bābar's wives, Bībī Mubārika (*Afghānī āghācha*) appears to me the most suitable to the time and task.

Bābar's body was still in its Āgra tomb in 1539. (Gul-badan, 34*b*.) Māham was then dead; Dil-dār's movements exclude her from consideration; Gul-rukh, if living, will have left Āgra with her son Kāmrān before the Tīmūrid exodus was enforced by defeat at Kanauj; Bībī Mubārika remains, the probable and appropriate agent for fulfilling Bābar's wish as to the final disposition of his body. She lived into Akbar's reign, and her character and respected position in the household add to the sum of probability that she would discharge this duty.

Bābar's body was not removed till after the *fiṭrat*, *i.e.*, the Tīmūrid downfall and exodus. Bega Begam, or, as we may call her with Jauhar for the sake of clearness, the Bībī, must therefore have remained behind the rest of the royal family. This may have occurred in one of two natural ways. She might have stayed in Āgra under the protection of one of the religious families and safeguarded by pious duty to Bābar's tomb, until Shīr Khān gave permission to remove the body and a safe escort for her journey to his frontier; or she may even have been in Bengal and at Chausa with Humāyūn, and, like Bega (*Ḥājī*) Begam, have been made captive. It would harmonize with Shīr Khān's known actions if he had allowed Bābar's widow to remove his bones, and if he had aided her pious task.

Tūzūk-i-jahāngīrī, lith. ed., 51.
Humāyūn-nāma, Jauhar, Pers. text, *s.a.* 951H. (November, 1545).
B. & H., II. 325 n..

XXXIII. Bega Begam *Mīrān-shāhī*. (No. 15.)

This Bega was a daughter of Mīrzā Ulugh Beg *Mīrān-shāhī* who was king of Kābul and known as *Kābulī*. She was Bābar's first cousin, and may be that daughter of her father who married Muḥammād Ma'ṣum Mīrzā *Bāyqrā*. Gul-badan styles her *'ama*, paternal aunt, of Humāyūn; *anglice*, she and he were first cousins, once removed. She was at the Mystic Feast in December, 1531.

Gul-badan, 24*b*.
Mems., 180.

XXXIV. Bega Begam *Mīrān-shāhī*. (? No. 22. Bega Kilān Begam.)

Daughter of Sulṭān Maḥmūd Mīrzā and Khānzāda II. *Termiẕī*; wife of Ḥaidar Mīrzā *Bāyqrā* and mother of Shād Begam (No. 28).

In 901H. (1496) Sulṭān Ḥusain *Bāyqrā* was besieging Ḥiṣār which was held for Bega's brother Mas'ūd, and in which she was. Ḥusain became apprehensive about the spring rains and patched up a peace, the seal of which was Bega's marriage with his son Ḥaidar, her first cousin through his mother, Pāyanda-sulṭān. The betrothal took place outside the fort, with assistance of such music as could be procured, and later when the bride was taken to Harāt, the marriage was celebrated with the splendour loved by Ḥusain and befitting a Tīmūrid alliance. Ḥaidar was a full Tīmūrid; Bega was one on her father's side, and probably as a Termiẕī sayyida's daughter, drew through her also a strain of the same blood.

Ḥaidar died before his father; *i.e.*, before 912H. (April, 1506).

Mems., 30, 38, 180.
Gul-badan, (?) 24*b*, No. 22.

XXXV. Bega (*Ḥājī*) Begam (?) *Begchik Mughal.* (? No. 50.)

She was a daughter of Uncle (*ṭaghāī*) Yādgār Beg who was, I think, a brother of Sulṭān ʿAlī Mīrzā, father of Kāmran's wife, Gul-rukh. Abūʾl-faẓl calls Bega Begam *dukhtar-i-ṭaghāī-i-wālida-i-Jannat-āshyānī.* Yādgār and ʿAlī *Begchik* are both styled *Mīrzā,* but this elevation is due, it seems, to their alliances with the royal house. Ḥaidar calls their brothers *mīrs.*

Bega married Humāyūn, her first cousin, and she was the wife of his youth. It is out of harmony with the custom of his house that his chief wife should be of less than royal descent. So far as I have been able to trace the matter, he never made an equal marriage. Gul-barg *Barlās,* 'Khalīfa's' daughter, whose second husband he was, had best claim to high birth.

The first son, perhaps first child, of Bega and Humāyūn was Al-amān, born 934H. or 935H. (1528) when his father was about twenty-one and was in Badakhshān. Bābar has commemorated his birth both by mentioning it and by preserving his own congratulatory letter to the young father. Al-amān died in infancy.

Bega came to India after Bābar's death (December, 1530), and her second and last-mentioned child, ʿAfīfa (ʿAqīqa) was born in 1531.

In 1534 (*circa*) Gul-badan's story (29*b*, 30*b*) shows Bega as resenting neglect by Humāyūn who accepts invitations to his sisters' quarters in camp in preference to hers and Gul-barg's. Some impressions of this story make one question whether the Bega it tells of is Humāyūn's wife or another. But the circumstances that she is associated with a wife, Gul-barg; that Gul-badan does not speak of her as being other than the 'Bega Begam' of the home circle; Humāyūn's allusions to the elder kinswomen; and the absence of the deference customary to an elder woman, seem sufficient justification for identifying the complaining Bega with the wife. (Gul-badan, it may be observed, mentions one other Bega Begam—*i.e.*, *Mīrān-shāhī*, daughter of Ulugh Beg *Kābulī*.)

Bega was with Humāyūn during the idleness of his decadence in Bengal, and with her was her sister, the wife of Zahīd Beg. Zahīd offended Humāyūn, and Bega tried in vain to obtain his forgiveness.

She was captured at Chausa by Shīr Khān, and here she lost her little girl, ʿAqīqa. The historians all call her *Ḥājī* Begam in recording her capture; it is only Gul-badan who calls her Bega Begam. She was returned in safety to Humāyūn under the escort of Shīr Khān's best general, Khawāṣ Khān. How soon she was returned I am not able to say. Support is to be found for the view that she was sent to Āgra directly after Humāyūn's arrival there, and also for the view that she was not returned to him until after a considerable time had elapsed. I do not know whether she went to Sind with the exiles or was sent later direct to Kābul. She was in Kābul with the royal family after 1545. She remained there with the other ladies when Humāyūn made his expedition to recover Hindūstān, and she came with Ḥamīda, Gul-badan, and the rest to join Akbar in 964H. (1557). After this she built her husband's tomb near Dihlī, and became its faithful attendant.

Akbar is said to have been much attached to her, and she was to him like a second mother. She went to Makka in 972H. (1564-65), and returned three years later. One thing raises the question whether this was her first pilgrimage, *viz.*, the fact that all the sources, except Gul-badan's, call her *Ḥājī* Begam. Why is she singled out to bear this title? It had been earned by many royal ladies before any one of the trio of great writers under Akbar had put pen to paper. The same unexplained distinction is conferred by the histories on a daughter of Kāmrān. In both these cases a renewed pilgrimage might serve as the explanation of the distinction.

Bega Begam died in 989H. (1581), shortly before Gul-badan's return from Makka. She had almost certainly passed her seventieth year, and was perhaps still older. Abū'l-faẓl says that her affairs were settled by one Qāsim ʿAlī Khān. He also records a visit of Akbar to her in her last illness, as well as an earlier visit of hers to him made from Dihlī in 981H..

Gul-badan, 22*a*, 23*b*, 29*b*, 30*b*, 78*b*, 83*a*.
Mems., 388, 390.
Akbar-nāma, *Bib. Ind.* ed., index, *s.n.*.
Āīn-i-akbarī, Blochmann, 465. (Confusion has been made here with Kāmrān's daughter.)
Badāyunī, Lowe, 308 n..
History of the Afghāns, Dorn, I. 103.

XXXVI. Bega *Kilān* Begam. (No. 22.)

She was at the Mystic Feast. No clue is given to her identification. The '*kilān*' of her title indicates a pre-eminence which would suit Bega *Mīrān-shāhī*, daughter of Sulṭān Maḥmūd Mīrzā. (*Cf. supra.*)

Gul-badan, 24*b*.

XXXVII. Bega Sulṭān Begam *Marvī.*

Daughter of Sanjar Mīrzā of Marv; first wife of Sulṭān Ḥusain Mīrzā *Bāyqrā;* mother of Badī'u-z-zamān Mīrzā. 'She was extremely cross-tempered, and fretted the mīrzā beyond endurance, till, driven to extremities by her insufferable humour, he divorced her. What could he do? He was in the right:

> A bad wife in a good man's house,
> Even in this world, makes a hell on earth.

May the Almighty remove such a visitation from every good Moslim; and God grant that such a thing as an ill-tempered, cross-grained wife be not left in the world.'

There is no later record of her.

Mems., 181, 182.

XXXVIII. Bega Sulṭān Begam *Mīrān-shāhī.* (No. 13.)

Daughter of Sulṭān Khalīl Mīrzā *Mīrān-shāhī;* grand-daughter of Sulṭān Abū-sa'īd; first cousin of Bābar.

Gul-badan, 24*b*.

XXXIX. Begam Sulṭān.

Daughter of Shaikh Kamāl. Died 945H. (1538).

Beale's 'Oriental Biography,' *s.n.*.

(Begam Sulṭān, Sa'ādat-bakht, *q.v.*.)

XL. Begī Sulṭān *āghācha.*

Inferior wife (*chāhar-shambihī*) of Sulṭān Ḥusain Mīrzā *Bāyqrā.*

Mems., 183.

XLI. Buwā Begam.

Mother of Sulṭān Ibrāhīm *Lōdī Afghān.* She attempted to poison Bābar in December, 1526 (933H.) in the manner which is told in most of the histories. The

Iqbāl-nāma adds the interesting detail that she was deported from India, and that on her enforced journey to Kābul she drowned herself in the Indus.

Mems., 347.
Gul-badan, 19*a*.

XLII. Chūlī Begam *Azāk*.

The Desert Princess; Pers. *chūl*, desert. The Memoirs have *Jūlī*, but the meaning of *chūlī* (which looks like a sobriquet) suits the descent of the begam better than anything which can be extracted from *jūl*. Ilminsky writes *Jūlī*, but for this the Mems. are his possible warrant. B.M. Pers. Or. 16,623, f. 123, l. 7., has a clearly-pointed *chūlī;* also on f. 124*b*.

Chūlī (Jūlī) Begam was a daughter of a beg of the Azāks, and married Sulṭān Ḥusain *Bāyqrā* before he conquered Khurāsān in 878H. (1473). She was the mother of Sulṭanām, his eldest girl and her only child, and she died before 912H. (1506).

Mems., 181, 182.
Ḥabību-s-siyār, 327 *et seq.*.

XLIII. Daulat-bakht *āghācha.*

(?) The lady of happy horoscope (*bakht*).

She may be the mother of Kāmrān's daughter 'Āyisha, with whom she was in flight for Qandahār. (*Cf.* 'Āyisha.)

Gul-badan, 78*b*.

XLIV. Daulat-bakht Bībī. (No. 85.)

She was clearly an active and working member of Humāyūn's household. She appeared to him in a dream (71*a*), and her name formed a part of Bakhtu-n-nisā''s. She went on before the main body of begams when they visited the waterfall at Farza, and saw to the commissariat. She is named as being at Hindāl's marriage feast.

She may be the Daulat-bakht *āghācha* of the preceding notice.

Gul-badan, 26*b*, 71*a*, 74*a*.

XLV. Daulat-kitta (?) *Arghūn*.

Kitta I find only as a Turkī word, meaning noble, powerful. With it the name would be a mongrel of Arabic and Turkī. Perhaps Daulat-gītī might be read.

She was a servant in Mīrzā Muḥammad Muqīm *Arghūn's* house, and was an intermediary in effecting the elopement of her master's daughter, Māh-chūchak *Arghūn*, from Kābul. Mr. Erskine tells the story admirably.

B. & H., I. 348 *et seq.*, and the sources there referred to.

XLVI. Daulat-nigār Khānam *Chaghatāī Mughal*.

Good-fortune itself; the very image of felicity. Ar. *daulat*, and Pers. *nigār*, effigy, image.

Daughter of Isān-būghā Khān *Chaghatāī;* wife of Muḥammad Ḥaidar Mīrzā *Dughlāt*.

Tār. Rash., E. & R., 88.

XLVII. Daulat-sulṭān Khānam *Chaghatāī Mughal*.

Ar. *daulat*, fortune, and *sulṭān*, sway. In many proper names, *sulṭān* does not appear to be a title, but rather to indicate the sway or dominance of the quality imputed by the first word of the name; *e.g.*, *Laṭīf-sulṭān*, *Daulat-sulṭān*. In giving these names, one might suppose the prophetic notion to be that the first child should be a regnant delight and the second a prevailing felicity.

Youngest child of Yūnas Khān *Chaghatāī* and Shāh Begam *Badakhshī;* half-sister of Bābar's mother; wife by chance of battle, of Tīmūr Sulṭān *Uzbeg;* mother by him of a daughter.

In 907H. (1501-2) she was in Tāshkand, and Qūt-līq-nigār Khānam went to visit her after thirteen or fourteen years of separation. Bābar, dejected and an exile, joined the family party in the next year. In 909H. (1503) Shaibānī sacked Tāshkand and forcibly married

Daulat-sulṯān to his son Tīmūr. She bore him a daughter, and she remained in his *ḥaram* until Bābar took possession of Samarqand in 917H. (1511), and she joined him. She went south with him in 1513, and remained several years in Badakhshān with another nephew, Mīrzā (Wais) Khān who behaved to her like a son.

Another nephew, Sa'īd, her own brother Aḥmad's son, then invited her, with costly gifts, to visit him in Kāshghar. She made the long and difficult journey; joined him in Yarkand; and with him she spent the rest of her life.

Bābar mentions that her foster-brother brought him news and letters from her in 925H. (September 8th, 1519). In the same year Manṣūr, Sa'īd's eldest brother, went to Kāshghar to visit her, his 'beloved aunt.'

The Persian text of the *Tārīkh-i-rashīdī* says that Manṣūr went so that by looking at her kind face his grief for the loss of his father might be mitigated. The Bible Society's Turkī version reads: 'Being prompted thereto by the extreme warmth of his affection for her.' Both statements illumine her character. The second seems the more appropriate, since the death of Sulṯān Aḥmad Khān took place in 909H. (1503) and Manṣur's visit in 926H. (1520).

There is no mention of her remarriage, and her story is that of an affectionate and leisured aunt.

Mems., 14, 99, 105, 274.
Tār. Rash., E. & R., 108, 117, 156, 160, 351, 352, 356.

XLVIII. Daulat-sulṯān (?) *Sakanj* Begam.

Sakanj I cannot explain. B. M. Add. 24,090 (44*b*) has no points, and the word may be S-k-n-gh. B. M., Or. 137 (48*a*) has k-m-n-j or b-k-n-j. The Turkī (Bible Society's MS. translations) has Daulat.

Daughter of Amīr Shaikh Nūru-d-dīn *Qibchāq Mughal*, governor of Turkistān; wife of Wais Khān *Chaghatāī Mughal*.

Tār. Rash., E. & R., 64 and 64 n..

XLIX. Dil-dār Begam. (No. 48.)

The Heart-holding Princess; Pers. *dil*, heart, and *dār*, holding.

Neither her husband, Bābar nor her daughter, Gul-badan gives any clue to her parentage. Her marriage is not spoken of in the Memoirs; it, as well as Gul-rukh's, probably occurred in the missing decade of 1509-19. If Bābar held the view that four wives were a lawful number, Dil-dār, of whatever parentage, may be counted amongst them, since in 1509 Māham only remained of his earlier wives, 'Āyisha, Zainab, and Ma'sūma having disappeared from the household by death or divorce.

Dil-dār is mentioned once in the Turkī text of Kehr and Ilminsky, and then as *āghācha*. I am too ignorant of the import of this word in the domestic circle to venture to draw from its use an inference as to social status. It, however, as used by Bābar and by Gul-badan, supports Pavet de Courteille's definition of a 'lady' in contradistinction to a 'begam,' and does not convey reproach to the woman as its occasional English rendering (concubine) does.

The *Akbar-nāma* (*Bib. Ind.* ed., II. 62) makes use of the words 'Dil-dār *āghācha* Begam,' and adds *āghā* as a variant (*cf.* App., *s.n.* *āghā*). Gul-badan always styles her mother begam, and sometimes *ḥazrat*. In enumerating her father's children and their mothers, she does not mention the parentage of any wife besides Ma'sūma *Mīrān-shāhī*, a Tīmūrid, but no deduction as to the lower birth of the others can be drawn safely from this, and there is some ground for supposing that Dil-dār was of *Mīrān-shāhī* birth. (*Cf. infra*, p. 277.)

Perhaps some indication of non-royal birth is given by Māham's forcible adoption of Dil-dār's son in 1519, but I am too ignorant of the *nuances* of Muḥammadan etiquette to venture on assertion or even on opinion in such a matter. That Māham did not take Gul-rukh's[1] son tells nothing, since the chief factors in the adoption, *i.e.*, Māham's loss of her own children and wish to adopt, may have become operative only when they were put into practice in 1519.

Five children of Dil-dār are mentioned by Gul-badan: Gul-rang, born between 1511 and 1515; Gul-chihra; Abū-n-nāṣir Muḥammad (Hindāl), born 1519; Gul-badan, born 1523; and Alwar, who died in India in 1529.

She is very frequently written of by her daughter; some other authors give of her a clear and pleasant impression; and she is always spoken of with respect and as a good and sensible woman.

Gul-badan, 6*b*, 16*a*, 23*a*, 25*b*, 29*b*, 30*a*, 35*a*, 35*b*, 38*a*, 42*a*, 50*b*, 51*b*, 65*a*, 70*b*.
Jauhar, Stewart, 30, 31.
Ilminsky, 281.
Akbar-nāma, *Bib. Ind.* ed., *s.n.*.
B. & H., II. 164, 220, 302.

L. Dil-shād Begam.

The Heart-rejoicing Princess; Pers. *dil*, heart, and *shād*, rejoicing.

Daughter of Shāh Begam and grand-daughter of Fakhr-jahān Begam *Mīrān-shāhī*. Of her paternal descent nothing is recorded.

Gul-badan, 24*b*.

LI. Dūdū Bībī.

Wife of Sulṭān Muḥammad Shāh *Lohānī*, Afghān King of Bihār; mother of Sulṭān Jalālu-d-dīn; regent for her son in his minority from 1529.

B. & H., *s.n.*.

LII. Fakhr-jahān Begam *Mīrān-shāhī*. (No. 1.)

The world's ornament. Ar. *fakhr*, ornament, and Pers. *jahān*, world.

She was a daughter of Sulṭān Abū-sa'īd Mīrzā; a paternal aunt of Bābar; the wife of Mīr 'Alā'u-l-mulk *Termiẕī*; and mother of Shāh and Kīchak Begams.

[1] For *erratum* in my Introduction as to Gul-rukh, *cf.* App. *s.n.*.

She went to India in 1526, the first year of Bābar's occupation, with her sister Khadīja, and stayed there nearly two years. She took leave of Bābar before starting on her return journey to Kābul on September 20th, 1528 (Muḥarram 5th, 935H.). She was again in Āgra and at the Mystic Feast in 1531.

Gul-badan, 11*a*, 24*b*.
Mems., 374, 382.
P. de Courteille, II. 453. (This is a fragment, supplied by Kehr and Ilminsky, which has the appearance of memoranda and which concerns a period already and variously written of in the *Bābar-nāma* of Kehr and contained in the Memoirs of Mr. Erskine.)
Aīn-i-akbarī, Blochmann, 322.

LIII. Fakhru-n-nisā'.

The ornament of womanhood; Ar. *fakhr*, ornament, and *nisā'*, woman.

She was a daughter of Bābar and 'Āyisha-sulṭān, and his first child, born when he was nineteen. She died when about a month old.

Mems., 90.
Gul-badan, 6*b*.

LIV. Fakhru-n-nisā' *anaga* and *māmā*.

Mother of Nadīm *kūka;* mother-in-law of his wife, Māham *anaga*.

She and Nadīm are several times mentioned by Gul-badan.

Gul-badan, 26*a*, 46*a*, 71*a*, 73*b*.
Journal of the Royal Asiatic Society, January, 1899, art. Māham *anaga*, H. Beveridge.
Akbar-nāma, *Bib. Ind.* ed., *s.n.* Nadīm.

LV. Fakhru-n-nisā' Begam *Mīrān-shāhī*. (No. 61.)

Daughter of Humāyūn and Māh-chūchak; sister of Muḥammad Ḥakīm; wife (1) of Shāh Abū'l-ma'ālī and (2) of Khwāja Ḥasan *Naqshbandī*. (*Cf.* Bakhtu-n-nisā'.)

Akbar-nāma, *Bib. Ind.* ed., *s.n.*.
Aīn-i-akbarī, Blochmann, *s.n.*.
Badāyunī, Lowe, 72.

LVI. Fāṭima Sulṭān *āghā.*

Ar. *Fāṭima*, a name given presumably in honour of the Prophet's daughter. The meaning of *sulṭān* here is not apparent. It does not seem as, *e.g.*, in *Daulat-sulṭān*, safe to consider it as a part of a compound word, and to read Faṭīma-sulṭān. Nor from the bearer's parentage does it suit to take it as a title, implying that she is of the sulṭāns of her tribe.

There are points in the use of the word *sulṭān* which require fuller discussion than is practicable here. One Fāṭima Sulṭān and her sister Bairām (Maryam) were the children of Ḥusain *Bāyqrā* by an Uzbeg servant of one of his royal wives. They are not given any further title, but their brothers are *mīrzās.*

Daughter of the chief of a Mughal *tumān* (10,000 men); first wife of ʿUmar Shaikh *Mīrān-shāhī;* mother of his second son, Jahāngīr who was two years the junior of Bābar.

Mems., 10, 14.

LVII. Fāṭīma Sulṭān *anaga* and Bībī. (No. 60.)

Mother of Raushan *kūka* and of Zuhra, wife of Khwāja Muʿaẓẓam. Bāyazīd *bīyāt* speaks of her as the *ōrdū-begi* of Humāyūn's *ḥaram,* a title which Blochmann translates 'armed woman.'

She was at Hindāl's marriage feast; she helped to nurse Humāyūn in 1546; and was an envoy to Ḥaram Begam for marriage negotiations; and she appears in Akbar's reign when her daughter is murdered.

Journal of the Royal Asiatic Society, October, 1898, art.
Memoirs of Bāyazīd *bīyāt*, H. Beveridge.
Ṭabaqāt-i-akbarī, Elliot, V. 291.
Akbar-nāma, *Bib. Ind.* ed., *s.n.*.
Gul-badan, 26*a*.

LVIII. Fāṭima Sulṭān *Bāyqrā.*

Daughter of Sulṭān Ḥusain Mīrzā *Bāyqrā* and of Mīnglī-bī *āghācha Uzbeg;* wife of Yādgār Muḥammad Mīrzā *Shāh-rukhī* (died 875—1470-71). She was dead before 912H. (May, 1506).

Mems., 182.
Ḥabību-s-siyār, 327 *et seq.*.

LIX. Fāṯima Sulṯān Begam.

A wife of Shāh Ḥusain Beg *Arghūn*, and mentioned in the *Tārīkh-i-sind*.

LX. Fauq Begam. (No. 31.)

Ar. *fauq*, superiority, excellence.

Gul-badan, 25b.

LXI. Fīroza Begam. (No. 35.)

The princess of victory; Pers. *fīroz*, victorious, prosperous.

Gul-badan, 25b.

LXII. Fīroza Begam *Mīrān-shāhī.*

She was a grand-daughter of Tīmūr, and married Manṣūr Mīrzā *Bāyqrā.* Their son Ḥusain was therefore a double Tīmūrid, fourth in descent through Manṣūr and third through Fīroza.

Mems., 176.

LXIII. Gauhar-shād Begam and *āghā, Turkomān.*

The jewel of joy; Pers. *gauhar*, jewel, and *shād*, joy, delight.

Wife of Shāh-rukh, son of Tīmūr; sister of Qarā Yūsuf *Turkomān;* founder of the Masjid which bears her name in Mashhad, and, with her husband, of the Bāgh-i-zāghān (Ravens' Garden) at Harāt. Bābar saw her tomb (dated 861H., 1457) and her mosque in 1506.

Mems., 207.
Northern Afghānistān, C. E. Yate, *s.n.*
Tār. Rash., E. & R., 83 *n.*.

LXIV. Gauhar-shād Begam *Dughlāt.*

Daughter of Muḥammad *Dughlāt Ḥiṣārī;* wife of Amīr Yār (*sic*); son of Amīr Jān-wafā, who was *darogha* of Samarqand under Shaibānī in 906H. (1500) when Bābar took the city, and who was an intimate of Muḥammad *Ḥiṣārī*, and saved his life by a warning word, as a reward for which Gauhar-shād was given in marriage to his son.

Mems., 86, 88, 239.
Tār. Rash., E. & R., 193.

LXV. Gauhar-shād Begam *Mīrān-shāhī*. (No. 5.)

Daughter of Sulṭān Abū-sa'īd Mīrzā and paternal aunt of Bābar. She was at the Mystic Feast.

Mems., 387.
Gul-badan, 11*a*, 24*b*.

LXVI. Gul-badan Begam *Mīrān-shāhī*. (No. 46.)

Cf. Biographical Introduction and her own *Humāyūn-nāma*.

LXVII. Gul-barg Begam *Barlās*. (No. 49.)

The rose-leaf princess; Pers. *barg*, leaf.

Daughter of Niẓāmu-d-dīn 'Alī *Barlās*, Bābar's *Khalīfa*; niece, therefore, of Sulṭān Junaid *Barlās*, a brother-in-law of Bābar. (*Cf.* Shahr-bānū.) She may be the child of that Sulṭānam who received Gul-badan at Kūl-jalālī. (14*a*) She married, first, Mīr Shāh Ḥusain *Arghūn*, in 930H. (1524). The alliance was not happy and a separation took place. She appears to have remarried Humāyūn at some time before the defeat at Chausa (1539). She was with him subsequently in Sind, and from there went with Sulṭānam to Makka previous to 1543.

She was buried in Dihlī. Mīr Ma'ṣūm writes of her death: 'She entrusted her soul to the guardians of the hour of death, and the leaves (*gul-barg*) of the rose-bush of her life were dispersed by the boisterous wind of mortality.'

Gul-badan, 21*a*, 25*b*, 29*b*, 30*b*, 49*b*.
Tārīkh-i-sind, Mīr Ma'ṣūm.
B. & H., I. 385.

LXVIII. Gul-barg, or - i̱zar, or -rang, or -rukh *Mīrān-shāhī.*

By these various names is mentioned the mother of Salīma-sulṯān Begam. There are difficult points as to her descent which are discussed *s.n.* Salīma-sulṯān.

LXIX. Gul Begam. (No. 30.)

The rose princess.

She was at the Mystic Feast, and may be one of the various ladies of the rose who are entered *infra.*

Gul-badan, 25*b*.

LXX. Gul-chihra Begam *Mīrān-shāhī.* (No. 45.)

The rosy-cheeked princess; Pers. *chihra*, face.

Daughter of Bābar and Dil-dār; their second child, and born between 1515 and 1517. She was full-sister of Gul-rang, Hindāl, and Gul-badan.

She married Bābar's first cousin (a son of his mother's brother Aḥmad), Sulṯān Tūkhta-būghā Khān *Chaghatāī Mughal.* The marriage was arranged by Bābar, and took place in 937H. (end of 1530). She would then be about fourteen years old.

She was widowed *cir.* 940H. (1533), and nothing as to her remarriage is recorded until 956H. (1549), when she was over thirty years old. It is improbable that she remained a widow so many years. (*Cf.* App. *s.n.* Salīma-sulṯān.) In 956H. she entered upon what looks like a *mariage de raison* with 'Abbās Sulṯān *Uzbeg*, just before Humāyūn set out on his expedition for Balkh. The bridegroom came to suspect that the Tīmūrid army was about to act against his own people and ran away. Probably he did not take Gul-chihra with him. Her name next appears in the histories when she accompanies Gul-badan and Ḥamīda to India in 964H. (1557).

Gul-badan, 6*b*, 16*b*, 18*b*, 23*b*, 25*b*, 29*b*, 38*a*, 65*a*.
Akbar-nāma, *Bib. Ind.* ed., *s.n.*

LXXI. Gul-'izār Begam *Mīrān-shāhī.*

The rosy-cheeked princess; Pers. *gul*, rose, and *'izār*, cheek, face.

Daughter of Bābar and Gul-rukh; full-sister of Kāmrān and 'Askarī.

Gul-badan names no marriage for her, but she may have been the wife of Yādgār-nāṣir.

Gul-badan, 6*b*.
Mems., 10.

LXXII. Gul-'izār Begam *Mīrān-shāhī.*

Daughter of Kāmrān Mīrzā; she accompanied Gul-badan Begam to Makka (983H., October, 1575). (*Cf.* App. *s.n.* 'Āyisha *Mīrān-shāhī.*)

Akbar-nāma, *Bib. Ind.* ed., III. 145.

LXXIII. Gul-nār *āghācha.* (No. 57.)

The red, red rose; Pers. *gul*, rose, and *nār* (*anār*), pomegranate, carnation red.

She was of Bābar's *ḥaram*, and may have been one of the two Circassian (Cherkis) slaves (the other being Nār-gul) who were presented to the Emperor by Shāh Ṭahmāsp in 933H. (1526).

She was at Hindāl's wedding-feast, and shared in the conferences of Humāyūn and his family; and she was one of Gul-badan Begam's pilgrim band (983H., 1575).

Gul-badan, 25*b*, 30*a*, 35*a*, 38*a*.
Mems., 347.
Akbar-nāma, *Bib. Ind.* ed., III. 145.

LXXIV. Gul-rang Begam *Mīrān-shāhī.* (No. 44.)

The rose-hued princess.

Daughter of Bābar and Dil-dār and her mother's first child. She was born in Khost, probably between 1511 and 1515, during Bābar's exile from Kābul after the Mughal rebellion. She was given in marriage to Isān-tīmūr *Chaghatāī* Mughal, her father's first cousin, during the last days of her father's life and in 1530.

Isān-tīmūr is last mentioned in 1543, and of Gul-rang there is no certain record after *cir.* 1534, when she was at Guālīār. (23*a*) (*Cf.* App. *s.n.* Salīma.)

Gul-badan, 6*b*, 16*b*, 18*b*, 23*a*, 25*b*, 29*b*.

LXXV. Gul-rukh Begam (?) *Begchik Mughal.*

The rose-cheeked princess.

Wife of Bābar; mother of Kāmrān, 'Askarī, Shāh-rukh, Aḥmad, and Gul-'iẕār. Outside Kābul there was in 1545 the tomb of Gul-rukh Begam. (64*b*) This may well have been hers.

She is perhaps a *Begchik*. This may be judged from the following notes:

(1) Kāmrān married a daughter of Sulṭān 'Alī Mīrzā *ṭaghāī*.[1] (Mems., 388.)

(2) Humāyūn married a daughter of Yādgār *ṭaghāī*. (Mems., 388.)

Amongst contemporary *Begchik* amīrs are Sulṭān Alī Mīrzā and Yādgār Mīrzā.

If one follows the recorded incidents of Sulṭān 'Alī's life, one sees that Gul-rukh may be his sister.

(*a*) In 914H. (1508-9) he was ordered to drown Khalīl Khān. (*Tār. Rash.*, 183.) Having done so, he took refuge with Bābar in Samarqand. (*l.c.*, 265.)

(*b*) In 917H. (1511) he was with Sayyid Muḥammad *Dughlāt* in Andijān, apparently at Bābar's instance. (*l.c.*, 248.) In the same year he was sent by Sa'īd

---

[1] This is a difficult word to deal with. It has a wider use than its usual translation 'mother's brother.' It is used for the uncle, great-uncle, etc., in ascending line. In other words, the mother's brother, in at any rate distinguished families, of one generation remains the mother's brother, *ṭaghāī*, in the next and the next. Once a *ṭaghāī*, always a *ṭaghāī*. The numerous uncles on the mother's side who appear in the Memoirs and the *Tārīkh-i-rashīdī* as so-and-so *ṭaghāī*, might be described as brothers of the mothers of a king's or chief's children.

To found opinion of relationship on the unsupported use of the word is to court disaster. Great wariness is needed. A quite perplexing *ṭaghāī* is the Machiavelli of Mīrzā Ḥaidar's life, 'Alī Mīrzā *ṭaghāī* (*Dughlāt*). He is constantly on the scene, and the one fact not mentioned which it is desirable to know is, whose brother was he? Only with much trouble can a surmise as to his parentage be hazarded.

Khān who had reinforced Andijān under Bābar's orders, to Kāzan.

(*c*) In 920H. (1514) he accompanied Sa'īd in his conquest of Kāshghar, and at this date is named amongst the Begchik amīrs of the Kāshghar army. (*l.c.*, 308, 326.)

(*d*) In 925H. (1519) he waited on Bābar, and is styled *ṭaghāī* of Kāmrān. (Mems., 274.) Bābar says here: 'Sulṭān 'Alī Mīrzā, the maternal uncle of Kāmrān (Ilminsky, 311, *Kāmrān-nīnak ṭaghāī*), who in the year in which I passed over from Khost to Kābul had proceeded to Kāshghar, *as has been mentioned*,[1] waited on me here.'

Bābar must several times have passed from Khost (Andar-āb) to Kābul. The *Tārīkh-i-rashīdī* fixes the occasion here alluded to as in 920H. (1514). This was Bābar's latest and last crossing of the northern passes to Kabul.

By thus bringing the statements of the Memoirs and the *Tārīkh-i-rashīdī* together, Sulṭān 'Alī Mīrzā *Begchik* is fairly-well identified with Sulṭān 'Alī Mīrzā, *ṭaghāī* of Kāmrān.'

(*e*) In 935H. (1528) Kāmrān married his daughter. (Mems., 388.)

Mems., 274, 388.
Tār. Rash., 183, 248, 264, 265, 280, 308, 326.

LXXVI. Gul-rukh Begam *Mīrān-shāhī*.

Daughter of Kāmrān Mīrzā; wife of Ibrāhīm Ḥusain Mīrzā *Bāyqrā;* mother of Muẓaffar Ḥusain who married Sulṭān Khānam, Akbar's eldest daughter, and of Nūru-n-nisā' who became a wife of Salīm (the Emperor Jahāngīr).

---

[1] Something interesting as to the *Tūzūk-i-bābarī* (Turkī text of the Memoirs) may lie here. The period of Sa'īd's Kāshghar conquest falls in a gap of the *Tūzūk*. Bābar referred to an incident of that time as having been already mentioned. This suggests, as a cause of the gap, lost leaves, and not an omission of record. (*Cf. Tār. Rash.*, 247 n..)

The story of her husband's rebellious pursuit and death (981H., 1573), and of her flight to the Dakhin with her son, is found at length in the histories.

She was living and visited by Jahāngīr in 1023H. (1614). (*Cf.* XIX. 'Āyisha-sulṭān.)

LXXVII. Gūn-war Bībī.

Wife of Humāyūn and mother of Bakhshī-bānū Begam.

Gul-badan, 39*b*.

LXXVIII. Ḥabība Begam *Mīrān-shāhī.*

The beloved or desired princess.

Eldest daughter of Kāmrān Mīrzā and probably of the daughter of Uncle (*ṭaghāī*) Sulṭān 'Alī Mīrzā *Begchik* whom Kāmrān married in 935H. (1528). She married Yasīn-daulat (the Fair Sulṭān) *Chaghatāī Mughal,* a brother of Gul-badan's husband, Khiẓr, and her own second cousin. It may be that she married a second time after she was forcibly parted from Yasīn-daulat in 1551-52. (*Cf.* App. *s.n. Ḥājī Mīrān-shāhī.*)

Gul-badan, 64*b*, 65*a*, 78*a*.

LXXIX. Ḥabība-sulṭān Begam *Arghūn.*

The desired of the desired; Ar. *ḥabība*, beloved, desired, and *sulṭān*, pre-eminence, sway.

'Brother's daughter of Sulṭān *Arghūn*' (? Muqīm, Shāh Shuja'a, or a brother of Ẕū'l-nūn); wife of Sulṭān Aḥmad Mīrzā *Mīrān-shāhī;* and mother of Bābar's wife, Ma'ṣūma. Bābar gave her a name of affection, *yanga.* (*Cf.* Index, *s.v.*.)

Mems., 22, 23, 208, 238.

LXXX. Ḥabība-sulṭān Khānish *Dughlāt.* (No. 21.)

Daughter of Muḥammad Ḥusain *Dughlāt* and Khūb-nigār *Chaghatāī;* full-sister of Mīrzā Ḥaidar; first cousin (maternal) of Bābar; wife (1) of 'Ubaidu-l-lāh *Uzbeg,* and (2) of her cousin, Sa'īd Khān *Chaghatāī.*

She was taken captive as a child by Shaibānī *Uzbeg*, and she lived in his household until he gave her in marriage to his nephew, 'Ubaidu-l-lāh. Shortly before Shaibānī murdered her father (914H., 1508-9), 'Ubaidu-l-lāh asked for Ḥaidar (*ætat.* 11) to come to him and Ḥabība in Bukhārā, and thus saved him from a general massacre of Mughal sulṭāns.

When 'Ubaidu-l-lāh retreated to Turkistān (*cir.* 1511), Ḥabība remained in Bukhārā. She then joined her uncle Sayyid Muḥammad *Dughlāt*, in Samarqand, and with him went to Andijān where he married her to her cousin Sa'īd. She reared one of Sa'īd's children, Rashīd whose mother was a 'tribeswoman,' Makhdūm *Qāluchī*, but he certainly did her training no credit. She was widowed in 939H. (July 9th, 1533), so that Gul-badan may be wrong in saying that she was at the Mystic Feast in 1531. She may have been a wedding guest in 1537.

Tār. Rash., E. & R., 140, 192, 193, 206, 268, 451, 453.
Gul-badan, 24*b*.

LXXXI. *Ḥājī* Begam *Mīrān-shāhī*.

She was a daughter of Kāmrān, and accompanied Gul-badan Begam to Makka in 983H., but it is to be inferred that this was not the pilgrimage which gave her her title of *Ḥājī*, since she is so entered before the *ḥaj* of 983H. (*Cf.* XIX., 'Āyisha-sulṭān.)

(*Ḥājī* Begam, Bega, *q.v.*)

(*Ḥājī* Begam, Māh-chūchak *Arghūn*, *q.v.*)

LXXXII. Ḥamīda-bānū.

Ar. *ḥamīda*, praised, laudable, and Pers. *bānū*.

Daughter of Sayyid Muḥammad Qāsim. She died 984H. (1576-77), and was buried at Andakhui.

The above information is given by Captain Yate,

and as Hamīda-bānū may be the daughter of one of Humāyūn's followers, I have inserted her name.

Northern Afghānīstan, Yate, p. 349.

LXXXIII. Ḥamīda-bānū Begam *Maryam-makānī.*

Posthumous style, *Maryam-makānī*, dwelling with Mary.

She was the mother of Akbar. There is difficulty in making precise statement as to her family relations. She was of the lineage of Aḥmad *Jāmī Zinda-fīl.*

(*a*). Gul-badan, whose long intimacy with Ḥamīda invests her statement with authority, states that Mīr Bāba Dost was Ḥamīda's father, and that Khwāja Mu'aẓẓam was her *barādar*, *i.e.*, brother undefined.

(*b*). The *Tārīkh-i-sind* states that her father was Shaikh 'Alī-akbar *Jāmī* who was one of the pillars of Mīrzā Hindāl. Niẓāmu-d-dīn Aḥmad says that 'Alī-akbar was father of Mu'aẓẓam.

If the statements of paragraphs (*a*) and (*b*) stood alone, 'Bābā Dost' and ''Alī-akbar' might be identified as the *petit-nom* and the name of one man.

There is a good deal to support this view, and there is something against it.

In favour of the identification of Bābā Dost with 'Alī-akbar are the following points:

(1). 'Bābā Dost' seems to be not a personal name, but a sobriquet of affection and domestic intimacy.

(2). Jauhar calls Ḥamīda the daughter of Hindāl's *akhund*, and Mr. Erskine (perhaps, however, inferentially) calls 'Alī-akbar Hindāl's preceptor.

(3). Mīr Bābā Dost was alive in 947H. (1540-41), the year preceding Ḥamīda's marriage, and was then with Hindāl. (*Akbar-nāma*, H. Beveridge, I. 360.)

(4). Niẓamu-d-dīn Aḥmad and *Badāyunī* contribute negative support to the identification by using the indefinite *khal*, maternal uncle, to describe the relation of Akbar and Muʻaẓẓam.

(5). *The Maʻāsiru-l-umarā'* confirms the identification by use of the words *barādar-i-aʻyānī*, full-brother. Its authority may not be of the best, but the choice of these words has some weight.

(6). ʻAlī-akbar was of the lineage of Aḥmad *Jāmī*. Humāyun had a dream which allowed him to know that the son prophesied in it by Aḥmad would be of the latter's lineage. There is, I think, nothing said on this point of Mīr Bābā Dost, but saintly descent was claimed for Ḥamīda's father.

(7). Gul-badan gives one the impression (it is little more) that Muʻaẓẓam was younger than Ḥamīda. He calls his sister *Māh-chīchām*, which may be read as 'Moon of my mother,' but also as 'Elder Moon-sister.' (*Cf.* 18*b* n.) If he were Ḥamīda's junior, and as Mīr Bābā Dost was alive in 1540-41, he could not have been an independent agent in 1543-44.

In opposition to the identification, there are two considerations :

(i.) A minor matter; two names are given by the sources : Mīr Bābā Dost and ʻAlī-akbar.

(ii.) The important fact that Abū'l-faẓl calls Muʻaẓẓam Ḥamīda's *ukhuwwat-i-akhyāfī*,[1] which, according to Lane, must be rendered 'uterine brother.'

Was, then, the name Bābā Dost a sobriquet of Shaikh ʻAlī-akbar ?

Were Ḥamīda and Muʻaẓẓam full brother and sister ? Were they the children of one father and two mothers, or were they uterine brother and sister ?

Shaikh ʻAlī-akbar's name I have not found in any

---

[1] Steingass does not recognise the force of 'uterine,' since he renders *barādar-i-aʻyānī* by 'uterine brother.'

passage except the one dealing with Ḥamīda's parentage. Mīr Bābā Dost may be the man so named by Bābar (Mems., 262), and who was then with Humāyūn in the year of the birth of Hindāl (1519). He may also have gone with Humāyūn, Ḥamīda (? his own daughter) and Mu'aẓẓam (? his son) to Persia, the *bakhshī* in the little party of exiles. He is mentioned by Abū'l-faẓl not only where already noted, but, we believe, also amongst Hindāl's servants who were transferred to Akbar in 1551 (958H.).

Two men with the name 'Alī-akbar are mentioned under Akbar, but neither appears to be a *Jāmī*, or to warrant identification with Ḥamīda's reputed father. (*Cf. Āīn-i-akbarī*, Blochmann, *s.n.* 'Alī-akbar.)

Whether there was any relationship more close than that derived from common descent from Aḥmad *Jāmī* between Māham Begam and Ḥamīda I am not able to say.

Ḥamīda was related to Bānū (Bābū) *āghā* who was the wife of Shihābu-d-dīn Aḥmad *Nishāpūrī* and a relation of Māham *anaga*. Bega (*Ḥajī*) Begam also had claim to descent from Aḥmad *Jāmī*, so that the saint's posterity was numerous in Akbar's court, and included the Emperor himself.

To Gul-badan's account of the discussion which preceded Ḥamīda's marriage, there may be added the following passage from the *Tazkiratu-l-wāqi'āt* of Jauhar. (I.O. MS. No. 221 and B.M. MS. Add. No. 16,711, f. 82.) After Humāyūn has asked whose daughter Ḥamīda is, he is told, perhaps by Dil-dār, that she is of the line of his Reverence the Terrible Elephant, Aḥmad *Jāmī*, and that her father, by way of blessing and benediction, has taught Mīrzā Hindāl, and that for this reason Ḥamīda is with the mīrzā's household.

The Persian (taken from the I.O. MS.) is as follows: *Pidar-i-īshān do sih kalma ba jihat-i-tabarruk wa tayammun ba Mīrzā Hindāl sabq farmudand. Az ān jihat ba mā hamrā and.*

Erskine (II. 220) and Stewart (Jauhar, 31 n.) both say that Ḥamīda was married at fourteen years of age. The incidents of her wedded life are set down in Gul-badan Begam's book and in the *Akbar-nāma* and other sources; but having regard to her interesting personality, they may be enumerated here also.

She was married at Pāt early in 948H. (summer, 1541), and remained in Sind until she made with Humāyūn the terrible desert journey to 'Umrkut where Akbar was born (October 15th, 1542). About the beginning of the following December she and her baby went into camp at Jūn, after travelling for ten or twelve days. In 1543 she made the perilous journey from Sind which had Qandahār for its goal, but in course of which Humāyūn had to take hasty flight from Shāl-mastān, 'through a desert and waterless waste.' She went with him, leaving her little son behind. She accompanied her husband to Persia, and it is recorded that on the way and at Sistān, its governor brought his mother and his wives to entertain her. With Humāyūn she made, amongst other pious visitations, one to Jām where was their ancestor Aḥmad's shrine. She was kindly treated by Shāh Ṭahmāsp and by his sister, and Gul-badan's details of the Persian episode can hardly have been learned from anyone but Ḥamīda. In 1544, in camp at Sabz-āwār, a daughter was born. She returned from Persia with the army given to Humāyūn by Ṭahmāsp, and at Qandahār would meet Dil-dār and Hindāl, her former protectors.

It was not until November 15th, 1545 (Ramẓan 10th, 952H.) that she again saw her son, who recognised her. She had shortly after this to accept Māh-chūchak as a co-wife. In June, 1548, she and Akbar accompanied Humāyūn on his way to Tāliqān as far as Gul-bihār, and thence returned to Kābul. This may be the expedition made by the ladies and chronicled by Gul-badan, to see the *rīwāj*. When Humāyūn, in November, 1554, set out for Hindūstān, she remained in Kābul.

Bāyazīd *bīyāt* mentions that at this time he fell under her displeasure, and was reproved because he had not cleared out a house for one of her servants. He pleaded the commands of Muʿnim Khān, and was forgiven. Early in the reign of Akbar, Khwāja Mīrak, Niẓāmu-d-dīn's grandfather and who was her *diwān*, was hanged by Muʿnim Khān because he had sided with Mīrzā Sulaimān.

She rejoined her son in the second year of his reign (964H., 1557), together with Gul-badan and other royal ladies. She is mentioned as in Dihlī in the fifth year, and she had a part in the plot for deposing Bairām Khān. She was closely associated with Gul-badan in Akbar's court and affection; together they interceded for Salīm with his father; together they received gifts from the Emperor; and their tents were side by side in his encampments. Ḥamīda was with Gul-badan in the latter's last hours.

Abū'l-faẓl says that when long fasts came to an end, the first dishes of dressed meat used to go to Akbar from his mother's house.

Ḥamīda died in the autumn of 1604 (19th Shahriyār 1013H.), sixty-three years after her wedding, and after almost fifty years of widowhood, passed as the proud mother of a great son. If she was fourteen in 1541, she must have been born in 1527 (*circa*), the year of Bābar's victory at Khānwa, and have been some seventy-seven years old at the time of death.

Gul-badan, 39*a*, 42*a*, 43*b*, 48*a*, 55*a*, 55*b*, 58*a*, 59*b*, 62*b*, 66*a*, 74*a*, 78*b*, 83*a*.
Akbar-nāma, *Bib. Ind.* ed., *s.n.*.
Aīn-i-akbarī. *Aīn*, 26, *Ṣufīyāna*, Blochmann, 61, 62.
Jauhar, *l.c.*, Niẓāmu-d-dīn Aḥmad, etc.
Maʿāsiru-l-umarā' Bib. Ind. ed., I. 618.
Journal of the Royal Asiatic Society, October, 1898, art. Bāyazīd *bīyāt*, H. Beveridge, 16.

LXXXIV. Ḥaram Begam *Qibchāq Mughal.*

Princess of the *Ḥaram.* Her name has been transliterated by some European workers as *Khurram*, 'blossoming, cheerful,' and this seems the more probable name to bestow on a child. But some of the Persian texts support *Ḥaram*, and the editors of the *Bib. Ind. Akbar-nāma* have adopted it. Gul-badan has *Ḥaram.*

Ḥaram Begam may be a sobriquet bestowed after the revelation of the facts of the bearer's character and dominance.

Daughter of Sulṭān Wais *Kulābī Qibchāq Mughal;* and sister of Chakr ʿAlī and Ḥaidar Begs and of Māh Begam, a wife of Kāmrān. She married Sulaimān Mīrzā *Mīrān-shāhī*, son of Khān Mīrzā (Wais). She had one son, Ibrāhīm (Abū'l-qāsim), and several daughters. Her children, through Shāh Begam *Badakhshī*, their paternal ancestress, claimed descent from Alexander the Great.

Most of the incidents of her career are given in the Introduction to this book, and her remarkable character is exhibited there. *Badāyunī* calls her *Walī-niʿamat*, and says she was known by this name. This may be a tribute to her pre-eminence in character and action and also to the fact of her belonging to an older generation than Akbar's, under whom he wrote. The elder men of royal birth were Lords and the elder women Ladies of Beneficence in those days.

Gul-badan, 65*a*, 75*b*.
Akbar-nāma, *Bib. Ind.* ed., *s.n.*.
Badāyunī, Lowe, 61, 89, 90, 217.
Journal of the Royal Asiatic Society, October, 1898, art. Bāyazīd *bīyāt*, H. Beveridge, 12, 16.
B. & H., *s.n.*.
Āīn-i-akbarī, Blochmann, *s.n.*.
Introduction, *supra*.

LXXXV. Hazāra Begam.

Princess of the tribe of the Hazāra. This is a title, and not a personal name.

She was the daughter of a brother of Khiẓr Khān *Hazāra* who was the chief of his tribe during the struggles for supremacy of Humāyūn and Kāmrān. She married Kāmrān.

Gul-badan, 64*b*.

LXXXVI. Ḥusn-nigār Khānam *Chaghatāī Mughal.*

The image of beauty; Ar. *ḥusn*, beauty, and Pers. *nigār*, image.

Daughter of Isān-būghā *Chaghatāī* and niece of Yūnas Khān; sister of Dost-muḥammad and wife of Abā-bakr *Dughlāt Mughal.*

Tār. Rash., E. & R., 89, 99.

LXXXVII. Isān-daulat Khānam and Begam *Qūchīn Mughal.*

Her name takes several forms. The *Bābar-nāma*, Turkī text (B.M. Or. Add. 26,324), has a clearly pointed *Ishān;* Ilminsky has *Isān passim.* An early Persian MS. (B.M. Or. 3,714) has *Isān* and *Isan.*

The Memoirs have *Isan* in all but two instances (p. 12), where *Ais* is used. But Mr. Erskine's Persian text (B.M. Add. 26,200), which is presumably his authority, can (I venture to think, after comparing the words he renders *Ais* with those he renders *Isan*) yield *Isan* in all places. Where he reads *Ais* (pp. 10 and 141) the *nūn* is not dotted; the letters closely correspond with those where it is dotted, and where he reads *Isan.*

The *Tārīkh-i-rashīdī* (B.M. Or. 157) writes *Isān.* The weight of authority is in favour of *Isān.*

Isān-daulat was Bābar's maternal grandmother and a daughter of Mīr Shīr-ʻalī Beg *Qūchīn* (*Kunjī*), chief of the Sagharīchī *tumān* (10,000) of the Qūchīn Mughals.

She married Yūnas Khān *Chaghatāī Mughal* when he was forty-one years old. He was born in 818H. (1415-16), so that the date of her marriage is, approximately, 1456. At this time Yūnas was made Great Khān of the Mughals.

Isān-daulat bore three daughters, who were named Mihr-nigār, Qūt-līq-nigār, and Khūb-nigār. She had many brothers, of whom three, Shīram, Mazīd, and

'Alī-dost, took leading parts in Bābar's affairs. Her chief co-wife was Shāh Begam *Badakhshī*.

She shared the vicissitudes of her remarkable husband's remarkable career for some thirty years; nursed him through two years of paralytic helplessness till his death in 892H. (1487) at the age of seventy-four, and survived him about eighteen years.

Four times at least she fell into the hands of an enemy:

(1) In Kāshghar, *cir.* 860H. (1455-56), when Mihr-nigār was an infant at the breast and when she was returned in safety to her husband.

(2) In Tāshkand in 877H. (1472-73), when Yūnas had gone to buy barley at a time of dearth in Mughalistān. It was then that there occurred the well-known episode which shows Isān-daulat's high spirit and decision of character and which is briefly narrated in the Introduction (p. 68). She was returned with honour to her husband.

(3) In Andijān in 903H. (1497-98), when the town was taken from her grandson Bābar by his kinsfolk. She was sent after him in safety to Khojand, and from there went on to the protection of her third daughter's home in Kāshghar.

(4) At Samarqand in 906H. (1500-1), when the town was taken by Shaibānī. She remained behind when Bābar left the place, and rejoined him in a few months with his 'family, heavy baggage, and a few lean and hungry followers.'

In the eighth year of her widowhood (900H.) she was guiding Bābar's affairs with decision and sense in Andijān. He says that few women equalled her for sagacity, far-sight and good judgment, and that many important affairs were carried out by her counsel.

News of her death reached Bābar in Kābul early in 911H. (June, 1505), during the forty days' mourning for his mother.

Two slight records of her remain for mention.

Desert-born and of a tribe which clamoured against settled life, she yet had a garden-house at Andijān. She reared a half-sister of Bābar, Yādgār, daughter of Aghā *āghācha*.

Mems., 10, 12, 16, 27, 58, 59, 100, 111, 169.
Tār. Rash., E. & R., 86, 94, 175, 197, 308.
B. & H., *s.n.*.

LXXXVIII. Jahān-sulṭān Begam.

The world-ruling princess; Pers. *jahān*, world, and Ar. *sulṭān*, sway.

Probably a child of Humāyūn. She died in Kābul, aged two, in 954H. (1547).

Gul-badan, 70*a*.

LXXXIX. Jamāl *āghā*.

Grace; Ar. *jamāl*, grace, beauty.

Wife (1) of Sanīz Mīrzā *Dughlāt*, and by him mother of ʿUmar and Abā-bakr and Jān (or Khān)-sulṭān Khānam.
(2) of Dost-muḥammad *Chaghatāī* in 869 H.
(3) of Muḥammad Ḥaidar *Dughlāt*, and by him mother of Muḥammad Ḥusain Mīrzā *Ḥiṣārī* (Ḥaidar's father) and Sayyid Muḥammad Mīrzā.

Her third marriage was made by the Mughal custom of *yanga-lik*, *i.e.*, marriage by a younger brother of an elder brother's widow. (*Cf.* Khān-zāda *Mīrān-shāhī*.)

Tār. Rash., E. & R., 88, 89, 99, 102, 104.

XC. Jān-sulṭān Begam. (No. 32.)

The soul-ruling princess; Pers. *jān*, life, soul, and Ar. *sulṭān*, sway.

She was at the Mystic Feast in 1531.

Gul-badan, 25*b*.

(Jūlī Begam, *Chūlī*, *q.v.*)

XCI. Khadīja Begam.

Presumably she was named after Muḥammad's first wife.

She was first a slave[1] of Sulṭān Abū-sa'īd Mīrzā, and upon his death in 873H. (1469) she betook herself to Harāt and there became the wife of Sulṭān Ḥusain *Bāyqrā*.

She had a daughter, known as Āq Begam, by Abū-sa'īd, and two sons, Shāh Gharīb and Muẓaffar Ḥusain, by her marriage with Ḥusain.

Hers is an instance where the conferring of a title is mentioned. Bābar says that Ḥusain was passionately fond of her and that he raised her to the rank of begam; also that she managed him entirely. To her are attributed the intrigues and rebellion which ruined Ḥusain's family. She acquired more influence than any other of his wives, and it was consequently round her surviving son Muẓaffar Ḥusain, that adherents gathered after his father's death. She forced on the joint-kingship which excited Bābar's ridicule. Mīrzā Ḥaidar when speaking of the death of Jahāngīr *Mīrān-shāhī*, said that he was generally reported to have been poisoned in his wine by Khadīja Begam after her old fashion.

In 912H. (1506-7) Bābar saw her in Harāt, and he was there unlawfully entertained by her at a wine-party. When Shaibānī conquered the city in 913H. she was cast down from her high estate and given up to be plundered, and was treated as one of Shaibānī's meanest slaves.

Mems., 179, 182, 183, 198, 204, 223.
Tār. Rash., E. & R., 196, 199.

---

[1] Turkī text (Ilminsky), *ghuncha-chī*, which Redhouse translates a seller of rosebuds and a young and good-looking female slave. The Persian text has the same word *ghuncha-chī*. The interest of these details is the light they may cast on the use of such words as *āghā* and *āghācha*.

XCII. Khadīja-sulṭān Begam *Chaghatāī Mughal.*

Fourth daughter of Sulṭān Aḥmad Khān *Chaghatāī.* After her father's death in 909H. (1503-4), Mīrzā Abā-bakr *Dughlāt* took possession of his capital, Aksu, in Farghāna, and with it of Khadīja-sulṭān, then a child. He however, says Mīrzā Ḥaidar, treated her kindly and when she was of age, he gave her in marriage to his son Jahāngīr who was her second cousin. She accompanied her husband to her full-brother Sa'īd's court, shortly after 920H. (1514), and while in Kāshghar, Jahāngīr was murdered by an unknown hand, in Yangī-ḥiṣār. She then remained, respected and honoured, in her brother Sa'īd's family circle. In 923H. (1517) she was married to Shāh Muḥammad Sulṭān *Chaghatāī,* a grandson of Sulṭān Maḥmūd Khān, through Muḥammad, the only son of Maḥmūd who survived the massacre of sulṭāns by Shaibānī. The marriage of one of Khadīja's brothers, Aiman, was celebrated at the same time.

When Rashīd succeeded his father Sa'īd, in Kāshghar (939H.—July, 1533) Khadīja was badly treated by him. She was then ill and confined to bed, but Rashīd banished her and her children and made her start on the weary journey for Badakhshān. She died on the road after much hardship of travel. She left four children, Ismā'īl, Ishāq, Ya'qūb, and Muḥtarima. They went on to Kābul, and were there received with fatherly kindness by their uncle, Isān-tīmūr.

Tār. Rash., E. & R., 161, 329, 352, 382, 451.

XCIII. Khadīja-sulṭān Begam *Mīrān-shāhī.* (No. 6.)

Daughter of Sulṭān Abū-sa'īd Mīrzā *Mīrān-shāhī* and paternal aunt of Bābar. I have not ascertained the name of her husband. She went to India in 934H. (1527), arriving in November, with Fakhr-jahān and their children. She planned to return with her sister and Bābar took leave of them both on

Muḥarram 5th, 935H. (September 20th, 1528), but various business detained her and Bābar paid her another of his dutiful visits on October 9th. When or if she returned to Kābul is not said, but she was at the Mystic Feast in Āgra in 1531.

Gul-badan, 11*a*, 24*b*.
Mems., 374, 382, 387.

XCIV. Khāl-dār *anaga*.

The nurse with a mole; *khāl-dār*, mole-marked.

Mother of Sa'ādat-yār *kūka*.

Akbar-nāma, *Bib. Ind.* ed., I. 44.

XCV. Khānam Begam. (No. 18.)

Daughter of Āq Begam; grand-daughter of Abū-sa'īd *Mīrān-shāhī*. The 'Khānam' may indicate that she is a Chaghatāī chief's child.

Gul-badan, 24*b*.

(Khānam, Muḥtarima, *q.v.*)

XCVI. Khānish *āghā Khwārizmī*.

Daughter of Jūjūq Mīrzā *Khwārizmī*; wife of Humāyūn; mother of Ibrāhīm who died as an infant. Bāyazīd calls her child Muḥammad Farrūkh-fāl, but Gul-badan and Abū'l-faẓl are against him. Farrūkh-fāl was the child of Māh-chūchak. Ibrāhīm was born on the same day as Muḥammad Ḥakīm, *i.e.*, Jumāda I. 15th, 960H. (April 19th, 1553).

Gul-badan, 71*a*, 71*b*, (?) 73*b*.
Bāyazīd (I. O. MS. 72*a*), *Journal of the Royal Asiatic Society*, October, 1898, art. Bāyazīd *bīyāt*, H. Beveridge, p. 14.
Akbar-nāma, *Bib. Ind.* ed., I. 331.

XCVII. Khān Sulṭān Khānam and Sulṭānam *Dughlāt*.

Both these names appear to be titles, and not personal.

Daughter of Sanīz Mīrzā *Dughlāt* and Jamāl *āghā*; full-sister of Abā-bakr.

She was a woman of life-long piety and devotion to good works. Perhaps for this reason her brother who seems to have been an incarnation of unjust cruelty, treated her with studied barbarity, as a consequence of which she died in torture and suffering.

Tār. Rash., E. & R., 88, 258.

XCVIII. Khān-zāda Begam *Bāyqrā.* (No. 16.)

The khān-born princess; Turkī *khān*, and Pers. *zāda*, born.

Gul-badan says she is a daughter of Sulṭān Mas'ūd Mīrzā *Mīrān-shāhī*, and through a daughter grandchild of Pāyanda Muḥammad (*sic*) Sulṭān Begam, paternal great-aunt of Humāyūn. Bābar names no such marriage of a daughter of Pāyanda. 'The second of the daughters [of Pāyanda] was Kīchak Begam [whose name is probably a sobriquet]. Sulṭān Mas'ūd Mīrzā was extremely attached to her, but whatever efforts he made, Pāyanda-sulṭān Begam, having an aversion to him, would not consent to the match. She was *afterwards*' (Turkī *sūngrā*, P. de C. *dans la suite*) 'married to Mullā Khwāja.'

A daughter of Ḥusain *Bāyqrā* and of Bābā *āghācha*, whose name was Sa'ādat-bakht and title Begam Sulṭān, was married to Mas'ūd after his blinding. Her daughter might be fitly described as of inferior rank to the great begams. Such a description is given by Bābar of 'Khān-zāda, daughter of Sulṭān Mas'ūd Mīrzā.' Ḥusain and Pāyanda's daughter would certainly rank as equal in birth to the daughters of Abū-sa'īd, since she was a full Tīmūrid.

The 'extreme attachment' of Mas'ūd to Kīchak fits Musalmān marriage better than Musalmān courtship. It may be that, spite of Pāyanda's opposition, Mas'ūd married Kīchak. The 'afterwards' of the Memoirs (*supra*) and the *de la suite* of Pavet de Courteille seem to demand some more definite antecedent than

Mas'ūd's attachment. Moreover, this presumably persisted with his wish to marry Kīchak.

Did he marry Kīchak, and was she divorced after his blinding or at some other time, and then was Sa'ādat-bakht given to him?

Mems., 181, 182, 387.
Gul-badan, 24*b*.

XCIX. Khān-zāda Begam *Mīrān-shāhī*.

Daughter of 'Umar Shaikh Mīrzā *Mīrān-shāhī* and of Qūt-līq-nigār Khānam; full-sister of Bābar and five years his senior. Eldest of her father's daughters. She is recorded as thrice married: first, to Shaibānī in 1501 (907H.); secondly, to a man of inferior rank, Sayyid Hada; and, thirdly, to Mahdī Muḥammad Khwāja,[1] son of Mūsa Khwāja. One child of hers is recorded, Shaibānī's son, Khurram-shāh Sulṭān.

She was born *circa* 1478 (883H.). This is known from the statement of her brother that she was five years his senior. In 1501 (907H.) she was married by Shaibānī when he captured Samarqand from Bābar. Gul-badan makes the marriage a condition of Shaibānī's peace with Bābar; Ḥaidar says she was given in exchange for Bābar's life, and Khāfī Khān, as a ransom (*ba tarīq-i-faida*). She was in Shaibānī's power and could have been married without consent of Bābar. As in 1501 she was twenty-three years old, she had almost certainly been married before, possibly to Mahdī. Her marriage arrangements with Shaibānī might include the divorce which the Musalmān law requires. Bābar does not go into details as to the marriage; he says she fell into Shaibānī's hands. Presumably as himself of Tīmūrid birth, Shaibānī would treat a Tīmūrid woman with respectful forms even when she was spoil of battle. To marry Khān-zāda, he divorced her maternal aunt, Mihr-nigār *Chaghatāī*.

[1] *Cf.* Appendix B., Mahdī Khwāja.

Khān-zāda's son by Shaibānī, Khurram-shāh, died a young man. Shaibānī divorced her because she leaned to her brother's side in disputed matters. He then gave her in marriage to a certain Sayyid Hada, who fell in the battle of Merv with Shaibānī himself (1510).

In 1511 and at the age of thirty-three, she was returned to Bābar by Shāh Ismā'īl. At what date she married Mahdī Muḥammad Khwāja I am not able to say. It is probable that the marriage would take place within no long time after her return. As Mahdī is never described by Bābar in any way (as is his custom when a new actor comes upon the scene of his Memoirs), it is probable that Mahdī's joining Bābar and his marriage with Khān-zāda took place in the decade 1509-19, of which no record is known to survive.[1] Mahdī was with Bābar in 1519 (925H.), and is frequently mentioned subsequently.

There are many references to Khān-zāda by Gul-badan who frequently calls her Dearest Lady (*ākajanām*). She died at Qabal-chak in 1545 (952H.), aged about sixty-seven years, and after a life full of sorrows and chagrins.

Gul-badan, 3*b*, 15*b*, 18*b*, 23*b*, 24*b*, 27*b*, 28*b*, 50*b*, 62*b*, 69*a*.
Mems., 10, 98, 241 (Supplement).
Tār. Rash., E. & R., 117, 155, 175, 196, 239, 400.
Ḥabību-s-siyār, under date 923H.
Khāfī Khān, I. 33 (here Khāna-zāda).

C. Khān-zāda Begam *Mīrān-shāhī*.

Daughter of Sulṭān Maḥmūd *Mīrān-shāhī* and Khān-zāda *Termizī* II.; wife (1) of Abā-bakr *Dughlāt*, and mother by him of (?) Jahāngīr, Turāngīr, and Bus-tāngīr; (2) of Sayyid Muḥammad *Dughlāt* who married

[1] There are some indications that a record of this decade once existed.

her in conformity with the custom of *yanga-lik*. (*Cf.* Jamāl *āghā*.)

Mems., 30.
Tār. Rash., E. & R., 330.

CI. Khān-zāda Begam *Termiẕī*.

Of the family of the Khāns of Termiẕ; wife of Sulṯān Aḥmad Mīrzā *Mīrān-shāhī*. She was a bride when Bābar was five, *i.e.*, in 893H. (1488) but, according to Turkī custom, was still veiled. Sulṯān Aḥmad desired Bābar to pluck off the veil and run away, a little ceremony which it was supposed would bring him good luck when his time for marriage should come.

Mems., 23.

CII. Khān-zāda Begam *Termiẕī* (*a.*).

Daughter of the chief (*mīr-i-buzurg*) of Termiẕ; wife of Sulṯān Maḥmūd Mīrzā *Mīrān-shāhī*; mother of Sulṯān Mas'ūd Mīrzā. She died apparently early in her married life. The mīrzā was greatly afflicted at her death.

Mems., 29, 30.

CIII. Khān-zāda Begam *Termiẕī* (*b.*).

Daughter of a brother of Khānzāda *Termiẕī* (*a.*); grand-daughter of the chief of Termiẕ; wife of Sulṯān Maḥmūd Mīrzā *Mīrān-shāhī*; mother of Ḥusain (who died, aged thirteen, before his father) and of five girls, Khānzāda, Bega, Āq, Āī, and Zainab.

Mems., 29, 30, 38, 128.

CIV. Khān-zāda Khānam.

'Épouse légitime' of Muẕaffar Mīrzā *Bāyqrā*, and illegally taken by Shaibānī.

Mems., 224.
Pavet de Courteille, II., 10.

CV. Khūb-nigār Khānam *Chaghatāī Mughal.*

The image of beauty. Here *khānam* has its full value, since Khūb-nigār was daughter of the *Khāqān*, the Khān emphatically.

Third daughter of Yūnas Khān *Chaghatāī* and Isān-daulat *Qūchīn;* wife of Muḥammad Ḥusain *Dughlāt Ḥiṣārī;* mother of Ḥaidar and Ḥabība.[1] She was a year older than her husband, and was married in 899H. (1493-94). Bābar, writing in 907H. (1501-2) mentions the reception of news of her death. Her husband was murdered in 914H..

Mems., 12, 99, 218.
Tār. Rash., E. & R., 117, 118, 153, 156, 197.

CVI. Khurshed *kūkī.* (Nos. 55 and 64.)

Pers., the sun, sunshine.

Gul-badan, 26*a*.

CVII. Kīchak Begam *Bāyqrā.*

The small princess; Turkī, *kīchak*, small. The name is probably a sobriquet.

Daughter of Sulṭān Ḥusain Mīrzā *Bāyqrā* and Pāyanda-sulṭān Begam *Mīrān-shāhī;* wife of Maulānā Khwāja who was of the family of Sayyid Atā one of her father's best vazīrs.

Khwānd-amīr reverses her marriage with that of her sister Bega, and makes her marry Bābar, son of Rabī'a.

Mems., 181.
Ḥabību-s-siyār, 327 *et seq.*.

CVIII. Kīchak Begam *Termiẓī.* (No. 23.)

Daughter of Mīr 'Alā'u-l-mulk *Termiẓī* and Fakhr-jahān *Mīrān-shāhī;* wife of Khwāja Mu'īn *Aḥrārī;* mother of Mīrzā Sharafu-d-dīn Ḥusain.

---

[1] The translation of the *Tārīkh-i-rashīdī* (E. & R., 159) has the statement that Khūb-nigār bore six sons (*farzandān*), and that two died at the breast and four survived. I believe it should read 'six children, of whom four died at the breast, and two survived her.'

She went to Hindūstān with her mother, and was at Hindāl's wedding feast.

Mems., without names. (*Cf.* Fakhr-jahān and Shāh Begam.)
Gul-badan, 25*a*.
Akbar-nāma (lith. ed.), *s.n.*.
Aīn-i-akbarī, Blochmann, 322.

CIX. Kīchak māham. (No. 80.)

Cf. s.n. Māham for meaning of the word.

She is named as at Hindāl's wedding.

Gul-badan, 26*b*.

CX. Kilān Khān Begam.

This is clearly not a personal name. Pers. *kilān*, elder, great, and Turkī *khān*, a title.

Daughter of Sulṭānam Begam *Mīrān-shāhī* and grand-daughter of Sulṭān Aḥmad Mīrzā. Which of Sulṭānam's three husbands was Kilān Khān Begam's father is not said; from her daughter's title, Tīmūr Sulṭān *Uzbeg* seems most probable.

Mems., 22.
Gul-badan, 24*b*.

CXI. Lād-malik *Turkomān*.

(?) Mistress of the Fort; Pers. *lād*, fortress, and Ar. *malik*, possessor, ruler.

Wife of (1) Tāj Khān *Sarangkhānī* and (2) of Shīr Khān *Sūr* (935H., 1528-29).

B. & H., II. 131, 132, and authorities there cited by Mr. Erskine.

CXII. Lāl-shād Khānam *Chaghatāī Mughal*.

Perhaps, with a lip like the gleam of a ruby; Pers. *lāl*, ruby, and *shād*, gleam, happy.

Eldest daughter of Sulṭān Aḥmad Khān *Chaghatāī* and of a 'slave' (*amm-i-wald*).

'Although she was outside the circle of distinction, she was finally married to Muḥammad Amīr Mīrzā *Dughlāt*.'

Tār. Rash., E. & R., 161.

CXIII. Laṭīfa-sulṭān *āghācha.*

Of pre-eminent delicacy or gentleness; Ar. *laṭīfa*, delicate, and a jest, and Ar. *sulṭān*, sway.

Chār-shambihī, a Wednesday wife, of Sulṭān Ḥusain Mīrzā *Bāyqrā;* mother of Abū'l-ḥasan and of Muḥammad Muḥsin (*kepek*, round-shouldered).

The *Ḥabību-s-siyār* says she was a relation of Jahān-shāh (? *Turkomān* or *Barlās*). She was dead before 912H. (1506).

Mems., 179, 183.

CXIV. Laṭīf Begam *Duladāī Barlās.*

Grand-daughter of Aḥmad Hājī Beg; wife (1) of Sulṭān Aḥmad Mīrzā *Mīrān-shāhī;* (2) of Ḥamza Sulṭān *Uzbeg*, and by him mother of three sons who fell into Bābar's hands at Ḥiṣār, and were released by him.

Both her grandfather Aḥmad and his paternal uncle, Janī Beg *Duladāī*, were amīrs of her first husband.

Mems., 23.

CXV. Māh-afroz Begam.

The princess who outshines the moon; Pers. *māh*, moon, and *afroz*, dazzling, illuminating.

She was a wife of Kāmrān and mother of *Ḥājī* Begam. Two of Kāmrān's wives are not known by their personal names, Hazāra Begam and the daughter of Uncle ʿAlī Mīrzā *Begchik*. Māh-afroz may be one of these.

Gul-badan, 64*b*.

CXVI. Māham *anaga.*

Nurse of Akbar; wife of Nadīm *kūka;* mother of Bāqī and Adham *kūkas*. *Cf.* Bābū *āghā*. Much of her story is given in the Introduction to this volume.

CXVII. Māham Begam : *ākā* and *ākām* (lady and my lady).

The word Māham is explained by Mr. Erskine (who did not know Gul-badan's book) as Bābar's name of endearment for his favourite wife, and as meaning 'my moon.' Mr. Schuyler also translates it by the same words. He says that a woman who was shot for political offences in Bukhārā was known as 'My moon (Māham) of Keninghez.'

But many Māhams are chronicled, and not only Bābar gives the name to Humāyūn's mother; Gul-badan speaks frequently of 'my lady who was Māham Begam,' and Māham seems to be her personal name. It is used at least once as a man's. (*Akbar-nāma*, I. 320, Māham 'Alī Qulī Khān.)

Whether māham is to be classed with sulṭānam, khānam, begam, shāham, I am unable to say.

Sir Douglas Forsyth (Mission to Yarkand, 84) translates khānam and begam by *my lord* and *my chief.* But neither is a domestic word; both are in common use in the sources to designate, for general readers, the wives or daughters of khāns and begs, or princes. Sulṭānam also is a common title, and from Gul-badan's use of it does not appear to be a personal name, but to answer to sulṭān as khānam to khān, etc..

Against reading khānam as *my lady*, with a sense of possession or admission of superiority (as is done by Sir Douglas Forsyth), there are the Turkī words formed from it, viz., *khānam-alī*, honeysuckle, and *khānam-būjakī*, ladybird. Shāham, which has the appearance of being formed from shāh like the others by the suffix *am* or *im*, is used both for man and woman. Shīram occurs as a man's name.

Māham was a wife of whom it was said that she was to Bābar what 'Āyisha was to Muḥammad, and she was Humāyūn's mother. Gul-badan mentions her often, yet no one of the numerous sources I have consulted, sets down her family or the name of her father.

At one time it appeared to me probable that she was a Begchik Mughal, because Bābar calls Yādgār *Begchik, ṭaghāī* when speaking of him in connection with Humāyūn. Further consideration led to the abandonment of the theory.

Uncle Yādgār, Uncle 'Alī, and Uncle Ibrāhīm (*Chapūk*, slashed-face) are named as being three of the eight brothers or half-brothers of Gul-rukh, the mother of Kāmrān; and Bega (*Ḥajī*) Begam is the daughter of Uncle Yādgār.

Amongst these eight Begchiks I do not find one named Uncle Muhammad 'Alī, and there is a good deal to lead one to regard a certain Khwāja Muḥammad 'Alī *ṭaghāī* as being Māham's brother.

He was associated with Khost, and it is on record that Humāyūn visited his maternal grandparents (*nanahā*) in Khost. The Begchiks do not seem to have been connected with Khost. Bābar speaks frequently of Khwāja Muḥammad 'Alī as being employed in the government of Khost (925H.); as coming from Khost for orders, etc., and the *mīr-zādas* of Khost also are recorded as visiting the court. One of Māham's children was born in Khost.

Bābar frequently mentions an 'Abdu-l-malūk *Khostī*, and he may be a connection of Māham. He, however, appears as *Khostī*, *Khwastī*, *Qastī*, *qūrchī*, *Qūrchīn*, and without a more complete good Turkī text no opinion can be formed as to his identity.

Gul-badan says that *Ākā* (Māham) was related to the owners of the New Year's Garden in Kābul, and this was made by Ulugh Beg *Kābulī Mīrān-shāhī*.

Abū'l-faẓl says Māham was of a noble Khurāsān family, related to Sulṭān Ḥusain Mīrzā (*Bāyqrā*), and, like Ḥamīda-bānū Begam, was of the line of Shaikh Aḥmad *Jāmī* (*az dūdman-i-a'yān wa ashrāf-i-Khurāsān and, wa ba Sulṭān Ḥusain Mīrzā nisbat-i-khwesh dārand*. Perhaps *nisbat-i-khwesh* implies blood-relationship on the father's side.

Gul-badan speaks of Māham's Mughal servants, but a Chaghatāī, a Begchik, a Qūchīn is also a Mughal, and Bābar often sinks the divisional tribe-name in the general one, Mughal (*e.g.*, Mems. 9 and 21).

Some considerations suggest that Māham was a *Dughlāt Mughal*, and of the family of 'Abdu-l-qadūs, but no valid opinion can be formed until a text as good as the Elphinstone is available for guidance.

Bābar married Māham in Harāt when he visited that city after Sulṭān Ḥusain Mīrzā's death, and in 912H. (1506). Humāyūn was born on March 6, 1508 (Zū'l-qa'da 4th, 913H.). Four other children were born to her, and all died in infancy. They were Bār-bul, Mihr-jahān, Isān-daulat and Fārūq.

The events of her career are detailed in the Introduction to this volume and in Gul-badan Begam's book.

Mems., 250, 405, 412, 423, 428 n..
Gul-badan, 4*a*, 6*b*, 7*a*, 8*b*, 11*b*, 13*b*, 14*b*, 16*a*, 16*b*, 17*a*, 18*b*, 21*a* and *b*, 22*a* and *b*, 23*a* and *b*, 24*b*.
Akbar-nāma, *Bib. Ind.* ed., and H. Beveridge, *s.n.* Māham and Māham 'Alī Qulī Khān.
Turkistān, Schuyler, 95 ff..

CXVIII. Māham *Kābulī*. (No. 81.)

At Hindāl's marriage feast.

Gul-badan, 26*a*.

CXIX. Māham Khānam *Chaghatāī Mughal*.

Second daughter of Sulṭān Aḥmad Khān *Chaghatāī* and full-sister of Manṣūr Khān. Their mother was Ṣaḥib-daulat *Dughlāt*, sister of Mīr Jabār *Bardī Dughlāt*. Māham married Builāsh Khān *Uzbeg Kazāk*, son of Awīq.

Ḥaidar Mīrzā names her as a hostage given, with her mother, by her brother Manṣūr to his half-brother Sa'īd at a time of their meeting in 1516. She had two other full-brothers, Bābājāk and Shāh Shaikh Muḥammad.

Tār. Rash., N. E. & R., 160, 344.

CXX. Māh Begam *Qibchāq Mughal*.

The moon princess; Pers. *māh*, moon.

Daughter of Sulṭān Wais *Qibchāq Mughal* and sister of Ḥaram Begam; wife of Kāmrān Mīrzā.

Gul badan, 64*b*.

CXXI. Māh-chachaq *Khalīfa.*

She is mentioned by Bāyazīd as interceding for him with Ḥamīda-bānū. She may be a servant (*khalīfa*).

J. R. A. S., October, 1898, art. Bāyazīd *bīyāt*, H. Beveridge p. 16.

CXXII. Māh-chūchak Begam *Arghūn*, *Ḥājī* Begam.

The word *chūchak* presents difficulties. Ilminsky writes *chūchūq;* Bāyazīd. *chachaq;* Gul-badan, *chūchak* and *jūjak;* the Memoirs, *chuchak.* Mr. Blochmann and Mr. Lowe transliterate, *jūjak.* There is a Turkī word *jūjūq*, but its meaning of sweet-savoured is less appropriate for a woman's name than a word which, spite of vowel variation it seems safer to take from the Persian; viz. *chachak*, a rose, and *chachak*, *chuchuk*, a lovely cheek, a mole.

Daughter of Mīrzā Muḥammad Muqīm *Arghūn* and of Bībī Zarīf *Khātūn;* wife (1) of Bābar's *kūkaltāsh* Qāsim; (2) of Shāh Ḥasan *Arghūn* of Sind (died 963H.); (3) of 'Īsā *Tarkhān Arghūn* of Tatta and Sind.

By Qāsim, she was mother of Nāhīd Begam and by Shāh Ḥasan of his only child, Chūchak or Māh-chūchak, Kāmran's wife.

She had an interesting story which Mr. Erskine tells at length. (B. & H., I. 348 *et seq.*.)

On the death of 'Īsā (975H.) his son and successor, Muḥammad Bāqī *Tarkhān*, who was a madman, ill-treated Mah-chūchak and Nāhīd who was then visiting her. This led to a plot against him, but in the end Māh-chūchak was imprisoned by him and starved to death. (*Cf. s.n.* Nāhīd.)

Mems., 233.
B. & H., I. 348 *et seq.*.
Tārīkh-i-sind, Mīr Ma'ṣūm, in the account of Shāh Ḥasan's family.
Aīn-i-akbarī, Blochmann, 420.
Ilminsky, 273.

XXIII. Māh-chūchak Begam *Arghūn.*

Daughter of Shāh Ḥasan and Māh-chūchak *Arghūn* and her father's only child; wife of Kāmrān; married 953H. (1546). Her wifely fidelity is commemorated by the historians. She went with Kāmrān to Makka after his blinding, and attended him until his death, October 5th, 1557. She survived him seven months.

Tārīkh-i-sind, Mīr Ma'ṣūm, in the account of Shāh Ḥasan's family.

CXXIV. Māh-chūchak Begam.

Sister of Bairām *Oghlān* and of Farīdūn Khān *Kābulī.*

She married Humāyūn in 1546. She had two sons, Muḥammad Hakīm (born 960H.—1553) and Farrūkh-fāl. Gul-badan says she had four daughters and then, with discrepancy frequently found in her writings, names three: Bakht-nisā', Sakīna-bānū, and Amīna-bānū. The name of the best-known of her girls, Fakhru-n-nisā', is omitted.

Māh-chūchak's story is told by her sister-in-law, in the Introduction of this volume, by Mr. Blochmann and by several Persian writers.

She was murdered by Shāh Abū'l-ma'ālī in Kābul in 1564.

Gul-badan, 71*a*, 71*b*, 73*b*, 78*b*, 83*a*.
Jauhar, Mr. William Irvine's MS., Part II., Chapter II..
Bāyazīd, I.O. MS., 72*a*.
Niẓāmu-d-dīn Aḥmad, 27th year of Akbar.
Badāyunī, Lowe, 54 *et seq.*.
Āīn-i-akbarī, Blochmann, *s.n.*.

CXXV. Makhdūma *āghā.* (No. 59.)

The Lady *āghā*; Ar. *makhdūma*, lady, mistress.

Wife of Hindū Beg.

Gul-badan, 26*a*.

CXXVI. Makhdūma Begam (*Qarā-gūz*).

Wife of 'Umar Shaikh *Mīrān-shāhī;* mother of Ruqaiya, a posthumous child; she was married at the end of 'Umar's days; she was tenderly beloved, and to flatter him her descent was derived from his uncle, Manūchahr *Mīrān-shāhī.*

Mems., 10, 14.

CXXVII. Makhdūma-jahān.

The mistress of the world; Ar. *makhdūma*, mistress, and Pers. *jahān*, world.

Mother of Sulṭān Bahādūr *Gujrātī.*

B. & H., II. 96.

CXXVIII. Makhdūma *Qāluchī.*

A wife of Sa'īd Khān *Chaghatāī;* a 'tribes-woman'; mother of Rashīd; sister of Suqār *Bahādūr Qāluchī.*

Tār. Rash., E. & R., 140, 187, 309.

CXXIX. Makhdūma Khānam.

The Lady Khānam; Ar. *makhdūma*, lady, mistress.

Daughter of Shīr 'Alī Khān *Chaghatāī Mughal;* sister of Wais Khān; wife of Amāsānjī Taishī *Qālmāq;* mother of Qadīr, Ibrāhīm, and Ilyās.

Her marriage was a ransom for her brother Wais of whom it was commonly reported that he was routed sixty times by the Qālmāqs. On her marriage, Wais made Amāsānjī become a Musalmān, and Makhdūma continued the work of her husband's conversion and that of his tribe.

She named one of her daughters Karīm *Bardī* in affection and respect for the Dughlāt amīr of this name.

Mems., 409.
Tār. Rash., E. & R., 67, 91.

CXXX. Makhdūma-sulṭān Begam.

Daughter of Sulṭān Maḥmūd Mīrzā *Mīrān-shāhī* and Zuhra Begī *āghā Uzbeg*; elder sister of Sulṭān 'Alī Mīrzā. 'She is now in Badakhshān.' (Mems., 30.) The 'now' may be in the late twenties of 1500, and she may have been with Mīrzā Khān (Wais *Mīrān-shāhī*).

Mems., 30.

CXXXI. *Makhfī.*

Hid, concealed.

This is the poetical name (*takhalluṣ*) of Salīma-sulṭān Begam *Chaqānīānī*, Nūr-jahān Begam, and Zību-n-nisā', a daughter of Aurang-zīb.

CXXXII. Malika-jahān.

The world's queen; Ar. *malika*, queen, and Pers. *jahān*, world.

Elliot and Dawson, V. 81, 87, 88.

CXXXIII. Ma'ṣūma-sulṭān Begam *Mīrān-shāhī.*

The very chaste princess; Ar. *ma'ṣūm*, chaste, innocent, and *sulṭān*, sway, pre-eminence.

Fifth and youngest daughter of Sulṭān Aḥmad Mīrzā *Mīrān-shāhī*. Her mother was Ḥabība-sulṭān Begam *Arghūn*. She married Bābar (her first cousin) in 913H. (1507), and from his account of the affair it was a love-match on both sides. She was half-sister of 'Āyisha, Bābar's first wife. She died in child-bed, and her infant received her name.

Gul-badan, 6*b*.
Mems., 22, 208, 225, 231, 429 Supplement.

CXXXIV. Ma'ṣūma-sulṭān Begam *Mīrān-shāhī*. (No. 43.)

Daughter of Bābar and Ma'ṣūma; wife of Muḥammad-zamān Mīrzā *Bāyqrā*.

Gul-badan, 6*b*, 23*a*, 25*b*, 29*b*.
Akbar-nāma, *s.n.*.
Mems., 22, 395, 429 Supplement.

CXXXV. Maywa-jān.

Fruit of life; Pers. *maywa*, fruit, and *jān*, life.

Daughter of Khazang *yasāwal* and a servant of Gul-badan Begam; an inferior wife of Humāyūn.

Gul-badan, 21*b*, 22*a*, 30*a*.

CXXXVI. Mihr-angez Begam. (No. 29.)

The princess who commands affection; Pers. *mihr*, affection, and *angez*, commanding, raising.

Daughter of Muẓaffar Ḥusain Mīrzā *Bāyqrā*; grand-daughter of Sulṭān Ḥusain *Bāyqrā* and Khadīja.

She was accomplished after the fashion of gentlemen-at-arms and she played polo.

She was married by ʿUbaidu-l-lāh *Uzbeg* when Harāt was taken by Shaibānī (913H., June, 1507).

She was at the Mystic Feast in 1531.

Gul-badan, 24*b*.
Ḥabību-s-siyār, 397 *et seq.*.

CXXXVII. Mihr-bānū Begam *Mīrān-shāhī*. (? No. 27.)

The beloved; Pers. *mihr*, affection, and *bānū*, possessing.

Daughter of ʿUmar Shaikh *Mīrān-shāhī* and of Umīd *Andijānī*; full-sister of Nāṣir and Shahr-bānū; born *cir*. 886H. (1481-82).

Gul-badan mentions a Mihr-līq Begam (No. 27.) who was a paternal aunt of Humāyūn, as being at the Mystic Feast. This may be Mihr-bānū. No aunt named Mihr-līq is mentioned elsewhere, and *līq* and *bānū* have the same sense.

Gul-badan, 25*a*.
Mems., 10.

CXXXVIII. Mihr-bānū Khānam.

I think she is a relative of Bābar, and she may be the daughter of ʿUmar Shàikh and Umīd, and thus Bābar's half-sister. (See *infra.*) From her title of Khānam, she is very possibly a Chaghatāī on her mother's side (Umīd was an Andijānī), or the style is due to her marriage with a khān. She appears to have married a man of high rank; perhaps Kūchūm (*Qūch-kunjī*) Khān who was Khāqān of his tribe from 1510 to 1530, or his son and successor (ruled from 1530 to 1533). She had a son Pulād whom Bābar mentions as fighting with 'Qūch-kunjī' and his son Abū-sa'īd *Uzbeg* at Jām (1528).

The Qūch-kunjī was the tribe of Isān-daulat.

Kūchūm, Abū-sa'īd, Mihr-bānū, and Pulād sent ambassadors and messengers to Bābar in the same year, and Bābar mentions his return gifts with quaint particularity. The envoys were entertained at a feast by him on December 12th, 1528 (935H.).

Mems., 10, 390, 395, 397, 399.
Tār. Rash., E. & R., *s.n.* Kuchum and Sulṭān and 206 n..
Muḥammadan Dynasties, Stanley Lane-Poole, 273.

CXXXIX. Mihr-jahān or -jān Begam *Mīrān-shāhī*.

Sun of the world or of life; Pers. *mihr*, sun, and *jahān*, world, or *jān*, life, soul.

Daughter of Bābar and Māham; born at Khost; died an infant.

Gul-badan, 6*b*.

CXL. Mihr-nigār Khānam *Chaghatāī Mughal*.

The image of affection, or a very sun.

Eldest daughter of Yūnas Khān *Chaghatāī* and Isān-daulat (*Qūchīn, Kunjī*); born *cir.* 860H. (1455-56); wife of Sulṭān Aḥmad Mīrzā *Mīrān-shāhī*; first cousin of Bābar.

In 905H. (early in July, 1500) she was captured by Shaibānī and married by him. In 906H. (1500-1) she was divorced when he wished to marry Khān-zāda, her niece. She then stayed awhile in Samarqand. In 907H. (1501-2) she went to Tāshkand and joined the large family party which assembled there. (Mems. 99.) In 911H. (middle of 1505) she came to Kābul with other kinsfolk, soon after the death of her grandmother (Isān) and of her father, and during the ceremonial mourning of Bābar for his mother. 'Our grief broke out afresh,' he writes.

Mīrzā Ḥaidar gives a pleasant account of the welcome she accorded her generous and kindly nephew Bābar in 912H. (1506-7), when he put down Khān Mīrzā's (Wais) rebellion in Kābul: 'The Emperor leapt up and embraced his beloved aunt with every manifestation of affection. The khānam said to him: "Your children, wives, and household are longing to see you. I give thanks that I have been permitted to see you again. Rise up and go to your family in the castle. I too am going thither."'

In 913H. (1507), when Khān Mīrzā set out for Badakhshān with his mother, Shāh Begam, to try his fortunes in her father's ancient lands, Mihr-nigār also 'took a fancy to go. It would have been better and more becoming,' writes Bābar, 'for her to remain with me. I was her nearest relation. But however much I dissuaded her, she continued obstinate and also set out for Badakhshān.

Mihr-nigār rued her self-will. She and Shāh Begam were captured on their way to Qila'-ẓafar by one of Abū-bakr *Dughlāt's* 'marauding bands,' and 'in the prisons of that wretched miscreant they departed from this perishable world.'

Mems., 12, 22, 99, 169, 232.
Tār. Rash., 86, 94, 117, 155, 196, 197, 200, 258.

CXLI. Mīnglī-bī *āghācha Uzbeg*.

A low-born wife (*ghūncha-chī*) of Sulṭān Ḥusain Mīrzā *Bāyqrā*. The *Ḥabību-s-siyār* calls her a Turk and a purchased slave (*mamlūqa*) of Shahr-bānū Begam

Mīrān-shāhī who brought her when she herself married Sulṭān Ḥusain, and presented her to him.

She was mother of three sons: Abū-tūrāb, Muḥammad Ḥusain, and Farīdūn Ḥusain; and of two daughters: Bairām (or Maryam) and Fāṭima.

Mems., 181, 182, 183.
Habību-s-siyār (lith. ed.), 327 *et seq.*.

CXLII. Mīng-līq *kūkaltāsh*.

She escaped from Samarqand with Bābar's mother on its capture by Shaibānī in 907H. (1501).

Mems., 98.

CXLIII. Mubārika Bībī; *Afghānī āghācha*. (No. 56.)

Ar. *mubārika*, blessed, fortunate.

She was a daughter of Shāh Manṣūr *Yūsufzai*, and was married by Bābar at Kehrāj on January 30th, 1519 (Muḥarram 28th, 925H.). The alliance was the sign and seal of amity between him and her tribe. A charming account of her and her marriage is given in the *Tārīkh-i-ḥāfiẓ-i-raḥmat-khānī*, and Mr. Beveridge has translated it in full under the title 'An Afghān Legend,' so that it need not be reproduced here.

Gul-badan never gives the name Mubārika (Blessed Damozel) as that of the Afghān lady (*Afghānī āghācha*) whom she so frequently and pleasantly mentions. Ḥafiẓ Muḥammad (*l.c.*) says that Mubārika was much beloved by Bābar, and this is borne out by the fact that she was one of the small and select party of ladies who were the first to join him in India. She went there, it is safe to infer, with Māham and Gul-badan in 1529.

She bore no child, and this misfortune Ḥafiẓ Muḥammad attributes to the envy of other wives who administered drugs to deprive her of motherhood and weaken her husband's affection.

She died early in Akbar's reign.

A brother of Mubārika, named Mīr Jamāl, accompanied Bābar to Hindustān in 1525, and rose to high office under Humāyūn and Akbar. Hindāl had a favourite follower of this name who passed, on his death, into Akbar's service. He may well be the Yūsufzai.

Gul-badan, 8*a*, 25*b*, 30*a*, 35*a*, 38*a*, 73*b*.
Mems., 250, 250 n., 251.
Akbar-nāma, *Bib. Ind.* ed., I. 315.
Asiatic Quarterly Review, April, 1901, art. An Afghān Legend, H. Beveridge.

(Mughal Khānam, 'Ayisha, *q.v.*)

CXLIV. Muḥibb-sulṭān.

The very loving khānam; Ar. *muḥibb*, a lover, one who loves, and *sulṭān*, pre-eminence.

Daughter of Sulṭān Ḥusain Mīrzā *Bāyqrā* and a 'handmaid' (*ghūncha-chī*).

Mems., 30.

CXLV. Muḥibb-sulṭān Khānam *Chaghatāī Mughal.* (No. 20.)

Third daughter of Sulṭān Aḥmad Khān *Chaghatāī;* wife of Mīrzā Ḥaidar *Dughlāt.*

Gul-badan, 11*a*, 24*b*.
Tār. Rash., E. & R., 161, 280,[1] 341.

CXLVI. Muḥtarima Khānam *Chaghatāī Mughal.*

The honoured khānam; Ar. *muḥtarim*, respected, honoured.

Daughter of Shāh Muḥammad Sulṭān *Kāshgharī Chaghatāī*, and Khadīja Sulṭān *Chaghatāī;* wife (1) of Kāmrān, (2) of Ibrāhīm *Mīrān-shāhī*, the son of Sulaimān and Ḥaram.

---

[1] There is some error here in the translation, as its statements do not agree with known facts.

She is occasionally spoken of simply as 'Khānam.'

Gul-badan, 62*b*.
Akbar-nāma, *s.n.*.
Aīn-i-akbarī, Blochmann, *s.n.*.
Tār. Rash., E. & R., 451.
Cf. Introduction.

CXLVII. Munauwar Sulṯān Begam *Bāyqrā.*

The illuminated princess; Ar. *munauwar*, bright illuminated.

Daughter of Sulṯān Ḥusain Mīrzā *Bāyqrā* and Bābā *āghācha;* wife of Sayyid Mīrzā of Andekhud who appears also to have married her niece. She was famed for her beauty. The Memoirs and Ilminsky's text do not give her name, and I have found it in the *Ḥabību-s-siyār*. From this same work is derived the information that Sayyid Mīrzā is a name given to a son of Ulugh Bēg Mīrzā *Mīrān-shāhī*.

Mems., 182.
Ḥabību-s-siyār, 327 *et seq.*

CXLVIII. Nāhīd Begam. (No. 54.)

Pers. *Nāhīd*, the name of the mother of Alexander; a name for the planet Venus, *etc.*.

Daughter of Māh-chūchak *Arghūn* by her marriage as a captive of Bābar, with his foster-brother Qāsim; wife of Muḥibb-'alī *Barlās*.

When her mother, resenting her position in a mis-alliance, ran away, Nāhīd, then eighteen months old, remained in Kābul.

When her mother was imprisoned in Sind by Muḥammad Bāqī *Tarkhān*, Nāhīd escaped to Bhakkar, and was protected, till her return to Akbar's court, by Sulṯān Maḥmūd *Bhakkarī* (975H.).

She was at Hindāl's wedding feast. Much of her story is contained in the Introduction of this volume.

Gul-badan, 4*a*, 26*a*.
Tārīkh-i-sind, Mīr Ma'ṣūm.
Bādshāh-nāma s.n. (fully used by Blochmann).
Aīn-i-akbarī, Blochmann, *s.n.*.
B. & H., I. 348, 351, 352, 385.

CXLIX. Nār-gul *āghācha*. (No. 58.)

(?) Red as a rose, pomegranate-red. For *nār* see *infra*. Pers. *gul*, a rose.

She was perhaps one of two Circassian slaves, of whom Gul-nār may be the other and who were sent to Bābar by Ṭahmāsp in 1526.

Mems., 347.
Gul-badan, 25*b*, 35*a*, 38*a*.

CL. Nār-sulṭān *āghā*. (No. 77.)

Presumably Pers. *nār*, a pomegranate; but it might be Ar. *nār*, advice, counsel, or even fire, and *sulṭān*, pre-eminence, a high degree of what is expressed by the first word of the compound name.

Gul-badan, 26*a*.

CLI. Nigār *āghā*. (No. 76.)

Pers. *nigār*, a mistress, a sweetheart.

Mother of Mughal Beg.

Gul-badan, 26*a*.

CLII. Nizhād-sulṭān Begam *Bāyqrā*.

The princess of highly distinguished race; Pers. *nizhād*, family, high-born; Ar. *sulṭān*, pre-eminence.

Eldest daughter of Sulṭān Ḥusain Mīrzā *Bāyqrā* and Bābā *āghācha;* wife of Sikandar Mīrzā, son of *Bāyqrā* Mīrzā who was her father's elder brother.

Mems., 182.
Ḥabību-s-siyār, 387 *et seq.*

CLIII. Pāpā (? Bābā) *āghācha*.

Mr. Erskine writes *Papa*, and Ilminsky, perhaps following him, *Pāpā*. *Bābā—i.e.*, darling—would seem a more fitting name for one who is said to have been much beloved.

She was a low-born wife of Sulṭān Ḥusain Mīrzā *Bāyqrā* and foster-sister of Āfāq Begam. The mīrzā 'saw her and liked her,' and she became mother of seven of his children, *i.e.*, four sons, Muḥammad

Ma'ṣūm, Farrūkh Ḥusain, Ibn Ḥusain, Ibrāhīm Ḥusain; of three daughters, Nizhād-sulṭān, Sa'ādat-bakht, and a third whose name Bābar does not give.

Mems., 181, 182, 183.

CLIV. Pāshā Begam *Bahārlū Turkomān* of the Black Sheep.

(?) Turkī *Pāshā*, a lord, or Pers. *pecha*, chief, before. The *Ma'āsir-i-raḥīmī* writes *pāshā*.

Daughter of 'Alī-shakr Beg *Bahārlū*; wife (1) of Muḥammadī Mīrzā of the Black Sheep; (2) in 873H. (1468-69) of Sulṭān Maḥmūd Mīrzā *Mīrān-shāhī*; mother by Maḥmūd of three daughters and one son, Bayasanghar (born 882H.).

Bābar does not give the name of any one of the three girls, nor does he mention that one of them was a wife of his own. One married Malik Muḥammad Mīrzā *Mīrān-shāhī*. The *Ma'āsir-i-raḥīmī* supplies the information that another was Ṣālḥa-sulṭān Begam and that she had a daughter by Bābar whose name was Gul-rukh; that Gul-rukh married Nūru-d-dīn Muḥammad *Chaqānīānī*, and had by him Salīma-sulṭān Begam. Abū'l-faẓl says that a daughter of Pāshā by Sulṭān Maḥmūd Mīrzā was married to Khwāja Ḥasan *Khwāja-zāda*, and that on account of this connection *Firdaus-makānī* (Bābar) married Mīrzā Nūru-d-dīn to his own daughter, Gul-barg Begam, and that Salīma-sulṭān Begam was the issue of this marriage.

(There are difficulties connected with the account here given of Ṣālḥa which are set forth under the name of her daughter, Salīma-sulṭān.)

Pāshā Begam was of the same family as Bairām Khān. (*Cf.* genealogical table *s.n.* Salīma-sulṭān.)

Mems., 29. 30, 31, 72.
Tār. Rash., E. & R., 93 n..
Ma'āsir-i-raḥīmī, Asiatic Society of Bengal MS. in year 1024H..

CLV. Pāyanda-sulṭān Begam *Mīrān-shāhī*.

(?) Of fixed pre-eminence; Pers. *pāyanda*, firm, stable, and Ar. *sulṭān*, pre-eminence.

Daughter of Abū-sa'īd Sulṭān Mīrzā *Mīrān-shāhī*; paternal aunt of Bābar; wife of Sulṭān Ḥusain Mīrzā *Bāyqrā*; sister of Shahr-bānū whom Sulṭān Ḥusain Mīrzā divorced; mother of Ḥaidar Mīrzā *Bāyqrā*; of Āq, Kīchak, Bega, and Āghā Begams.

When the Uzbegs took Khurāsān, 913H. (1507-8), she went to 'Irāq, where 'she died in distress.'

Mems., 30, 180, 181, 182, 204, 208 and n., 223.
Gul-badan, 25*a* (here a *Muḥammad* is inserted after Pāyanda in the name).

CLVI. Qadīr Khānam *Qālmāq*.

Daughter of Amāsānjī Taishī *Qālmāq* and Makhdūma Khānam *Chaghatāī*.

Tār. Rash., E. & R., 91.

CLVII. *Qarā-gūz* Begam *Bāyqrā*.

The black-eyed princess. *Qarā-gūz* is a sobriquet, and I have not found her personal name.

Daughter of Sulṭān Ḥusain Mīrzā *Bāyqrā* and Pāyanda-sulṭān Begam *Mīrān-shāhī*; wife of Nāṣir Mīrzā, Bābar's half-brother.

Mems., 181.

(*Qarā-gūz* Begam, Rabī'a, *q.v.*)

(*Qarā-gūz* Begam, Makhdūma, *q.v.*)

CLVIII. Qūtūq *āghācha* and Begam.

Ilminsky writes *Qūtūq*; Mems., *Katak*.

Foster-sister of *Terkhān* Begam; wife of Sulṭān Aḥmad Mīrzā *Mīrān-shāhī*; mother of four daughters: (1) Rabī'a (*Qarā-gūz*), (2) Salīqa (Āq), 'Āyisha (wife of Bābar, (4) Sulṭānam.

She was married 'for love,' and Aḥmad was 'prodigiously attached' to her. She drank wine; her co-wives were neglected from fear of her. At length her husband put her to death, and 'delivered himself from his reproach.'

Mems., 22.

CLIX. Qūt-līq (Qutluq) Khānam *Chaghatāī Mughal.*

(?) The image of happiness; from Turkī *qūtla*, happy, and *līq*, endowed with.

Daughter of Sulṭān Maḥmūd Khān *Chaghatāī;* wife of Jānī Beg Khān *Uzbeg.*

Her marriage was a sequel of victory by Shaibānī over her father. *Cf.* 'Āyisha (her sister).

Tār. Rash., E. & R., 160, 251.

CLX. Qūt-līq-nigār Khānam *Chaghatāī Mughal.*

Second daughter of Yūnas Khān *Chaghatāī* and Isān-daulat *Qūchīn;* chief wife of 'Umar-shaikh *Mīrān-shāhī;* half-sister of Maḥmūd and Aḥmad Khāns; mother of Khān-zāda and Bābar.

She accompanied her son in most of his wars and expeditions, and lived to see him master of Kābul. She died in Muḥarram, 911H. (June, 1505).

Mems., 10, 11, 12, 30, 90, 94, 98, 99, 104, 105, 134, 169.
Gul-badan, 4*a*.
Tār. Rash., *s.n.*.
Akbar-nāma, *s.n.*.

CLXI. Rabī'a-sulṭān Begam *Bāyqrā* and Bedka Begam *Bāyqrā.*

These two names may indicate the same person.

The Memoirs (176 and 177) say that Sulṭān Ḥusain Mīrzā *Bāyqrā* had two full-sisters, Āka and Bedka, and that Bedka married Aḥmad *Hājī Tarkhān*, and had two sons who served Sulṭān Ḥusain.

These statements are contained also in the Turkī texts (B.M. Add. 26,324, and Ilminsky), and also in a considerable number of good Persian texts in the British Museum and Bodleian.

There is, however, this difference of statement. The Turkī texts write: *Bedka Begam ham mīrzā nīnak aīkā-chī sī aīdī.* P. de C. translates: *était aussi l'ainée du mīrzā.* The Persian texts have: *Bedka Begam ki khwāhar-i-khurd mīrzā būd;* and from this Mr. Erskine translates: . . . *the mīrzā's younger sister.*

The Turkī, it should be observed, uses of Āka precisely the same word as of Bedka, *aīkā-chī sī.*

It may be right to regard Bedka as the younger of the two sisters of the mīrzā, and not as the sister younger than the mīrzā.

To pass now to what has led me to make a tentative identification of Bedka with Rabī'a-sulṭān.

The Memoirs (181) mention Rabī'a-sulṭān as the younger sister of the mīrzā (Ḥusain) and as having two sons, Bābar and Murād who were given in marriage to two daughters of Ḥusain.

The Turkī texts do not describe Rabī'a-sulṭān in any way, or say that she was Ḥusain's sister. They simply mention the marriages.

The Persian texts say of Ḥusain's two daughters (Bega and Āghā): *ba pisarān-i-khwāhar-i-khurd-i-khudrā Rabī'a-sulṭān Begam, Bābar Mīrzā wa Sulṭān Murād Mīrzā, dādā būdand.*

The Persian texts which state that Rabī'a-sulṭān was Ḥusain's own sister, have greater authority than most translations can claim for such additional information as is here given, because the Persian translation of the *Tūzūk-i-bābarī* was made in a court circle and at a date when such additional statements were likely to be known to many living persons.

Ḥusain *may* have had a younger and half-sister, but the words in the Persian texts which are used of Rabī'a-sulṭān are those used of Bedka, and they are more applicable to a full than a half sister.

The *Āka* of the passage in which Bedka is mentioned has no personal name recorded. Bedka may be a word of the same class as *āka, i.e.*, a title or sobriquet, and Rabī'a-sulṯān may be the personal name of Bedka. Perhaps the word *Bedka* is *Bega*.

The facts of Bedka's descent are as follows: she was a daughter of Manṣūr Mīrzā *Bāyqrā* and of Fīroza Begam *Mīrān-shāhī*, and thus doubly a Tīmūrid. She was full-sister of Bāyqrā and Ḥusain Mīrzās and of Āka Begam. She married Aḥmad Khān *Hājī Tarkhān*, and had two sons whose names (if Bedka be Rabī'a-sulṯān) were Bābar and Murād and who married two of her nieces, Bega and Āghā.

Mems., 176, 177, 181.
Ilminsky, 203, 204, 208.
B.M. Turkī Add. 26,234, f. 48*a* and *b*; 53.
Other texts under 911H..

CLXII. Rabī'a-sulṯān Begam (*Qarā-gūz*) *Mīrān-shāhī.*

Daughter of Sulṯān Aḥmad Mīrzā *Mīrān-shāhī* and Qūtūq (Katak) *āghācha* (Begam); wife (1) of Sulṯān Maḥmūd Khān *Chaghatāī* and mother of Bābā Sulṯān, and (2) of Jānī Beg *Uzbeg* who married her after the murder of her father and her son by his cousin Shaibānī in 914H. (1508).

Mems., 22.
Tār. Rash., E. & R., 114, 116.

CLXIII. Rajab-sulṯān *Mīrān-shāhī.*

Ar. *rajab*, fearing, worshipping. *Sulṯān* may here be a title.

Daughter of Sulṯān Maḥmūd Mīrzā and a concubine (*ghūncha-chī*).

Mems., 30.

CLXIV. Ruqaiya Begam *Mīrān-shāhī.*

Ruqaiya was the name of a daughter of Muḥammad, and conveys the notion of bewitching or of being armed against spells.

Daughter of Hindāl; first wife of Akbar; she died Jumāda I. 7th, 1035H. (January 19th, 1626), at the age of eighty-four. She had no children of her own, and she brought up Shāh-jahān. Mihru-n-nisā' (Nūr-jahān) lived 'unnoticed and rejected' with her after the death of Shīr-afkan.

Āīn-i-akbarī, Blochmann, 309, 509.

CLXV. Ruqaiya-sulṭān Begam *Mīrān-shāhī.*

Daughter of 'Umar Shaikh *Mīrān-shāhī* and Makhdūma-sulṭān Begam (*Qarā-gūz*). She was a posthumous child. She fell into the hands of Jānī Beg *Uzbeg, cir.* 908-9H. (1502-4), and bore him 'two or three' sons who died young. 'I have just received information that she has gone to the mercy of God.' The date of this entry in the Memoirs is about 935H. (1528-9).

Mems, 10.

CLXVI. Sa'ādat-bakht (Begam Sulṭān) *Bāyqrā.*

Of happy fortune; Ar. *sa'ādat*, happy, and Pers. *bakht*, fortune.

Daughter of Sulṭān Ḥusain Mīrzā *Bāyqrā* and Papa (Bābā) *āghācha*. She was married to Sulṭān Ma'sūd after the loss of his eyesight.

Mems., 182.
Ḥabību-s-siyār, 327 *et seq.*

CLXVII. Ṣāḥib-daulat Begam *Dughlāt.*

The princess of good fortune; Ar. *ṣāḥib*, enjoying, and *daulat*, fortune.

Sister of Mīr Jabār *Bardī Dughlāt*; wife of Sulṭān Aḥmad Khān *Chaghatāī*; mother of Manṣūr, Bābājāk, Shāh Shaikh Muḥammad and Māham.

Tār. Rash., E. & R., 125, 344.

CLXVIII. Sakīna-bānū Begam *Mīrān-shāhī.*

The princess guardian of tranquillity; Ar. *sakīna*, tranquillity of mind, and Pers. *bānū*, keeper.

Daughter of Humāyūn and Māh-chūchak; wife of Shāh Ghāzī Khān, son of Naqīb Khān *Qazwīnī*, a personal friend of Akbar.

Gul-badan, 71*a*.
Blochmann, 435, 449.

CLXIX. Sālḥa-sulṭān Begam *Mīrān-shāhī.*

Cf. Salīma-sulṭān *Chaqānīānī.*

CLXX. Salīma-sulṭān Begam *Chaqānīānī.*

Daughter of Mırzā Nūru-d-dīn Muḥammad *Chaqānīānī* and of a daughter of Bābar, as to whose name the sources ring changes upon the rose. She appears as Gul-rang (B. and H. *s.n.*), Gul-barg, Gul-rukh. As her mother was a full Turkomān or Turk by descent, it has occurred to me that she may have borne a Turkī name, and that the various forms it assumes in the Persian may have their origin in this.

As to her maternal parentage there are difficulties. From the *Ma'āsir-i-raḥīmī*, under 1024H., the following information is obtained. Pāshā Begam *Bahārlū Turkomān* married (873H., 1469) as her second husband, Sulṭān Maḥmūd Mīrzā *Mīrān-shāhī*. By him she had three daughters and one son: Bayasanghar (b. 882H., 1477). One daughter whose name was Sālḥa-sulṭān Begam, married Bābar and bore him a daughter, Gul-rukh (*sic*). Gul-rukh married Nūru-d-dīn Muḥammad *Chaqānīānī*, and their daughter was Salīma-sulṭān Begam who married first, Bairām *Khān-i-khānān*, and secondly, the Emperor Akbar.

Abū'l-faẓl (*Bib. Ind.* ed., II. 65) adds the particular that *Firdaus makānī* gave his daughter Gul-barg (*sic*), to Nūru-d-dīn because a daughter of Maḥmūd and Pāshā had been given to Nūru-d-dīn's grandfather Khwāja Ḥasan, known as Khwāja-zāda *Chaqānīānī*. He also states that Salīma-sulṭān Begam was the issue of Gul-barg's marriage.

In the Memoirs, as we have them, there is no mention of Sālḥa-sulṭān nor of Nūru-d-dīn's marriage with a daughter of Bābar. Yet Abū'l-faẓl states that *Firdaus-makānī* arranged Gul-barg's marriage. The first omission is the more remarkable because Bābar (Mems., 30) states that Pāshā had three daughters. He does not give their names, and specifies the marriage of the eldest only. On the same page he tells of his marriage with Sālḥa's half-sister Zainab and of her death. The omission is remarkable and appears to have no good ground, since he chronicles his other Tīmūrid marriages. Of Pāshā's daughters it may be noted here that one married Malik Muḥammad *Mīrān-shāhī*, another Khwāja Ḥasan *Chaqānīānī*, and the third, Bābar.

It appears to me tolerably clear that Bābar's marriage with Sālḥa-sulṭān took place at a date which falls in a gap of the Memoirs, *i.e.*, from 1511 to 1519. This is the period which contains the exile from Kābul after the Mughal rebellion.

Not only does Bābar omit Sālḥa-sulṭān's name and his marriage with her (Mems., 30), but Gul-badan is also silent as to name, marriage and child of Sālḥa-sulṭān. This silence is in every way remarkable. She enumerates her father's children and gives their mothers' names, and she enumerates some of his wives in more places than one. From her lists a Tīmūrid wife cannot have escaped, and especially one whose child became the mother of Gul-badan's associate Salīma-sulṭān.

An explanation of Gul-badan's silence and also of a part of Bābar's has suggested itself to me; it is conjectural merely and hypothetical. The absence of mention of Sālḥa-sulṭan and of her child suggests that she appears under another name in Gul-badan's list of her father's children and their mothers. She may be Gul-badan's own mother, Dil-dār Begam without undue wresting of known circumstantial witness.

The principal difficulty in the way of this identification is Abū'l-faẓl's statement that Nūru-d-dīn's marriage was made by *Firdaus-makānī*, whereas Gulbadan states that her father arranged two Chaghatāi marriages for her sisters.

If we might read *Jannat-āshyānī* (Humāyūn) for *Firdaus-makānī* much would fall into place; the marriage with Nūru-d-dīn could be a re-marriage of Gul-chihra who was widowed in 1533, and of whose remarriage nothing is recorded until her brief political alliance with 'Abbas *Uzbeg* in 1549. It is probable that she remarried in the interval.

To pass on to recorded incidents of Salīma-sulṭān's life:

There is an entry in Hindāl's guest-list which may indicate her presence.

She accompanied Ḥamīda-bānū and Gul-badan to Hindūstan in 964H. (1557), and she was married at Jalindhar shortly after Ṣafar 15th, 965H. (middle of December, 1557) to Bairām *Khān-i-khānān*. It is said that the marriage excited great interest at Court. It united two streams of descent from 'Alī-shukr Beg *Bahārlū Turkomān*. Salīma-sulṭān was a Tīmūrid through Bābar, one of her grandfathers, and through Maḥmūd, one of her great-grandfathers.

A few words must be said about her age at the time of her marriage, because the question has been raised through Jahāngīr's statement that she died at the age of sixty in 1021H., and commented upon by the *Darbār-i-akbarī*. If Jahāngīr gives her age correctly she must have been born in 961H., and this would make her a child of five when she married Bairām, and needs her betrothal by her father to Bairām to date from babyhood.

The *Darbār-i-akbarī* says that it is clear from Jahāngīr's statement of her age at death that she was married to Bairām *ætat.* 5, and that her memory is thus cleared from the reproach of two marriages!

Whatever is concealed in Jahāngīr's 'sixty,' nothing is said to indicate that he desired to bring Salīma-sulṭān into the circle of Hindū propriety. He may have had the wish; he was a Hindū mother's son. The comment of the modern author of the *Darbār-i-*

akbarī witnesses to the Hindūizing action to which Moslim custom and thought have submitted. Adult remarriage was no reproach to Islām in Salīma's day.

It does not, however, seem correct to accept Jahāngīr's statement that Salīma-sulṭān was sixty only at death. To have betrothed her as a baby and to have married her to a man of, at least, middle-age at five, is not in harmony with the Muḥammad custom of Humāyūn's day. Moreover, Jahāngīr himself speaks of her as married (*kad-khudā*) to Bairām. She is said by Abū'l-faẓl to have been betrothed (*nāmzād*) by Humāyūn, and married (*sipurdan*) by Akbar to Bairām Khān.

Badāyunī's words indicate adult and not child marriage; *sābiqā dar ḥabāla-i-Bairām Khān Khān-i-khānān būd, b'ad azān dakhl-i-ḥaram-i-pādshāhī shūd.*

After the murder of Bairām in 968H. Salīma-sulṭān was married by Akbar. She was probably a few years his senior.

In 983H. she made her pilgrimage with Gul-badan. Particulars of the expedition are given in the Introduction to this volume.

Her name appears in the histories as a reader, a poet who wrote under the pseudonym of *makhfī*, and as pleading with Akbar for Salīm's forgiveness.

Her death is chronicled by Jahāngīr who heard of it on Ẕū'l-qa'da 2nd, 1021H. (December 15th, 1612). He gives particulars of her birth and descent, and of her marriages; and he states that she was sixty at the time of her death. By his orders her body was laid in a garden which she herself had made.

Jahāngīr praises her both for her natural qualities and her acquirements. She creates an impression of herself as a charming and cultivated woman.

Gul-badan, (?)26*a*.
Akbar-nāma s.n..
Badāyunī, Lowe, 13, 216, 389.
Tūzūk-i-jahāngīrī, Sayyid Ahmad, Aligarh, 113.
Khāfī Khān, *Bib. Ind.* ed., I. 276.
Āīn-i-akbarī, Blochmann, *s.n.*.
Darbār-i-akbarī, 736.

The genealogical table on the next page illustrates Salīma-sulṭān's descent, and the following dates bear also upon the topic:

Pāshā married Maḥmūd	873H.—1469.
Bayasanghar born	882H.—1477.
Maḥmūd died	900H.—Jan. 1495
Bābar married Zainab, d. of Maḥmūd ...	910H.—1504.
Zainab died	913H.-914H.—1507-8.

Sālḥa's child, the wife of Nūru-d-dīn, was not born in 911H.—1511, because she is not in the list of children who left Kābul with Bābar in that year. (Gul-badan, 7*a*.)

CLXXI. Salīma Khānam *Chaghatāī Mughal.*

Daughter of Khiẓr Khwājā, but whether also of Gul-badan is not recorded.

She went with Gul-badan to Makka in 983H. (1575).

Āīn-i-akbarī, Blochmann, 441.

CLXXII. Salīqa-sulṭān Begam (Āq Begam) *Mīrān-shāhī.*

(Ilminsky, 25, reads Ṣālḥa.) The princess of excellent disposition; Ar. *salīqa*, of good disposition, and *sulṭān*, pre-eminence.

Daughter of Sulṭān Aḥmad Mīrzā *Mīrān-shāhī* and Qūtūq (Katak) Begam; wife of her cousin Maʿsūd. The marriage was announced to Bābar in 900H. (1494) with gifts of gold and silver, almonds, and pistachios. She was captured by Abū-bakr *Dughlāt* with Shāh Begam and Mihr-nigār Khānam.

Mems., 22, 27.

CLXXIII. Sāmiḥa Begam *Barlās.*

The gentle princess; Ar. *sāmiḥ*, gentle.

Daughter of Muḥibb ʿAlī *Barlās* (son of Niẓāmu-d-dīn ʿAlī *Khalīfa*), and presumably of Nāhīd Begam; mother of Mujāhid Khān.

Mujāhid (who is named in the *Ṭabaqāt-i-akbarī* as commander of 1,000, but is not in the *Āīn*) was a son

GENEALOGICAL TABLE OF SALĪMA-SULṬĀN *CHAQĀNĪĀNĪ*.

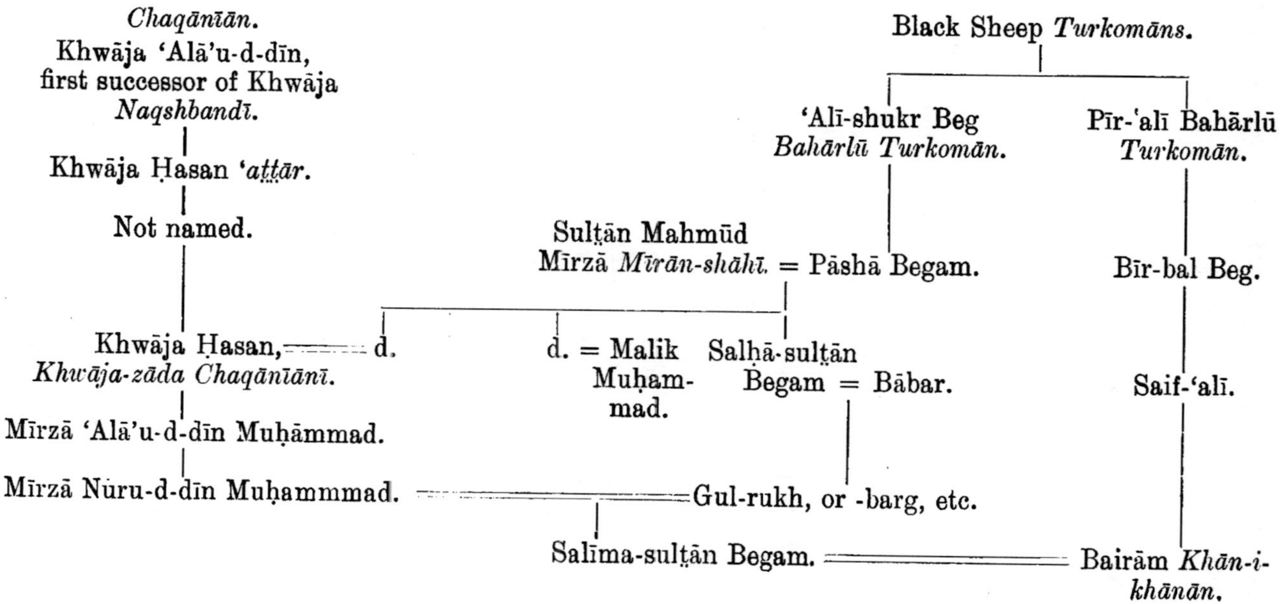

of Muṣāhib Khān, son of Khwāja Kilān (Bābar's friend).

Aīn-i-akbarī, Blochmann, 421, 533.

CLXXIV. Sarv-qad and Sarv-i-sahī.

Straight as a cypress; Pers. *sarv*, a cypress, and *qad*, form, or *sahī*, erect.

Sarv-i-sahī, to use Gul-badan's word, was a singer and reciter. She belonged to the households both of Bābar and Humāyūn, and was subsequently married, with full *nisbat*, to Mu'nim *Khān-i-khānān*.

She acted as go-between of Mu'nim and Khān-i-zamān ('Alī Qulī *Uzbeg-i-shaibānī*) during the rebellion of the latter—probably in the tenth year of Akbar, and Bāyazīd calls her a reliable woman and the *ḥaram* of the *Khān-i-khānān*. She sang on the way to Lamghān by moonlight in 958H. (1551); she was with Mu'nim at the time of his death in Gaur (Ṣafar, 983H., 1575), and in Rajab of the same year accompanied Gul-badan to Makka.

Gul-badan, 82*a* (inserted in the translation after 73*b*).
Bāyazīd, I.O. MS., 122*b*, 147*b*.
Akbar-nāma, *Bib. Ind.* ed., III. 145.

CLXXV. Shād Begam *Bāyqrā*. (No. 28.)

Daughter of Ḥaidar *Bāyqrā* and Bega *Mīrān-shāhī*; wife of 'Adil Sulṭān.

Gul-badan, 25*a*.
Mems., 180.

CLXXV (*a*). Shād Bībī.

Wife of Humāyūn; lost at Chausa.

Gul-badan, 33*b*.

CLXXVI. Shāham *āghā*.

(?) My queen; from Pers. *shāh*, king, ruler.

Of the *ḥaram* of Humāyūn. She went with Gul-badan Begam to Makka in 983H..

Aīn-i-akbarī, Blochmann, 441.

CLXXVII. Shāh Begam *Badakhshī.*

The princess of royal blood.

She was one of six daughters of Shāh Sulṭān Muḥammad, King of Badakhshān, the last of a long line of hereditary rulers of his country who claimed descent from Alexander of Macedon. Her mother was a sister of Sulṭān Sanjar *Barlās.*

She was given in marriage to Yūnas Khān *Chaghatāī* and was the mother of Maḥmūd and Aḥmad Khāns and of Sulṭān-nigār and Daulat Khānams. She was widowed in 892H. (1487), and survived Yūnas more than twenty years.

She dwelt in Mughalistān with her elder son, Maḥmūd, the then Khāqān of the Mughals, from the time of Yūnas' death until about 911H. (1505-6). Then 'base advisers provoked a quarrel between the mother and son—a son so obedient that he had never even mounted for a ride without her permission. . . . They [the base advisers] decided to send Shāh Begam to Shāhī Beg Khān to solicit a country for herself, because she found living in Mughalistān distasteful. . . . Now, as the Begam was a very sensible woman, she went under this pretext, and thus left her son before those base advisers could bring about an open rupture, which would have caused endless scandal and reproach to herself. The rumour was that she had gone to entreat Shāhī Beg Khān while she was really enjoying in Samarqand the company of her children.' (*Tar. Rash*, E. & R., 180.)

Shāhī Beg did not permit her to remain in Samarqand but banished her to Khurāsān. From Khurāsān she went with other connections and relations to Bābar in Kābul. They arrived early in 911H. (June, 1505), during the ceremonial mourning for Bābar's mother, Shāh Begam's stepdaughter. With Shāh Begam was Ḥaidar Mīrzā's father and also Bābar's aunt, Mihr-nigār. Ḥaidar says that Bābar gave the party a warm welcome and showed them all possible honour; and that they spent some time in Kābul in the greatest ease and comfort.

Bābar's kindness fell on ungrateful ground, since in the following year, 912H. (1506-7), Shāh Begam fomented a rebellion against him in favour of her grandson, Mīrzā Khān. Ḥaidar says that during Bābar's absence in Harāt her motherly love (it was grandmotherly) began to burn in her heart, and persuaded her that Bābar was dead, and that room was thus made for Mīrzā Khān. The story of Bābar's magnanimity to her when he had put down the rising she had stirred, is well known and is detailed in the histories.

In 913H. (1507-8) she laid claim to Badakhshān, saying that it had been her family's hereditary kingdom for 3,000 years; that though she, a woman, could not attain to sovereignty, her grandson would not be rejected. Bābar assented to her scheme, and she set off for Badakhshān, together with Mihr-nigār Khānam and Mīrzā Khān.

The latter went on in advance to Qila'-ẓafar. The ladies and their escort were at once attacked and plundered by robber bands in the employ of the ruler of Kāshghar, Abā-bakr *Dughlāt*, and were by them conveyed to him in Kāshghar. They were placed in confinement, and 'in the prison of that wicked miscreant they departed from this perishable world' (*cir.* 913H.).

Mems., 12, 13, 22, 32, 60, 74, 99, 104, 105, 106, 169, 216, 217, 231.
Tār. Rash., E. & R., *s.n.*.

CLXXVIII. Shāh Begam *Termiẕī*. (No. 24.)

Daughter of Fakhr-jahān Begam and of Mīr Alā'u-l-mulk *Termiẕī*. She may be 'Kīchak' Begam, and if not, is her sister.

She was the mother of Dil-shād Begam. If she be

Kīchak, she was the wife of Sharafu-d-dīn Ḥusain. (*Cf.* Kīchak.)

She was at the Mystic Feast.

Gul-badan, 24*b*.

CLXXIX. Shāh Khānam. (No. 17.)

Daughter of Badī'u-l-jamāl Begam.

Gul-badan, 24*b*.

CLXXX. Shahr-bānū Begam *Mīrān-shāhī*.

(?) Ar. *shahr*, the moon, the new moon.

Daughter of Sulṭān Abū-sa'īd Mīrzā *Mīrān-shāhī*; wife of Sulṭān Ḥusain Mīrzā *Bāyqrā*, and married to him before his accession in 873H. (March, 1469).

Bābar gives an entertaining detail about her married life. Once at Chekmān her husband was engaged in a battle with her brother Maḥmūd. All his ladies except herself alighted from their litters and mounted on horseback, presumably for rapid flight if the day went against Ḥusain. Shahr-bānū, however, 'relying on her brother,' remained in her litter. This being reported to her husband, he divorced her and married her younger sister, Pāyanda-sulṭān.

Of her subsequent history nothing seems recorded. (*Cf.* Mīnglī-bī *āghācha*.)

Mems., 182.

CLXXXI. Shahr-bānū Begam *Mīrān-shāhī*. (No. 7.)

Third daughter of 'Umar Shaikh Mīrzā *Mīrān-shāhī* and Umīd *Andijānī*; half-sister of Bābar and eight years his junior; born *cir*. 1491; full-sister of Nāṣir and Mihr-bānū; wife of Junaid *Barlās* (brother of Niẓāmu-d-dīn 'Alī *Khalīfa*); mother by him of Sanjar Mīrzā; widowed *cir*. 944H. (1537-38).

She seems to have gone to Sind with her nephew,

Yādgār-nāṣir Mīrzā, in 1540 and after the *débacle* in Hindūstān, for when Yādgār-nāṣir had fled from Sind to Kāmrān in Qandahār (a traitor cast aside by his employer, Shāh Ḥusain *Arghūn*), Kāmrān sent ambassadors to Shāh Ḥusain to request that the begam and her son might be returned to his charge. [Shahr-bānū was Kāmrān's paternal (half)-aunt and full-aunt of Yādgār-nāṣir.]

She was at once started on her journey, but was insufficiently provided with necessaries for traversing the difficult desert tract which stretches towards the western mountain barrier of Sind. Numbers of her party perished before reaching Shāl (Quetta); and many died in that town from 'malignant fever.' Amongst its victims was Shahr-bānū, at the age of about fifty-one years.

Gul-badan, 24*b*.
Mems , 10.
Akbar-nāma, *s.n.*.
B. & H., I. 526 and II. 253. (Here occur errors of statement, *i.e.*, that Shahr-bānū was Yādgār-nāṣir's wife and Kāmrān's sister.)

CLXXXII. Shāh Sulṭān Begam.

(?) Wife of Abū-sa'īd Mīrzā *Mīrān-shāhī;* mother of 'Umar Shaikh Mīrzā.

The news of her death in Andijān reached Bābar in 907H. (1501).

Mems., 20, 99.

CLXXXIII. Shāh-zāda Begam and Sulṭānam Khānam *Ṣafawī*.

The daughter of kings.

Sister of Shāh Ṭahmāsp of Persia. Her protection of the Emperor Humāyūn during his sojourn in Persia is named by many of the historians.

Gul-badan, 58*a*, 58*b*.

CLXXXIV. Shāh-zāda Khānam *Mīrān-shāhī.*

Daughter of Sulaimān Mīrzā *Mīrān-shāhī* and Ḥaram Begam. She was betrothed to Humāyūn in 958H. (1551), but the affair went no further.

Journal of the Royal Asiatic Society, 1898, art. Bāyazīd *bīyāt*, H. Beveridge.
B. & H., II. 397.
Cf. appendix *s.n.* Ḥaram and Fāṭima.

CLXXXV. Sulṭānam Begam *Bāyqrā.*

For meaning of *Sulṭānam*, *cf.* app. *s.n.* Māham.

Daughter of Sulṭān Ḥusain Mīrzā *Bāyqrā* and Chūlī Begam *Azāk*; her father's eldest girl and her mother's only child. She married, first, her cousin Wais, son of her father's elder brother Bāyqrā, and, secondly, 'Abdu-l-bāqī Mīrzā *Mīrān-shāhī.* By her first marriage she had a son, Muḥammad Sulṭān Mīrzā, and a daughter who married Isān-qulī *Shaibānī*, younger brother of Yīlī-bārs Sulṭān. Through her son Muḥammad she was ancestress of those numerous rebel Bāyqrās whom history knows as 'the mīrzās.'

When the Uzbegs took Harāt in 1507 (913H.) she went to Khwārizm, and there her daughter was married. On April 12th, 1519 (Rabī' II. 12th, 925H.), Bābar records her arrival with her daughter in Kābul. He gave her the Garden of Retirement (*Bāgh-i-khilwat*) for her residence, and waited upon her with the ceremony due to an elder sister. He bowed and she bowed; he advanced, they embraced; and having established this form of greeting, they kept to it.

Sulṭānam started from Kābul for India in 1527 with a grandson (her sons had six sons), but she died at the Indus and her body was taken back to Kābul for burial.

There are curious discrepancies of the texts in the passage about Sulṭānam which occurs at Mems., 181.

The first point to note is contained in the words: 'Her elder brother gave her in marriage to Sulṭān

Wais Mīrzā, the son of Miāngī Bāyqrā Mīrzā.' (Mems., 181.)

Barādar kilānash ba pisar miāngī Bāyqrā Mīrzā Sulṭān Wais Mīrzā dāda būd. (*Waqiʿāt-i-bābarī*, Persian text, B.M. Or. 16,623, 123*b*.)

Āghā sī Bāyqrā Mīrzā nīnak ortānchī oghalī Sulṭān Wais Mīrzāgha chīqārīb aidī. (*Tūzūk-i-bābarī* or *Bābar-nāma*, Turkī text, B.M. Add. 26,324, f. 52*b*, and Ilminsky, 209.)

'Son frère ainé l'avait donnée en mariage à Sulṭān Wais Mīrzā, fils cadet de Bāyqrā Mīrzā.' (Pavet de Courteille, I. 375.)

Both the English and French versions make the elder brother of Sulṭānam give her in marriage. But she was an only child, and her father was living to act for her. The French version, here as in so many other places, appears to have relied upon Mr. Erskine. The Turkī text appears to yield something more probable, *i.e.*, 'His elder brother, Bāyqrā Mīrza's middle son, Sulṭān Wais Mīrzā. . . .'

Mr. Erskine has read *miāngī* as part of Bāyqrā's name. Comparison with the Turkī makes appear as the more probable reading: 'the middle son'—*pisar-i-miāngī.*

M. Pavet de Courteille's *fils cadet* lets slip the notion of *mīyān*. Redhouse gives for the *ortānchī oghal* of the Turkī text, 'the middle son out of an odd number' —*e.g.*, the third out of five, the second of three, etc..

In the same passage the Memoirs have: 'Sulṭānam Begam set out along with her grandson. . . .' Here the Persian words *ba hamīn tārīkh* (Turkī, *ushbū tārīkh*) are omitted, with loss of precision, for they fix the date of her journey by conveying the information that it occurred at the time of her son's appointment to the government of Kanauj, *i.e.*, April, 1527.

Mems., 181, 190, 266.
Habību-s-siyār, 327 *et seq.*.
Also the places mentioned in the notice above.

CLXXXVI. Sulṭānam Begam *Mīrān-shāhī*. (No. 12.)

Daughter of Sulṭān Aḥmad Mīrzā.

A Sulṭānam of this parentage is mentioned by Bābar (Mems., 22), by Ḥaidar (E. & R., *s.n.*), and by Gulbadan (24*b*). These appear to be at least two, and perhaps are three women. Their record is as follows:

(1). Sulṭānam, fourth daughter of Sulṭān Aḥmad Mīrzā. (Mems., 22.) She was the child of Qūtūq (Katak) Begam. She married her cousin 'Alī, son of Maḥmūd Mīrzā. 'Alī was murdered by Shaibānī (*cf. s.n.* Zuhra) in 906H. (July, 1500), and his widow was taken to wife by Shaibānī's son, Muḥammad Tīmūr. A third marriage is mentioned by Bābar, viz., to Mahdī Sulṭān. By this style the histories mention the Uzbeg chief who was associated with Ḥamza (Khamza) Sulṭān. But this Mahdī was put to death by Bābar in 1511, and Tīmūr was living in 1512 (918H.). Either Sulṭānam was divorced, perhaps to make marriage with some other kinswoman and later captive legal; or Mahdī Sulṭān may be the father of 'Adil Sulṭān; or he may be Maḥdī Muḥammad Khwāja.

(2). Sulṭānam, daughter of Sulṭān Aḥmad Mīrzā, married Muḥammad Ḥusain *Dughlāt* in the autumn of 1503. She was given to her husband by Khusrau Shāh who describes her as daughter of Sulṭān Aḥmad Mirzā *wa pādshāh-zāda-i-man*, by which Mr. Ross has understood that she was of Khusrau's 'family.' There was a son, issue of this marriage and named 'Abdu-l-lāh.

It is difficult to regard No. 1 and No. 2 as one woman, both because of their marriage dates and of the circumstance that No. 1 was an Uzbeg captive and No. 2 in Badakhshān. Bābar mentions no marriage of a Sulṭānam with Muḥammad Ḥusain *Dughlāt*. A surmise—it is nothing more—has occurred to me, namely: No. 2 was married to the Dughlāt mīrzā shortly after the destruction of Tāshkend; Bābar's wife 'Āyisha, third daughter of Sulṭān Aḥmad *Mīrān-shāhī*, had left Bābar shortly before that disaster. She might be Sulṭānam No. 2.

(3). Sulṭānam, or Sulṭānī, daughter of Sulṭan Aḥmad Mīrzā, was at the Mystic Feast in 1531. She is said to be the mother of Kilān Khān Begam. This title is not appropriate for the child of any of the marriages mentioned for No. 1 or No. 2. It is quite appropriate for the child of the marriage of Sulṭan Aḥmad and Qūtūq's firstborn daughter, Rabī'a-sulṭān, because Rabī'a married Sulṭān Maḥmūd Khān who was the Elder Khān (*kilān*) and also the Great Khān (*Khāqān*) of the Mughals. Shaibānī murdered five of Maḥmūd's six sons, but probably his girls escaped because of their value as wives.

The above notes make for the opinion that Sulṭānam is a title, and not a name. *Cf.* app. *s.n.* Māham.

Mems., 22.
Gul-badan, 24*b*.
Tār. Rash., E. & R., 164, 170, 193.

CLXXXVII. Sulṭānam. (No. 52.)

Wife of Niẓāmu-d-dīn 'Alī *Khalīfa*.

Gul-badan, 14*a*, 14*b*, 26*a*, 50*a*.

CLXXXVIII. Sulṭān-nigār Khānam *Chaghatāī Mughal*.

Daughter of Yūnas Khān *Chaghatāī* and Shāh Begam *Badakhshī*; wife of Sulṭān Maḥmūd Mīrzā *Mīrān-shāhī*; mother of Sulṭān Wais (Khān Mīrzā); widowed in 900H. (January, 1495).

On Maḥmūd's death in Samarqand she joined her brothers in Tāshkand, going off 'without giving any notice of her intentions,' says Bābar. Later on she married Awīq (Adīk) Sulṭān *Jūjī*, the chief of the *Uzbeg Qazāqs*. Her story is somewhat confused in the Memoirs (13 and 14) by a double mention of her marriage to Awīq. Ḥaidar Mīrzā throws some light, and it seems that when Shaibānī had murdered her brother, Mahmūd Khān, Awīq left him and joined the Uzbeg Qazāqs, his own people, and Sulṭān-nigar followed him into Mughalistān.

She had two daughters by Awīq, one of whom married ʿAbdu-l-lāh *Qūchīn* and died a young wife, and the other married Rashīd Sulṭān *Chaghatāī*.

On Awīq's death, Sulṭān-nigār was married to his brother Qāsim, presumably in consonance with the Turkī custom of *yang-lik*.

With Qāsim's death, the khānship of the *Qazāqs* devolved on Sulṭān-nigār's stepson (*i.e.*, Awīq's by a co-wife) named Ṭāhir. 'He was,' says Ḥaidar, 'very much attached to her, and even preferred her to the mother who had given him birth.'

What follows is full of colour and feeling. Nigār-sulṭān showed her appreciation of Ṭāhir's affection, but petitioned him, saying: 'Although you are (as) my child, and I neither think of nor desire any son but you, yet I wish you to take me to my nephew, Sulṭān Saʿīd Khān. For I am grown old, and I have no longer the strength to bear this wandering life in the deserts of Uzbegistān. Take me where I may enjoy some quiet and repose.' She then offered to mediate for him and to obtain the support for him of the Mughal Khāqāns against his foes. Ṭāhir accordingly escorted her to the Mughalistān borders, and with her waited upon Saʿīd. 'The latter, from love of his aunt, rose, saying that although his rising to receive Ṭāhir was contrary to the rules of Chingīz (their common ancestor), yet that he did it out of gratitude because Ṭāhir had brought his aunt.'

Sulṭān-nigār died of a hæmorrhage in the summer of 934H. (1528).

Mems., 13, 14, 30, 31, 99, 105.
Tār. Rash., E. & R., *s.n.*

CLXXXIX. *Tarkhān* Begam.

This is a title, and not a personal name.

In Bābar's time, according to Mr. Erskine (Mems., 24 n.), the ancient title of *Tarkhān* had come to belong to a particular family or clan. This may be well seen by consulting Professor Blochmann's *Āīn-i-akbarī*, 361, where the genealogical table of the Arghūns of Tatta shows the title to have become hereditary in their branch of the Arghūns.[1]

The Tarkhān Begam whose name stands above this notice was linked with these Tarkhān Arghūns in the way shown below. She married her first cousin, Aḥmad *Mīrān-shāhī*, and Qūtūq Begam was her foster-sister.

Urda-būghā *Tarkhān Arghūn.*

Daughter = Abū-sa'īd *Mīrān-shāhī.* — Darvish Muḥammad *Tarkhān.* — Daughter = 'Abdu-l-'alī *Tarkhān Arghūn*, d. *cir.* 1490. — Muḥammad Mazīd *Tarkhān.*

Maḥmūd, b. 1453. — Aḥmad, b. 1451; d. 1490. = Tarkhān Begam. — Bāqī *Tarkhān.*

Mems , 22, 24.
Āīn-i-akbarī, Blochmann, 361.
B. & H., I. and II. *s.n.* Sind, Arghūn, etc..

CXC. *Tarkhān* Begam and Bega.

Gul-badan, 75*b*.

(Tarsūn-sulṭān, Yūn, *q.v.*)

---

[1] Professor Blochmann (*l.c.*) states that 'Abdu-l-'alī and five sons were murdered by Shaibānī, but Bābar and the Sind historians give no support to the story. It looks as though by some clerical error the account of the murder of Sulṭān Maḥmūd Khān and his sons had crept in here. Shaibānī drove Bāqī out of his late father's government of Bukhārā.

CXCI. Ulugh Begam. (No. 10.)

Daughter of Zainab Sulṭān Begam ; grand-daughter of Sulṭān Abū-sa'īd ; first cousin of Bābar.

Gul-badan, 24*b*.

CXCII. Ulūs (Anūsh and Alūsh) *āghā Turkomān*. (? No. 53)

Turkī, *ūlūs*, tribe. Clearly a title.

Daughter of Khwāja Ḥusain Beg *Turkomān* of the White Sheep, an amīr of 'Umar Shaikh *Mīrān-shāhī* ; wife of 'Umar Shaikh ; mother of a girl who died in infancy. She was removed from the *ḥaram* a year or eighteen months after her marriage. Gul-badan mentions a begam of this name as at Hindāl's wedding-feast ; whether she is Ūlūs *āghā* promoted, I have no means of knowing.

Mems., 14.
Gul-badan, 26*a*.

CXCIII. Ūmīd *āghācha Andijānī*.

Pers. *ūmīd*, hope.

An inferior wife of 'Umar Shaikh Mīrzā *Mīrān-shāhī* whom she predeceased. She was the mother of Mihr-bānū who was two years older than Bābar and will have been born therefore in 1481 ; of Nāṣir who was born in 1487 ; and of Shahr-bānū who was born in 1491.

Mems., 10, 14.

CXCIV. Umm-kulṣūm Begam *Mīrān-shāhī*.

A surname of Fāṭima, daughter of Muḥammad ; Ar. *umm*, mother, and *kulṣūm*, plumpness.

Grand-daughter of Gul-badan Begam and a member of the Ḥaj of 983H..

Akbar-nāma, III. 145.

CXCV. Ūzūn-sulṭān Khānam *Chaghatāī Mughal.*

(?) Pers. *auzūn*, or *ūzūn*, ample, increase.

Daughter of Shīr 'Alī Khān *Oghlan Chaghatāī*; sister of Wais Khān and Makhdūma Khanām; paternal aunt of Yūnas Khān; wife of Amīr Sayyid 'Alī *Dughlāt;* mother of Muḥammad Ḥaidar *Dughlāt* and great-grandmother of Ḥaidar Mīrzā, the historian.

She was widowed in 862H. (1457-58), and then, in conjunction with her son, received Kāshghar and Yangī-ḥiṣār from her stepson, Sāniz.

Tār. Rash., E. & R., 64, 87, 88.

CXCVI. Yādgār-sulṭān Begam *Mīrān-shāhī.* (No. 8.)

Pers. *yādgār*, remembrance.

Daughter of 'Umar Shaikh *Mīrān-shāhī* and Āghā Sulṭān *āghācha;* half-sister of Bābar, and brought up by his grandmother, Isān-daulat. She was a posthumous child, and, if one may draw an inference from her example and others similar, is for this reason called Yādgār (Souvenir). Her father died Ramẓan 4th, 899H. (June 9th, 1494). When a child of not more than ten, and in 908H. (1503), she fell into the hands of 'Abdu-l-laṭīf *Uzbeg*, after the conquest of Andijān and Akhsī by Shaibānī, and in 916H. (1511) Bābar's successes at Khutlān and Ḥiṣār enabled her to return to him and her own people.

I do not find any marriage mentioned for her by her name.

She is in the list of the guests at the Mystic Feast, and her mother is named (as such) as present at Hindāl's wedding festivities.

Mems., 10.
Gul-badan, 24*b*, 26*b*.

CXCVII. Yūn (Tarsūn)-sulṭān *Mughal.*

Ilminsky, 15, writes *Tarsūn*.

Inferior wife of 'Umar Shaikh, and married at the end of his life.

Mems., 14.

CXCVIII. Zainab-sulṭān Begam *Mīrān-shāhī.*

(?) From Ar. *zain*, adorning.

Fifth daughter of Sulṭān Maḥmūd Mīrzā and Khān-zāda Begam (*b.*) *Termiẕī;* first cousin and wife of Bābar.

She was married at the instance of Qūt-līq-nigār, in the year of the capture of Kābul, *i.e.*, 910H. (1504-5), perhaps at the time that Jahāngīr Mīrzā, Bābar's half-brother, married her half-sister, Āq Begam. The marriage was not happy. Two or three years later Zainab died of small-pox.

Mems., 30.

CXCIX. Zainab-sulṭān Khānam *Chaghatāī Mughal.*

(No. 19.)

Daughter of Sulṭān Maḥmūd Khān *Chaghatāī Mughal;* favourite wife of Sulṭān Sa'īd Khān *Kāshgharī*, her first cousin; aunt of Shāh Muḥammad Sulṭān whom Muḥammadī *Barlās* put to death; mother of Ibrāhīm who was born 930H. (1524), Sa'īd's third son and favourite child, of Muhṣin, and of Maḥmūd Yūsuf.

On her husband's death in 939H. (July, 1533), she was banished by her stepson Rashīd, and went with her children to Kabul where she met Ḥaidar Mīrzā and where she was under the protection of Kāmrān.

Gul-badan mentions her in the guest-list, and places her name as present at the Mystic Feast (1531), but this can hardly be right. She could easily have been at the marriage festivities in 1537.

Tār. Rash., E. & R., 146, 375, 383, 467.
Gul-badan, 11*a*, 24*b*.

CC. Zainab-sulṭān Begam *Mīrān-shāhī.*

Gul-badan describes her as the paternal aunt or great-aunt (*'ama*) of Humāyūn. Bābar had no such sister, and no Zainab is mentioned by Gul-badan as a daughter of his grandfather Abū-sa'īd. An Āq Begam, however, is spoken of by her, and Zainab may be her personal name. Zainab had a daughter Ulugh Begam.

Gul-badan, 24*b*.

CCI. Zainab-sulṭān Begam.

There is a difficulty in identifying the begam of this name, whom Bābar mentions (Mems., 387) as coming to India. It will be seen by comparing the sources and their French and English interpretations:

Mems., 387. 'another, by name Zainab-sulṭān Begam, the granddaughter of Bikeh Chichām.'
P. de C., II. 355. 'et la petite-fille de Yenga-Tchetcham, autrement dite Zeineb-sulṭān Begam.'
B. M. Or., 3714, Pers., p. 482. *dīgar nabīra yanga chichām ki Zainab-sulṭān Begam būshad.*
Bodleian, Elliot, 19, f. 180*a*. *dīgar nabīra bega chichām ki Zainab-sulṭān Begam.*
Ilminsky, Turkī text, 447. *yana, yanga chichām ki Zainab-sulṭān Begam būlaghā'ī nabīra sī kīlīb.*

It seems safer to take Zainab as the name of Bābar's relation (*i.e.*, the *yanga* of his *chicha*) than as that of the granddaughter (*nabīra*).

It may be observed here that the best authorities quoted above, *i.e.*, Ilminsky, behind whom is Kehr, and Or., 3714, have *yanga* where Mr. Erskine and Elliot, 19, have *bega*. This exchange may occur in the case of other *begas* of this appendix. Until a good Turkī text more complete than that in the B. M. is found, this must be left an open question.

If *Zainab* be taken as the name of the *yanga*, she may be identifiable with one of the other women already entered in the appendix, but for deciding this point more examples are necessary of Bābar's application of the word *yanga*.

Mems., 387.

CCII. Zobaida *āghācha Jalāīr*.

The marigold; Ar. *zubaida*.

Grand-daughter of Ḥusain Shaikh Tīmūr of the Shaibān Sulṭāns. According to the *Ḥabibu-s-siyār*, she was a *Jalair*.

She was an inferior wife of Sulṭān Ḥusain Mīrzā and the mother of 'Āyisha Begam. She predeceased her husband who died April, 1506.

CCIII. Zuhra Begī and Āghā *Uzbeg*.

Ar. *zuhra*, beauty, a yellow flower, the star Venus.

An inferior wife of Sulṭān Maḥmūd Mīrzā; mother of Makhdūma-sulṭān Begam and of Sulṭān 'Alī Mīrzā.

She was married during the lifetime of Maḥmūd's father, and therefore before Rajab 873H. (January, 1469), and was widowed Rabī II., 900H. (January, 1495). In 905H. (1499-1500) she entered into an intrigue with Shaibānī, a fellow-tribesman, of which the ultimate aim was dominance in Samarqand for her son 'Alī. A part of her scheme and offer was her own remarriage with Shaibānī. Bābar stigmatizes her action as 'stupidity and folly,' and says, further, 'the wretched and weak woman, for the sake of getting herself a husband, gave the family and honour of her son to the winds. Nor did Shaibānī Khān mind her a bit, or value her even so much as his other handmaids, concubines, or women. Sulṭān 'Alı Mīrza was confounded at the condition in which he now found himself, and deeply regretted the step he had taken. Several young cavaliers formed a plan for escaping with him, but he would not consent. As the hour of fate was at hand, he could not shun it. They put him to death in the meadow of Kulba. From his overanxiety to preserve this mortal and transitory life, he left a name of infamy behind him; and, from following the suggestions of a woman, struck himself out of the list of those who have earned for themselves a glorious name. It is impossible to write any more of the transactions of such a personage (? Zuhra), and impossible to listen any further to the recital of such base and dastardly proceedings.'

Mems., 29, 30, 31, 83, 84.

APPENDIX B.

Mahdī Khwāja.

Niẓāmu-d-dīn Aḥmad has included in his *Ṭabaqāt-i-akbarī* a story which he heard from his father Muḥammad Muqīm *Harāwī*, and of which the purport is that Bābar's *Khalīfa* (Niẓāmu-d-dīn 'Alī *Barlās*) had at one time thought of placing a certain Mahdī Khwāja on the throne in succession to Bābar.

Two circumstances cast doubt on the story: (1) It was customary in Bābar's family for a son to succeed his father; (2) Bābar left four sons, the youngest of whom, Hindāl, was eleven years old.

Moreover, there were Tīmūrids both of the Bāyqrā and Mīrān-shāhī branches in India with Bābar whose claims to a Tīmūrid throne would be strongly enforced.

But Niẓāmu-d-dīn Aḥmad has left us the story in circumstantial detail and it cannot be passed over unnoticed, and this the less because Gul-badan Begam throws some light on the identity of the Mahdī concerned, and also because in an important particular, *i.e.*, the relation of Mahdī to Bābar, I am able, through Mr. Beveridge's study of the *Ḥabību-s-siyār*, to give more accurate information than was at Mr. Erskine's disposal.

The story was old when Niẓāmu-d-dīn set it down and it is not necessary to accept all its details as exact. It is sufficient to consider its minimum contents which are, that in the royal household there had been a rumour of a plan of supersession of Bābar's sons by Mahdī Khwāja at the instance of Khalīfa.

The question naturally arises, who was the man

concerning whom such intention could be attributed to the wise and experienced Khalīfa?

Niẓāmu-d-dīn calls Mahdī Bābar's *damād*, and Mr. Erskine, amongst other translators, has rendered this by son-in-law. It is unnecessary to consider why any Mahdī Khwāja known in history should have been preferred to those sons-in-law who were of Bābar's own blood, because Gul-badan calls Mahdī Bābar's *yazna*. For this word the dictionaries yield only the meaning of 'brother-in-law' and 'husband of the king's sister.' Both these meanings are also attributed to *damād*. But the *Ḥabīb* settles the verbal question by a statement that Mahdī Khwāja was the husband of Khān-zāda Begam, Bābar's full sister.

It is not improbable that he had another close link with the Emperor, namely that of relationship to Māham Begam, but I am not yet able to assert this definitely.

Bābar never mentions Mahdī Khwāja's parentage. This is learned from Khwānd-amīr who states that he was the son of Mūsa Khwāja and grandson of Murtaza Khwāja. He was a sayyid; and from the circumstance that his burial-place was chosen as that of Sayyid Abū'l-ma'ālī *Termiẕī*, it may be inferred that he belonged to the religious house of Termiẕ. If so, he had probably Tīmūrid blood in his veins, since intermarriage between the families was frequent.

Bābar mentions a Khwāja Mūsa who is perhaps Mahdī's father, in 914H., 1508. He immediately afterwards names Khwāja Muḥammad 'Alī, Māham Begam's brother, in suggestive sequence.

Bābar's first surviving record of Mahdī is made in 925H. (February, 1519) when 'Mīr Muḥammad Mahdī Khwāja' brings in a prisoner. It is in *cir.* 923H. (1517) that Khwānd-amīr speaks of the marriage of Mahdī and Khān-zāda, but this is probably a good deal after the fact, because Khān-zāda was returned to Bābar in 917H. (1511).

Mahdī Khwāja, as Bābar invariably calls him after his first appearance, went to Hindūstān with Bābar and is frequently mentioned. It is significant of his high position and presumably not only by marriage but by birth, that on military duty he is always associated with men of royal blood, either Tīmūrid or Chaghatāī. He is sometimes given precedence of them, and is never named last in a list of officers. Chīn-tīmūr *Chaghatāī*, Muḥammad Sulṭān Mīrzā *Bāyqrā*, Sulṭān Mīrzā *Mīrān-shāhī*, and 'Ādil Sulṭān are constantly associated with him. It seems clear that he was a great noble and ranked amongst the highest. Khāfī Khān calls him Sayyid Khwāja, and so does Khwānd-amīr. Whether the 'Khwāja' indicates anything as to his mother's marriage I am not able to say.

Khāfī Khān (I. 42) has a passage which *may* relate to him: *Sulṭān Mīrzā wa Mahdī Sulṭān binī a'māmrā* (of Bābar) *ki asīr-i-ān juma' būdand khalāṣ sakht.* The date of the occurrence is *cir.* 1511, the year in which another Mahdī, *i.e.*, *Uzbeg*, was killed by Bābar. Mr. Erskine appears to think that the two men, named here as released, were Ḥamza and Mahdī Sulṭāns *Uzbeg*, but the sources do not give the style of Mīrzā to either of these chiefs. They appear to have had marriage connections with Bābar in an earlier generation, and a son of Mahdī seems to have been 'Ādil Sulṭān (Mems., 363) who was father of 'Āqil Sulṭān *Uzbeg* (*Akbar-nāma*, I. 221).

A Mahdī Khwāja who was undoubtedly of Bābar's family, appears both in the *Tārīkh-i-rashīdī* and in Gul-badan Begam's *Humāyūn-nāma.* He is the son of Aiman, and grandson of Sulṭān Aḥmad Khān *Chaghatāī*, Bābar's mother's brother. But his age places him out of the question; he was about ten in 1530, and the hero of Niẓāmu-d-dīn's story stroked his beard, and was either a *damād* or a *yazna.* Mahdī

Chaghatāī, moreover, reached India after Bābar's death.[1]

The *Ṭabaqāt* states that Mahdī Khwāja had long been connected with Khalīfa; the latter was himself a sayyid.

Niẓāmu-d-dīn calls Mahdī a *jūwan* and Mr. Erskine has accentuated all the faults and characteristics of youth in his version of the story. But Gul-badan calls Hindāl an uninjurious youth at thirty-three, and there seems good ground to read often in *jūwan* the notion of vigour and strength rather than exclusively of fewness of years. In 1530 Mahdī had served Bābar eleven known years.

Like many other such small problems, that of the family connections of Mahdī Khwāja and the other men of his name may be solved by some chance passage in a less known author, or by a closer consideration of the personages of the Memoirs.

Mems., 255, 303, 305-307, 338, 340-342, 344, 345, 349, 352, 363, 370, 371, 401, 426.[2]
Akbar-nāma, *s.n.*, 'Áqil Sulṭān and Mahdī.
Khāfī Khān, *Bib. Ind.* ed., *s.n.*.
Ḥabibu-s-siyār, Khwānd-amīr, under date *cir.* 923H..
Cf. Index to this volume, *s.n.* Mahdī.

---

[1] The rough estimate of Mahdī *Chaghatāī's* age is made as follows: Aiman was married to Ḥaidar Mīrzā's cousin in 923H. (1517). (*Tār. Rash.*, E. and R., 144, 352.) He had five sons by this wife. (l. c. 144 and 401). Of these Ma'sūd is named as the eldest. The rest are Khiẓr (Gul-badan's husband) Mahdī, Isān-daulat (Ḥabība's husband), and another. Khiẓr is inferentially the second son, but if Mahdī were the second, he could hardly have been born before 926H. (1520). This would make him about ten in 1530, but he may have been younger and the third son, as is indicated by the enumeration of Ḥaidar Mīrzā.

[2] At p. 424 Mr. Erskine has an entry of a Sayyid Mahdī who arrives from Guālīār in July, 1529. That this is a mis-reading for Mashhadī is shown by collation with other texts than his own.

INDEX (OTHER THAN OF PLACES).

NOTE.—This index is full for the pages down to 201. It gives the Roman-numbered names only of Appendix A.

Reference to the Persian imprint is by folio numbering. This is reproduced accurately from the MS., in the Persian imprint, and as closely as the sentences permit in the translation.

Words in *'āīn*, *ghain*, etc., are classed with their nearest equivalents.

INDEX OF PLACES.

همایون نامه

تصنیف گلبدن بیگم بنتِ بابر بادشاه*

* (Note to بادشاه) *This title is inscribed on the first fly-leaf of the volume containing the M.S. It is upon paper of colour and kind differing from that of the M.S. and identical with four blank pages bound up at the end of the volume, possibly with the intention of writing up the missing terminal portion of the work.*

احوال همایون بادشاه

جمع کرده گلبدن بیگم بنتِ بابر بادشاه عمهٔ اکبر بادشاه*

Copied from the British Museum Persian M.S. (Or. 166),
by Annette S. Beveridge.

* (بادشاه) *This title stands on the first page of the M.S. and on paper like that of the M.S.. The page is numbered 15 in the Arabic and 2 in the B.M. marking. The M.S. is numbered by folios, and both with Arabic figures—inscribed in India—and with Roman, added by the B.M.. This reproduction and the translation of the M.S. are numbered in agreement with the Roman figures. A subdivision of folios into pages (1a, 1b &c.) allows easier reference. One index serves for both parts (Persian text and translation).*

(2 b)

بســم الله الرحمن الرحيم

حکم شده بود که آنچه از واقعهٔ فردوس مکانی وحضرت جنّت آشیانی میدانسته باشید بنویسید* وقتی که حضرت فردوس مکانی از دار الفنا بدار البقا خرامیدند ـ این حقیر هشت ساله بود و بیان* واقع شاید کمترك بخاطر مانده بود* بنابر حکم پادشاهی آنچه شنیده و بخاطر بود نوشته میشود*

در اوّل این جُزو از واقعهٔ حضرت بادشاه بابام نوشته میشود ـ اگرچه در واقعه نامهٔ حضرت بادشاه بابام این سخنان مذکور است ـ بنابر تیمنًا و تبرکًا نوشته میشود*

از زمان حضرت صاحب قرانی تا زمان حضرت فردوس مکانی از سلاطین ماضیه هیچکس برابر ایشان ترددات نکرده* در دُوازده سالگی بادشاه شدند و بتاریخ پنجم شهر رمضان المبارك سنه نهصد ونه در خطّه** اندجان (3a) که پای تخت ولایت فرغانه است ـ خطبه خوانده* مدّت یازده ساله کمال در الکه ماور النهر با سلاطین چغتیه و تیموریه و اوزبکیه جنگها و ترددات نموده اند که زبانِ قلم از شرح تعداد آن عاجز وقاسر است* وآنقدر محنت و مهالك که در باب جهانگیری بحضرتِ مَا رُوی نموده ـ کم کس را روی نموده باشد* وآن قدر دلیری و مردانگی

* (بیان) Misread in translating as به این.

** (خطه) A.F. (Bib. Ind. 87) has خطّهٔ دلکشای.

1*

وتحمّل که بانحضرت معارک* ومهلك روی نموده — ازکم بادشاهی منقول
است * دو نوبت بضرب شمشیر فتح سمرقند کرده * مرتبه اوّل حضرت بادشاه
بابام دوازده ساله بوده اند ومرتبه دویم نوزده ساله بوده اند ومرتبه سیوم
٢٢ بیست ودو ساله بوده اند — وشش ماهه قبلی شده اند ومثل سلطان حسین
میرزا بایقرا عموی ایشان در خراسان بوده اند — بایشان کومك نفرستادند
وسلطان محمود خان در کاشغر بودند که طغائ ایشان باشند — ایشان نیز
کومك نفرستادند * چون مدد ومعاونت ازهیچ جا نرسیده — مایوس شدند *

درین طور وقت شاهی بیگ خان گفته فرستاد که اگر (3b) خانزاده بیگم
خواهر خودرا بمن نسبت کنید میان ماو شما صلح شود ورابطه اتحاد بجا باشد *
آخر ضرورت شد خانزاده بیگم را بخان مذکور نسبت کرده خود بر آمدند *
با دویست کس پیاده ودرکتف چپان** ودر پائ آنها چاروق — ایلیك***

---

* (معارك) Comparing this passage with A. F.'s parallel passage (*Bib. Ind.* I. 67), we find a curious resemblance, e. g. وآن قدر مشقّت وتردد که — — آنحضرت‌را پیش آمده کم پادشاهی‌را رو نموده باشد — وآن قدر دلیری — — وتحمّل که آنحضرت — — در معارك — — —

** Pavet de Courteille and Steingass render *chapān* by *haillons* and „tattered garments", Erskine (127 and n.) by "long frocks". Vambéry gives no *chapān* but *chāpān*, which he translates *Oberrock* and *pardessus.* Steingass has no *chāpān*.

*** (چاروق) The words of the next phrase present difficulty. The sense is "with clubs in their hands", and that this is so, is shewn by the parallel passages from the Turkī and Persian texts of Bābar's Memoirs. (Turkī) اکثر یایاق وایلیك لاریدا تایاق و ایاق لاریدا چاروق و ایکین لاریدا چاپان ایردی (B.M. Add. 26, 324 p. 4. Ilminski has verbal variants). (Persian) در دستهای ایشان چوبها و در پاهای ایشان چاروق و بر کتفهای ایشان چاپان. The difficult words may be a Turkī interpolation in Gul-badan's text. The word which follows چاروق may be read المسك leathern, but چاروق includes the notion of leathern and neither the Turkī nor the Persian text uses any such qualifying word. I propose to read the words as a Turkī phrase — ایلیك لاریدا چوباق. It may be that when Gul-badan was writing she had her Father's book before her. Her close reproduction of his words points to this or to intimate recollection of his words.

لاریه چویاق — باین طور حال بی یراق توکّل بحضرت حق سبحانه کرده متوجه بدخشانات وکابل شده *

در قندز وبدخشانات لشکر ومردمِ خشرو شاه بُودند * آمده حضرت بادشاه بابام‌را ملازمت کرده * باوجود گناهان که بدکرده — مانند بایسنغر میرزارا شهید کرده وسُلطان مسعُود میرزارا میل کشیده بودند واین هردو میرزا عموزادهٔ بادشاه بابام بوده اند — وقبل از آن که عبورِ آن حضرت در ایّام قزّاقیها بولایتِ او افتاده بود — از ضرورت رفته بودند — بمحصّلیها ودرشتیهاء آنحضرت‌را از ولایت خود بدر کرده بود * وحضرت بادشاه که مفهوم مردی ومردمی ومُروّت بوده اند — اصلاً وقطعًا در مقام انتقامِ آن نشدند وفرموده اند که ازجواهر وطلا آلات هرچند که دلش خواهد بردارد — وپنجشش قطار شتر وپنجشش (4a) استر بار همراه برده بصحت وسلامت رخصت یافته بخراسان رفته وحضرت بادشاه متوجه کابل شدند *

در آن وقت تحکم کابل محمّد مقیم — پسرِ ذو النون ارغون که پدر کلانِ ناهید بیگم بود — داشت * کابل‌را بعد از وفات الغ بیگ میرزا — ازعبد الرزاق میرزا گرفته واز (?آن) میرزا عبد الرزاق مذکور عموزادهٔ بادشاه بوده *

بادشاه بدولت بکابل آمدند * دوسه روز قلعگی شد وبعد از چند روز بعهد وقول کابل‌را به بندگان حضرت بادشاه سپُرده با مال واسباب خود بقندهار پیش پدرِ خود رفت *

وفتح کابل در اواخر ماه ربیع الثانی سنه ۹۱۰ نهصد وده بوده * بعد از میر شدن کابل به بنگش رفتند ویکباره الجه کرده بکابل آمدند *

وحضرت خانم که والدهٔ حضرت بادشاه باشند — در شش روز تب کرده — از عالم فانی بدار البقا رحلت نمُودند * ودر باغ نوروزی حضرت

خانم‌را ماندند[*] * صاحبانِ باغ که مردم وصیل[**] انکه[***] باشند — یکهزار تنکه مشقالی داده گذاشتند *

درین اثنا فرمانهائ سلطان حسین میرزا بتاکید آمدند که ما (4b) خیال جنگ باوزبک[†] داریم * اگر شما هم بیائید بسیار خوبست * حضرت آنمعنی‌را از خدا میطلبیدند * عاقبت الامر بسوی ایشان روانه گشتند * در اثنای طی طریق خبر آمد که سُلطان حسین میرزا شنقار شدند * امرای حضرت بادشاه بعرض رسانیدند که چُون سُلطان حسین میرزا شنقار شدند — مناسب آنست که برگشته بکابل باید رفت * حضرت فرمودند که چون اینمقدار راه آمده ایم بمیرزا عزاپرسی نموده بر بردیم * عاقبت الامر متوجه خراسان شدند * چون از تشریف آوردن بادشاه که میرزایان شنیدند هر همه باستقبال روان شدند — غیر بدیع الزمان میرزا که برنتوق[††] بیگ وذو النون بیگ که امرائ سُلطان حسین میرزا بودند — چنین گفتند که چون بادشاه از بدیع الزمان میرزا خوردند پانزده ۱۵ ساله — مناسب چنان است که پادشاه زانوزده دریابند * درین اثنا قاسم بیگ گفته که بسال خوردند امّا بتوره کلانند — از برای آنکه چند مرتبه بضرب شمشیر فتح سمرقند کرده اند * آخر چنین قرار دادند (5a) که یکمرتبه بادشاه زانوزده

---

* (ماندند) Used transitively. So too at 59a &c..

** (وصیل) Text ویصل.

*** (انکه) This word may be *atka* or *anaga* and is to be explained by the known ownership of the garden which was made by Bābar's paternal uncle, Ulugh Beg. But for the undotted "prop", it might have been read as اکه and as referring to Khān-zāda Begam or Māham, Bābar's wife, both of whom, as will be noticed, are styled *āka* (*janām*) and *āka* respectively. Cf. a use of انکه p. 28b.

† (باوزبک) Vambéry's derivation of this multiform word, "Özbeg, his own master, independent" (History of Bokhara, 245) is at least *ben trovato* and in congruity with the acts of the tribe. But several careful writers, Blochmann amongst them, have chosen the form *Uzbak*.

†† (برنتوق) Text, *sic* for برندوق.

دریابند* بدیع الزمان میرزا از جهة تعظیم بادشاه پیش آمده دریابند* در این اثنا بادشاه از در درآمدند* میرزا غافل بودند که قاسم بیگ فوطهٔ حضرت بادشاه را گرفته کشیده با برنتوق بیگ و ذو النون بیگ گفت که قرار چنین داده بودند که میرزا پیش درآمده دریابند* درین اثنا میرزا باضطراب تمام پیش درآمده حضرت پادشاه‌را دریافتند*

وچند روزی که در خراسان بودند میرزایان هرکدام تکلیفِ میزمانی می نمودند وجشنهای میکردند وتمامی باغات و محلات‌را سیر مینمودند* میرزایان تکلیفِ زمستان نمودند که توقّف نمایند که بعد از زمستان باوزبک جنگ میکنیم* امّا اصلاً وقطعًا نتوانستند بجنگ قرار داد*

مدّت هشتاد سال خراسان‌را سُلطان حسین میرزا ابادان ومعمُور ساخته بُود — امّا میرزایان تا شش ماه نتوانستند که جای پدررا نگاه دارند*

وچون پادشاه ایشان‌را بی پروا دیدند بجهة خرج وخراجات ایشان (5 b) جاها تعین نموده بودند وببهانهٔ دیدن آنجاها بجانب کابل روان شدند*

ودر آن سال برف بسیار باریده بود* راهها غلط کردند* حضرت و قاسم بیگ از برای نزدیکئ راه — این راه‌را اختیار نموده بودند والا امرای دیگر کنگایش داده بودند* چُون که گفته امراها نکردند — این‌ها هر یك تغافل کرده — میرفتند* حضرت وقاسم بیگ مع پسران خود تا سه چهار روز برف دور کرده راه‌را طیار میکردند ومردم لشکر از عقب میگذشتند* باین روش تا بغوربند رسیدند ودر آنجا از هزارهای باغی بحضرت ور خورده جنگ کردند* از گاو و گوسفند بسیار واشیای بیشمار از مردم هزارها بدست مردم بادشاهی افتاد وباولجه بیحد متوجه کابل شدند*

در پای منار که رسیدند — شنیدند که میرزا خان ومیرزا محمّد حسین کورکان باغی شده اند وکابل‌را قبل دارند* بمردم کابل حضرت بادشاه فرمانهای دلداری ودلاسای نوشته فرستادند که مردانه باشید — ما هم آمدیم*

در بلای (6a) کوه بیبی ماه روی آتش خواهم انداخت وشما هم در بالای خزانه‌خانه آتش اندازید تا دانیم که از آمدن ما خبردار شده اید * وقت صُبح از آنجانب شما و از این‌جانب ما مقابله غنیم خواهیم شد * امّا تاآمدن مردم قعله حضرت جنگ کرده وفتح کرده بودند *

میرزا خان در خانهٔ والدهٔ خود که خالهٔ بادشاه بودند — پنهان شدند * آخر خانم پسر خودرا آورده — گناه طلبیدند — ومیرزا محمّد حسین در خانهٔ کوچ خود که خالهٔ خورد بادشاه بود — از وهم جان خودرا در مفرش انداخته خدمتگاری را گفت که بربند * عاقبت الامر مردم بادشاهی خبردار شده — میرزا محمّد حسین‌را از مفرش بر آورده پیش بادشاه آوردند * عاقبت الامر حضرت بخاطر خالهای خود گناهٔ میرزا محمّد حسین‌را بخشیدند — وبخانهٔ خالی خالهای خود بدستور سابق آمد ورفت هر روزه ورعایت خاطر بیشتر از بیشتر میکردند تا غبار خاطر کلفت بخاطر خالهای ننشینید ودر ساحت جا وجاگیر تعین نمودند *

وکابل‌را (6b) از قبل میرزا خان خلاص ساخته خدای تعالی بایشان ارزانی داشت — ودر آنوقت بیست وسه ساله بودند وهیچ فرزندی نداشتند ودر آرزوی فرزند بسیار بودند — ودر هفتده سالگی از عایسه سلطان بیگم دختر سلطان احمد میرزا — دختری تولّد شده بود ودر سر ماهگی فوت شد — وگرفتن کابل خدای تعالی مبارك کرده که هشت فرزند شد *

اوّل ازآکم که ماهم بیگم باشند — حضرت همایون بادشاه وباربول میرزا ومهرجهان بیگم وایشان دولت بیگم وفاروق میرزا *

دیگر معصومه سلطان بیگم دختر سلطان احمد میرزا — درحین زائیدن فوت شد * نام مادررا بدختر ماندند *

واز گلرخ بیگم کامران میرزا وعسکری میرزا وشاهرخ میرزا وسلطان احمد میرزا وگلعذار بیگم *

واز دلدار بیگم گلرنگ بیگم وگلچهره بیگم وهندال میرزا وگلبدن بیگم والور میرزا ٭

غرض که گرفتن کابل‌را شگون گرفته بودند که همه فرزندان درکابل شده اند غیر دو بیگم که در خوست شده اند مهرجان (sic) (7a) بیگم از ماهم بیگم وگلرنگ بیگم از دلدار بیگم ٭

تولّد حضرت همایون پادشاه که پسر کلان حضرت فردوس مکانی اند — ولادت مبارك ایشان در شب سه شنبه چهارم ذی قعده سنه ۹۱۳ نهصد وسیزده — در ارك کابل در وقت که آفتاب در برج حوت بود — تولّد شدند — ودر همان سال حضرت فردوس مکانی خودرا فرمودند به امرا وسایر الناس که مرا بابر بادشاه گوئید والا اوایل قبل از تولّد حضرت همایون بادشاه میرزا بابر موسوم ومرسوم بودند بلك همه بادشاه‌زادهای‌را میرزا می‌گفتند ودر سال تولّد ایشان خودرا بابر بادشاه گویانیدند ٭ تاریخ تولّد حضرت جنّت آشیانی سلطان همایون خان یافته اند — ودیگر شاه فیروز قدر یافته اند ٭

و بعد از تولّد فرزندان خبر آمد که شاهی بیگ خان‌را شاه اسماعیل کشت ٭

حضرت بادشاه کابل‌را بناصر میرزا داده خود اهل وعیال وفرزندان که همایون بادشاه ومهرجهان بیگم (7b) وباربول میرزا ومعصومه سلطان بیگم ومیرزا کامران باشند — همراه گرفته متوجه سمرقند شدند — وبامداد شاه اسماعیل فتح سمرقند کردند — وتا هشت ماه تمامی ماور النهر در تحت تصّرف ایشان بود — واز ناموافقی برادران و مخالفت اهل مغل درکول ملك از عبید الله خان شکست یافتند ونتواستند در آن ولایت بود ٭ پس جانب بدخشان وکابل متوجه شدند — ودیگر خیال ماور النهر از سر بدر کردند — ودر سنه ۹۱۰ نهصد وده ولایت کابل میسّر شده بود ٭

دایم درین هوس بودند که در هندستان (*sic*) درآیند واز سُپِست رائ امرا و ناموافقی برادران مُیسَّر و مسخَّر نمی‌شد * آخر الوقت که برادران رفتند واز امرایان هیچ‌کسی نماند که خلاف مقصود ایشان توانند حکایتی کرد — در سنه نهصد وبیست وپنج ۹۲۵ بجوررا بجنگ در دو سه گری گرفتند — ومردم بجوررا قتل عام کردند *

ودر روز مذکور ملك منصور یوسفزی که پدر افغانی آغاچه باشد — آمده حضرت‌را ملازمت (8a) کرد * حضرت بادشاه دخترش افغانی آغاچه‌را گرفته در عقد خود در آوردند وملك منصورررا رخصة دادند — واسپ وسروپای پادشاهانه* عنایت فرمودند که رفته مردم و رعایا و غیره‌را آورده بوطن‌های خود ابادان سازد *

وقاسم بیگ که در کابل بود عرضه داشت فرستاد که شاه زاده نو تولّد شد * بشگون فتح هند وتخت املش گستاخی کرده نوشته ام * دیگر بادشاه صاحب اند — هرچه رضای ایشان * بادشاه در ساعت میرزا هندال نام نهادند *

وبعد فتح بجور بجانب بهیره روان شدند ودر بهیره آمدند وتالان نکرده الامان داده چهار لك شاهرخی گرفته بمردم لشکر بعدد نوکر تقسیم کرده متوجه کابل شدند *

درین اثنا از مردم بدخشان عرضه داشت آمد که میرزا خان فوت شد — میرزا سلیمان خورد سال واوزبگ نزدیك — فکر این ولایت بکنید که مباده بدخشان از دست برود * تا فکر بدخشان کردن والدهٔ میرزا سلیمان میرزای (8b) مذکوررا گرفته آورده بود * حضرت بادشاه حسب المدعا وخاطر خواهٔ ایشان جای نشپست وجاگیر پدر تعین نمودند

---

* (پادشاهانه) The M.S. writes indifferently بادشاه and پادشاه. With equal caprice it inserts *zamma*, *hamza*, under-dotted *sīn*, &c..

و بدخشان‌را بهمایون پادشاه دادند — وهمایون بادشاه متوجه آنصوبه گشتند *

حضرت بادشاه و آکم هم متعاقب ببدخشان رفتند وچند روزی با یکدیگر بهم گذرانند * حضرت همایون بادشاه آنجا ماندند وبادشاه بابام وآکم بکابل آمدند *

و بعد چند گاه متوجه قلات وقندهار شدند ودر ساعت که بقلات رسیدند فتح کرده متوجه قندهار شدند — ومردم قندهار تا یکنیم سال در قلعه بندی بودند * بعد یکنیم سال بجنگ وجدل بسیار قندهاررا بعنایت آلهی فتح نمودند و زر بسیار بدست افتاده وبسپاهی و مردم لشکر زرها و شترها بخش کردند — وقندهاررا بمیرزا کامران دادند — وخود متوجه کابل شدند *

روز جُمعه غره صفر سنه ۹۳۲ نهصد وسی ودو که آفتاب در برج قوس بود — پیش‌خانه بر آورده از پشته یك لنگه گذشته (9a) در جلگه دیه یعقوب نزول اجلال فرمودند * دیگر از آنجا مقام کردند و روز دیگر کوچ بکوچ متوجه هندستان شدند *

و از سنه نهصد وسی وپنج درین هفت هشت سال چند مرتبه لشکر بجانب هندوستان (*sic*) که کرده اند در هر مرتبه ولایتی و پرگنه تسخیری نموده اند — مثل بهیره وبجور وسیالکوت ودیپالپور ولاهور وغیره تا آنکه مرتبه پنجم روز جُمعه غره صفر سنه ۹۳۲ نهصد وسی ودو از دیه یعقوب نزول اجلال کوچ بکوچ متوجه هندستان شدند ولاهور وسرهند وهر ولایت که در سر راه بود فتح کردند — بتاریخ هشتم ماه رجب روز جمعه سنه ۹۳۲ در پانی‌پت بسلطان ابراهیم بن سلطان سکندر بن بهلول لودی جنگ صف کرده — بعنایت آلهی غالب آمدند — وسلطان ابراهیم در آن جنگ کُشته گشته — واین فتح محض از عنایت آلهی بود — از برای آنکه سلطان

ابراهیم یك لك وهشتاد هزار سوار داشت وتا هزار پنجصد زنجیر فیل مست (9b) ولشکر حضرت بادشاه خود مع سوداگر ونیك وبدر دوازده هزار کس بوده وسپاهی کار آمدنی نهایتش شش هفت هزار کس بود *

وخزانهٔ پنج بادشاه بدست ایشان افتاد وهمه‌را بخش کردند * دربن اثناء امرای هندستان عرض کردند که درهندستان عیب است خزینهٔ پادشاهان ماضی‌را خرج کردن بلك خزینه‌را اضافه نموده نموده جمع کنند وحضرت برعکس آن کردند که تمامی خزینه‌هارا بخش کردند *

وخواجه کلان بیگ چند مرتبه رخصت کابل طلبیدند که مزاج من بهوای هند موافق نیست * اگر رخصت شود چند گاه درکابل آنجا باشم — وحضرت بجدای خواجه اصلاً اصلاً وقطعاً راضی نبودند * آخر چون دیدند که خواجه بسیار مبالغه دارند رخصت دادند وفرمودند که چون میروید تحفه وهدیهٔ هندرا که از فتح سلطان ابراهیم بدست افتاده بولی نعمتیان (sic) وهمشیرها واهل حرم میخواهم فرستیم (sic) — همراه برید ومفصل نوشته میدهیم * از روی مفصل (10a) تقسیم نمائید وبگوئید که درباغ ودیوانخانه هرکدام بیگمان سراپردها وچادرها علاحده بزنند — ومعرکه خوبی کرده وسجدهٔ شکر حق سبحانه به جا آورند که فتحی کلی روی نموده و بهر بیگمی بدین تفصیل رسانند — یك پاتر خاصه از پاتران سلطان ابراهیم با یك رکیبی طلا پر جواهر ولعل ومروارید ویاقوت والماس وزمرّد وفیروزه وزبرجد وعین الهر — ودر خوانچه صدفی پر اشرفی ودر دو خوان دیگر شاهرخی وهر جنسی پارچهای توقوز توقوز که چهار خوان ویك رکیبی ویك پاتر ویك رکیبی جواهر وهریك خوان از هر جنس اشررفی وشاه‌رخی که حکم کرده بود ورکیبی جواهر وهمان پاتررا که به ولی نعمتان خود پیشکش کرده ام برده گذرانند ودیگر پیشکش کرده ام آنهارا در عقب آن گذرانند — وخواهران وفرزندان وحرمان وخویشاوندان

وبیگمان وآغه‌ها وانگها وکوکها وآغه‌چه‌ها وهمه دعاء گویان از جراؤ* واشرفی (10b) وشاهرخی وپارچه جُدا جُدا بدهند* از روی مفصل بدین ترتیب دادند* تا سه روز در باغ ودیوانخانه مذکور خوشحالی ومعرکه داشتند* سرافرز گشتند وبدعا ودولت حضرت فاتحه خوانده — وخوشحال شده سجدات شکر بجا اوردند*

وبدستِ خواجه کلان بیگ بعموی عپس** یك اشرفی کلان بوزن سه سیر بادشاهی که پانزده سیر هند باشد وبخواجه گفته بودند — اگر عپس از شما پرسد که حضرت بادشاه بمن چه فرستاده است — خواهید گفت که یك اشرفی — وچون فی الحقیقه یکی بوده تعجب کرده تا سه روز کاهید* حکم بود که اشرفی‌را سوراخ کرده وچشمشرا بسته ودر گردنش انداخته درون حرم فرستید* بمجرّدی که اشرفی سوراخ کرده در گردنش انداخته از گرانی طرفه بیطاقتی واضطراب وخوشحالی میکرد وبه دو دست اشرافی‌را گرفته طرفگیها میکرد که کسی اشرفی مرا نگیرد — واز بیگمان هم هرکدام ده دوازده اشرفی دادند تا قریب هفتاد و (11a) هشتاد اشرفی شد*

وبعد از آمدن خواجه کلان بیگ بکابل — در آگره همایون بادشاه وهمه میرزایان وسلطانان وامرا از خزانها بخش کردند — وباطراف وجوانب وولایتها فرمانهای بتاکید فرستادند که هرکس که در ملازمت ما بیاید رعایتهای کلّی خواهیم کرد* علی الخصوص آنهائی که پدر وابا واجداد مارا خدمت کرده اند — اگر بیایند در فراخور انعامات خواهند یافت — واز نسل صاحب قران یا چنگیز خانی هرکه باشد متوجه درگه

---

* (جراو) *Sic*; but presumably جواهر.

** (عپسپس) For remarks on this passage cf. note to translation.

ما گردد* حق سبحانه ممالك هندوشتان‌را بما عطاکرده بیایند تا دولت‌را بهم بینیم*

واز دختر سلطان ابو سعید میرزا هفت بیگم آمده بودند — گوهر شاد بیگم وفخر جهان بیگم وخدیجه سلطان بیگم وبدیع الجمال بیگم وآق بیگم وسلطان بخت — وزینب سلطان خانم دختر تغائی پادشاه سلطان محمود خان ومحب سلطان خانم دختر الاچه خان تغائی خورد حضرت پادشاه بودند* قصه مختصر همه بیگمان وخانمان نود وشش (11b) کس بودند* بهمه آنها جای وجاگیر وانعامات خاطرخواه تعین کردند*

ومدّت چهارسال که در آگره بودند هر روز جمعه بدیدن عمهای خود میرفتند* یك روز هوا بغایت گرم بود وحضرت آکم گفتند که هوا بغایت گرم است — اگریك جمعه نروید چه شود؟ بیگمان ازین سخن نخواهند رنجید* بادشاه با آکام* گفتند — ماهم از تو عجب است که این سخنان بگوئی* دختران حضرت ابو سعید سلطان میرزا که از پدر وبرادران خود جدًا شده اند — من اگر خاطرجوی ایشان نکنم چون شود؟

بخواجه قاسم معمار حکم کردند — خدمتی خوبت میفرمایم وآن آنست که عمهای ما هرکاری ویا مهمی در دریخانه داشته باشد — بجان ودل خود خدمات دریخانهٔ ولی نعمتان‌را بتقدیم رسانی*

ودر آگره آنروی آب عمارتها فرمودند وخانهٔ سنگین که خلوتخانهٔ ایشان میانه حرم وباغ ودر دیوانخانه هم خانهٔ سنگین راست کرده بودند — ودر میانهٔ خانه حوضی وچهار حُجره در چهار برج خانه — ودر کنار دریا (12a) چوکندی راست کرده بودند — ودر دهولپور هم از یك

* (آکام) Up to this point this alternative name of Māham has been written آکم. Now (as elsewhere in some other words) the orthography of the writer improves and the correct spelling is given آکام=آکه ام = my Lady.

پارهٔ سنگ حوض ده در دهی فرموده بودند و می‌گفتند که هرگاه این حوض طیار شود بشراب پر خواهم کرد* چون قبل از جنگ رعنا* سنگا که از شراب توبه کرده بودند بشربت لیمون پر کردند*

بعد از فتح سلطان ابراهیم بعد از یکسال رعنا از طرف مندو** (or هندو) پیدا شد بلشکر بی حد*

از امرا و راجها و رانا هرکدام که آمده حضرت بادشاه‌را ملازمت کرده بودند — هرهمه یاغی شده برعنا رفته پیوستند تا کول جلالی و سنبهل و راپری همه پرگنهارای و راجها وافغانان یاغی شدند* قریب دو لك سوار جمع شده*

درین ولا محمّد شریف منجّم با مردم لشکر گفته که مناسب دولت آنست که حضرت بادشاه جنگ نکنند — که ستاره شکر*** یلدوز در برابر است* لشکر بادشاهی‌را عجب هیرانی دست داد وبسیار متفکر ومتألم

---

* (رعنا) Perhaps a sarcasm is intended by changing the title *rānā* into the epithet *ra'nā*—a foolish admirer of himself. Sangā is always so stigmatized, but so too are other and friendly *Rānās*. Cf. 48 b.

** (مندو) Text uncertain. The enemy came from the side which from a military stand-point, was emphatically Hindū and also may be said colloquially to have come from the direction of Mandū.

*** (شکر) I am indebted to Mr. Beveridge for the interesting information in the following note. The شکر (Venus) of the text is, he believes, a mistake for سکّز, *Sakkiz*, eight, the Eight Stars being regarded as unpropitious by Persians. Gul-badan has perhaps confused the portents of a defeat by Shaibānī at Khwāja Kārdzīn in 1501 and the battle of Khānwa in 1527. Bābar's statement about Khānwa is that Sharīf gave warning that Mars was in the west and that whoever should come from the east, would be defeated.

Bābar has a characteristic story of his having precipitated the fight at Kārdzin (1501) because the Eight Stars were exactly between the opposing armies and if he had delayed, they would have favoured Shaibānī for 13 or 14 days. "These observances were all nonsense and my precipitation was without the least solid excuse." He lost the battle. Cf. Steingass Pers. Dict. 689; Vullers II. 310 a; Mems. 92, 353, 368.

شدند واظهار بی دلی مینمودند و (12b) مردم لشکررا چون باین حالت دیدند ملاحظه کلی نمودند* چون غنیم نزدیك رسید تدبیری که بخاطر مبارك ایشان رسید این بود که جمیع اُمرا وخوانین وسلاطین ووضیع وشریف وصغیر وکبیرکه ازگریخته گان وباغی آنچه مانده بودند باقی‌را حکم فرمودند که همه جمع شوند* هریك جمع شده آمدند* فرمودند که هیچ میدانند که میانه ما و وطن وشهر مالوف ما چند ماهه* راه است* خدا از آن روز نگهدارد که اگر مردم شکست خورند — نعوذ بالله — ما کجا ووطن وشهر ما کجا که کار بمردم اجنبی وبگانه می افتد* پس همان بهتر که خودرا باین دو شق قرار باید داد که اگر غنیم‌را می کشیم — غازی می شویم و اگر کشته می شویم — شهید می شویم* بهر دو تقدیر بهبود ما است ودرجهٔ عظما ومرتبهٔ علیاست*

همه یك دل شده قبول کردند* بزن طلاق و مصحف سوگند خوردند و فاتحه خواندند وگفتند — پادشاه انشاء الله تعالی تا رمقی درجان ودر بدن خواهد بود — درجان سپاری وجان نثاری خودرا معاف (13a) نمیداریم*

وقبل ازجنگ رعنا سنگا به دو روز پیشتر حضرت بادشاه از شراب توبه کرده بودند — بلك از جمیع مناهی توبه کردند — وبجهة موافقت و متابعت چهارصد جوان نامی که دعوی مردانگی ویکدلی ویك جهتی می نمودند — در آن مجلس بطفیل حضرت بادشاه آنها نیز توبه کردند وجمیع آلات مناهی وطلا آلات ونقره آلات از پیاله وصراحی وغیره همه‌را شکسته بفقرا ومساکین بخش کردند*

وفرمانها باطراف وجوانب بتاکید تمام فرستادند که از باج وتمغا وزکاة حبوبات وتکلیفات نا مشروع همه‌را معاف کردیم — که هیچ احدی وفردی

---

* (ماهه) Cf. 3a.

مزاحمت بمحال آمد و رفت سوداگر و غیره نرساند وگذارند تا مرفه الحال وفارغ البال آمد و رفت نمایند*

روزی که به رعنا سنگا جنگ خواهد شد در شب آن قاسم حسین سلطان نواسهٔ دختری سلطان حسین میرزا که پسر عایشه سلطان بیگم باشد — در شب مذکور خبر آمد که قاسم حسین میرزا از خراسان آمده در ده کروهی رسید* (13 b) حضرت را از استماع این خبر خوش حالی کلّی روی نمود* فرمودند که چه مقدار کس همراه دارد؟ چون تحقیق نمودند سی چهل سوار بود فی الحال هزار سوار مسلّح ومکمل نیم شب فرستادند که همان شب همراه شده آمدند — تا مردم غنیم و بیگانه دانند که کومك آمده رسیده وبوقت آمده* هر که این رای وتدبیررا شنید بسیار پسندید*

وصباح آن که ماه جمید الاوّل سنه ٩٣٣ نهصد وسی وسه بود در دامن کوه سیکری که الحال فتح‌پور بر بالای آن کوه آبادان شده — به رعنا سنگا جنگ صف شده بعنایت آلهی فتح کردند وغازی شدند*

بعد از فتح رعنا سنگا بعد یك سال آکام که ماهم بیگم باشند از کابل بهندوستان آمدند واین حقیر هم همراه ایشان پیشتر از همشیرها آمده حضرت بادشاه بابام‌را ملازمت کردم وآکام در کول رسیدند که حضرت بادشاه دو محافهٔ سه رکیب فرستادند* از کول باگره ایلغار کرده رفتند وحضرت بادشاه خیال داشتند که تا کولجلالی پیشواز روند* (14 a) نمازشام یکی آمده گفت که حضرت‌را در دو کروهی گذاشته آمدم* حضرت بادشاه بابام تا اسپ آوردن تحمّل نکردند وپیاده روان شدند ودر پیشخانهٔ ننجهٔ ماهم در خوردند* آکام میخواستند که پیاده شوند* پادشاه بابام نماندند وخود در جلوی آکام تا خانهٔ خود پیاده آمدند*

وقتی که آکام پیش بادشاه بابام می آمدند مرا حکم کردند که در روز روشن آمده حضرت‌را ملازمت کنید ٭

*نه رکیب ودو توقوز اسپ ودو محافهٔ کوتل که بادشاه بابام فرستاده بودند و یك محافه که از کابل آورده بودند — قریب صد مغلانی خدمتگاران آکام بر اسپان تپوچاق سوار پر زیب و زینت ٭

وخلیفهٔ بابام با سلطانم کوچ خود تا نوگرام پیشواز آمدند ومن در محافه بودم ٭ مامهای من در باغچه مرا فرود آورده بودند و زلچه (*sic*) انداخته بالای زلچه مرا نشاندند وبمن اموختند که وقتی خلیفهٔ بابام بیایند شما استاده شده دریابید ٭ چون خلیفهٔ بابام آمد من استاده دریافتم ٭ درین ضمن سُلطانم (14 b) کوچ ایشان هم آمد ٭ من نادانسته میخواستم که برخیزم که خلیفهٔ بابام بنیاد مبالغه پیش نهادند که این پیر داه شما است — باین برخاستن حاجت نیست ٭ پدر شما این پیر غلام خودرا سرافراز کرده اند که در باب او اینچنین حکم فرموده اند ٭ روا باشد بندهارا چه مجال است؟

پیشکش خلیفهٔ بابام پنج هزار شاهرخی وپنج اسپ گرفتم وسُلطانم کوچ ایشان سه هزار شاهرخی وسه اسپ پیشکش کرد وگفت — ما حاضری طیّار است اگر نوش‌جان کنند سرافرازی بندها خواهد بود ٭ قبول کردم — در جای خوب صُفهٔ کلان راست کرده وچادر سقرلات سرخ اندرون زربفت گجراتی وشش شامیانه سقرلات و زربفت — هرکدام بیك رنگ وچهار چوقهٔ سراپرده سقرلات وچوبهای سراپرده همه رنگ بود ٭ در منزل خلیفهٔ بابام نشستم — ما حاضری کشید تا قریب پنجاه (*sic*) گوسفند بریان و نان و شربت و میوه بسیار ٭ عاقبت الامر طعام خورده در محافه در آمده در ملازمت حضرت بادشاه بابام آمده ملازمت (15 a) کردم

---

* (نه) What follows appears to be an incomplete and perhaps misplaced description of Akām's *cortêge*.

و درپای افتادم وحضرت پرسش بسیار نمودند * زمانی در بغل نشانند و این حقیررا درآن اثنا آنقدر خوشحالی روی نمود که مزیدی بر آن متصور نباشد *

بعد از آمدن آگره سه ماه گذشته بود که حضرت بادشاه متوجه دهولپور شدند وحضرت ماهم بیگم و این حقیر به سیر دهولپور رفتم * در دهولپور حوضی ده در ده راست کرده بودند از یك پرچه * از آنجا بسیکری رفتند * صفهٔ کلانی در میانهٔ کول حکم کردند که راست بکنند * وقتی که آن راست شد درکشتی نشسته آنجا میرفتند و سیر می کردند و می نشستند — که تا حال هم آن صُفهٔ مذکور هست * ودر سیکری در باغ چوکندی هم راست کرده بودند * حضرت بادشاه بابام در آن چوکندی * تورخانه برپا کرده درآن نشسته مصحف می نوشتند *

و من و افغانی آغاچه در پیش در پایان نشسته بودیم که آکام بنماز رفتند * من با افغانی آغاچه گفتم که دست مرا بکشید * افغانی آغاچه دست مرا کشیدند * دست من بر آمد و من (15 b) بیطاقتی وگریه کردن گرفتم * آخر کمان گررا آورده دست مرا بسته متوجه آگره شدند *

ودر آگره رسیده بودند که خبر آوردند که بیگمان از کابل می آیند * حضرت بادشاه بابام پیشواز آکه جانم که عمهٔ کلان من وخواهر کلان حضرت بادشاه بابام بودند تا نوگرام پیشواز رفتند وهمه بیگمان در ملازمت آکه جانم در منزل ایشان ملازمت کردند * خوشحالیها نمودند و

---

* (تور خانه) Erskine (202 n.) says "perhaps a space enclosed by a low railing." Chardin (*Voyage en Perse*) has a picture of a grandee seated within an enclosure (at sides and back) which as he sits, appears to reach his shoulders. Perhaps this is a *tūr-khāna*. Zenker describes it as a seat of honour of the nature of a throne. It would supply a necessity of Indian life, if one might read *ṭaur*, net, and allow the royal author a mosquito-room.

سجدات شکر بجا آوردند و متوجه آگره شدند — و بهمه بیگمان حویلیها عنایت فرمودند و بعد از چند روز بسیر باغ زرافشان رفتند *

و در باغ مذکور وضوخانه بود * آن‌را که دیدند فرمودند — دل من از سلطنت و بادشاهی گرفته در باغ زرافشان بگوشه بنشینم — و از برای خدمتگاری طاهر آفتابچی بمن بسیار است — و بادشاهی‌را به همایون بدهم * درین اثنا حضرت آکام و همه فرزندان گریه و بیطاقتی کرده گفتند که خدای تعالی شمارا در مپسند پادشاهی سالهای بسیار و قرنهای بیشمار در امان خود نگاه دارد و همه فرزندان (16 a) در قدم شما بکمال پیری برسند *

بعد از چند روز آلور میرزا بیمار شدند و بیماریٔ ایشان بدرد شکم کشید که هر چند حکیم ها و اطبا علاج کردند — بیماریٔ ایشان پیشتر از پیشتر شد * آخر بهمان بیماری از عالم فانی بعالم جادوانی خرامیدند * حضرت بادشاه بسیار تأسّف و غم خوردند * والدهٔ میرزا آلور که دلدار بیگم باشند — از غم و غصهٔ آن فرزند — که نادر جهان و یگانهٔ عصر بود — سودا پیدا کردند * چون دلگیری از حد گذشت حضرت بادشاه باکام و بیگمان گفتند — بیائید — بسیر دهولپور برویم — و خود درکشتی نشسته بسعادت وسلامت از آب گذشتند و بدهولپور مذکور رفتند * بیگمان نیز میخواستند که درکشتی نشسته از آب بگذرند *

که در این اثنا عرضه داشت مولانا محمّد فرغرلی* از دهلی آمد * نوشته بود که همایون میرزا بیمار اند و حالی عجبی دارند بشنیدن این خبر حضرت بیگم زودی زود متوجه دهلی می باید شوند که میرزا (16 b) بسیار بیطاقتی میکنند * بمجرّد شنیدن این خبر حضرت آکام بیطاقتی کرده * مانند تشنهٔ که مهجور آب باشد — بجانب دهلی متوجه شدند * در متهره رسیدند چنانچه شنیده بودند از آن ده چند مضعوف و مجهول بچشم جهان بین

---

* (فرغرلی) *Sic.* Parghālī is the usual form.

خویش دیدند — و از آنجا هر دو — مادر و پسر — مانند عیسی و مریم متوجه آگره شدند *

ودر حینی که باگره در رسیدند — این حقیر همراه همشیرها ملازمت آن حضرت فرستهٔ خصال رفته کردم — چون ضعیف ایشان بیشتر از پیشتر بود در این وقت هرگاه که آن حضرت بهوش خویش می آمدند از زبان درافشان خویش پرسش می فرمودند که خواهران خوش آمدید — بیائید تا یکدیگررا دریابیم که شمارا در نیافته ایم * قریب سه مرتبه سرافرازکرده از زبان گوهرافشان خود باین عبارت سرافراز فرمودند * وچون حضرت آمدند ودریافتند — بمجرّد دیدن آن چهرهٔ نورافشان درکلفت و رقت شد و ایشان بیشتر از پیشتر اظهار بیدلی کردن گرفتند *

درین اثنا حضرت (17a) آکام گفتند که شما از فرزند من غافلید — و پادشاه اید چه غم دارید — وفرزندان دیگر نیز دارید * مرا غم است که فرزند یگانه دارم * حضرت جواب دادند که ماهم اگرچه فرزندان دیگر دارم — امّا هیچ فرزندی برابر همایون تو دوست نمی دارم — از برای آنکه سلطنت وبادشاهی ودنیای روشن از برای یگانهٔ جهان ونادرهٔ دوران کامگار برخوردار فرزند دلبند همایون میخواهم — نه برای دیگران *

وقتی که ایشان بیمار بودند حضرت روندهٔ حضرت مرتضی علی کرم الله وجه نگاه داشتند — وآن روندهٔرا از روز چهار شنبه نگاه میدارند * ایشان از اضطراب وبیطاقتی از روز سه شنبه نگاه داشتند * هوا بغایت گرم بود * دل وجگر ایشان تفید — ودر روندهٔ مذکور دعا خواستند که خدایا — اگر بعوض جان جان مبدل شود — من که بابر ام — عمر وجان خودرا بهمایون بخشیدم — و در همان روز حضرت فردوس مکانی‌را تشویش شد (17b) وهمایون بادشاه بر سر خود آب ریختند وبیرون آمده بار دادند وحضرت بادشاه بابام‌را از جهة تشویش درون بردند *

قریب دو سه ماه صاحب فراش بودند ومیرزا همایون بجانب کالنجر رفته بودند* چون تشویش حضرت بادشاه پیشتر شد — بطلب حضرت همایون بادشاه کس فرستادند* ایشان بایلغار رسیدند* چون حضرة را ملازمت کردند — ایشان‌را بسیار ضعیف دیدند* حضرت همایون بادشاه رقت تمام نموده — بیطاقتی کردن گرفتند و بخدمتگاران می گفتند که یکبارگی چرا ازین قسم زارنزار گشته اند — واطبا وحکمارا طلبیدند وگفتند که من ایشان‌را تندرست گذاشته رفته بودم — یکبارگی چه شده؟ حکما واطبا چیزها می گفتند*

وحضرت بادشاه بابام هر زمان وهر ساعت می پرسیدند که همایون* کجا است؟ وچه کار می‌کند؟ درین اثنا یکی آمده گفت که پسر میر خورد بیگ میر بردی بیگ کورنش میرساند* فی الحال حضرت بادشاه (18a) بابام باضطراب تمام طلبیده پرسیدند که هندال کجا است؟ کی خواهد آمد؟ چه بلا انتظار داد* میر بردی گفت که شاهزاده کامگار بدهلی رسیده اند — امروز فردا بخدمت خواهند رسید* درین اثنا حضرت بادشاه بابام به میر بردی بیگ گفتند که مردك بدبخت — شنیده ام که خواهر ترا درکابل کدخدا کردند وترا در لاهور کدخدا کردند — برای این طوهای پسر مرا زودتر نمی** آوردی — که انتظار از حدّ گذشت — ومی پرسیدند که هندال میرزا چه مقدار شده است وبه که مانند است؟ چون میر بردی بیگ جامهٔ میرزا پوشیده بود نمود که این جامهٔ شاهزاده است که به بنده عنایت فرموده اند* حضرت پیشتر طلبیدند که به بینم قد وقامت هندال چه مقدار شده است — وهر زمان هر ساعت می گفتند که هزار دریغ که هندال‌را ندیدم* هرکس که می آمد می پرسیدند که هندال کی خواهد آمد؟

---

* (همایون) This is probably a clerical error for *Hindāl*.

** (نمی) The text has no negative but it is required by the context.

و در حین بیماری حکم کردند باکام که گلرنگ بیگم و گلچهره بیگمرا کدخدا باید کرد (18b) و هرگاه که حضرت عمه جیو* تشریف ارزانی فرمایند معلوم ایشان بکنید که بادشاه میگویند بخاطر من میرسد که گلرنگرا به ایسن تیمور سلطان و گلچهرارا به توخته بوغا سلطان نسبت بکنم * آکا جانم تبسم کنان آمدند * به ایشان گفتند که حضرت بادشاه این قسم می فرمایند که بخاطر من چنین رسیده — باقی آنچه رضای ایشان باشد — همان طور بکنند * حضرت آکه جانم نیز گفتند که خدا مبارك وسازکاری کناد — بسیار خوب بخاطر ایشان رسیده * جیجم** خود وبدیع الجمال بیگم وآق بیگم هر دو عمه بردالان بردند * صفا*** داده و بساطها انداخته ساعترا ملاحظه کرده نیچه ماهم هر دو سلطانانرا زانوزنانیده به دامادی سرافراز بکنند *

درین ضمن تشویش سکم ایشان پیشتر شد * حضرة همایون بادشاه که احوال پدر خرابتر دیدند — باز بیطاقت شدند * اطبا و حکمارا طلبیده گفتند نیك ملاحظه کرده علاج تشویش حضرت نمائید * اطبا وحکما (19a) جمع شده گفتند که کم طالعی مایان است که داروی کارگر نمی شود * امیدواریم از حضرت حق سبحانه که از خزانهٔ غیب شفای عاجل عطا کند * درین حین چون نبض آنحضرت دیدند — اطبا بعرض رسانیدند که علامت همان زهر است که والدهٔ سلطان ابراهیم داده بود — و آنچنانست که بیده بدبخت بدست داهٔ خود یك توله زهر داده بود که برده

---

* (جیو) By this term of endearment Ḥamīda-bānū, Akbar's mother addressed the dying Gul-badan.

** (جیجم) I believe this should be جیجام. A similar omission of the *alif* is not infrequent in the M.S. Cf. مامها for ماماها (14b.). So also of the points of the *yā* and the *che*.

*** (صفا) As in this M.S. *alif* is several times written for *hā'i hauwaz*, I translate صفه, estrade, raised seat and not صفا.

بدست احمد چاشنی گیر بده وبگوکه هرطورکرده درآش خاصه بادشاهی اندازد وباو وعده بسیار کرده بود* با وجود آنکه حضرت بادشاهٔ آن بیده بدبخت‌را مادر می گفتند وجا وجاگیر تعین کرده رعایت کلیّ فرموده بودند — وفرموده بودند که مرا بجای سلطان ابراهیم خود بدان* امّا از آنجا که جهل در آن قوم غالب است رعایتهارا منظور نداشت* مشهور است — ع باز گردد باصل خود همه چیز* قصّه مختصر آن زهر که با آن باورچی آورده داده بود باورچی‌را الله تعالی کور وکر ساخته بود که زهررا بالاء نانِ پاشیده بود کمتر تناول کرده بودند* امّا اصل بیماری از اثرهمان بود که روز بروز ضعیف و نحیف میشدند وهر روز تشویش (19b) ایشان در تزاید بود وچهرهٔ مبارك ایشان در تغیر که فرداش همه امرایان‌را طلبیده فرمودند که سالهای بود که در دل داشتم که بادشاهی خودرا بهمایون میرزا بدهم وخود در باغ زرافشان بگوشه نشینم* ازکرم آلهی همه چیز مُیسَّر شد امّا آن نشد که در تندرستی خود این امررا بکنم* الحال این تشویشِ مرا زبون کرده وصیت میکنم که همه ایشان همایون‌را بجای من دانند — ودر دولت خواهی او تقصیر نکنید وبه او موافق ویکجهة باشید* از حق سبحانه امیدوارم که همایون هم بمردم خوب پیش خواهد آمد* دیگر همایون ترا و برادران ترا و همه خویشان و مردم خودرا و ترا بخدا می سپارم و این هارا بتو می سپارم* از این سخنان حاضران و ناظران‌را گریه و زاری دست داد وخود هم چشمان مبارك پرآب گردند*

این واقعه‌را اهل حرم ومردم درون شنیدند* طرفه حالی و بیطاقتی وگریه و زاری دست داد* بعد از سه روز از عالم فانی بعالم جاودانی خرامیدند* بتاریخ پنجم ماه جمید الاوّل روز دو شنبه سنه نهصد وسی وهفت بود که شنقار شدند*

(٩٣٧)

عمه مارا ومادران مارا (20a) به بهانهٔ برآوردند که طبیبان وحکیمان

برای دیدن می آیند ٭ همه برخواستند همه بیگمان‌را ومادران مرا بخانهٔ کلان بردند ٭ وفرزندان وخویشان وغیره مردم‌را روز سیاه افتاد وطرفه زاری وفریاد وفغان وبیطاقتی کردن گرفتند — وهرکس بگوشهٔ پنهانی این روز سیاه داشتند ٭

وواقعهٔ ایشان‌را پنهان میکردند ٭ آخر الامر آرایش خان نام یکی امرای هند بود — او عرضه داشت که پنهان کردن این امر خوب نیست از برای آنکه در هندوستان رسم است که اگر بادشاهان‌را واقعهٔ چنین دست میدهد — مردم بازاری تاراج میکنند ٭ مباده مُغلان نا دانسته در خانهای ودرحویلهای در آمده تاراج بکنند ٭ مناسب آنست که بیك کسی جامهٔ سرخ پوشانند وبرفیل سوار بکنند واز بالاء فیل منادی بکند که حضرت بابر بادشاه درویش شدند وپادشاهی خودرا بهمایون بادشاه دادند ٭ وحضرت همایون پادشاه حکم فرمودند که چنین بکنید ٭ بمجرّد مُنادی کردن مردم‌را خیلی تسلّی شد (20 b) وهمه مردم دعای دولت ایشان میکردند ٭ بتاریخ نهم شهر مذکور روز جمع حضرت همایون پادشاه بتخت نشستند — وپادشاهی ایشان‌را همه عالم مبارك باد گفتند ٭

بعد از آن بدیدن مادران وخواهران ومردم خود آمده — پرسش ودلداری داده نوازش وغم خواریها فرمودند — وحکم فرمودند هرکس هر منصبی وخدمتی وجاگیری وجای که داشت — همه بحال خود باشد وبخدمتِ خود بدستور صابق قیام نماید ٭

ودر روز مذکور میرزا هندال از کابل آمده حضرت بادشاه‌را ملازمت کرد ٭ برو مهربانی ها کردند وبسیار خوشحال شدند ٭ از خزاین که از پدر مانده بود چیز بسیار بمیرزا هندال عنایت فرمودند ٭

بعد از وفاتِ حضرت بادشاه بابام برات وایّام متبرکهٔ اوّل معرکه بر سر مزارِ حضرت بادشاه بابام می شد ومحمّد علی عسس‌را متولیٔ مزار حضرت

کردند — وشصت حافظِ خوشخوان و خوشالحان قاری‌را مقرر فرمودند که پنج وقت نماز بجماعت بخوانند وختم قران بکنند وفاتحه بارواح حضرت فردوس مکانی میخوانده باشند* وسیکری که الحال (21a) فتح پور مشهور است دروبست ومع زیادتی پنج لك از بیانه وقفِ مزارِ حضرت کردند که برای خرج علما وحفاظ وغیره که تعلقِ مزار دارند صرف می شده باشد* دو وقت آش آکام تعین فرمودند — صباح یك گاو و دو گوسفند و پنج بز — ونماز دیگر پنج بز* تا دو نیم سال که آکام در قید حیاة بودند این طعام دو وقته از سرکار ایشان بر سر مزار بخش میکردند*

وتا زمانی که آکام حیات بودند در دولتخانهٔ آکام حضرت بادشاه‌را میدیدم* وقتی که آکام بد حال شدند بمن گفتند که بسیار مشکل مینماید که بعد از فوتِ من دخترانِ پادشاه برادر خودرا در خانهٔ کلبرگ بیبی به بینند* گویا که سخن حضرت آکام در دل وهوشِ حضرت بادشاه بود — تا در هندوستان بودند — دایم در خانهٔ ما آمده مایان‌را میدیدند و مهربانی و عنایت و شفقت بیحد میکردند — وبمصمومه سلطان بیگم وگلرنگ بیگم وگلچهره بیگم وغیره — همه بیگمان که کدخدا شده بودند — حضرة پادشاه در خانهٔ این حقیر می آمدند — وهمه بیگمان در خانهٔ این حقیر آمده ملازمت حضرت بادشاه میکردند (21b) غرض که حضرت بادشاه خاطرجوی این شکسته‌را بعد از وفات پادساه بابام وآکام به چنین عنایت میکردند و شفقتِ بیحد در بارهٔ این بیچاره میفرمودند که یتیمی و بی سری خودرا ندانستم*

مدّة ده سال که بعد از وفات حضرت فردوس مکانی — حضرت جنّت آشیانی در هند بودند همه مردم در رفاهیت وامنیّت وفرمانبرداری واطاعت بودند* بعد از واقعهٔ فردوس مکانی ببّن* وبایزید بعد از شش

* (ببّن) Text has *tashdīd*.

ماه از طرف گور رسیدند ٭ بمجرّد استماع این خبر حضرت پادشاه از آگره متوجه آنها شدند و ببّن و بایزیدرا شکست داده به چناده آمدند — و چناده‌را نیز گرفته به آگره آمدند ٭

و آکام که ماهم بیگم باشند بسیار در طلب و آرزو بودند که فرزندِ همایون‌را به بینم — و هر جا که دخترِ صاحب حُسن و جمال می‌بود — در خدمتِ حضرت بادشاه می آوردند ٭ و میوه جان که دخترِ خدنگ یساول بود در خدمتِ من بود ٭ (بعد) از قضا حضرت فردوس مکانی روزی در حیاۀ خود فرمودند — همایون — میوه جان بد نیست — چرا در خدمت خود نمی گیری ؟ — آخر بگفتۀ ایشان همایون (22 a) پادشاه همان شب عقد بسته میوه جان‌را گرفتند — و بعد از سه روز بیگه بیگم از کابل آمدند و حامله شدند ٭ بعد از یك سال دختر تولّد شد و نامش‌را عقیقه بیگم نهادند ٭ و آکه ماهم بیگم‌را میوه جان میگفت که من نیز حامله ام ٭ آخر آکام دو طربقِ* یراق طیار کردند و می گفتند — هر کدام که از شمایان پسر بزاید یراق نیك‌را بان میدهم — و یراق بسته و بدام و چار مغز از طلا و نقره راست کرده بودند — و یراق** یلقان نیز راست کرده بودند و خوشحال بودند که شاید یکی از این ها پسر زاید — و چشمِ انتظار داشتند که بیگه بیگم عقیقه بیگم‌را زائیدند ٭ الحال چشم براۀ میوه جان داشتند که ده ماه شد و یازدهم ماه نیز گذشت ٭ میوه جان میگفت که خالۀ من حرم میرزا الغ بیگ بودند ٭ در دوازده ماه پسر زائیدند ٭ من هم شاید که بدان مانند شده باشم ٭ و خرگاها دوخته و توشك ها پر کرده ٭ آخر همه معلوم شد که هوپسك*** بوده ٭

* (طربق) The text has no points to the *yā* of my reading. If the prop were absent the word could be read طرق, *ṯaraq*, ply, fold *i. e.* sets. The sense of the two passages is, I think, that Māham got together two sets of arms of which one included of those a Mughal Commander.

** (یراق) Text *yarāq-yalqān* for *yarāq-i-īlkhān*.

*** (هوپسك) ؟ an ambitious little person or a little mad-woman.

و پادشاه که بجانبِ چنّاده رفته بودند بدولت و سعادت آمدند* آکام که ماهم بیگم باشند — توئ کلان دادند وبازارهارا (22b) آیین بستند — وپیش ازین آیین بندی مردم بازار میکردند آخر ایشان مردم آدمی وسپاهی را هم حکم کردند تا جایهای خوب ومکانهای مرغوب راست بکنند* از آن پس آیین بندی در هند شایع شد*

وتخت مرصّع که بچهار زینه می بر آمدند بالای او ادسقهٔ* زردوزی و توشك وتکیهٔ زردوزی انداختند و پوشش خرگاها و بارگاه اندرون زربفت فرنگی و بیرون از سقلات پرتگالی* چوبهای خرگاه وبارگاه بطلا ملمّع کرده بودند* آن بسیار بزیب شده بود ونعرلی** خرگاه از زرکش گجراتی وکنّت وسرکنّت وآفتابه جلابجن*** وشمع دان ها ومشربها وگلاب چاشها همه از طلا و مرصّه راست کرده بودند — واز همه اسبابِ مرتّب ساخته توئ خوبی و مرغوبی دادند* ودوازده قطارِ شتر ودوازده قطارِ خچّر وهفتاد راسِ اسپِ تپوچاق وصد راسِ اسپِ بارگیر —

---

* (ادسقه) This word occurs thrice in the M.S. *i. e.*, at 22b (here), at 26b—in the plural—, and at 28b. It is written clearly and confidently. Nothing like it has been yielded to our search by the Dictionaries. Mr. Beveridge suggests (1) that it may be a corrupt and domestic form of an Arabic word '*alāqaha*' which he finds as what may be termed a corresponding word, in a description of the Peacock Throne and from this we assume the "hangings" of the translation. Or (2) it may be a corruption of the Turkī *aṣqī* "*tout qui est suspendu pour ornement*". Zenker 58b.

** (نعرلی) ؟ توغورلوق There are no points. Mr. A. G. Ellis has kindly helped me with the suggestion I have accepted. The meaning of توغورلوق is "*feutre qui recouvre la tente*". (P. de C. Turkī Dict. 237.) As the lining of the festal tents is described in the preceding paragraph, I have placed the second among the gifts. Vambéry translates the word: *die obere Filzdecke des Zeltes.*

*** (جلابجن) I suggest جلابجن on the analogy of گلابگن. One looks for *bason* after *ewer* but the word following آفتابه cannot be read as *chilumchī* or any other equivalent for *bason* which I can find. *Chilumchī*, i. e. *chilānchī* occur at 72a and does not resemble the doubtful word here rendered *julābjan.*

وهفت هزار کس خلعتِ خاص پوشانیدند و چند روز شادیها کردند ✲

و درین اثنا شنیدند که محمّد زمان میرزا پدر حاجی محمّد خان کوکی‌را کشت (23a) وخیال باغی شدن دارد ✲ حضرت بادشاه برای طلب آنها کس فرستادند وآنهارا گرفته در بیانه بند کرده بیادگار طغای سپردند — ومردم یادگار طغای یکی شده محمّد زمان میرزا گریزانیدند* ✲ درین اثنا سلطان محمّد میرزا ونیخوب سلطان میرزارا حکم شد که بچشم هر دو میل کشند ✲ در میل کشیدن نیخوب کور شد وبمحمّد سلطان میرزا کسی که میل کشید بچشم مشارالیه اسیب نرسانید ✲ بعد از چند روز محمّد زمان میرزا ومحمّد سلطان میرزا وپسرانش والوغ میرزا وشاه میرزا گریختند — و درین چند سال که در هند بودیم همیشه غوغای آنها بود ✲

وحضرت بادشاه که از لشکر ببنّ و بایزید آمدند قریب یکسال در آگره بودند ✲ به آکام عرض کردند که درین روزها دلگیرم ✲ اگر حکم شود در ملازمت شما بسیر گوالیار برویم ✲ حضرت آکام وآجم وهمشیرها معصومه سلطان بیگم‌را که ماه چیچه میگفتیم وگلرنگ بیگم‌را گل چیچه میگفتیم در ملازمتِ ولی نعمتان در گوالیار بودیم ✲

وگلچهره بیگم در اوده بودند چراکه شوهر ایشان توخته بوغا سلطان برحمت حق پیوستند (23b) ومردم که در ملازمت بیگم بودند — از اوده بحضرت عرضه داشت کردند که توخته بوغا سلطان فوت شدند — بیگم‌را چه حکم میشود؟ حضرت بادشاه میرزاچه‌را حکم فرمودند که رفته بیگم‌را در آگره بیارد — ما نیز در آگره می آئیم ✲

درین اثنا حضرت آکام گفتند که اگر حکم شود بیگه بیگم وعقیقه‌را

---

* (گریزانیدند) The rebellious Mīrzās were of the house of Bāyqrā with which Māham Begam had relationship.

طلبم که اینها هم گوالیاررا به بینند* نوکار و خواجه کبیررا فرستادند که بیگه بیگم و عقیقه سلطان بیگمرا از آگره آوردند — ودو ماه در گوالیار با یکدیگر بهم گذرانیدند* بعد از آن متوجه آگره شدند — ودر ماه شعبان در آگره آمدند*

ودر ماه شوال به آکام تشویش شکم شد* در سیزدهم شهر مذکور سنه ۹۴۰ نهصد وچهل از عالم فانی بعالم جاودانی خرامیدند — وفرزندان حضرة بادشاه بابامرا داغ یتیمی تازه شد — بتخصیص بمن که ایسان خود مرا پرورش فرموده بودند* مرا طرفه حالی و بیطاقتی ومصیبت صعب دست داده بود* شب و روز گریه وفغان و زاری میکردم* حضرت بادشاه چند مرتبه آمده دلداری‌ها وغمخواری‌ها ومهربانی‌ها کردند* دو ساله بودم که حضرة آکام مرا در منزل (24a) خود بردند و پرورش کردند وده ساله شدم که ایشان از عالم رحلت نمودند* تا یك سال دیگر هم در منزل آکام بودم*

وقتی که حضرت بسیر دهولپور رفتند — در سال یازدهم همراه آجم شدم و پیش از آنکه بگوالیار روند وعمارات‌را بنا کرده رفتند*

وبعد از آشِ چلهٔ آکام پادشاه بدهلی تشریف بردند وبنای قلعه دین پناه نهادند وبه آگره آمدند — وآکه جانم* بحضرت بادشاه گفتند که توئ میرزا هندال کی می کنید؟ حضرت گفتند بسم الله — ودر آن اثنا آکام حیات بودند که میرزا هندال نکاح کردند — امّا موقوف باسبابِ توی بودند که سپارند — فرمودند که اسباب توئ طلسم هم طیار است — اوّل توئ طلسم بدهم* بعد از آن توئ میرزا هندال بکنم* حضرت بادشاه به آکه جانم گفتند که حضرة عمه چه میفرمایند؟ ایشان گفتند خدا مبارك وخیر گرداند*

---

* (جانم) Cf. 15b n. .

شرح توی خانه که در لبِ دریا راست کرده بودند — ونام آنرا طلسم نهاده بودند*

اوّل خانهٔ کلانِ مثمّن بود ودر میانهٔ خانه حوض (24 b) مثمّن وباز در میانهٔ حوض صُفهٔ مثمن وبالای آن گلیمهای ولایتی انداخته — واکثر جوانان وصاحبِ حسن دختران وزنانِ صاحب جمال وسازندها وگویندهاء خوش آوازرا حکم کردند که در حوض بنشینند ودر پیشگاهٔ خانه تخت مرصّع که آکام در توی عنایت کرده بودند نهاده وتوشك زردوزی در پیش انداخته بودند*

حضرت پادشاه وآکه جانم در پیش تخت در یك توشك نشستند* ودر دست راستِ آکه جانم عمهای ایشان دختران سلطان ابو سعید میرزا فخر جهان بیگم وبدیع الجمال بیگم وآق بیگم وسلطان بخت بیگم وگوهر شاد بیگم وخدیجه سلطان بیگم نشستند*

ودر توشك دیگر عمهای ما که خواهران حضرت فردوس مکانی باشند — شهربانو بیگم ویادگار سلطان بیگم وعایشه سلطان بیگم دختر سلطان حسین میرزا والوغ بیگم دختر زینب سلطان بیگم عمه حضرت پادشاه وعایشه سلطان بیگم وسلطانی بیگم دختر سلطان احمد میرزا عموی پادشاه (25 a) ومادرِ کلان خان بیگم بیگه سلطان بیگم دخترِ سلطان خلیل میرزا عموی پادشاه وماهم بیگم وبیگی بیگم دخترِ الغ بیگ میرزاء کابلی عموی بادشاه — وخانزاده بیگم دخترِ سلطان مسعود میرزا از جانبِ مادری نواسهٔ پاینده محمّد *(sic)* سلطان بیگم عمهٔ پادشاه وشاه خانم دخترِ بدیع الجمال بیگم — وخانم بیگم دخترِ آق بیگم وزینب سلطان خانم دخترِ سلطان محمود خان طغائ کلانِ پادشاه — ومُحبه سلطان خانم دخترِ سلطان احمد خان که به الاچه خان مشهور بودند طغائ خوردِ پادشاهٔ کلان وخانش خواهر میرزا حیدر دخترِ خالهٔ پادشاه وبیگه کلان بیگم

وکیچك بیگم وشاه بیگم مادرِ دلشاد بیگم دخترِ فخرجهان بیگم عمۀ پادشاه وکچکنه بیگم وآپاق بیگم دخترِ سلطان بخت بیگم ومهرلیق بیگم عمۀ بادشاه وشاد بیگم نواسۀ سلطان حسین میرزا از جانبِ مادری عمۀ پادشاه — ومهرانگیز بیگم دخترِ مظفر میرزا نواسۀ سلطان حسین میرزا — بسیار دوست میداشتند (25 b) ولباسِ مردانه می پوشیدند وبانواع هنرها آراسته همچو زهگیری* تراشی وچوگان بازی وتیر اندازی واکثرسازها می نواختند — وگل بیگم وفوق بیگم وجان سلطان بیگم وافروزبانو بیگم وآغه بیگم و فیروزه بیگم وبرلاس بیگم ✲

وبیگمانِ دیگرهم بسیار بودند که بتفصیل نود وشش بیگم — همه علوفه‌دار بودند — وچندان دیگر هم بودند ✲

بعد از طوئ طلسم طوئ میرزا هندال شد — از بیگمان مذکور بعضی بولایت رفتند وبعضی که در آن مجلس حاضر بودند اکثر در دست راست نشسته بودند ✲ از بیگمان مایان — آغه سلطان وآغاچه مادرِ یادگار سلطان بیگم — وآتون ماما وسلیمه وسکینه وبیبی حبیبه وحنیفه بیگه ✲

ومردم دیگر که بدستِ چپِ پادشاه نشسته بودند بر توشك زردوزی — معصومه سلطان بیگم وگلرنگ بیگم وگلچهره واین حقیرِ شکسته گلبدن وعقیقه سلطان بیگم وآجم والدۀ ما که دلدار بیگم باشند — وگلبرگ بیگم و بیگه بیگم (26 a) ونچه ماهم وسلطانم کوچِ امیرخلیفه والوش بیگم وناهید بیگم وخورشید کوکه وکوکه زادهای پادشاه بابام — افغانی آغاچه وگلنار آغه ونازگل آغه چه وکوچِ هندو بیگ مخدومه آغه وفاطیمه سلطان انگه مادرِ روشن کوکه — فخرنسّاء انگه مادرِ ندیم کوکه کوچِ میرزا قلی کوکه — کوچِ محمّدی کوکه — کوچِ مؤیّد بیگ وکوکهای بادشاه — خورشید

---

* (زهگیری) I read *wa* before *tarāshī*.

کوکه وشرف نشا کوکه وفتح کوکه ورابعه سلطان کوکه وماه لقا کوکه و انگهای ما وکوکهای ما ومردمِ بیگمان وکوچ امرایان و مردم که در دست راست بودند — سلیمه بیگه وبیبی نیکه وخانم آغه دخترِ خواجه عبدالله مروارید ونگار آغه مادرِ مغل بیگ ونار سلطان آغه وآغه کوکه کوچِ منعم خان ودخترِ میرشاه حسین (؟) عیبِس بیگه وکیسك ماهم وکابلی ماهم وبیگی آغه وخانم آغه وسعادت سلطان آغه وبیبی دولت بخت ونصیب آغه وعیپس کابلی و دیگر بیگه‌ها وآغها کوچِ امرایان بدین طرف نشستند (26 b) وهمه در آن مجلس طوی حاضر بودند*

وطرحِ خانهٔ طلسم بدین تفصیل — خانهٔ کلان مثمن که در آن جا طوی دادند — خانهٔ خورد دیگر برابر آن هم مثمن بود — ودر هر دو مثمن انواع تکلف وآرایش نموده بودند — ودر مثمن کلان که طوی خانه باشد — تختِ مرصّع نهاده — در بالا و پایانِ تخت ادسقهای زردوزی انداخته وشدهای مروارید اویخته بمقدارِ یك نیم گز درازی — هرلری دو کرهٔ آینه در پایان قریب سی چهل لری‌ها ساخته وآویخته — ودر مثمن خورد چهپرکتِ* (*sic*) مرصّع نهاده وپاندان وصراحی ومشربهٔ مرصّع وطلا آلات ونقره آلات ساده در طاق‌ها نهاده وبجانبِ دیوانخانه قبله رویه و دیگری بجانب باغ مشرق رویه ودر سیوم بجانب مثمنِ کلان جنوب رویه ودر چهارم بجانبِ مثمن خورد شمال رویه — در بالای این سه خانه مذکور سه بالاخانه بود که یکی‌را خانهٔ دولت میگفتند — ودر آن خانه نه اسباب سپاه‌گری می بود — مثل شمشیرِ مرصّع وقورِ مرصّع وکمر خنجرِ مرصّع وجمدهر وکهپوهٔ مرصّع وترکش — همه مرصّع وقورپوش (27 a) زردوزی انداخه — وخانهٔ دویم که آن خانهٔ سعادت میگفتند در آن خانه جای نماز وکتابها وقلمدانهای مرصّع و جزدانهای خوش ومرقّهای لطیف مع

* (چهپرکهت) Several Hindustānī words occur in the M.S..

3

تصویرهای و خطّهای خوش نهاده بودند* و خانهٔ سیوم که آن‌را خانهٔ مراد می‌گفتند در آن خانه خهپرکت از مرصّع و ظرفی از صندل انداخته و توشکهای خیال انداخته و در پایان نیز نهالچهای خاصگی انداخته در پیش نهالچهاء دسترخانهای انداخته همه از زربفت خیال بود و میوهای الوان و شربتهای گوناگون — وهمه اسبابِ عیش وطرب تنعّم مهیا ساخته بودند*

و روزی که طوی خانهٔ طلسم شد حکم فرمودند که تمام میرزایان و بیگمان وامرایان همه ساچق سازند* بفرمودهٔ ایشان همه آوردند — حکم فرمودند که این ساچق‌را سه توده بکنند — سه خوان اشرفی شد و شش خوان شاهرخی — یکخوان اشرفی ودو خوان شاهرخی‌را به هندو بیگ دادند که این حصّهٔ دولت است — بمیرزایان و امرایان و وزرا و سپاهی‌ها بخش بکن — و یکخوان اشرفی و دو خوان شاهرخی‌را (27b) بملازمت مولا محمّد فرغری دادند که این حصّهٔ سعادت است — این‌را به آکابران و اشراف و علما وصلحا و زهّاد و مشایخ و درویش و عبّاد وفقرا ومساکین بخش بکنند — ویکخوانِ اشرفی ودو خوانِ شاهخی‌را فرمودند که این حصّهٔ مراد است — از ما است — پیش بیارید* آوردند — فرمودند که شمردن چه حاجت است* اوّل خود دستِ مبارك رسانیدند وفرمودند که اوّل در یکخوانچه اسرفی ودر یکخوانچه شاهرخی پیش بیگمان به برند* هرکسی مشت مشت خودها بگیرید وباقی دو خوانِ شاهرخی — وهمه اشرفی‌را قریب دو هزار بود — وشاهرخی قریب ده هزار باشد* همه‌را پاشیدند ونثار کردند اوّل پیش ولی نعمتان ودکر(؟ دیگر) بحاضرانِ مجلس از صد وصد پنجاه کم هیچکس نیافته بود — بتخصیص جماعهٔ که در حوض بودند — بسیار یافتند*

وحضرت بادشاه فرمودند که آکه جانم اگر حکم شود در حوض آب بمانند* آکه جانم گفتند بسیار خوب* خود آمده برسر زینه نشستند ومردم غافل که بیکبارگی شراس زده آب آمد — جوانان‌را طرفه اصترابی دست داده (28a) حضرت بادشاه فرمودند دخل ندارد — هرکدامِ شمایان که یك گلولهٔ شیبت* ویك پارچهٔ معجون بخورید وازینجا بدر روید — ودر ان میان هرکه معجون خورد زود برآمد وآب تا شتالنگ رسیده بود* الحاصل همه معجون رسا خوردند وبرآمدند* وآشِ طوی کشیدند وسروپاها بمردم نهادند وانعامها وسروپاها بمردم معجون خورده وغیره دادند* در لب حوض تالاری بود ودر تالار دریچه ها ابهرك گرفته بودند که جوانان درآن تالار نشستند وبازی گران بازی می‌کردند* بازار زنانه نیزکرده بودند وکیشتی‌هارا آئین بسته بودند* ودر یك کشتی مثل شش کسی وشش کنج بسته بودند ودرکشتی بالاخانه ساخته بودند وپایان باغی ساخته بودند از قسم قلغه وتاج خروس ونافرمان ولاله کاشته بودند ودر یك جا هشت کشتی کرده بودند که هشت پرچه میشد* غرض که خدای تعالی ازین قسم اختراعات در دل مبارك ایشان عطا کرده بود — هرکه میدید متحیّر ومنحصر می‌ماند*

دیگر شرح (28b) طویٔ میرزا هندال آنکه** سلطانم بیگم خواهرِ مهدی خواجه بودند*

یزنهٔ بابام غیرجعفرخواجه فرزندِ دیگر نداشتند وفرزند نمی‌شد* آکه جانم سلطانم‌را بفرزندی نگاه داشته بودند ودو ساله بود که خانزاده بیگم نگاه کرده بودند وعجایب دوست می‌داشتند وبه برادرزاده خود داند و طوی‌را درکمال لطافت وخوبی کردند*

---

* (شیبت) This word has only the *yā* points and might yield also *sīb*, apple. Anise seems the safer remedy against chill.

** (آنکه) Translated as *ān ast ki*.

کوشکه و ادسقه و پنج توشك و پنج بستوق و یك تکیهٔ کلان و دو تکیهٔ گلوله و قوشقه و نقاب مع خرگاه جباغ (؟) مع سه توشك همه زردوزی و سروپاهای میرزا چارقب و ناج زردوزی و فوطه و روپاك و رومالِ زردوزی و قورپوش زردوزی *

وبسلطانم بیگم نه نیمتنهٔ تکمه‌دارِ جواهر — یکی از لعل ویکی از یاقوت ویکی از زمرّد و یکی از فیروزه و یکی از زبرجد و یکی از عین الهرة * دیگر (ا)ز نحرگوهرنه* (؟) — و یك چارقب وچارقرنیچی تکمه‌دار — ویك جفت حاقه لعل و یك جفت حلقه درّ — سه پنخه و یك چترشاهی یکدرخت و دوخطب و دیگر اسباب واسیا و رخت و رخوت وکارخانها از همه (29a) جنس که آنچه خانزاده بیگم جمع کرده بودند — همه‌را دادند و بنوعی طوی کردند که مثل آن طوی فرزندان پادشاه بابام‌را دیگر مُیسّر نشد * همه مُهیّا کرده سپُردند — و نه اسپِ تپوچاق مع زین ولجامِ مرصّع کاری و زردوزی وطلا آلات ونقره آلات وغلامانِ ترك وچرکس واروس وحبشی واز هرکدام تقوز تقوز پیشکش *

وآنچه بزنهٔ بابام بمیرزا پیشکش کرده بودند — یك تقوزِ اسپِ تپوچاق مع زین ولجامِ مرصّع و زردوزی وطلا آلات ونقرهٔ آلات — ودو تقوز دیگر اسپانِ بارگیر مع زین ولجام مخمل و زربفت وسقرلات پرتگالی و غلامانِ ترك وحبشی وهندی — همگی سه تقوز وسه زنجیر فیل *

وبعد از آنکه از طوی فارغ شدند — خبر آمد که وزیرِ سلطان بهادر — خراسان خان نام — به بیانه تاخت آورده است * حضرت بادشاه میرزا عسکری‌را با چند امرای دیگر که فخر علی بیگ ومیر تردی بیگ وغیره‌را فرستادند * اینها در بیانه رفته جنگ کردند * خراسان خان‌را

---

* ? of neck (نحر)—jewels nine. *Naḥr* is the part of the neck on which the necklace rests. زنحر might also be read as *zingīr* but I have found no help to this reading in dictionaries.

شکست (29b) دادند* وبعد از چند گاه حضرت پادشاه خود متوجه گجرات بسعادت وسلامت شدند* بتاریخ پانزدهم شهر رجب المرجّب سنه نهصد وچهل ویك عزم جزم گجرات نمودند — وپیشخانه در باغ زرافشان برپا کردند — وخود در باغ مذکور تا جمع شدن لشکرها یکماه بودند*

روزهای دیوان که یکشنبه و سه‌شنبه باشد — آنروی آب می‌رفتند وتا در باغ بودند اکثر روزها آچم وهمشیرها وحرمان در ملازمتِ حضرت می‌بودیم* واز همه بالا چادرِ معصومه سلطان بیگم — بعد از آن چادرِ گلرنگ بیگم وچادر آچم یکجا بود* بعد از آن چادرِ مادرم* گلبرگ بیگم وبیگه بیگم وغیره بیگمان*

وکارخانها برپا کردند وطیار نمودند* مرتبهٔ اوّل که خیمه و خرگاه وبارگاه در باغ برپا کردند بجهة دیدن یورت وترتیب فروز آمد بیگمان وهمشیرها تشریف آوردند* چون معصومه سلطان بیگم نزدیکتر فروز** آمده بودند بخانهٔ ایشان تشریف آوردند* همه بیگمان وهمشیرها در ملازمتِ حضرت بودیم* بخانه هر بیگمی وهمشیرهٔ (30a) که تشریف می‌بردند همه بیگمان وهمه همشیرها همراه میرفتند — وفرداش در خانهٔ این حقیر تشریف فرمودند* تا سه پهرشب مجلس بود واکثر بیگمان وهمشیرها وبیگه‌ها وآغاها وآغچها وسازندها وگویندها بودند* بعد از سه پهر حضرت آسایش فرمودند* همشیرها وبیگمان همه در ملازمتِ حضرت تکیه کردند*

وبیگه بیگم بیدار کردند که وقتِ نماز است* حضرت فرمودند که آبِ وضورا در همان خانه طیار سازند* بیگم دانشتند که پادشاه بیدار شدند*

---

* (مادرم) Cf. n. to trs.

** (فروز) فروز occurs elsewhere where فرود might be looked for.

بنیاد گله کردند که چند روز است که درین باغ تشریف آورده اید — یك روز بخانهٔ ما نه آمدید* در راهٔ خانهٔ ما خوخار نکاشته اند — امیدواریم که در خانهٔ ما نیز تشریف بیارید و معرکه ومجلس سازید* تا کی اینهمه بی التفاتها در بابهٔ این بیچاره روا خواهید داشت* ما هم دلی داریم — در جایهای دیگر سه مرتبه تشریف بردید و شب و روز در آنجاها بعیش وعشرت گذرانیدید* آخر (30b) پادشاه هیچ نگفتند وبنماز رفتند — و یك پهر روز برآمده بود که همشیرها وبیگمان ودلدار بیگم وافغانی آغه‌چه وگلنار آغه‌چه ومیوه جان وآغه جان وانیگه هارا (sic) طلبیدند — وحالاً که همه رفتیم پادشاه هیچ نگفتند وهمه دانشتند که پادشاه در قهر اند* بعد از آن گفتند — بعد از زمانی — که بیبی سحر چه بلا از من گلها کردی — و — آن همچو جای نبود که گله بایست کرد* شما میدانید که در خانهٔ ولی نعمتانِ شمایان بوده ام* بمن ضرورت است خاطر جوئ ایشانان کردن وبا* جود آن از روی ایشان شرمنده ام که دیر می بینم — و دایم در خاطرم بود که از شمایان** بجلی طلبم* خوب شد که شما خود بزبان آوردید — من افیونی — اگر در آمد و رفتِ من دیرتر واقع شود از من نرنجید — وگرنه خطّی نوشته بدهید که رضائ شما خواه بیائید خواه نیائید که ما راضی وشاکر ایم از شما* گلبرگ بیگم فی الحال بهمین مضمون نوشته دادند وبه گلبرگ بیگم دریافتند وبیگه بیگم پاره مبالغه کردند که عذر بدتر از گناهش (31a) نگرید — غرضِ ما از اظهارِ گله آن بود که مارا از التفاتِ خود سرافراز سازند — ایشان کاررا تا اینجا رسانیدند — ما چه چاره داریم — پادشاه اند* خطّی نوشته دادند* حضرت بادشاه هم دریافتند*

---

* (با) Read as *bā wujūd-i-ān.*

** (بجلی) Read in translating for سبجلی; an attested writing.

و چهاردهمِ شهرِ شعبان از باغ زرافشان کوچ کرده متوجهٔ گجرات شدند وبر سرِ سلطان بهادر رفتند ودر منحسور مقابل شدند و جنگ کرده سلطان بهادررا بشکست او گریخته بجانب چنپانیر رفت * آخر حضرت خود مقیّد شدہ تعاقب کردند چنپانیررا گذاشته بطرف احمداباد رفت *

حضرة ولایتِ احمدابادرا هم گرفتند و بمردم تمام گجراترا تقسیم کردند واحمدابادرا بمیرزا عسکری عنایت فرمودند — وبهروچرا بقاسم حسین سلطان دادند — وپتن‌را به یادگار ناصر میرزا دادند — وحضرة خود از چنپانیر بمردم اندك بطریقِ سیر به کنمبایت رفتند * بعد از چند روز یك عورتی خبر اورد که — چه نشسته اید — مردمِ کنمبایت جمع شدہ به سرِ شما خواهد ریخت — یا حضرت سُوار شوند * امرایانِ حضرت برسرِ آنجماعت تاختند وآنها (31 b) گیرکردند و پاره‌را قتل کردند — و بعد از آن به برود آمدند * از آنجا بطرفِ چنپانیر رفتند *

نشسته بودیم که فترات شد و مردم میرزا عسکری احمدابادرا ماندہ پیش بادشاه آمدند — و بعرض رسانیدند که میرزا عسکری و یادگار ناصر میرزا متّفق شده اند و به آگره میخواهند بروند * چون حضرت شنیدند ضرور شد متوجه آگره شدند — وبهمّ ومعاملهٔ گجرات نپرداختند — گجرات‌را پرتافته کوچ کرده بجانبِ آگره آمدند * تا یکسال در آگره بودند *

بعد از آن بجانبِ چناده رفتند وچناده‌را وبنارس‌را گرفتند * شیر خان در پرکنده بود و بخدمتِ حضرت عرضه داشت کرد که بندہ پیر غلامِ شما است — بیکجارا سر حدّی سدّ بسته بدهند — که در آنجا نشسته باشم *

درین فکر بودند که پادشاهٔ گور بنگاله زخمی شدہ گریخته پیس حضرت آمد و بدان حضرة مقیّد نشدند — وکوچ کرده متوجه گور بنگاله شدند * شیر خان دانست که پادشاه بگور بنگاله رفتند * خود هم جریدہ ایلغار کرده بگور رفت و همراه پسرِ خود بیکجا شد * پسرِ او و خواص

خان غلام او در گور بودند* خواص خان (32a) و پسرِ خودرا فرستاد که بروید وگرهی‌را مضبوط کنید* ایشانان آمدند وگرهی‌را گرفتند — وآنحضرت جهانگیر بیگ‌را پیش نوشته بودند که یك منزل پیشتر می رفت* بر سر گرهی رسید* جنگ شد* جهانگیر بیگ زخمی شد وکس بسیار کشته شد*

آخر حضرة در کهل گانو سه چهار روز بودند و مصلحت چنان شد که کوچ کرده پیشتر بروند و نزدیك گرهی فرود آیند* چون کوچ کرده پیشتر رفته نزدیك گرهی فرود آمدند شب شیر خان و خواص خان گریختند* فردا آنحضرت به گرهی در آمدند واز گرهی گذشته به گور بنگاله رفتند وگوررا گرفتند*

تا نه ماه در ولایت گور بودند — وگوررا جنّت آباد نام کردند باز بدولت در گور بودند که خبر رسید امرا گریخته بمیرزا هندال ملحق شدند*

خسرو بیگ و زاهد بیگ وسید امیر میرزا ملازمت کرده بعرض رسانیدند که پادشاه بدولت دور رفته اند — و میرزایان که محمّد سلطان میرزا وپسرانش اولغ میرزا وشاه میرزا باز سر بر آورده اند — وهر زمان در یکجا نشان میدهند (32b) ومشیخت پناهی بندگی شیخ بهلول درین وقت جیبه وکجیم واسباب سپاهگری در تخته پنهان کرده و در ارابها بار کرده بشیر خان و میرزایان میفرستد* میرزا هندال باور نمی کردند* آخر بجهة تفحّص این امر میرزا نور الدین محمّدرا فرستادند* جیبه وکجیم‌هارا یافتند* بندگی شیخ بهلول‌را بقتل رسانیدند* این خبر که به پادشاه رسید متوجه آگره شدند وآن روی آب گنگ‌را گرفته می آمدند*

برابر منگیر که رسیدند امرا بعرض رسانیدند که شما بادشاهٔ کلان اید — بهمان راهی که آمده بودید بهمان راه متوجه شوید — تا شیر خان نگوید که راهٔ آمدن خودرا مانده براهٔ دیگر رفتند* باز آنحضرت متوجه

منگیر شدند واکثر مردم اهل وعیال خودرا درکشتی بالا رویه آب می‌کشیدند تا بحاجی‌پور پتنه رسیدند *

در حین رفتن قاسم سلطان در آنجا ماندند * درین اثنا خبر آمد که شیرخان آمد — وهر بار که جنگ میکردند مردم حضرت غالب می آمدند * ودرین اثنا بابا بیگ از جونپور آمد و میرك بیگ از چناده آمد و مغل بیگ از (33 a) اوده آمده این سه امرا که همراه شدند غله قیمت شد *

آخر خواستِ خُدا چنین بود — غافل نشسته بودند که شیرخان آمده ریخت * لشکر شکست یافت واکثر اهل ومردم در اسیری ماندند — وبدستِ مبارکِ حضرة زخم رسید * سه روز درچناده بودند * بعد ازآن به اریل آمدند وچون بر سرِ دریا آمدن درگذشتن حیران ماندند که بی کشتی چطور درگذرند * درین اثنا راجه با پنج شش سوار آمده ایشان‌را از پای آب گذراند * مدّت چهار پنج روز مردم بی طعام وشراب بودند * عاقبت الامر راجه بازار برپا کرد تا مردم لشکر چند روز بعیش وعشرت گذرانیدند واسپان نیز آسوده شدند — وهر که پیاده بوده اسپِ تازه خرید * غرض راجه خدماتِ شایسته وبایسته بجا آورد — و روز دیگر راجه‌را رخصت فرمودند وخود بسعادت وسلامت نماز پیشین برلبِ آبِ جمنه آمدند * یك جا گذر یافته مردم لشکر از آب گذشتند — وبعد از چند روز دیگر به کرّه* آمدند * در آنجا دانه وگاه وافر بود (33 b) از برای آنکه ولایتِ خود بود * مردم لشکر آسوده شده بکالپی رسیدند — واز کالپی کوچ کرده متوجه آگره شدند * قبل از آمدن آگره خبر شنیدند که شیرخان طرفِ چوسه می آید * مردم‌را طرفه اضطرابی دست داد *

از بعضی‌ها در آن فطرات اصلاً وقطعاً نام ونشان یافته نشد * از آن

---

* (کرّه) Text اگره. Clearly an error. Humāyūn was marching up the Dūāb from the junction of the Jamna and Ganges, towards Āgra.

جمله عایشه سلطان بیگم دختر سلطان حسین میرزا و بچکا که خلیفهٔ بادشاه بابام بود و بیگه جان کوکه وعقیقه بیگم وچاند بیبی که هفت ماهسه شکم داشت وشاد بیبی که این هر سه حرمانِ پادشاه بودند* ازین چند کس اصلاً وقطعاً خبر هم نیافتند که در آب رفتند یا چه شدند* هرچند تفحّص وتردّد کردند اصلاً معلوم نشد که چه شدند*

وتشویش ایشان تا چهل روز کشید* بعد از آن صحّت یافتند*

درین ضمن خشرو بیگ ودیوانه بیگ وزاهد بیگ وسید امیر از پیش حضرة پادشاه که آمدند از طرف میرزایان محمّد سلطان میرزا وپسرانش باز خبر رسید که کنوج آمده اند*

ومیرزا هندال بعد از (34 a) قتلِ شیخ بهلول بدهلی رفتند* میر فقر علی ودولتخواهانِ دیگررا همراه گرفته تا دفع ورفع محمّد سلطانِ میرزا وپسرانش بکنند* میرزایان از آنطرف گریخته بطرفِ کنوج آمدند* میرفقر علی میرزا یادگار ناصررا در دهلی درآورد* چون در میانِ میرزا هندال و میرزا یادگار ناصر اتحاد واخلاص نبود — میرفقر علی که این طور حرکتی کرد میرزا هندال از قهر دهلی‌را قبل کرده نشستند*

میرزا کامران که این خبرها شنیدند — در ایشان هم داعیهٔ پادشاهی پیدا شد* با دوازده هزار سوار مسلّح متوجه دهلی‌را شدند* بدهلی که رسیدند میر فقر علی و میرزا یادگار ناصر دروازهٔ دهلی بستند — وبعد از دو سه روز میر فقر علی قول وقرار گرفته آمده میرزا کامران‌را دید — وعرض کرد که خبرهای حضرت بادشاه وشیر خان‌را باین روش شنیده میشود — ومیرزا یادگار ناصر از ملاحظهٔ خود شمارا ملازمت نمی کند — مناسبِ دولت آنست که درین طور وقت شما میرزا هندال‌را گرفته متوجه آگره شوید وخیالِ نشستن (34 b) دهلی نکنید* میرزا کامران سخن میر فقر علی‌را پسندید وسروپا داده بدهلی رخصت کردند — وخود میرزا هندال‌را گرفته به آگره

آمدند و فردوس مکانی‌را زیارت کرده والده و همشیرهارا دیده در باغ گل افشان منزل کردند *

درین اثنا نور بیگ آمد و خبر آورد که حضرة بادشاه می آیند * چون از جهة کشتن شیخ بهلول میرزا هندال محجوب بودند خودرا جانب الور کشیدند *

و میرزا کامران حضرت بادشاه‌را ملازمت کردند * بعد از چند روز از باغ گل افشان آمده حضرت پادشاه‌را ملازمت میکردند * همان روز که حضرت آمدند شب بود که رفته ملازمت کردیم * این حقیررا دیدند فرمودند که اوّل ترا نشناختم از برای آنکه وقتی که لشکر ظفراثر به گور بنگاله کشیده بودم — طاقی پوش بودی * الحال که لچك قصابه دیدم نشناختم — وگلبدنِ من ترا بسیار یاد میکردم وگاهی پشیمان شده می گفتم که کاشکی همراه می آوردم — امّا وقتی که فطرات شد (35 a) شکر میکردم ومیگفتم الحمد الله که گلبدن‌را نیاوردم — با وجودی که عقیقه خورد بود صد هزار غم وافسوس میخوردم که چرا بلشکر آوردم *

وبعد از چند روز حضرت بادشاه بدیدنِ والده آمده بودند * آن حضرت هیکلِ مصحف همراه داشتند * فرمودند که ساعتی مردم کناره شوند * مردم برخاستند * خلوت شد * آخر حضرة به آچم و این حقیر وافغانی آغه چه وگلنار آغه چه ونارگل آغه چه وانگهٔ من گفتند که هندال قول وقناتِ من است بنوعی که مارا روشنائ چشم مطلوبست قوتِ بازو هم مطلوب و مرغوبست * روا باشد — بجهة قضیهٔ شیخ بهلول من بمیرزا محمّد هندال چه خواهم گفت — آنچه تقدیر الٰهی بود شد * الحال من هیچ غبار خاطري به هندال ندارم — واگر باور نکنید — مصحف‌را برداشته بودند که حضرت والده و دلدار بیگم و این حقیر مصحف‌را از دستِ ایشان گرفتیم وهمه گفتند — روا باشد — چرا چنین

میگوئید * وباز فرمودند که گلبدن چه شود (35 b) که برادرِ خود محمّد هندال میرزارا تو رفته بیاری؟ حضرت والدہ ام گفتند که این دخترك خورد سال است — هرگز صفر نکرده است * اگر حکم شود من بروم * آنحضرت فرمودند که من بشما این تصدیعات چون دهم این خود ظاهر است که غمخواری فرزندان بر مادر و پدر لازم است * اگر تشریف ببرید غمخواریست که بر مایان میکنید *

آخر امیر ابو البقارا بهمراهی حضرت والدہ ام بطلبِ میرزا هندال فرستادند — و محمّد هندال میرزا بمجرّد شنیدن این خبر تشریف آوردند و حضرت والدہ خوشحالی‌ها کردند و پیشواز آمدند و همراهٔ حضرت والدہ میرزا هندال از الور آمدند وحضرت پادشاه‌را ملازمت کردند وقصّهٔ شیخ بهول مذکور گفتند که جیبه وکجیم واسباب سپاه‌یگری‌را بشیر خان میفرستاد * چون بتحقیق رسید شیخ مذکوررا بنابر آن کشتم *

غرض بعد از چند روز خبر رسید که شیر خان نزدیك لکهنو رسید * درین اثنا حضرت پادشاه یك غلام سقّا داشتند * از جهة آنکه بادشاه درآب چوسه از اسپ جُدّا شدہ بودند (36 a) وغلام سقّا خودرا رسانید وبه مددِ او از گرداب بسعادت وسلامت برآمدند — آخر حضرت سقای مذکوررا بر تخت نشانند — ونامِ آن غلام مشخّص نشنیدیم * بعضی نظام میگفتند وبعضی سُنبل میگفتند * غرض آن غلام سقّارا بر تخت نشانند وحکم فرمودند که همه امرایان کورنش بغلام سقّا بکنند و غلام بهرکس هرچه خواهد بخشد ومنصب بدهد * تا دو روز به آن غلام پادشاهی دادند * میرزا هندال در آن مجلس حاضر نه بودند * رخصت شده باز بالور رفته بودند از برای یراق کردن — و میرزا کامران نیز در آن مجلس نیامدند * بیماری داشتند وبحضرت گفته فرستادند که غلام‌را بخشیش و رعایتهای دیگر بایست کرد — چه لازم بود که بر تخت نشیند *

درین وقت که شیر خان نزدیك رسیده این چه کار است که حضرت میکنند ×

در آن روزها میرزا کامران بیماریٔ عجب زور کرده × چنان ضعیف ولاغر شدند و از بس که لاغر شده بودند اصلاً چهره برجا نبود و امیدِ زیستن نبود × بعنایت (36 b) آلهی بهتر شدند — و میرزا کامران‌را گمانِ آن شد که بمصلحتِ حضرت بادشاه والدها به ایشان زهر دادند × حضرت بادشاه این سخن‌را شنیدند × یکمرتبه بدیدنِ میرزا کامران آمدند و سوگند خوردند که هرگز در خیال ما نگذشته و بکس نفرموده ایم × با وجودِ سوگند خاطرِ میرزا کامران صاف نشد و بیماریٔ میرزا باز روز بروز بدتر شد چنانچه قوتِ سخن کردن نداشتند ×

تا آنکه خبر رسید که شیر خان از لکهنو گذشت حضرت کوچ کردند ومتوجه کنوج شدند و میرزا کامران‌را بجای خود در آگره ماندند × بعد از چند روز میرزا کامران شنیدند که حضرت بادشاه پل بسته از آب گنگ گذشتند × میرزا کامران شنیدند — از آگره کوچ کردند ×

بطرف لاهور نشسته بودیم که میرزا کامران فرمانِ بادشاهی‌را فرستادند که شمارا حکم است که همراهٔ من به لاهور بروید × از جهةِ من میرزا کامران بحضرت بادشاه گفته باشند که بیماریٔ من بسیار قوی است و بسیار غریب و بیکس و بی غمخوارم (37 a) اگر گلبدن بیگم‌را حکم شود که بمن همراه بلاهور برود عین عنایت وکرم خواهد بود × حضرت بروی ایشان گفته باشند که برود × چون بادشاه بدولت وسعادت جانب لکهنو دو سه منزل رفتند میرزا فرمان پادشاهی‌را نمودند ومحصّل شدند که البته شما همراهٔ من بیائید × والدهٔ من درین اثنا گفته باشند که هرگز از مایان جُدًا سفر نکرده است × ایشان فرمودند اگر تنها سفر نکرده است شما نیز همراه بروید × تا پانج صد از سپاهی و مهتران حرم و هر دو انکه وکوکهٔ

خودرا فرستادند که اگر همراه نمیرود تا یك منزل خود بیائید* آخر در آن منزل که آمده شد دیگر بنیادِ سوگند خوردن کردند که من ترا نخواهم گذاشت*

آخر بصد گریه و زاری و فغان از والدها و از والدهٔ خود و از همشیرها و از مردمِ پدر و برادران که از خوردی یك‌جا کلان شده بودیم—از همه جُدّا کرده بزجر و زور بردند* دیدم که فرمان پادشاهی هم درین باب هست* لا علاج شدم و بحضرت عرضه داشت (37 b) نوشتم که از حضرت چشم داشتِ آن نداشتم که این حقیررا از ملازمت خود جُدا سازند و به میرزا کامران به بخشند* آخر در جواب عریضهٔ حقیر حضرت پادشاه سلام نامه نوشته فرستادند به این مضمون که من دل نداشتم که ترا از خود جُدّا کنم—امّا چون میرزا بسیار مبالغه کرد و عجز و الحاح نمود ضرور شد که ترا به میرزا سپردم چرا که الحال ما هم بر سرِ مهم ایم—انشاالله تعالی هرگاه که این مهم صورة پذیرد اوّل ترا خواهم طلبید*

چون میرزا متوجه لاهور شدند اکثر مردم از امرا و سوداگران وغیره هرکسی‌را استعداد بود* گرایه* کرده واهل وعیالِ خودهارا همراهٔ میرزا کامران کوچانیده بلاهور بردند*

بعد از آمدن بلاهور خبر رسید که براب آبِ گنگ جنگ شد وشکست بر لشکرِ حضرت افتاد* باری این قدر شد که حضرت با برادران و خویشان از آن ورطهٔ بصحت وسلامت برآمدند*

دیگر خویشاوند که در آگره بودند براهٔ الور شده متوجه لاهور شدند* در آن اثنا حضرت بمیرزا هندال (38 a) فرمودند که در آن فترتِ اوّل عقیقه بیبی غایب شدند* آخر بسیار پشیمان شدم که چرا بحضورِ خود نکشتم* الحال هم عورات‌را درین طورِ وقت همراه بجای رسانیدن مشکل

* (کرایه) Misread as گرای in the translation.

است* آخر میرزا هندال عرض کردند که قتل کردنِ مادر و خواهر بحضرت روشن است* تا جان دارم در خدمت آنها تردّد میکنم و امیدوارم از حضرت حق سبحانه که در قدمِ حضرت والده و همشیره این حقیر جانِ خودرا نثار کنم*

آخر حضرت بادشاه با میرزا عسکری و یادگار ناصر میرزا و امرای که از جنگ گاه سلامت بر آمده بودند متوجه فتح پور شدند*

و میرزا هندال حضرة والدهٔ خودرا که دلدار بیگم باشند و همشیره که گلچهره بیگم باشند و افغانی آغه چه وگلنار آغه چه و نارگل آغه چه و اهل و عیالِ امرا و غیره‌را در پیش انداخته می بردند که گواران بسیار بر ایشان تاختند* از سپاهیان ایشان چند کس اسپ انداخته اند و گواران‌را (38 b) شکست دادند — و یك تیر به اسپِ مبارك ایشان رسید* جنگ و جدّل بسیار کردند* ضعفارا از اسیرئ گواران خلاص کرده حضرت والده و همشیره خودرا و بسی امرا و غیره مردم‌را در پیش انداخته به الور آمده رسیدند*

چادر و خیمه و غیره بعضی اسباب که درکار بود گرفته متوجه لاهور شدند* میرزایان و امرایان‌را آنچه درکار بود همراه گرفته در اندك روز آمده بلاهور رسیدند*

حضرت در باغ خواجه غازی نزدیك بیبی حاج تاج فرود آمدند* هر روز خبرِ شیر خان میرسید* مدّت سه ماه در لاهور بودند و روز بروز خبر می آمد که شیر خان دو کروه سه کروه می آید — تا انکه خبر رسید که نزدیك سرهند رسید*

وحضرة مظفّر بیگ نام امرا *(sic)* داشتند* ترکمان بود* اورا همراه قاضی عبد الله پیش شیر خان فرستادند که چه انصافست — تمام ملك هندوستان‌را بتو گذاشتم* یك لاهور مانده میانِ ما و شما حد همین

سرهند باشد٭ آن بی انصاف (39a) خدا نا ترس قبول نکرده وگفت که کابل‌را بشما گذاشتم — در آنجا باید رفت٭

مظفّر بیگ در ساعت کوچ کرد و پیشتر کس فرستاد که کوچ می باید کرد٭ همین که خبر رسید حضرت کوچ کردند گویا روز قیامت بود که جای هارا آرسته همراهٔ اسباب همان نوع گذاشتند٭ مگر نقد آنچه بود همون‌را توانستند گرفت٭ شکر خدا درین بود که از آبِ لاهور گذر یافتند٭ همه مردم پای آب گذاَشتند — وچند روز در کنارِ دریای منزل کردند که ایلچیٔ شیر خان آمد٭ قرار دادند که صباح به بینند که میرزا کامران التماس نمودند که فردا معرکه خواهد بود و ایلچیٔ سیر خان خواهد آمد٭ اگر در نوك زلچهٔ حضرت نشینم تا فرقی میانِ من و برادران باشد باعثِ سرافرازی من خواهد شد٭

همین بانو بیگم میگویند بمیرزا این رباعی‌را پادشاه نوشته فرستادند ومن شنیده بودم که در جوابِ شیر خان بدستِ ایلچی نوشته فرستادند٭ رباعی این است —

در اینه گرچه خود نمائی باشد — پیوسته زخویشتن جُدّائی باشد — (39b)
خودرا بمثالی غیر دیدن عجب است — این بوالعجبی کار خدای باشد٭

ایلچیٔ شیر خان که آمده ملازمت کرد٭

خاطرِ مبارك ایشان ملول شد٭ دلگیر شده در خواب شدند و در خواب دیده اند که عزیزی آمده از سرتا پا لباس سبز پوشیده وعصای در دست٭ گفت مردانه باش وغم مخور و عصای خودرا بدستِ مبارکِ حضرت داده اند وگفته اند خدای تعالی بتو فرزندی خواهد داد — نامش جلال الدین محمّد آکبر بمانی٭ حضرت پرشیدند که اسمِ شریفِ شما چیست؟ فرموده اند که ژنده فیل احمدِ جام — وفرموده اند آن فرزند ازنسل من خواهد شد٭

و در آن ایام بیبی گونور حامله بود* همه میگفتند که پسر تولّد خواهد شد* در همان باغ دوست منشی از بیبی گونور در ماه جمید الاوّل دختر تولّد شد ببخشی بانو بیگم نام کردند*

و در آن روزها میرزا حیدررا بگرفتنِ کشمیر تعین نموده اند* درین اثنا خبر آمد که شیر خان رسید* عجب اضطرار می دست داد* قرار دادند که صباح کوچ کنند* (40 a)

درین مدّت که برادران در لاهور بودند هر روز مصلحت و مشورت و کنگاش میکردند* اصلاً بیك چیز قرار نمی دادند* آخر الامر خبر آمد که شیرخان آمد* دیگر بی علاج شده یکپهر روز بود که کوچ کردند و حضرت داعیهٔ کشمیر داشتند — و میرزا حیدر کاشغریرا فرستاده بودند* امّا هنوز خبرِ فتح کشمیر نیامده بود* کنگاش دادند که اگر حضرة متوجه کشمیر شوند وکشمیر فی الحال میُسَّر نشود و شیر خان در لاهور باشد — آن زمان بسیار مشکل میشود*

خواجه کلان بیگ در سیال کوت بود — متوجه ملازمتِ حضرت شد* مؤید بیگ همراهٔ خواجه بود* بحضرت عرضه داشت کرد — خواجه دغدغهٔ ملازمت دارد و می آید امّا ملاحظهٔ میرزا کامران دارد — اگر حضرت بسرعت بیایند ملازمتِ خواجه بحضرت با حسن وجه مُیسَّر می شود* حضرت از شنیدن این خبر فی الحال جیبه پوشیده مسلح و مکمل شده متوجه خواجه شدند و خواجه‌را همراه گرفته آوردند*

و حضرت فرمودند که باتفاقِ برادران به بدخشان رویم وکابل (40 b) تعلق بمیرزا کامران داشته باشد* امّا میرزا کامران برفتن کابل راضی نشدند وگفتند که کابل‌را حضرت فردوس مکانی در حیاتِ خود بوالدهٔ من داده اند — رفتن کابل لایق نیست* حضرت فرمودند که در بابِ کابل اکثر حضرت فردوس مکانی میفرمودند که کابل‌را من بهیچ کس نخواهم داد —

بلکه فرزندان طمعِ کابل نکنند — چرا که همهٔ فرزندان‌را خدای تعالی بمن در کابل داده و اکثر فتح‌ها از نشستن کابل شده بلکه در واقعه نامهٔ فردوس مکانی هم متشهد این معنی بسیار مذکور است * چه شد که من از روی مهربانی و برادری بمیرزا انسانیت کردم — میرزا الحال چنین میگوید *

هرچند حضرت دلاسا و یکانگی میفرمودند — میرزا بیشتر از پیشتر مبالغه مینمودند * چون حضرت دیدند که همراهٔ میرزا جمعیت بسیار است و بهیچ وجه رفتن کابل میرزا راضی نیست لا علاج شده ضرور شد بطرفِ بکهر وملتان متوجه شدند * در ملتان که رسیدند یك روز منزل (41a) نمودند * غلهٔ کمترك پیدا شد واندك غله که در قلعه پیدا شده بود بمردم قسمت کرده کوچ کردند و بر سر دریای که هفت دریا یکجا شده است رسیدند * حیران ماندند * کشتی بهم نمیرسد وأردوی عظیم همراه * درین اثنا خبر آمد که خواص خان با چند امرا از عقب می آید * بخشو نام بلوچی بود که جاهای متمکن داشت وکسی (؟ کشتی) بسیار هم داشت * حضرة کسی‌را پیش او فرستادند وعلم ونقاره واسپ وسروپا نیز فرستادند وطلب کشتی نمودند وغله هم طلب نمودند * آخر الامر بخشو بلوج قریب یك صد کشتی نمودند پر غله هم بملازمتِ حضرت فرستادند * ازین خدمت شایسته حضرت بسیار خوشحالی کردند وکشتی غلهٔ مذکوررا بمردم لشکر قسمت کردند و بسعادت وسلامت از آب گذشتند * رحمت باد بر بخشوْ مذکور که خدمتِ شایسته بجا آورد *

وآخر الامر بعد از طی مسافت به بکهر رسیدند — وقلعهٔ بکهر در میانِ دریا واقع شده وقلعه مضبوط دارد — وپادشاهٔ قلعه مذکور که سلطان محمود (41b) باشد متحصّن شده بود وحضرت به پهلوی قلعه بسعادة وسلامت فرود آمده بودند — ونزدیك قلعه باغی بود که میرزا شاه حسین سمندر راست کرده بود *

آخر میر سمندررا* پیش شاه حسین میرزا فرستادند که از ضرورت بولایتِ تو آمده ایم و ولایتِ تو بتو مبارك باشد — ما دخل نخواهیم کرد — باری تو خود آمده مارا ملازمت بکن و خدمت که لازمه باشد بجا بیار — که ما داعیهٔ گجرات داریم و ولایتِ ترا بتو میگذاریم * آخر شاه حسینِ مذکور بمکر وحیله تا پنج ماه حضرت‌را در سمندر نگاه داشت وبعد از آن کس بخدمت حضرت فرستاد که سامانِ طویٔ دختر خودرا کرده بخدمتِ حضرت میفرستم وخود نیز بملازمت خواهم آمد *

حضرت سخنِ اورا باور کردند — سه ماه دیگر انتظار کشیدند * غله گاهی پیدا میشود وگاهی پیدا نمی شود * مردم سپاه اسپان و شتران خودرا کشته میخوردند * باز حضرت شیخ عبد الغفوررا فرستادند — تا کی انتظار میدهی — مانع (42a) آمدن کیست وباعث توقّف چیست؟ این مرتبه داشت که کار تنگ شده است ومردم بسیار گریخته می روند * جواب فرستاد که دخترِ من نامزدِ میرزا کامران است ودیدنِ من هم امر محال است — شمارا ملازمت کرده نمی توانم *

درین اثنا محمّد هندال میرزا از آب گذشتند که بعضی مردم میگفتند که متوجه قندهار میشوند * حضرت پادشاه که شنیدند از عقبِ میرزا چند کس فرستادند که رفته ترسید (؟ پرسید) که شنیده شد که قصد قندهار دارند * چون از میرزا پرسیدند میرزا گفتند که غلط بعرض رسانیده اند * حضرت بادشاه این خبررا شنیده بدیدنِ حضرت والده آمدند *

حرمهای میرزا وهمه مردمِ میرزا حضرت بادشاه‌را درین مجلس ملازمت

* (سمندررا) Text, آخر میرزا شاه حسین سمندررا. This is clearly the scribe's error. Mīr Samandar was a confidential servant of Humāyūn and is named in the histories as the envoy. Cf. note to translation.

کردند* حمیده بانو بیگم‌را پرسیدند که این چه کس است؟ گفتند که دخترِ میر بابا دوست* خواجه معظّم روبروی حضرت استاده بود* گفتند — این پسر بما خویش میشود* حمیده بانو بیگم‌را گفتند که این هم خویشِ ما است*

در آن ایام حمیده بانو بیگم (42 b) آکثر در محلِ میرزا می بود* روز دیگر باز حضرت بدیدنِ حضرت والده دلدار بیگم آمدند* فرمودند — میر بابا دوست خویشاوند ما است — مناسب آنست که دخترِ اورا بما نسبت بکنید* میرزا هندال عذرها می‌گفتند که این دختررا من مثل خواهر و فرزند خود میدانم — حضرت پادشاه اند — مبادا معاشِ نیك نشود تا باعثِ کلفت شود* حضرت پادشاه خشم کرده برخواسته رفتند*

بعد از آن حضرت والده خطی نوشته فرستادند که مادرِ دختر ازین هم پیشتر ناز میکند — عجبست که به اندك سخن رنجیده رفتند* حضرت پادشاه در جواب نوشته فرستادند که این حکایتِ شما بما بسیار خوش آمد هر نازی که می کنید بسر و چشم قبول داریم* دیگر از جهة معاش که نوشته اند انشا الله — حسب المدّعا خواهد شد — چشمِ انتظار در راه است* حضرت والده رفته حضرت پادشاه‌را آوردند* آن روز مجلس دادند* بعد از مجلس بمنزلِ خود تشریف بردند* روزِ دیگر حضرت پیش والده‌ام آمدند وگفتند که کس (43 a) فرستید حمیده بانو بیگم‌را طلبیده بیار و حضرت والده که کس فرستادند حمیده بانو بیگم نه آمدند — گفتند — اگر غرض ملازمت است خود آن روز بملازمت مشرف شده ام — دیگر برای چه بیایم؟ مرتبهٔ دیگر حضرت سبحان قلی‌را فرستادند که میرزا هندال‌را رفته بگو که بیگم‌را بفرستید* میرزا گفتند — هرچند من گفتم نمیرود — تو خود رفته بگو* سبحان قلی که رفته گفت — بیگم جواب دادند که دیدنِ بادشاهان یك مرتبه جایز است — در مرتبهٔ دیگر نا محرمست — من نمی

آیم ٭ سبحان قلی که از بیگم این حرف شنیده آمده بعرض رسانید ٭ حضرت فرمودند اگر نا محرم اند محرم می‌سازیم ٭

غرض که تا چهل روز از جهةِ حمیده بانو بیگم مبالغه و مناقشه بود و بیگم راضی نشدند ٭ آخر حضرة والده‌ام دلدار بیگم نصیحت کردند که آخر خود بکسی خواهی رسید — بهتر از پادشاه که خواهد بود — بیگم گفتند که آری بکسی خواهم رسید که دستِ من بگریبانِ او برسد — نه آنکه بکسی برسم که دستِ من میدانم بدامنِ او نرسد ٭ آخر باز (43b) والده ام نصیحت بسیار کردند ٭

غرض که بعد از چهل روز در ماه جمید الاوّل سنه[۹۴۸] نهصد و چهل و هشت در مقام پاتر روز دوشنبه نیم روز بود که اسطرلاب‌را حضرة پادشاه بدستِ مبارکِ خود گرفته اند و ساعتْ سعدرا اختیار کرده میر ابو البقارا طلبیده حکم فرمودند که نکاح بستند ٭ مبلغ دو لك نکاحانه بمیر ابو البقا دادند ٭ بعد از عقد سه روز دیگر آنجا بودند — بعد از آن کوچ کرده در کشتی نشستند و متوجه بکهر شدند ٭

و یکماه در بکهر بودند ٭ میر ابو البقارا در پیش سلطان بکهری فرستادند ٭ آنجا تشویش شده برحمتِ حق پیوستند ٭

آخر میرزا هندال‌را رخصتِ قندهار کردند ٭ میرزا یادگار ناصررا بجای خود در لری گذاشتند و حضرت خود متوجه سیاه‌وان شدند که از سیاه‌وان تا تهته شش هفت روزه راهست ٭ سیاه‌وان قلعه مضبوط دارد و میر علیکه ملازم حضرت پادشاه در آن قلعه بود و توپچی چندی بود که هیچ کس‌را مجالِ نزدیك قلعه رفتن نبود ٭ چند کس از مردمِ حضرت پادشاه مورچال (44a) کرده نزدیك رسیدند و اورا نصیحت کردند که حرام نمکی درین طور وقت خوب نیست ٭ میر علیکه قبول نکرد ٭ آخر نقب کندند و یك برج قلعه‌را انداختند ٭ امّا قلعه‌را نتوانند گرفت

وغله قیمت بوده است واکثر مردم گریختن گرفتند* مدّت شش هفت ماه در آنجا بودند ومیرزا شاه حسین حرام نمکی کرده مردمِ لشکررا از هر طرف گرفته بمردمِ خود می سپرد که برده در دریای شور اندازید* سیصد چهار صد کس‌را یکجا کرده در کشتی انداخته به دریای شور می‌انداختند تا ده هزار کس‌را در دریای شور انداخت*

بعد از آنی که در پیش حضرت هم کس کم ماند چند کشتی پر توپ وتفنگ کرده خود از تهته بر سرِ حضرت آمده* سیاه‌وان نزدیك بدریا واقع شده است* آمد کشتی‌های حضرت پادشاه‌را همراه اسباب برد وکس فرستاد که حق نمك نگاه میدارم زود کوچ بکنید* حضرت لاعلاج شدند و باز برگشته متوجه بکهر شدند*

چون نزدیك بکهر شدند میرزا حسین سمندر پیش ازآن که حضرت در بکهر (44b) برسند کس پیش میرزا یادگار ناصر فرستاده بود که اگر حضرت برگشته بجانب بکهر میایند آمدن نگذارند که بکهر تعلق بشما دارد* من از شما ام و دخترِ خودرا بشما میدهم* میرزا یادگار ناصر سخنِ اورا باور کرده حضرت پادشاه‌را در بکهر آمدن نگذاشت ومیخواست که بحیله یا بجنگ پیش آید*

حضرت کس فرستادند که بابا شما بجای فرزندِ ما اید و بجای خود شمارا نشانده رفتم که اگر بما واقع پیس آید شما کوملكِ ما باشید — والحال از بدرائ نوکرانِ شما بما چنین سلوك می کنید* ابن نوکرانِ حرام نمك بشما هم وفا نخواهند کرد* هر چند حضرت نصیحت کرده فرستادند فایده نکرد* آخر حضرت فرمود که خوب ما بجانب راجه مال دیو میرویم واین ولایت‌را بشما دادیم* امّا شاه حسین شمارا از اینجا نخواهد گذاشت* سخنِ مارا یاد خواهید کرد*

بمیرزا یادگار ناصر این سخن‌را گفته کوچ کرده متوجه مال دیو شدند وبراهٔ

جیسلمیر شدند* بعد از چند روز بقلعهٔ دلاور رسیدند که سرحدِ ولایتِ راجه مالدیو است (45a) دو روز آنجا بودند — دانه وگاه پیدا نشد — و از آنجا بجانب جیسلمیر روان شدند* چون نزدیك جیسلمیر رسیدند راجهٔ جیسلمیر جمعی را فرستاد و سرِ راه گرفت و جنگ شد — و حضرت باچندی از راه کناره میرفتند* درین جنگ چند کسی زخمی شدند — (۱) لوش بیگ برادرِ شاهم خان جلایر و پیر محمّد اخته و روشنگ توشکچی و چند دیگر زخمی شدند* آخر فتح کردند* کافران گریخته بقلعه درآمدند — و حضرت آن روز تا شصت کروه راه رفتند و در سر تالابی منزل واقع شد* بعد از آن بساتلمیر رسیدند* آنمردم آن روز تشویش دادند تا آنکه در پلودی نام پرگنه که تعلق به مالدیو داشت رسیدند* راجه مالدیو در جودهپور بود — یك جیبه و یك شتربار اشرفی بخدمتِ حضرت فرستادند و دلاسائی بسیار نمود که خوش آمدید — بیکانیررا بشما میدهم* حضرت با دل جمع نشسته بودند و اتکه خان‌را پیش مالدیو فرستادند که چه جواب میدهد ملا سرخ کتابدار درآن شکست و ویرانئ هند بجانب (45b) ولایتِ مالدیو رفته ملازم شده بود* او عریضه فرستاد که زنهار هزار زنهار حضرت پیش نیایند و در هر جا که منزل دارند در ساعت کوچ کنند که مالدیو در صددِ گرفتنِ شما است و اعتماد بر قولِ او نکنید که ایلچئ شیر خان آمده و شیر خان نوشته فرستاده که هر نوعی که دانید و توانید آن حضرت‌را بگیرید — اگر این کار کردید ناگور و الور و هر جائی که خواهید بشما میدهم* و اتکه خان هم آمده گفت که وقتِ استادن نیست* نماز دیگر بود که حضرت کوچ کردند و در وقتِ سوارئ حضرت دو جاسوس‌را گرفته آوردند* هر دورا بسته نزدیك آورده سخن میپرسیدند که دست‌های خودرا فی الحال خلاص کرده شمشیر از کمرِ محمود کردباز کشیده اوّل محمودرا زده — بعد از آن باقی گوالیاری‌را زخمی کرده —

و آن دیگری خنجری از میانِ یکی کشیده رو بجانب مردم کرده * چند کس را زخمی کرده و اسپ سواریٔ حضرت کشته * غرض تلاش بسیار کردند تا آنکه آن هر دورا کشند (46a) و درین ضمن غوغا شد که مالدیو رسیده * حضرت بادشاه اسپ سواری نداشتند که لایقِ سواریٔ حمیده بانو بیگم باشد * برای سواریٔ بیگم از تردی بیگ اسپ طلبیده باشند * غالباً تردی بیگ اسپ نداده * حضرت فرمودند — برای من شترِ جواهر* افتابچی را طیار بکنند — من بشتر سوار خواهم شد و بیگم به اسپِ من سوار شوند * ظاهرًا ندیم بیگ شنیده است که حضرت بادشاه اسپِ سواریٔ خودرا بسواریٔ بیگم تعین کرده اند و خود خیال دارند که بشتر سوار شوند * او والدهٔ خودرا بر شتر سوار کرده اسپ سواریٔ والدهٔ خود بحضرت پادشاه پشکش کرده *

حضرت سوار شده متوجه عمرکوت شدند * از جای رهبر گرفتند که راه‌را سر کند * هوا بغایت گرم بود و اسپ و چاروا تا زانو درریگ فرو میرفت و در عقب لشکرِ مالدیو نزدیك رسید * باز کوچ کردند و تشنه وگرسنه روان شدند * اکثر از زن و مرد پیاده بودند * چون لشکر (46b) مالدیو نزدیك رسید حضرت ایشان تیمور سلطان و منعم خان و جمعی دیگررا فرمودند که شمایان آهسته بیائید و غنیم‌را نگاه دارید تا ما چند کروه بر آمده رویم * ایشان ماندند و شب شد — راه گم کردند * حضرت تمام شب راه رفتند * چون صبح شد سه روز بود که اسپان آب نیافته بودند که جائ آب یافتند * حضرت فرود آمدند که کس دویده آمد که هندوان بسیار اسپ سوار و شتر سوار رسیدند *

حضرت شیخ علی بیگ و روشن کوکه و ندیم کوکه و میر پاینده محمّد

---

* (جواهر) The M.S. writes the name of this jewel of chroniclers in the plural.

برادرِ میرولی و جمعی دیگررا رخصت کردند و فاتحه خواندند که رفته با کافران جنگ کنید — و یقینِ حضرت شد که ایشان تیمور سُلطان و منعم خان و میرزا یادگاررا با جمعی که گذاشته بودیم کشته شدند یا بدستِ کافران افتادند که این جماعیت آنهارا کشته بر سرِ ما آمده اند ٭ حضرت باز خود سوار شده همراه چند کس اُردورا گذاشته پیش رفتند ٭ وآن جماعیت که حضرت فاتحه خوانده بجنگ فرستاده بودند شیخ علی بیگ سردارِ (47a) آن راجپوتان‌را به تیرزده از اسپ انداخت و چند کسِ دیگررا مردمِ دیگر به تیر زدند ٭ کافران رو بگریز نهادند و فتح شد ٭ چند کس‌را زنده هم گرفته آوردند ٭ اُردو آهسته آهسته میرفت ٭ امّا حضرت پادشاه دور رفته بودند ٭ این مردم فتح کرده به اُردو آمده رسیدند ٭

بهبود نام چوبداری بود ٭ اورا از عقبِ حضرت دوانیده فرستادند که حضرت آهسته روند که بعنایت آلهی فتح شد وکافران گریختند ٭ بهبود خودرا بحضرت رسانیده وخبرِ خوش برد ٭ حضرت فرود آمدند — و اندك آبی هم می پیدا شد ٭ امّا در فکرِ امرا بودند که آنهارا چه واقع شد؟ که از دور چند سوار پیدا شدند ٭ باز دغدغه شد که مبادا مالدیو باشد ٭ کس فرستادند که خبر بیارد — دویده آمد که ایشان تیمور سُلطان و میرزا یادگار ومنعم خان همه بصحّت وسلامت می آیند ٭ راه گم کرده بودند ٭ بعد از رسیدن آنها حضرت خوشحال شدند و شکرِ حق بجا آوردند ٭

و صباح کوچ کردند — سه روزِ دیگر آب نیافتند (47b) بعد از سه روز بر سر چاها رسیدند وچاهای مذکور بسیار عمیق بودند ٭ بر سرِ آن چاها مقام کردند ٭ آبِ آن چاه بغایت سُرخ بود — بر سرِ یك چاه حضرت فرود آمدند — بر سرِ یك چاهٔ دیگر تردی بیگ خان — و بر سرِ یك چاه میرزا یادگار و معنم خان و ندیم کوکه — و بر سرِ یك چاه ایسان تیمور سلطان و خواجه غازی و روشن کوکه ٭

و هر دلوی که از چاه بیرون می آمد چون نزدیك می‌رسید مردم خودرا در میانِ دلو می‌انداختند و ریسمان گسسته می شد و پنج شش کس همراه دلو در چاه می‌افتادند* مردم بسیار از تشنگی مردند و هلاك می‌شدند* حضرت دیدند که مردم از تشنگی خودها در چاه می‌اندازند — از کروئ خاصهٔ خود بهمه مردم آب میخوراندند — آخر مردم‌را سیرِاب کرده نمازِ پیشین بود که کوچ کردند و یك شبانه روز راه رفتند* در سرای رسیدند* تالابی کلانی بود* اسپان وشتران که درونِ تالاب در آمدند چندان آب خوردند که اکثر مردند* اسپ کم مانده بود — استر وشتر بودند* از آن باز (48a) هر روز آب پیدا می‌شد تا به عمرکوت رسیدند که جای خوبست و تالابِ بسیار دارد* رعنا* پیشوازِ حضرت آمد و درون قلعه برد و منزلِ خوب داد و مردمِ امرارا بیرون قلعه جا داد*

اکثر چیز در کمال ارزانی بود — یك روپیه‌را چهار بز میدادند* از بز غاله و غیره رعنا پیشکشِ بسیار آورد وچنین خدماتِ شایسته بجا آورد که بکدام زبان تقریر توان کرد؟ و چند روزی در آنجا بخیر وخوبی گذرانیدند*

و بعد از آنی که خزینه تمام شد تردی بیگ خان زرِ بسیار داشت حضرت بطریقِ قرض ازو مبلغی طلبیدند* او بحسابِ ده دو هشتاد هزار اشرفی قرض داد* حضرت گرفته حصّه رسد تمام لشکر بخش کردند*

وکمر خنجرها و سروپاها به رعنا و فرزندانِ او عنایت فرمودند* و بعضی مردم اسپانِ تازه خریدند*

وپدرِ رعنارا میرزا شاه حسین کُشته بود* بوجودِ آن هم دو سه هزار سوار جرّار بهم رسانیده در ملازمتِ حضرت همراه کرد* باز حضرت متوجه

* (رعنا) Text, *passim*, spells thus.

بکهر شدند وبسی واهل وعیال‌را (48 b) درعمرکوت گذاشتند ـــ وخواجه معظّم‌را نیز گذاشتند که از حرم خبردار باشد * حمیده بانو بیگم حامله بودند * بعد از متوجه شدن حضرت سه روز گذشته بود که بتاریخ چهارم شهر رجب المرجب سـنه ۹۴۹ نهصد وچهل و نه وقتِ سحر روز یکشنبه بود که تولّدِ حضرت بادشاه عالم پناه عالمگیر جلال الدین محمّد اکبر بادشاه غازی شد * قمر در برج اسد بود * تولّد در برج ثابت شده بغایت خوبست و منجمان گفتند فرزندی که درین ساعت شود صاحبِ اقبال ودراز عمر می‌شود *

حضرت در پانزده کرو می‌بودند که تردی محمّد خان خبر رسانید * حضرت بسیار بسیار خوشحال شدند ـــ واز مژده و بشارت این خبر تقسیرات ماتقدمِ تردی محمّد خان معاف کردند *

و آن خواب که در لاهور دیده بودند همون نامِ جلال الدین محمّد اکبر بادشاه نام نهادند * واز آنجا کوچ کرده متوجه بکهر شدند ـــ واز مردمِ رعنا واطرافی وسودمه وسمیچه تا ده هزار کس جمع شدند ـــ در پرگنهٔ چون رسیدند (49 a) یك غلامِ شاه حسین میرزا با چند سوار در چون بود ـــ گریخته رفت * در آنجا باغِ آینه بسیار خوب بصفا بود * در آن باغ حضرت فروز آمدند و مواضعاتِ آن‌را بمردم جاگیر تعین فرمودند * از جون تهته شش روزه راه بود * تا شش ماه حضرت در آنجا بودند و بعمرکوت کس فرستادند اهلِ حرم و بسیٔ تمام مردم‌را طلبیدند * در آن وقت جلال الدین اکبر بادشاه شش ماه بودند که در چون آوردند *

وجماعه که از اطراف وجانب همراهٔ اهلِ حرم آمده بودند متفرق شدند ورعنارا از جهة گفت وگوی که به تردی محمّد خان واقع شده بود شکر رنگی در میانِ تردی بیگ واو بود * نیم شبی بود که کوچ کرده بجانب ولایتِ خود رفت وجماعهٔ سودمه وسمیچه نیز بدو موافقت کرده رفتند * حضرت بهمان جمعیتِ خود ماندند *

وشیخ علی بیگ که مردِ مردانه بود حضرت اورا همراه مظفّر بیگ ترکمان بجانب جاجکا پرگنهٔ کلان بود فرستاده بودند* میرزا شاه حسین جمعی‌را بر سرِ او فرستاد (49 b) در میانِ هر دو لشکر جنگ عظیم شد* آخر الامر مظفّر بیگ منهزم شده گریخته وشیخ علی بیگ بجمعی کشته شد ضیاع شد*

ودر میانِ خالد بیگ ولوش بیگ برادرِ شاهم خان جلایر گفت وگوی شد* آخر جمعی رعایت لوش بیگ کردند* ازین سبب خالد بیگ با جمعی گریخته پیش میرزا شاه حسین رفت* حضرت پادشاه والدهٔ اورا که سلطانم نام داشت بندی خانه فرمودند* ازین واسطه گلبرگ بیگم رنجیده بودند* آخر گناهٔ اورا بخشیدند وهمراهٔ گلبرگ بیگم رخصتِ مکّه معظمه کردند* بعد از چند گاه لوش بیگ هم گریخت وحضرت اورا بدعای بد یاد کردند که ما برای خاطرِ او خالد بیگ‌را درشتی کردیم* با وجودِ آن از دایرهٔ حلال نمکی برآمده بدایرهٔ حرام نمکی در آمد* جوانه مرگ خواهد شد* آخر همون طور شد که بعد از پانزده روز در کشتی خواب کرده بود که غلامش بکاردزده کشت — وحضرت بعد از شنیدن بسیار متالم ومتفکر شدند (50 a) شاه حسین کشتی‌هارا نزدیك چون بدریا آورده بود ودر خشکی* هم آکثر اوقات مردمِ حضرت بمردمِ شاه حسین جنگ می‌کردند واز جانبین مردم کشته می‌شدند — وآکثر مردمِ پادشاهی هر روز گریخته بطرفِ شاه حسین میرفتند* از جمله ملّا تاج الدین که درِّ علم وبر آن عنایتِ کلّی داشتند در آن جنگ کشته شد*

ودر میانِ تردی محمّد خان ومنعم خان گفت وگوی شد* منعم خان هم گریخت* امرای معدودی ماندند* از جمله تردی محمّد خان ومیرزا

* (خشکی) Misread in translating as کشتی.

یادگار و میرزا پاینده محمّد و محمّد ولی و ندیم کوکه و روشن کوکه و خدنگ ایشك آغاچی* وجمعی دیگر در ملازمتِ حضرت بودند که خبر آمد که بیرم خان از جانبِ گجرات می آید و پرگنهٔ جاجکاه رسیده است ✲ حضرت خوشحال شدند وکدنگ ایشك آغاچی‌را بجمعی حکم کردند که باستقبالِ بیرم خان روند ✲

درین اثنا شاه حسین شنید که بیرم خان می‌آید ✲ چند کس‌را فرستاده که بیرم خان‌را بگیرند ✲ غافل در جائ فروز (50 b) آمده بود که آمده ریختند ✲ خدنگ ایشك آغا کشُته شد وبیرم خان با چندی خلاص شده در ملازمتِ حضرت آمده مشرف شد ✲

درین اثنا عرضه داشتهای قراچه خان آمد بحضرت پادشاه (؟و) میرزا هندال که مدتیست که در نواحیٔ بکهر نشسته اید ✲ درین مدّت از شاه حسین میرزا اثرِ دولتخواهی ظاهر نشد بلکه بد پیش آمد ✲ دیگر بعنایتِ آلهی کارِ آسان خواهد شد اگر پادشاه بدولت و سعادت بیایند بهتر و عین مصلحت است واگر حضرت نیایند شما البته بیائید ✲ چون حضرت توقف کرده بودند و میرزا هندال (؟) به اسقبال برآمده و قندهار‌را پیشکش بمیرزا هندال کرده بود ✲

میرزا عسکری در غزنین بودند ✲ میرزا کامران عرضه داشت کردند که قراچه خان قندهار‌را بمیرزا هندال داد ــ فکرِ قندهار‌را باید کرد ✲ میرزا کامران در صددِ این شدند که قندهار‌را از میرزا هندال بگیرند ✲

درین صمن حضرت این خبرهارا شنیده پیش عمهٔ خود خانزاده بیگم آمده مبالغه بسیار (51 a) نمودند که مرا سرافراز کرده بقندهار بروید و میرزا هندال‌را و میرزا کامران‌را نصیحت کنید که اوزبك و ترکمان

---

* (اغاچی) Cf. Turkī *īshīk aghāṣī*, usher.

نزدیك شمایان است ــ درین طور وقت که بر ما و شمایان است در میانِ خودها باتفاق باشید بهتر است وکتابةها که من بمیرزا کامران نوشته ام اگر قبول کنند و بعمل آرد هرچه خاطرِ او خواهد ماهم همان نوع می کنم*

بعد از رسیدنِ حضرت بیگم بقندهار بعد از چهار روز میرزا کامران هم رسیدند و هر روز مبالغه‌ها می‌کردند که خطبه بنامِ من بخوانید* میرزا هندال می‌گفتند که تغیر دادنِ خطبه چه معنی دارد؟ حضرت فردوس مکانی در حیاتِ خود پادشاهی‌را به همایون پادشاه داده اند و ولی عهدِ خود کردانیده اند و مایان همه قبول کرده و خطبه بنامِ ایشان تا این مدّت خوانده ایم ــ الحال تغیر دادنِ خطبه صورة ندارد* میرزا کامران بحضرت دلدار بیگم خطی نوشتند که ما از کابل شمارا یاد کرده آمدیم عجب است که یك زمان آمده مارا ندیدید ــ (51b) چنانچه والدهٔ میرزا هندال اید بهمون طور والدهٔ ما اید* آخر الامر دلدار بیگم بدیدنِ ایشان آمدند* میرزا کامران گفتند الحال شمارا نمی گذارم تا میرزا هندال‌را تطلبید* دلدار بیگم گفتند که خانزاده بیگم ولی نعمتِ شما اند وکلان و بزرگ همه شمایان اند* حقیقتِ خطبه‌را از ایشان پرسید* آخر به آکه گفتند* حضرت خانزاده بیگم جواب دادند ــ اگر از من می‌پرسید بطریقی که حضرت فردوس مکانی قرار داده اند و پادشاهی خودرا به همایون پادشاه داده اند و شمایان همه خطبه‌را تا حال بنامِ ایشان خوانده ائد ــ الحال هم کلانِ خود دانسته فرمان بردارِ ایشان باشید* غرض تا چهار ماه میرزا کامران قندهاررا قبل کرده و مبالغهٔ خطبه می نمودند* آخر قرار دادند ــ خوب ــ الحال پادشاه دور اند ــ خطبه‌را بنامِ من بخوانید ــ هرگاه پادشاه بیایند بنامِ ایشان خواهد خواند* چون قبل بدور ودراز کشیده بود ومردم تنگ آمده آمده بودند ضرور شد خطبه‌را خواندند*

و قندهاررا بمیرزا عسکری (52 a) دادند و غزنین‌را وعده کردند بمیرزا هندال ✲ حالا که بغزنین آمدند لمغانات و تنگیهاررا بمیرزا هندال دادند ✲ این طور وعدهای دروغ ✲ میرزا هندال ببدخشان رفته در خوست و اندراب نشستند ✲ میرزا کامران بدلدار بیگم گفتند که شما رفته بیارید ✲ حضرت دلدار بیگم که رفتند میرزا جواب دادند که من خودرا از دغدغهٔ سپای گری گذرانده ام و خوست هم گوشه ایست ✲ نشسته ام ✲ بیگم گفتند اگر غرضِ درویشی و گوشه نشینی باشد هم کابل گوشه ایست با اهل و عیال و فرزندان یکجا باشید — بهتر است ✲ آخر بیگم میرزارا بزور آوردند و در کابل مدت‌ها بوضع درویشی می بودند ✲

در اینجا میرزا شاه حسین پیش حضرت پادشاه کس فرستاد که لایقِ دولت آنست که از اینجا کوچ کرده بجانبِ قندهار بروید — بهتر است ✲ حضرت راضی شدند و جواب فرستادند که در اُردوی ما اسپ و شتر کم مانده است — شما اسپ و شتر بما بدهید تا ما بقندهار برویم ✲ شاه حسین میرزا قبول (52 b) کرد و گفت که هرگاه شما از آب گذرید هزار شتر آن روی آب هست — همون‌را بشما خواهم فرستاد ✲

اکر (?اکثر) سخنان که در راهٔ بکهر و سند از خواجه کیپك خویشِ خواجه غازی مذکور بود نقل از نوشتهٔ خواجه کیپك مذکور است ✲ آخر حضرت به اهل و عیال لشکر و غیره برکشتی‌ها سوار شدند ✲ تا سه روز بحررا طی کردند ✲ از سرحدِ ولایتِ او گذشته نواسی نام موضعی بود آنجا فرود آمدند و سُلطان قلی نام ساربان باشی‌را فرستادند تا شتران‌را بیارد ✲ سلطان قلی مذکور رفته هزار شتر آورد ✲ حضرت همه شتران‌را به امرایان و سپاهی و غیره مردم لشکر دادند و قسمت فرمودند ✲ آن شتران بنوع بودند که گویا هفت پشت بلکه هفتاد پشت آن شتران مذکور شهر و ادم و باررا ندیده بودند ✲ چون در لشکر قحط الفرس بود اکثر مردم شتر

سوار بودند وآنچه تتمه باقی مانده بود برای بار تعین فرمودند* وهرکه سوار می شد بمجرّد سوارشدن سواررا بزمین میزدند (53a) و راهٔ جنگل میگرفتند واز شتران بارخانه هرکدام که بار میکردند بمجرّد شنیدنِ اوازِ سُمِ اسپ جسته جسته باررا بر زمین انداخته خود بجنگل در آمده میرفتند — و بر هرکدام شترکه باررا محکم بسته می‌شد هرچند می جست بار نمی افتاد بمع بار راهٔ جنگل پیش گرفته میگریخت* بدین نوع بجانبِ قندهار می‌رفتند تا قریب دویست شتر گریخته باشد وچون نزدیك سیوی رسیدند محمود ساربان باشی ملازمِ شاه حسین میرزا در سیوی بود — قلعه‌را مصبوط کرده متحصّن شد* حضرت درشش کروهی سیوی فروز آمدند* درین اثنا خبر آمد که میر الله دوست و بابا جوجوك از کابل دو روز است که سیوی آمده اند و پیش شاه حسین میرزا میروند* سروپا واسپان تپوچاق ومیوهٔ بسیار میرزا کامران برای شاه حسین میرزا فرستاده ودخترِ اورا برای خود طلب نموده اند* خود حضرت بخواجه غازی فرمودند که چون در میانهٔ تو والله دوست نسبتِ پدر و فرزندی (53b) است کتابتی نوشته فرست که میرزا کامران بچه طریق بما پیش می آید واگر ما بدانجا رویم چون سلوك بکند* وحضرت بادشاه خواجه کیپسك‌را فرمودند که بجانبِ سیوی رفته به میر الله دوست بگوکه اگر آمده مارا به بیند* خوبست* خواجه کیپك مذکور بجانبِ سیوی روان شد* حضرت فرمودند که تا آمدنِ تو ما کوچ نخواهیم کرد* او چون نزدیك سیوی رسیده بود که محمود ساربان باشی گرفته پرسید که بچه کار آمدی؟ او گفت بجهتِ اسپ و شتر خریدن* گفت دست در بغل اندازید وتاجِ اورا بپالید که مبادا به الله دوست و بابا جوجوك فرمان استمالت آورده باشد*

چون تفحّص کردند کتابت از بغلِ او بر آمد* فرصت نیافت که کتابت‌را

* (ببیند) Misread in translating as پند.

بگوشهٔ پرتابد * گرفته خواند و اورا نسپرده در ساعت الله دوست و بابا جوك‌را بدرونِ قلعه برد و انواع درشتی کرده * اینها سوگند خوردند که مارا از آمدن این خبر نیست و این (54a) پیش من سبق خوانده است و خواجه غازی جهت ما داشت و پیش کامران میرزا بود — باین سبب کتابت نوشته است * محمود قرار داد که کیپك‌را با جمعی همراه پیش شاه حسین فرستد * میر الله دوست و بابا جوجوك تمام شب پیش محمود بودند و ملائمیت کرده اورا درخواست نموده از بند خلاص کردند و سیصد انار وصد بهی میر الله دوست برای حضرت فرستاد و عریضه از ترش نه نوشت که مباده بدستِ کسی افتد — امّا زبانی گفته فرستاد که اگر عرضه داشتِ میرزا عسکری یا امرا آمده باشد رفتن کابل بد نیست و اگر نه مصلحت در رفتن کابل نیست که حضرت بادشاه‌را بخواهد دید و حضرت کس کم دارند آخر تا چه روی دهد * کیپك آمده بعرض رسانید *

حضرت مُتحیّر و متفکر شدند که چه باید کرد و بکجا باید رفت * کنگاش کردند * تردی محمّد خان و بیرم خان کنگاش دادند (54b) که غیر از شمالیان وشال مستان که سرحدِ قندهار است بجای دیگر عزم جزم کردن ممکن نیست — چراکه درآن حُدود افغان بسیار اند بجانبِ خود خواهیم کشید وامُرا وملازمانِ میرزا عسکری نیز گریخته پیش ما خواهند آمد *

آخر چنین قرار با یکدیگر داده فاتحه خواندند وکوچ بکوچ متوجه قندهار شدند * چون نزدیك شال مستان رسیدند ودر موضع رلی نام موضعی فروز آمدند وچون برف و باران باریده بود وهوا بغایت خنك بود وقرارداد چنین بود که ازین منزل بشال مستان خواهم رفت * وقتِ نمازِ عصر بود که جوانیٔ اوزبك بریابوی قله رهوار کپك (؟) رسید ونعره زد که حضرت سوار شوند که در راه سخنی عرض خواهم کرد که وقتِ تنگ است والحال وقتِ سخن گفتن نیست *

حضرت در همان ساعت سوار شدند که غوغا افتاد و پادشاه روان شدند* دو تیر پرتاب (55 a) راه رفته بودند که حضرت بادشاه خواجه معظم و بیرم خان‌را فرستادند که حمیده بانو بیگم‌را بیارند* این‌ها آمده بیگم‌را سوار کردند و فرجهٔ آن نشد جلال الدین محمّد اکبر بادشاه‌را هم همراه ببرند* همین که بیگم از اُردو بر آمده بودند که همراهٔ پادشاه شوند که درین اثنا میرزا عسکری با دو هزار سوار رسید وشور شد* بمجرّد رسیدن بدر اُردو آمد وگفت که پادشاه کجا اند* مردم گفتند دیر است که بشکار رفته اند و دانست که بر آمده رفته اند* آخر جلال الدین محمّد اکبر پادشاه‌را گرفته وهمه مردم پادشاهی‌را کوشانیده در قندهار برو (or برد) ومحمّد اکبر پادشاه‌را بسلطانم بیگم کوجِ خود سپرد* سلطانم بیگم کوجِ میرزا عسکری بود* بسیار مهربانی وغمخواری میکرد*

و پادشاه که سوار شدند رو بجانبِ کوه نهادند تا چهار کروه رفتند و بعد از آن بسرعت تمام روان شدند* و در آن وقت این جماعت در ملازمت بودند — بیرم خان و خواجه معظم وخواجه نیازی (55 b) و ندیم کوکه و روشن کوکه وحاجی محمّد خان و بابا دوست بخشی ومیرزا قلی بیگ چولی وحیدر محمّد اخته بیگی وشیخ یوسف چولی وابراهیم ایشك آغا و حسن علی ایشاك آغا و یعقوب قورچی وعنبر ناظر وملك مختار وسنبل میر هزار* وخواجه کیپك* خواجه غازی میگوید که من هم در ملازمت بودم* این جماعت همراه حضرت روان شدند — وحمیده بانو بیگم میگویند که با سی کس بودند* واز ضعفا کوجِ حسن علی ایشك آغا هم بوده*

نمازِ خفتن گذشته بود که در پای کوه رسیدند وکوه‌را انبوع برف گرفته

---

* (هزار) Text, *wa mīr hazār;* clearly a clerical error.

بود که راه نبود که بالای کوه روند و این دغدغه برداشتند که مبادا میرزا عسکری بی‌انصاف از عقب رسد * و آخر راه‌را یافته بهر روش بالای کوه رفتند و تمام شب درمیانِ برف بودند * در ان وقت هیزم هم بهم نرسید که آتش کنند و برای خوردن هم چیزی نبود * گرسنگی بغایت تنگ کرد * مردم بیطاقتی شدند (56 a) حضرت فرمودند که یك اسپ بکشید * حالا اسپ‌را که کشتند دیگ نی که آش بپزند * در دبلغه گوشت بپختند وکباب کردند و چهار طرف آتش کردند و بدستِ مبارکِ خود کباب کرده نوش کردند * بزبانِ مبارکِ خود می‌فرمودند که سرِ من از زمهریر هم سرد شده بود * باری چون صبح شد کوهٔ دیگررا نشان دادند که در آن کوه ابادانی هست و جماعهٔ بلوچان در آنجا می باشند در آنجا می باید رفت * راهی شدند * دَر دو روز بدانجا رسیدند * خانهٔ چندی دیدند * در آن خانها چند بلوچ وحشی که عبارت که از غولِ بیابان آن مردم اند در دامنِ کوه نشسته بودند * همراهٔ حضرت قریب سی کس بودند * بلوچان که دیدند همه جمع شده آمدند * حضرت در خرگاه بدولت نشسته بودند که از دور دریافتند که حضرت نشسته اند با یکدیگر می‌گفتند که اگر ما این‌هارا گرفته پیش میرزا عسکری ببریم البته یراقِ این‌هارا بما (56 b) می‌دهد بلکه انعاماتِ زیادتی هم خواهد داد * حسن علی ایسك آغا زنِ بلوچی داشت * او زبانِ بلوچی میدانست * او معلوم کرد که این غولهای بیابان خیالِ فاسد دارند — وصباح خیالِ کوچ داشتند * بلوچان گفتند که بلوچی که سردارِ ما است اینجا حاضر نیست * وقتی که او بیاید کوچ بکنید * چون وقت هم بیگاه شده بود تمام شب باحتیاط تمام بودند * پاره از شب گذشته بود که آن بلوچ سردار آمده حضرت‌را ملازمت کرد وگفت که فرمانِ میرزا کامران ومیرزا عسکری بما آمده است * در آن نوشته اند که شنیده شد که پادشاه در خانهای شما تشریف دارند — اگر در آنجا باشند زنهار هزار

زنهار که نخواهید گذاشت — گرفته پیش ما بیارید — مال و اسپان تعلق بشما دارد و پادشاه‌را بقندهار برسانید* اوّل که من حضرت‌را ندیده بودم خیالِ فاسد داشتم* الحال که حضرت‌را ملازمت کردم جانِ من و خاندانِ من (57 a) پنج شش فرزندان دارم همه صدقهٔ سرِ حضرت بلك صدقهٔ یکتارِ موئ حضرت* حضرت هرکجا که میخواهند تشریف فرمایند پناه خدا میرزا عسکری مرا هرچه خواهد بکند* آخر یك پارهٔ لعل و مروارید وچیزهای دیگر به آن بلوچ عنایت فرمودند وصباح کوچ کرده بجانبِ قلعهٔ بابا حاجی تشریف فرمودند*

بعد از دو روز رسیدند* آن قلعه داخلِ ولایتِ گرم سیر است و در کنارِ دریا واقع شده است وجمعی از سادات در آنجا می باشند* آمده حضرت‌را ملازمت کردند ومیزبانی بجا آوردند* صباح او خواجه علاول الدین محمود از میرزا عسکری گریخته آمد وقطارِ استر واسپ وشامیانه وغیره که داشت آورده پشکشِ حضرت کرد* دیگر بی دغدغه شدند*

روزِ دیگر حاجی محمّد خان کوکی با سی چهل سوار آمد وقطارِ استر پشکش نمود* آخر از ناموافقی برادران و نا هم پای امرا لا علاج شده مصلحت (57 b) چنان دیدند که توکل بحضرت مسبب الاسباب کرده عزم جزمِ خراسان باید کرد* وبعد از قطعِ منازل وطئ مراحل بنواحئ خراسان رسیدند* باب هلمند که رسیدند شاه طهماس از استماع این خبر در تحیر و تفکر فرو ماند که همایون بادشاه از گردشِ فلك غدّار کج رفتار نا سازکار به این حدود رسیدند وحضرت واجب الوجود باینجاها رسانید*

جمیع اهالی وموالی واشراف واکابر ووصیع وشریف وکبیر وصغیررا باستقبالِ حضرت پادشاه فرستادند* همه این‌ها تا آبِ هلمند پیشواز آمدند وبهرام میرزا والقاس میرزا وسام میرزا که برادرانِ شاه باشند — همه‌را

باستقبال فرستاد * این‌ها همه آمده دریافتند و به اعزاز و اکرام تمام حضرت‌را آوردند وچون نزدیك رسیدند برادرانِ شاه بشاه خبر فرستادند * شاه نیز خود سوار شده باستقبالِ حضرت آمد * با یکدیگر دریافتند واشنائی (58a) ویك جهتی آن دو بادشاهٔ عالی مقام مانند دو مغز در یك پوستِ بادام قرار یافت واتحاد واخلاص بحدی رسیده بود که ایام چندی که حضرت آنجا تشریف داشتند اکثر اوقات شاه در منزلِ حضرت می‌آمدند و روزی که شاه نمی آمدند حضرت می رفتند *

در خراسان که بودند هر باغ و بوستان که بود عماراتِ عالی که سلطان حسین میرزا بنا کرده بودند و عماراتِ عالئ سابق و غیره همه‌را سیر می‌نمودند وتا در عراق بودند هشت مرتبه بشکار رفته بودند وهرگاه که بشکار میرفتند هر مرتبه حضرت‌را هم تکلیف میکردند — وحمیده بانو بیگم در کجاوه یا در محافه از دور تماشاه میکردند — وشاه‌زاده سلطانم خواهرِ شاه بر اسپ سوار شده بعقبِ شاه می‌ایستاد * حضرت گفته بودند که در شکار عقبِ شاه ضعیفهٔ بر اسپ سوار بود — جلوش‌را مرد محاسنِ سفید گرفته ایستاده بود * مردم چنین می گفتند که شاه‌زاده سلطانم (58b) خواهر شاه است * قصه مختصر شاه بحضرت بسیار مهربانی و مروت پیش می‌آمد وتکلیف کرده مهربانی و غمخواری مادرانه وخواهرانه می نمود *

روزی شاهزاده سلطانم حمیده بانو بیگم‌را تکلیف مهمانی نموده بود * شاه بخواهر خود گفت که چون مهمانی می کنید در بیرونِ شهر معرکه سازید * از شهر دو کروه دور پیشترك خیمه وخرگاه و بارگاه در صحنِ میدانِ خوب برپا کردند * چتر وطاق نیز برپا کردند * در خراسان ودر آن حدود سراپرده میگرفتند ودر عقب نمی گرفتند وحضرت پادشاه سراپرده مدور می گرفتند مثل هندوانه * مردم شاه خرگاه و بارگاه چتر وطاق برپا کرده درگرداگرد چغ‌های رنگارنگ مدور گرفته بودند وتمامی خویشاوندان شاه

و عمهٔ شاه و خواهرانِ شاه و حرم‌های شاه و کوچ خانانِ و سلطانان و امرایان همه قریب هزار زن حاضر بودند همه پر زیب و زینت آراسته *

در آن روز شاهزاده سلطانم پرسید از (59 a) حمیده بانو بیگم که در هندوستان همچو چتر و طاق بهم میرسد * بیگم در جواب گفتند که خراسان‌را دو دانگ می‌گویند و هندوستان‌را چهار دانگ — هرگاه که در دو دانگ بهم رسد در چهار دانگ خود بطریقِ اولی بهم خواهد رسد * شاه سلطانم که خواهرِ شاه باشد نیز در جواب بعمهٔ خود مقویٔ سخنِ حمیده بانو بیگم گفت که عمه از شما عجب است که این سخن‌را گفتند دو دانگ کجا و چهار دانگ کجا ظاهر است که بهتر و خوبتر بهم میرسیده باشد* *
و تمام روز معرکه و مجلس‌را خوب گذرانیدند * در وقتِ طعام همه زنانِ امرا ایستاده خدمت میکردند * و حرمانِ شاه پیش شاه‌زاده سلطانم آش می‌ماندند * دیگر از هر جنسِ پارچای زردوزی و غیره چندان که باید و شاید به حمیده بانو بیگم مهمانی کرده * شاه خود پیش رفته تا نمازِ خفتن در خانهٔ پادشاه بوده * بعد از آن شنید که همیده بانو بیگم بخانهٔ خود آمدند از پیش پادشاه (59 b) برخواسته بخانهٔ خود رفت * تا این حد رعایت و خاطرجوی خوب میکرد *

در آن اثنا روشن کوکه با وجودِ وفاداری و خدماتِ سابقه در آن ملكِ بیگانه و پر مخاطره بی وفائی کرد که چند پاره لعلِ قیمتی که در طومارهای حضرت پادشاه می‌بود که حضرت خود یا حمیده بانو بیگم میدانستند و ثالث‌را بان اطلاع نبود * اگر پادشاه بجائی تشریف می بردند آن طوماررا به حمیده بانو بیگم می‌سپردند * روزی بیگم بسر شپشتن رفتند * آن طومارر‌ا در بقچهٔ روپاك بپیچیده بر بلای پلنگِ پادشاهی نهادند * روشن کوکه فرصت‌را

---

* (باشد) The translation of Sulṭānam's speech is doubtful.

غنیمت دانسته است و پنج لعل‌را دزدیده و بخواجه غازی یکجهة شده وبخواجه غازی سپرده و بمرورِ ایام صرف میخواستند صرف نمایند*

حمیده بانو بیگم که سرِ خودرا شسته آمدند حضرت پادشاه آن طومار را به بیگم دادند* بیگم از هوای دست فلحال دریافتند که آن طومار سبك ظاهر میشود* بیگم به پادشاه گفتند* حضرت فرمودند این چه معنی دارد (60a) غیر ما وشما ثالثی اطلاع ندارد چه شده باشد وکه گرفته باشد* حیران شدند* بیگم برادرِ خود خواجه معظم‌را گفتند که همچو امری واقع شده — اگر درین طور وقت برادری‌را بجا آرید و تفحّص این بیك روشی که شور نشود بکنید گویا مرا از خجالت می برآرید* والا تا زنده ام از روئ پادشاه خجل خواهم بود*

خواجه معظم گفت — بیچیزی بخاطرِ من می رسد که مرا با وجودِ تقربِ حضرت پادشاه قوتِ آن نیست که تانوی لاغر توانم خرید بخلاف خواجه غازی و روشن کوکه که هرکدام اینها برای خودها اسپان تپوچاق خریده اند وهنوز زرِ اسپان‌را نداده اند* این خریدِ اینها بی یك امیدواری نیست* بیگم گفتند — ای برادر وقتِ برادری است — البته تفحّصِ این معامله باید کرد* خواجه معظم گفت — ماه چیچم* شما بکسی نگوئید — انشا الله تعالی امیدوارم که حق (60b) بحقدار برسد* از آنجا برآمده بخانهٔ همون سوداگران پرسیده که این اسپان‌را بچند فروختید؟ در بهای اسپان بشما زرکی وعده کرده اند واداى این زرهارا بچه روش خاطرِ نشان کرده اند؟ سوداگران گفتند که بما این هر دو شخص وعدهٔ لعلها کرده اند واسپان برده اند* خواجه معظم از آنجا پیش نفرِ خواجه غازی آمد وگفت که بقچهٔ سرو‌پای وناری و پرئ خواجه غازی درکجا می شد؟ ودرچه جا نگاه میدارد* یتیم خواجه غازی جواب داد که خواجهٔ ما بقچه

* (چیچم) Cf. 18b.

و ناری پری ندارد — یك طاقی دارد که وقتِ خواب گاهی زبر سرِ خود وگاهی در بغلِ خود نگاه میدارد* خواجه معظم فهمید و در دل جزم و یقین کرد که آن لعلها در پیش خواجه غازی هست و در همان طاقی نگاه داشته است* پیش حضرت آمد و عرض کرد که من نشانِ لعلهارا در طاقی خواجه غازی یافته ام* بیك روشی میخواهم ازو آن‌را ربایم* اگر (61 a) خواجه غازی پیش حضرت آمده از من استغاثه کند حضرت بمن چیزی نگویند* حضرت شنیده تبسّم فرمودند* خواجه معظم از آن باز بخواجه غازی هزل و مطایبه ومزاق (?ك) میکرد* خواجه غازی آمده بعرضِ حضرت پادشاه رسانید که من مرد غریب واسم و رسمی دارم ودر ولایتِ بیگانه خواجه معظمِ خورد سال این چه معنی دارد که بمن هزل ومطایبه ومزاق (?ك) بکند وبمن اهانت رساند* حضرت پادشاه فرمودند که باکی ندارد — خورد سال است باری بخاطرش رسیده باشد واز دلگیری‌ها بی ادبی کرده باشد* شما چیزی بخاطر نرسانید که او خورد سال است*

روزِ دیگر خواجه غازی آمده در دیوانخانه نشسته بود که خواجهِ معظم غافل ساخته بیك بار طاقی‌را از سرش ربود ولعل بی بدل از طاقی برآورده پیش حضرت پادشاه وحمیده بانو بیگم آورد ونهاد* حضرت تبسّم کردند وحمیده بانو بیگم خوشحال شدند وبخواجه معظم شاباش ورحمت (61 b) باد گفتند* خواجه غازی و روشن کوکه از افعال‌های خود شرمسار شده هر دو پیش شاه رفته وسخنانِ مخفی بعرضِ شاه رسانیدند تا بجدی چیزی‌ها گفتند که خاطرِ شاه مکدّر شد* حضرت پادشاه معلوم کردند که اخلاص واعتقادِ شاه به دستور سابق نیست* فی الحال از لعل وجواهر هر چه داشتند بشاه فرستادند* شاه بپادشاه گفت که گناهٔ خواجه غازی و روشن کوکه است که مارا از شما بیگانه کرده بودند والا ما شمارا یگانه

میدانستم* باز هر دو پادشاه یکدل شدند و با یکدیگر خاطررا صاف کردند* وآن هر دو حرام خور مردود هر(fault) پادشاه شدند* وآن هر دورا پادشاه به شاه سپردند*

آن لعل هارا بهر نوعی و وقتّی که دانست و توانست گرفت وآن هارا فرمود که در قید نگاه دارند ــ وحضرت پادشاه تا در عراق بودند خوشحالی گذرانیدند وشاه انواع خاطرجوئی مینمودند وهر روز تحفه وهدیهٔ عجیب و غریب (62 a) بحضرت بادشاه میفرستادند* آخر الامر پسرِ خودرا با خانان وسلطانان وامرایان بکومك همراهٔ حضرت پادشاه کرده با یران (؟ق) خاطرخواه وخرگاه و بارگاه وچتر وطاق وشامیانهای پرکار وگلیم‌های ابریشمی وزلچهای کلابتون دوزی از هر بابِ اسباب چنانچه باید وشاید واز توشکخانه وخزینه خانه واز هرکارخانه وباورچیخانه ورکابخانهٔ پادشاهانه‌را طیار کرده بساعتِ نیك آن دو پادشاهٔ عالیمقدار از یکدیگر رخصت شدند واز آنجا حضرت پادشاه متوجه قندهار شدند*

وحضرت پادشاه درآن وقت گناهٔ آن هر دو بی وفارا از شاه طلبیده وبخشیده همراه گرفته متوجه قندهار شدند*

میرزا عسکری که شنید که حضرت پادشاه از خراسان مراجعت نموده بجانب قندهار می آیند جلال الدین محمّد اکبر پادشاه‌را بکابل پیش میرزا کامران فرستادند* میرزا کامران به آکه جانم که (62 b) خانزاده بیگم عمهٔ ما اند سپردند ــ ودر آن وقت جلال الدین محمّد اکبر پادشاه دو نیم ساله بودند که آکه جانم گرفته نگاه داشتند وبسیار دوست میداشتند ودست و پای ایشان‌را می‌بوسیدند ومی‌گفتند که بعینه گویا دست و پای برادرِ من بابر پادشاه است وشباهتِ تمام دارد*

بعد از تحقیق شدنِ آمدنِ حضرت پادشاه بقندهار میرزا کامران بحضرت خانزاده بیگم زاری وعجز بسیار ومبالغه بی شمار می کردند که شما بدولت

پیش پادشاه بقندهار بروید و میان مایان صلح بکنید * و بعد از آمدنِ حضرت خانزاده بیگم آکبر پادشاه‌را بمیرزا کامران سپردند و میرزا کامران بکوچِ خود خانم سپردند و بسرعتِ تمام بقندهار آمدند *

وحضرت پادشاه که بقندهار آمدند چهل روز میرزا کامران و میرزا عسکری در قندهار قبل داشتند و بیرم خان‌را به ایلچی‌گری پیش میرزا کامران فرستادند (63 a) میرزا عسکری عاجز و زبون شده گناهٔ خودرا درخواست نموده بیرون آمده حضرت پادشاه‌را ملازمت کرد — وحضرت پادشاه قندهاررا گرفته فتح نمودند و به پسرِ شاه دادند * بعد از چند روز پسرِ شاه بیمار شده مُرد * حضرت پادشاه قندهاررا بعد از آمدنِ بیرم خان ببیرم خان سپُردند *

وحمیده بانو بیگم‌را نیز در قندهار گذاشته متعاقبِ میرزا کامران متوجه شدند *

وآکه جانم خانزاده بیگم که همراه بودند در مقامِ قبلچاك که رسیدند تا سه روز تپ کردند * هرچند که اطبّا علاج کردند مفید نشد * روز چهارم در سنهٔ ٩٥١ نهصه و پنجاه و یك برحمتِ حق پیوستند * در همان منزل قبلچاك دفن کردند * بعد از سه ماه آورده در مقبرهٔ حضرت پادشاه بابام نگاه داشتند *

ومیرزا کامران در آن چند سال که در کابل بودند هرگز بتاخت نرفته بودند * بیکبار آمدنِ حضرت پادشاه شنیده در آن وقت (63 b) ایشان‌را هوسِ تاخت شد بجانبِ هزاره بتاخت رفته بودند *

ودرین اثنا میرزا هندال که گوشهٔ درویشی‌را اختیار کرده بودند مراجعتِ حضرت پادشاه‌را از عراق وخراسان وفتحِ قندهار شنیده فرصت‌را غنیمت داشته میرزا یادگار ناصررا طلبیده گفتند که پادشاه قندهاررا آمده فتح کردند و میرزا کامران خانزاده بیگم‌را برای صُلح فرستاده بودند *

پادشاه به آن روش صلح‌را قبول نکردند وحضرت پادشاه بیرم خان‌را برای یلچی‌گری فرستاده بودند* میرزا کامران سخنِ بیرم خان‌را قبول نکردند و الحال پادشاه قندهاررا به بیرم خان سپرده متوجه کابل شده اند* بیائید ما وشما شرط وعهد با یکدیگر کرده بحیله خودرا بحضرت پادشاه رسانیم* میرزا یادگار ناصر قبول کرد* این هر دو شرط وعهد کردند* میرزا هندال گفتند که شما فراررا بر خود قرار بدهید* میرزا کامران که می‌شنوَد البته مرا خواهد گفت (64 a) که یادگار ناصر گریخته شما رفته دلاسا کرده بیارید* تا آمدنِ من شما آهسته آهسته بروید* بعد ازآنی که من آمده رسیدم همراه شده بسرعتِ تمام خودهارا بملازمتِ حضرت پادشاه خواهیم رسانید* همین‌را قرار داده میرزا یادگار ناصر گریخت* خبر بمیرزا کامران رفت* میرزا کامران فی الحال گشته بکابل آمدند و میرزا هندال‌را طلبیده گفتند که شما بروید ومیرزا یادگار ناصررا دلاسا کرده بیارید* ایشان فی الحال سوار شده بسرعتِ تمام آمده همراه شدند* دیگر از آنجا یلغار کرده در پنج شش روز آمده بملازمتِ حضرت مشرف شدند وبحضرت عرض کردند که براهٔ تکیهٔ حمار* باید متوجه شد*

در سنه ٩٥١ نهصد وپنجاه ویك نهم شهر رمضان المبارك در تکیهٔ حمار* نزول اجلال فرمودند* همان روز بمیرزا کامران خبر رسید* میرزا کامران‌را اضترابئ عجبی دست داد* در ساعت چادر برآورده در پیش گذرگاه فروز آمدند وحضرت (64 b) پادشاه در یازدهم شهر رمضان در جلگهٔ تیپه** نزولِ اجلال فرمودند ومیرزا کامران هم آمده در برابر فروز آمدند بقصدِ جنگ* درین اثنا همه امرایان و سپاهیان میرزا

---

* (حمار) خمار؟.

** (تیپه) Perhaps the Tibāh of Bābar (Mems: L. & E. 139 & 136 n.) which Mr. Erskine says is 3 m. s. of Ak-serāi and to the left of the road from that place to Kābul. Abū'l-fażl (A. N. I. 243) gives Julga-i-dūrī as the meeting place.

کامران گریخته آمده بپابوسئ حضرت پادشاه مشرف شدند — و باپوس که یکی از امرای نامئ میرزا کامران بود وی نیز بجماعهٔ خود گریخته بقدم‌بوسئ حضرت آمده مشرف گشت * میرزا کامران یکی و تنها ماندند و چون دیدند که در گرد و نواحئ من کس نماند — منزلِ باپوس که امرای نامئ ایشان بود نزدیك بود — در و دیوار مشارالیه‌را انداخته ویران کرده و آهسته آهسته از پیش باغ نوروزی وگورخانهٔ گلبرخ بیگم شده این دوازده هزار سوارِ خود طلاق داده رفتند * چون تاریك شد بهمان راه به بابا دشتی در پیش کول آمده ایستادند و دوستی کوکه وجوکی خان‌را فرستادند که حبیبه بیگم دخترِ کلانِ میرزا و ابراهیم سلطان میرزا پسرِ میرزا کامران وهزاره بیگم برادرزادهٔ خضر خان وماه بیگم (65 a) خواهر حرم بیگم ومهر افروز* بیکه مادرِ حاجی بیگم وباقی کوکه که این جمله‌را بیارید * آخر این جماعه بمیرزا کامران همراه شدند ومیرزا متوجه تهته وبکهر شدند *

در ولایتِ خضر خان که در سرِ راهٔ بکهر واقعست در آنجا که رفتند حبیبه بیگم‌را باق سلطان نکاح بسته سپردند وخود بجانبِ بکهر وتهته شدند *

حضرت پادشاه فتح کرده در شب دوازدهم پنج گهری شب گذشته بود که در بالای حصار نزولِ اجلال بدولت وسعادت واقبال نزول فرمودند ومردمِ میرزا کامران که بخدمت مشرف شده بودند همه نقاره نواخته در خدمتِ حضرت در کابل در آمدند * و روز دوازدهم ماه مذکور حضرت والده دلدار بیگم وگلچهره بیگم واین حقیر حضرت‌را ملازمت کردیم * چون مدّتِ پنج سال بود که از دولتِ ملازمت محروم ومهجور بودیم واز محنت دوری ومشقت مهجوری خلاص شده بدولتِ وصالِ آن ولی‌نعمت مشرف شدیم وبمجرّد دیدن دل غمزده‌را حضوری (65 b) وچشم رمد دیده‌را نوری تازه حاصل گشت واز خوشحالی هرزمان سجداتِ شکر بجا می‌آورد *

---

* (مهرافروز) Erroneously read as ماه افروز in translating.

واکثر اوقات معرکه و مجلس بود و شبها تا صباح می‌نشستند وسازندها وگویندها دایم در نوازش بودند* واکثر بساط نشاط بازی میکردند ــ از آن جمله ــ دوازده کس بودند بهرکس بیست ورق و بیست بیست شاهرخی میدادند وکسی که پای میداد همین بیست شاهرخی پای میداد که پنج مثقالی باشد واگر می برد هرچند که بازی میکردند زیاده می‌بردند*

ومردم که در جنگِ چوسه وکنوج وبکهر ودر آن فطرانها در تودهٔ حضرت کشته وخسته گشته بودند بیوها ویتیمان واهل وعیالِ آن جماعت‌را وطیفه ورانبه وآب وزمین وقلبها عنایت می فرمودند ومردم سپاهی و رعیت وغیره‌را بسیار اسودگی وفراغت در ایامِ دولتِ حضرت روی داد* همیشه بفراغت میگذرانیدند وبجان درازئ حضرت اکثر بفاتحه خیریت قیام واقتدام (66 a) می‌نمودند*

بعد از چند روز بقندهار برای طلبِ حمیده بانو بیگم کسان فرستادند* بعد از آمدنِ حمیده بانو بیگم جلال الدین محمَّد اکبر پادشاه‌را ختنه سور کردند واسبابِ طوی سنّت‌را طیار میکردند* وبعد از نوروز هفت ده روز همایونی میکردند ولباسهای سبز می‌پوسیدند وقریب سی چهل دختررا حکم می‌شد که لباسهای سبز پوشند وبرکوه‌ها برآیند ــ ودر یك نوروز برکوه هفت دادران برآمدند* اکثر در حضور وعیش وفراغت میگذرانیدند ووقتی که محمَّد اکبر پادشاه پنج ساله شدند در شهر کابل ختنه سور کردند ودر همان دیوان‌خانهٔ کلان طوئ سنّت‌را دادند ــ وتمام بازاررا آئین بستند ومیرزا هندال ومیرزا یادگار ناصر وسلطانان وامرایان بجهة آئین بندی جاهاء خوب ومرغوب راست کرده بودند ودر باغ بیگه بیگم بیگمان وضعفا جاهای عجیب وغریب راست کرده بودند ــ وساچق‌را همه میرزایان وامرایان در (66 b) همان باغ دیوان‌خانه آوردند* بسیار طوئ

نغز و معرکهٔ خوب گذرانیدند و بمردمان خلعت‌های فاخر و سروپاهای وافر عنایت فرمودند* و مردم رعیّت و علما و صلحا و فقرا و غربا و شریف و وضیع و صغیر و کبیر در امنیّت و رفا روز بعیش و شب بعشرت میگذرانیدند*

و بعد از آن متوجه قلعهٔ ظفر شدند و در قلعهٔ مذکور میرزا سلیمان بودند* برای جنگ بر آمدند* چون مقابل شدند مقاومت نتوانستند کرد و فرار را بر خود قرار دادند* وحضرت پادشاه بدولت و ساعدت در قلعهٔ ظفر در آمدند* و در کشم پادشاه خود تشریف داشتند*

در آن زمان اندك تشویش در وجودِ مبارکِ ایشان غالب شد و صباح آن روز خفّت یافتند — و بهوشِ خود که آمدند فضایل بیگ برادرِ منعم خان‌را بکابل فرستادند که برو و مردمِ کابل‌را تسلی و دلداری داده بنوعی دلجوئی ایشان بکن که برهم نخورند و بگو — ما رسیده بود بلائ ولی بخیر گذشت*

بعد از رفتنِ فضیل بیگ (67 a) بکابل یکروز پیشترك بکابل رفته بودند و از کابل خبرِ دروغ در بکهر بمیرزا کامران رسید میرزا کامران در ساعت از بکهر ایلغار کرده متوجه کابل میشود و در* وقتی که زاهد بیك‌را آمده کشتند و متوجه کابل شدند*

و در سحری بود که مردم کابل غافل بودند و دروازها‌را بدستور سابق کشادند و مردم آب‌کش و علف‌کش و غیره می‌در آمدند و می‌بر آمدند که همراه همون مردم عام در قلعه در آمدند و محمّد علی تغائ‌را که در حمّام بوده فی الحال کشتند — و در مدرسهٔ ملا عبد الخالق فروز آمدند*

وقتی که حضرت بجانب قلعهٔ ظفر تشریف می‌بردند نوکاررا بر درِ

---

* (در) I propose to read here — در غزنیین که آمده زاهد بیگرا کشتند which agrees with other sources.

حرم گذاشته بودند* میرزا کامران پرسیدند که بر بالای حصار کیست؟ یکی گفته باشد که نوکار است — و این خبررا نوکار شنیده در همان ساعت لباسِ زنانه پوشیده برآمده بود که مردم میرزا کامران دربانانِ حصاررا گرفتند و پیش میرزا کامران بردند* ایشان فرمودند که در بند بکنید (67b) بعد ازین مردم میرزا کامران بالای حصار رفتند واشیاء واسباب بی‌شمارِ اهلِ حرم تالان وتاراج کرده در سرکارِ میرزا کامران ضبط و ربط نمودند و بیگمانِ کلان‌را در خانهٔ میرزا عسکری نشانند* و درِ آن خانه‌را از خشت وگچ و ماس* مسدود ساختند — واز بالای چهار دیواری خانه مذکور بیگمان‌را آب وطعام می‌دادند* و در خانه که میرزا یادگار ناصر می‌بودند خواجه معظم‌را نشانند — و در محلی که حرمانِ حضرت و بیگمانِ دیگر بودند در آن محل اهل و عیالِ خودرا فرمودند — واهل وعیال و اطفالِ سپاهیانی که گریخته در ملازمتِ حضرت رفته بودند به آنها بسیار بد پیش آمدند — وخانهٔ هرکدام آنهارا تاراج و تالان کردند — واهل وعیالِ هرکدام‌را بیکی سپردند* چون استماع نمودند که میرزا کامران از بکهر آمده چنین کارها کردند حضرت باز از قلعهٔ ظفر واندراب بدولت وساعدت متوجه کابل شدند وقلعهٔ ظفر بمیرزا سلیمان عناعت فرمودند*

چون حضرت بنواحیٔ کابل رسیدند میرزا (68a) کامران حضرت والده‌را ومرا از خانه طلبیدند وحضرت والده‌را حکم کردند که در خانهٔ قوربیکی باشند — ومرا گفتند که این هم خانهٔ شماست — همین جا باشید* من گفتم که برای چه اینجا باشم — در جای که والدهٔ من خواهد بود من نیز آنجا خواهم بود* ایشان در جواب من گفتند که پس شما بحضر خواجه خان خطی نویسید که آمده بما ملحق شوند وخاطر جمع دارند — بنوعی که میرزا

---

* (ماس) ؟ مایس Armenian, cakes of dung. The word is current in Turkī. The translation should read "He closed the door of that house" *&c.*.

عسکری و میرزا هندال برادرانِ من اند ایشان نیز برادرِ من اند که این وقتِ مدد است * من در جوابِ ایشان گفتم که خضر خواجه خان سواد ندارد که خطِ مرا شناسد و من هرگز خود نه نوشته ام * در بیرون از زبانِ فرزندانش می نویسند — هرچه بخاطرِ شما برسد بنویسید * آخر الامر مهدی سلطان‌را و شیر علی‌را بطلبِ خان فرستادند ومن در اوایل گفته بودم بخان که برادرانِ تو پیش میرزا کامران می باشند — مبادا تو هم خیالِ آن کنی و پیش ایشان (68 b) روی و به برادرانِ خود ملحق شوی — زنهار الف زنهار که از حضرت جدای‌را خیال نکنی * باری شکر الحمد الله بنوعی که گفته بودم خان هم تجاوز نه نمود — و حضرت پادشاه که شنیدند که مهدی سلطان و شیر علی‌را میرزا کامران بآوردن خضر خواجه خان فرستاده حضرت نیز قنبر بیگ پدرِ میرزا حاجی‌را بطلبِ خضر خواجه خان فرستادند *

در آن اوان خان در جاگیرِ خود بود * گفته فرستادند — زنهار الف زنهار که بمیرزا کامران ملحق نشود — در ملازمتِ ما بیائید * آخر خضر خواجه خان بمجرّد شنیدنِ این خبر و پیغام فرح‌انجام متوجه درگاهٔ فلک بارگاه گشت و در عقابین آمده ملازمت کرد *

آخر حضرت از منار که گذشتند درین اثنا شیر افکن پدرِ شیرویه‌را میرزا کامران ترتیب داده و ترتیب کرده تمام لشکرِ خود همراه کرده پیش فرستادند که رفته جنگ کند * مایان از بالا میدیدیم که او نقاره زده از پیش بابا دستی میگذشت و مایان میگفتیم که خدا نصیب نکند که (69 a) تو رفته جنگ کنی و گریه میکردیم *

آخر چون در برابر دیه افغانان که رسید و قراولان روبرو که شدند بمجرّد روبرو شدن قراولانِ حضرت پادشاه قراولانِ میرزائی‌را برداشتند و اکثر دستگیر کرده پیش حضرت آوردند * حضرت حکم کردند بمغولان که آنهارا پاره پاره کردند و اکثر مردمِ میرزا کامران که بجنگ رفته بودند

بدستِ مردم پادشاهی اسیر شدند ودستگیر گشتند وآن حضرت بعضی‌را کشتند وبعضی‌را در بند کردند* ازآن میان جوکی خان که ازامرایانِ میرزا کامران بود او نیز بدست افتاد*

حضرت پادشاه ومیرزا هندال در ملازمتِ حضرت بفتح وفیروزی شادیانه نواختند وبکوکبه ودبدبه درعقابین درآمدند — واز برای خود خیمه وخرگاه وبارگاه برپا کردند* ومیرزا هندال‌را مورچالِ پلِ مستان تعین نمودند وبامرایان هرجا هرجا مورچال تعین کردند*

تا مدّتِ هفت ماه محاصره داشتند* از قضا یك روزی (69 b) میرزا کامران از حویلی در دالان میرفتند که شخصی از عقابین تفنگ انداخت وایشان دویده خودرا درکناره گرفتند وآکبر پادشاه‌را گفتند که در روبرو بُرده نگاه دارید* آخر مردم بعرض اقدس اشرف رسانیدند که میرزا محمّد آکبررا در روبرو نگاه داشته اند* حضرت فرمودند که تفنگ نه اندازند* بعد ازین مردم پادشاهی در بالای حصار تفنگ نمی‌انداختند واز شهرِ کابل مردم میرزا کامران بعقابین در لشکرِ حضرت تفنگ می‌انداختند — ومردم بادشاهی میرزا عسکری‌را در برابر روبرو ایستاده می‌کردند وسپاهیان پادشاهی شوخی مینمودند ومردم میرزا کامران هم از قلعه برآمده جنگ میکردند واز جانبین مردم کُشته می‌گشتند* اکثر مردمِ حضرت غالب می آمدند — دیگر از قلعه دلیر نمی برآمدند — وحضرت از ملاحظهٔ عیال واطفال وبیگمان ومردم وحرمان وجماعهٔ دیگر توپ وضربِ جنگ نمی انداختند — وبجانها (?) اب‌را (70 a) تنگ نمی کردند*

چون محاصره بدور دراز انجامشد خواجه دوست خاوند مداریچه‌را در پیش حضرت فرستادند که از برای خدا میرزا کامران هرچه التماس می‌کنند قبول فرمایند وبندهای خدارا از محنت خلاص بکنند*

حضرت از بیرون از برای ایشان نه گوسفند وهفت شیشهٔ گلاب ویك

شیشهٔ آبِ لیمون و هفت توقوز پارچه و چند نیمه دوخته فرستادند و نوشتند که از جهةِ ایشان نمی توانم بقلعه زور آورد که مبادا بدشمنانِ ایشان بنوعی دیگر پیش آید*

و در آن ایام جهان سلطان بیگم دو ساله شده درهمان قبل فوت شد و می‌نوشتند که اگر بقلعه زور آوریم زمانی میرزا محمّد اکبررا پنهان خواهد کرد*

غرض دائم در بالای حصار مردم از نمازِ شام تا صبح حاضرباش و غوغا داشتند* شبی که میرزا کامران میگریزند نمازِ شام گذشت بلکه خفتن شد که (70 b) هیچ غوغای ظاهر نشد — وکوتلی بود که از آنجا مردم پایان ببالا می برآمدند* در آن حین مردم شهر آرام وتسکین یافته بودند که بیکبار آوازِ جیبه و جوشن و زره برآمده که بهمدیگر خبر کردیم که غلو می‌نماید* در پیش جلوخانه قریب هزار کس استاده باشند* مایان همه در وهم بودیم بیکبار بی خبر برآمدند و پسرِ قراچه خان بهادر خان آمده خبر کردند که میرزا فرار نموده و خواجه معظم‌را از راهٔ دیوار ریسمان انداخته بر آوردند*

ومردم مایان و بیگمان وغیره که در بیرون بودند ودری که بالای مایان برآورده بودند وا کردند* بیگه بیگم مبالغه کردند که برویم بخانهای خود* من گفتم که زمانی صبر کنید — از راهٔ کوچه باید رفت وشاید که از پیش حضرت هم کسی آید — که درین ضمن عنبر ناظر آمد وگفت که حضرت فرموده اند که تا من نیایم از آن خانها نه برآیند* زمانی گذشته بود که حضرت آمدند و به دلدار بیگم وبمن دریافتند بعد از آن به بیگه بیگم و بحمیده بانو بیگم دریافتند وفرمودند که زود ازین (71 a) خانه برآئید که دوستان‌را خدا ازین تورخانه نگاه دارد ونصیبِ دشمنان شود* بناظر فرمودند که در یك طرف تو باش ودر یك طرف تردی بیگ خان باشد وبیگمان‌را بگذرانند* آخر همه آمدند وآن شب در ملازمتِ حضرت بودیم — واز

خوشحالی تمام شب در یکزمان صباح شد — ماه چوچك بیگم و خانش آغا و حرمان که در لشکر همراهٔ حضرت آمده بودند دریافتیم ٭

و وقتی که حضرت به بدخشان رفتند ماه چوچك بیگم دختر زائیدند ٭ در همان شب حضرت در خواب دیدند که فخرالنسا مامام و دولت بخت هر دو از در درآمده اند و چیزی آوردند و پیش من گذاشتند ٭ هرچند تفکر کردند فرمودند که تعبیرِ آن چه باشد ٭ آخر در خاطر رسانیدند که چون دختر شده است از نام هر دو یکی نسا و از دیگری بخت بطریق اختصار بخت نسا بیگم نام نهادند ٭

ماه چوچك بیگم چهار دختر و دو پسر زائیدند — بخت نسا بیگم و سکینه بانو بیگم و امنه بانو (71 b) بیگم و محمّد حکیم میرزا وِ فرّخ فال میرزا — و وقتی که حضرت متوجه هندوستان شدند ماه چوچك بیگم حامله بودند ٭ در کابل پسر زائیند — فرّخ فال میرزا نام نهادند ٭ و بعد از چند گاه از خانش آغا پسر توّلد شد — ابراهیم سلطان میرزا نام نهادند ٭ و مدّت یکنیم سال کامل بدولت و سعادت در کابل بعیش و عشرت گذرانیدند ٭

و میرزا کامران که از کابل فرار نمودند بجانبِ بدخشان رفتند و در طالقان می بودند — و حضرت در اورته باغ می‌بودند ٭ صباح که بنماز برخاستند خبر شد که اکثر امرای میرزا کامران که در ملازمتِ حضرت بودند گریخته رفتند — از جمله قراچه خان و مصاحب خان و مبارز خان و بابوس و اکثر نا مرادان شب گریخته به بدخشان رفتند و بمیرزا کامران ملحق شدند ٭ حضرت در ساعتِ نیك متوجه بدخشان شدند و میرزا کامران‌را در طالقان محاصره کردند ٭

بعد از چند گاه میرزا کامران اطاعت و فرمان‌برداری قبول کرده و آمده حضرت‌را (72a) ملازمت کرده ٭ کولاب‌را حضرت بمیرزا کامران دادند

و قلعهٔ ظفررا بمیرزا سلیمان دادند و قندهاررا* بمیرزا هندال و طالقان‌را بمیرزا عسکری عنایت فرمودند ✲

روزی در کشم خرگاه دوخته بودند و اجتماع برادران شد — حضرت همایون پادشاه و میرزا کامران و میرزا عسکری و میرزا هندال و میرزا سلیمان ✲

چند توره که در ملازمتِ حضرت پادشاه نشپته اند فرمودند که آفتابه چلانچی بیارید که دست شسته همه بیکجا طعام بخوریم ✲ حضرت پادشاه دست شستند و میرزا کامران دست شستند ✲ بسالِ نسبت میرزا عسکری و میرزا هندال میرزا سلیمان کلان بودند ✲ بجهةِ تعظیم آفتابه و چلانچی هر دو برادران پیش میرزا سلیمان نهادند ✲ و بعد از دست شپتن میرزا سلیمان بینی خودرا حرکتی بدی کرد ✲ میرزا عسکری و میرزا هندال بسیار درشت پیش آمدند (72b) وگفتند که این چه روستای کریست؟ اولا مایان چه حد داریم که در حضورِ حضرت پادشاه دست بشویم — امّا چون عنایت فرمودند و حکم نمودند نتوانستم تغیر حکم کرد — این اداهای بینی جنبانی چه معنی دارد ✲ آخر میرزا عسکری و میرزا هندال بیرون برآمده دست شسته آمده نشپتند — و میرزا سلیمان بسیار شرمنده شده — و همه دریك دستارخان طعام خوردند ✲ و حضرت درین مجلس این حقیررا یاد فرمودند و به برادرانِ خود گفته اند که در لاهور کلبدن بیگم گفته بودند که این آرزو دارم که همهٔ برادران‌را بیکجا به بینم و از صباح که نشپته ایم همان سخن بخاطرم میرسد انشا الله تعالی جمعیت مارا حق سبحانه تعالی در امانِ خود دارد ✲ بخدا روشن است که در ضمیرِ من این نیست که زیانِ مسلمانی بطلبم چه جای آنکه زیانِ برادران‌را می طلبیده باشم — انشا الله تعالی بهمهٔ شمایان خدای تعالی همین توفیق کرامت کند که موافق و بیکجهة باشد (73a) و در میانهٔ

---

* (قندهاررا) So too Jauhar. Kundūz appears right.

مردم عجب شوقی و خوشحالی روی داده بود — چراکه اکثر امرایان و نوکران هم خویش و برادر یکدیگر بودند از ممر جُدای صاحبانِ خود آنها هم از یکدیگر جُدا بلك تشنهٔ خونِ یکدیگر بودند* الحال همه یکجا خوشحالی تمام میگذرانیدند*

و از بدخشان که آمدند یکنیم سال در کابل بودند* بعد از آن عزم جزمِ بلخ نمودند و در باغ دلکشا منزل فرمودند و دولتخانهٔ حضرت‌را در پایانِ باغِ مذکور روبرو برپا کردند و بیگمان در حویلی کلی بیگ چون نزدیك بود آنجا فرود آمدند* بحضرت باز عرض رسانیدند که ایا رواج چطور می برآمده باشد* حضرت فرمودند — چون که بلشکر میرویم براهٔ کوه دامن رویم تا شمایان برآمد رواج‌را به بینید* نماز دیگری بود که حضرت سوار شده در باغ دلکشا آمدند و حویلی کلی بیگ که بیگمان در آن بودند نزدیك بود و آنجا سرکوب بود*

حضرت آمده استادند* بیگمان همه دیدند و برخواستند (73 b) وکورنش کردند — و بمجرّد کورنش کردنِ بیگمان حضرت بدستِ مبارکِ خود اشهارت کردند که بیائید* فخر النسا ماما و افغانی آغاچه پیشترك میرفتند — و در دامنِ کوهٔ باغ دلکشا جوی بوده است* افغانی آغاچه از جوی مذکور نتوانست گذست و افغانی آغاچه از اسپ افتاد* از برای آن ساعتی معطل کردند* آخرالامر بعد از ساعتی بملازمت اشرف اقدس مشرف گشتیم و ماه چوچك بیگم نا دانسته اسپش اندك بلند رفت* از برای آن حضرت بسیار اعراض کردند — باغ مذکور در بلندی بود و هنوز دیوارها نکرده بودند* درین اثنا در چهرهٔ مبارکِ حضرت کلفتی پدید آمده* فرمودند که شمایان بروید و من افیون خورده و این کلفت‌را تسکین داده خواهم آمد* مایان بفرمودهٔ حضرت اندك راهی رفته بودیم که حضرت تشریف آوردند* در واقع کلفت بالکلیه بر طرف شده و خوشحال و فرخناك آمدند* شب

مهتاب بود* حرف و حکایات کرده* (M.S. 83a) میرفتند وخانش آغاچه و ظریف گوینده و سروسهی و شاهم آغا آهسته آهسته نقش** می گفتند* تا که بلغمان رسیدند خیمه و خرگا و بارگاه پادشاهی وچادرهای بیگمان هنوز نیامده بود* درآنوقت چادرِ مهر آمیز آمده بود* حضرت و همهٔ مایان و حمیده بانو بیگم نیز در همان چادر در ملازمتِ حضرت تا دو پهر وسه گهری شب نشسته بودیم* آخر در چادر مذکور در ملازمتِ آن قبلهٔ حقیقی خواب کردیم — وصباح میخواستند که رفته در کوه رواج‌را به بینید* چون اسپانِ بیگمان در دیه بودند تا آمدنِ اسپان وقتِ سیر گذشت* حکم کردند که در بیرون اسپِ هرکس که باشد بیارید* اسپان‌را که آوردند فرمودند سوار شوید*

بیگه بیگم وماه چوچك بیگم هنوز سروپا می‌پوشیدند* من بحضرت عرض کردم که اگر حکم شود من رفته آنهارا بیارم* فرمودند — زودتر برو و بیار* من به بیگم وماه چوچك بیگم وغیرهٔ حرمهای دیگر گفتم — بندهٔ سرِ حضرت شوم — چه بالا انتظار میدهد* اینهارا بمحصلی تمام می‌آوردم (M.S. 83b) که حضرت از روبروی ما تشریف آوردند و فرمودند — کلبدن حالا خود وقتِ سیر گذشت تا به آنجا رسیدن هوا گرم خواهد شد — انشا الله تعالی نماز پشین‌را ادا کرده خواهم رفت*

---

* (کرده) It seems to me that in binding the M.S. in India; fol. 83 has been misplaced and that it should follow at this point where its contents are *à propos*. The catchwords are wanting on it and on 74 a.

This emendation has been made only since the preparation of my article on Gulbadan Begam (Calcutta Review, April 1898) and contradicts and modifies some statements of that article.

The account of the journey to Laghmān (fol. 83) is appropriate here and is out-of-place in the story of Kāmrān's blinding and of Humāyūn's subsequent movements.

It is possible that another page also is missing and that the quiet singing was not on the road.

** (نقش) Ar. *naqs*, an air with its variations. (Pavet de Courteille.)

وخرگاهی که بهمان خرگاه حمیده بانو بیگم آمده نشپتند* بعد از نماز پیشین تا اسپان‌را آوردن میان دو نماز شد* درین طور وقت تشریف بردند* در دامنِ کوه هرجا رواج برگ برآورده بود در آن درها گشت وسیر میکردند که شام شد* در همان جا چادر و خرگاه برپا کرده آمده نشپتند* آن شب در آنجا نیز بعیش و عشرت بهم گذرانیدیم ومایان همه در ملازمتِ آن قبلهٔ حقیقی بودیم* صباح وقتِ نماز بیرون تشریف بُردند — واز بیرون به بیگه بیگم وحمیده بانو بیگم وماه چوچك بیگم وبمن و بهمه بیگمان علحده خطً نوشتند که بگناهٔ خود قایل شده عذرخواهی نوشید* انشا الله در فرضه یا در استالیف خیرباد کرده متوجه لشکر خواهم شد واگرنه (74a) بُخدا (? بجدا) سپردیم* آخر همه عذرخواهی نوشته بخدمت اقدس اشرف فرستادند* عاقبت الامر حضرت و همه بیگمان سوار شده از لغمان به بهزادی آمدیم وشب هرکس بمنزلِ خود رفت وصباح آن طعام نوش جان کردند ونماز پیشین سُوار شده بفرضه آمدند*

حمیده بانو بیگم بخانهٔ مایان نُه نه گوسپند فرستادند — ویك روز پیشترك بیبی دولت بخت در فرضه آمده بود وخوردنیٔ وافر وشیر وجغرات و شیره وشربت وغیره طیار کرده بودند* آن شب بعیش گذرانیده صباح بر بالای فرضه ثرثرآب خوبست* آنرا (fault) استالیف رفته وسه روز دیگر در استالیف بودند وبعد از آن کوچ کرده در سنه ۹۵۸ نهصد و پنجاه هشت متوجه بلخ شدند*

واز کوتل که گذشتند بمیرزا کامران ومیرزا سلیمان ومیرزا عسکری فرمانهای طلب فرستادند که ما متوجه جنگِ اوزبك شدیم وقتِ یکجهتی وبرادریست می‌باید که بسرعتِ تمام برسید* میرزا سلیمان و میرزا عسکری آمده (74b) بحضرت ملحق شدند* کوچ به کوچ متوجه شده به بلخ رسیدند*

پیر محمّد خان در بلخ بود ودر همان روز اِوّل مردمِ پیر محمّد خان برآمده جنگ صف کردند* لشکر پادشاهی غالب آمد ومردم پیر محمّد خان شکست خورده در شهر در آمدند* صباح آن پیر محمّد خان قرار داده بود که چغتای زور است — من نمی توانم جنگ کرد — بهتر است که برآمده بروم — که امرایان پادشاهی یکی بعرض رسانید که یورت چرکین شده است — اگر ازین منزل برخواسته دشت منزل نمایند مناسب است* حضرت حکم فرمودند چنین بکنند* بمجرّد که دست به بار و بارخانه نهادند دیگر مردم تلاتوف شدند وچند کس منادی کرد بمردم کسی بس نیامد* چون خواست آلهی چنین بود بی جهة غنیم وتقریب وبی واسطه مردم راهی شدند* به اوزبك خبر رسید که لشکرِ پادشاهی کوچ کرد* اوزبك در تعجب شد ویساولان پادشاهی هرچند که سعی کردند به ریزه پاپس نه آمدند (75a) وبمنع کردن نشد* مردم راهی شدند* حضرت مدّتی استادند* آخر دیدند که کس نماند* ضرور شد حضرت هم روان شدند ومیرزا عسکری ومیرزا هندال‌را خبر نبود که لشکر پادشاهی برهم خورده است* اینها سوار شده آمدند — دیدند که در لشکرگاه کسی نمانده واوزبك در پی برآمدن است* اینها نیز بطرف قندوز راهی شدند* حضرت اندك راهی آمده بودند که ایستادند وگفتند که برادران تا حال نه آمدند* من چطور پیش روم* به بعضی امرا وغیره که در ملازمت بودند فرمودند که کسی باشد که از میرزایان خبر بیارد* هیچکس جواب نداد ونرفت* بعد ازآن از قندوز از مردم میرزا خبر آمد — عرض داشت کرده اند که شنیده شد که شکست واقع شده — ندانستم که بکدام طرف رفتند* این خط که بدستِ حضرت افتاد بسیار بی طاقتی کردند* خضر خواجه خان گفته اگر حکم شود من خبر بیارم* پادشاه فرمودند — رحمت باد — انشا الله باشد که میرزا بقندوز رفته باشد* بعد از (75b) دو روز خضر خواجه

خان خبرِ میرزا هندال‌را بحضرت آورد که بصحت و سلامت در قندوز رسیدند* این خبررا که حضرت شنیدند بسیار خوشحال شدند*

و میرزا سلیمان‌را بجای خود که قلعه ظفر باشد رخصت کردند و خود بکابل آمدند* میرزا کامران که در کولاب بودند ترخان بیگه نام عورتی عیّار مکّاره بود بمیرزا کامران راه نموده که به حرم بیگم اظهارِ عاشقی بکنید که درین مصلحتهاست* میرزا کامران هم بگفتهٔ آن ناقص العقل خطی و روپاکی بدستِ بیگی آغا بحرم بیگم فرستادند* این عورت خط و روپاک‌را برده پیش حرم بیگم نهاد و ملازمتِ میرزا کامران و اشتیاقِ بسیار اظهار کرد* حرم بیگم گفت که حالا این خط و روپاک‌را نگاه دارید هرگاه میرزایان از بیرون بیایند این خط و روپاک‌را بیارید* بیگی آغا در پی گریه و زاری و ملایمت که میرزا کامران این خط و روپاک بشما فرستاده و مدتهاست که برشما عاشق است و شما ازین بابت بی مروتی می کنید* حرم بیگم (76 a) بنیاد اعراض و شدت تمام نموده فی الحال میرزا سلیمان و میرزا ابراهیم‌را طلبیده گفت که میرزا کامران نا مردی‌های شمایان‌را دانسته است که بمن همچو خطی نوشته واقع که من لایق این بودم که مرا چنین نویسد* میرزا کامران برادرِ کلانِ تو باشد و من بجای کلینِ ایشان باشم* مرا ازین بابت خطی فرستد* بگیرید و این زنکه‌را پاره پاره سازید تا بر دیگران عبرت شود و هیچکس بر اهل و عیال کسی بچشم بدخیال فاسد نکند و از زن آدمی‌زاده چه مناسب که همچو چیزهای نالایق بیارد و از من و پسرِ من نترسد* و فی الحال بیگی آغا بیبی دولت‌خون گرفته‌را پاره پاره کردند و میرزا سلیمان و میرزا ابراهیم ازین جهة بمیرزا کامران بد شدند بلکه دشمن شدند و بخدمتِ حضرت نوشتند که قصدِ مخالفت دارد و مخالفت ازین صریح‌تر نمی باشد که درحین توجهٔ بلخ در ملازمت همراه نرفته* بعد از آن میرزا کامران در کولاب از توهم هراسیده هیچ علاجی

بهتر ازین (76b) نیافتند که خودرا بگوشهٔ بکشند* ابوالقاسم میرزا پسر خودرا پیش میرزا عسکری فرستادند وعایشه سلطان بیگم دختر خودرا میرزا کامران همراه گرفته بجانبِ طالقان میرفت وخانم کوچ میرزا کامران بود* باو گفتند که شما ودخترِ شما ازعقب بیائید* در هرجا که قرار خواهم گرفت شمارا خواهم طلبید* امّا تا آن زمان شما در خوست واندرآب رفته نشینید* خانم مذکور با خانان اوزبك قرابت داشت* در میانِ آن اوزبکان از خویشان آن بوده به اوزبکان معلوم کرده وفهمانیده که اگر غرض اوانچه است مال وداه وغلام دارم ببرید وضعفارا گذارید که برادرزادهٔ عایشه سلطان خانم اگر فردا شنود از شما البته خواهد رنجد* بصد مکر وحیله وبصد حیرانی وبی سامانی از بندِ اوزبك خلاص شده در خوست واندرآب رسیده در آنجاها می‌بودند*

ومیرزا کامران از شکستِ بلخ اطلاع یافته که حضرت در بارهٔ من چنانچه ملتفت بودند نیستند واز کولاب (77a) برآمده بهر طرف می‌گشت*

در این اثنا حضرت از کابل برآمده بطرف دشت قبچاق که رسیدند غافل در جائی پشت فرود آمده بودند که میرزا کامران از جای بلندی بیکبار مُسلح ومکمل شده آمده برسر دشمنان حضرت ریختند* چون خواست آلهی چنین بود یك کور باطن گردن شکسته ظالم ستمکار بدبخت تابکار بحضرت پادشاه زخم انداخت وبسرِ مبارکِ ایشان رسیده وتمام پیشانی وچشمهای مبارکِ ایشان بخون آلوده شده بود* بطریقی که در جنگ مغولان بسرِ مبارکِ حضرت فردوس مکانی بابر پادشاه مغولی زخم زده وطاقی ودستار بریده نشد امّا سرِ مبارکِ ایشان مجروح شده — حضرت همایون پادشاه دایم تعجب‌ها می‌نمودند ومی‌گفتند که عجب سر است که طاقی ودستار بریده نشود وبسر زخم رسد* غرض بسر مبارکِ ایشان هم همان طور شد* حضرت بعد از شکستِ دشت قبچاق به بدخشان رفتند ومیرزا هندال ومیرزا

سلیمان و (77b) میرزا ابراهیم آمده حضرت‌را ملازمت کردند و حضرت بکابل رفتند و میرزایان در دولتخواهی یکدل و یکجهة شده در ملازمت بودند که میرزا کامران متوجه شدند* حضرت پادشاه بحرم بیکم گفته فرستادند که کلین‌را بگوئید که بزودی زود لشکر و مردم بدخشان‌را سامان نموده فرستید و بیگم در اندك روز اندك فرصتی چند هزار کس‌را اسپ و یراق دادند واهتمام وسامان نموده وبهمراهٔ خود تا کوتل آورده واز آنجا لشکررا پیش فرستادند — خود مراجعت نمودند ولشکر مذکور آمده بحضرت پادشاه ملحق شد* در چارکاران یا قراباغ بمیرزا کامران جنگ شد لشکرِ حضرت غالب آمده وفتح کردند ومیرزا کامران‌را شکست دادند* میرزا کامران گریخته به تنگیها ولمغانات رفت*

وآق سلطان که دامادِ میرزا کامران بود گفته باشد که شما دایم بحضرت همایون پادشاه مخالفت پیش می آئید — چه معنی دارد؟ مناسب نیست — یا اطاعت وفرمان برداری حضرت بکنید یا مرا (78a) رخصت بدهید که مردم از مایان می‌دانند* میرزا کامران به آق سلطان درشتی کرده گفت که کارِ من بجای رسیده که تو بمن نصیحت کنی* آق سلطان هم از روی درشتی گفت اگر من در پیش شما باشم حلالِ من حرام باشد* وآق سلطان همان زمان جُدا شده در بکهر رفت و بکوچِ خود همراه شده بود که فرمانِ میرزا کامران بشاه حسین میرزا رسید که آق سلطان مارا رنجانیده رفته است* اگر در آنجا آمده باشد اورا نگذرایدکه به زنِ خود همراه شود وکوچِ اورا ازو جُدا سازید واورا بگوئید که هر جامیخواهی برو* بمجرّد رسیدنِ فرمان شاه حسین میرزا حُبیبه بیکم‌را از تصرفِ آق سلطان جُدا ساخته و سلطان‌را بمکهٔ معظمه رخصت کرده*

درهمان جنگ چارکاران قراچه خان و آکثر مردم نامیٔ میرزا کامران کشته شدند*

و عایسه سلطان بیگم و دولت بخت آغاچه گریخته بجانبِ قندهار میرفتند که از تکیهٔ حمار مردم پادشاهی گرفته آوردند (78 b) و میرزا کامران به افغانان همراه شده در میانِ افغانان می بوده *

و حضرت پادشاه گاه گاهی بدیدن باغ نارنج میرفتند * در آن سال نیز بدستور سابق بدیدنِ نارنج در تنگیها رفتند و میرزا هندال در ملازمت بودند و از حرمان بیگه بیگم و حمیده بانو بیگم و ماه چوچك بیگم و غیره اکثر حرمان همراه بودند * و پسرِ من سعادت یار در آن روزها بیمار بود بنابر آن من نتوانستم رفت * روزی در نواحی تنگیها حضرت پادشاه در شکار بودند و میرزا هندال در ملازمت بود * بسیار شکارِ خوب بود * طرفی که میرزا شکار رفته بودند حضرت هم آن طرف آمدند * میرزا شکارِ بسیاری کردند * میرزا بدستور چنگیز خان همه شکار خودرا بحضرت پیشکش کردند که در توره چنگیز خان رسم چنین است که خوردان به بزرگان خود چنین پیش می آیند * غرض همه شکارهای خودرا پیشکشِ حضرت کرده * بعد از آن به خاطرِ میرزا رسیده که حصهٔ خواهران هم بماند (79 a) باز خواهران گله نکنند * پاره دیگر شکار بکنم که برای خواهران حصه ببرم * میرزا باز بشکار مقید شده اند * یکپاره شکار کرده برگشته می‌آمدند که میرزا کامران کسی‌را تعین کرده بودند آن کس سر راه‌را گرفته و میرزا ازین غافل تیری زد و آن تیر به کتفِ مبارکِ ایشان رسیده — از ملاحظه آنکه مبادا خواهرانِ من یا حرمانِ من شنیده بیطاقتی بکنند * فی الحال نوشته فرستادند که — ه رسیده بود بالائی ولی بخیر گذشت * شمایان خاطرها خودرا جمع دارید که من بصحت و عافیت هستم * غرض هوا که گرم شد حضرت برگشته بکابل آمدند و مدّتِ یکسال گذشت زخم تیر بهتر شد *

بعد از یکسال خبر آمد که میرزا کامران باز جمعیّت کرده استعداد جنگ دارد * حضرت نیز سامانِ جنگ نموده متوجه تنگیها شدند و میرزا

هندال در ملازمتِ حضرت‌را می‌شدند٭ وقتی که به تنگیها بدولت و سعادت رفته نزول اجلال فرمودند (79b) و جاسوسان هر زمان هر ساعت خبر می‌آوردند که میرزا کامران قرار داده است امشب شبخون باید ریخت٭ میرزا هندال آمده بعرضِ حضرت رسانیدند وکنگایش دادند که حضرت درین بلندی باشند و برادرم جلال الدین محمّد اکبر پادشاه در ملازمت همراه باشند تا درین بلندی مردم باحتیاط چوکی بدهند — و خود مردمِ خودرا طلبیده بهرکدام علیحده علیحده دلداری و دلاسا کرده که — همه آن خدمتها یکطرف و خدمت امشب یکطرف انشا الله آنچه حسب المدعای شمایانست بهمون روش سر افراز خواهید شد٭ همه‌را جابجا نشانده و برای خود جیبه جامه و طاقی و دبلغه طلبیدند٭ توشکچی بقچه‌را برداشته بود که شخصی عطسه زد٭ توشکچی بقچه‌را ساعتی نگاه داشت٭ چون معطل شد کسی‌را برای تاکید فرستادند٭ چون بتاکید تمام آوردند خود پرسیدند که چرا معطل کردی؟ توشکچی عرض کرد که بقچه‌را برداشته بودم که شخصی عطسه زد — بنابر آن بقچه‌را باز ماندم وازین (80a) سبب معطل شد٭ فرمودند که غلط کردی بگو انشا الله شهادتِ مبارك باشد — و باز گفتند — یاران همه گواه باشند که از جمیع چیزهای حرام و از افعال‌های ناشایسته توبه کردم٭ حاضران فاتحه خواندند ومبارك باد گفتند٭ فرمودند — نیمچه جامه جیبه بیار٭ پوشیده در پیش خندق رفتند و بسپاهیان مردانگی و تسلی دادند٭ درین اثنا طبقچیٔ میرزا هندال آوازِ میرزارا که شنیدند فریاد برآورد که مرا به شمشیر گرفتند٭ میرزا بمجرّد شنیدن از اسپ فروز آمده و بدو گفتند — یاران این از مردانگی دور است که طبقچیٔ مارا در تهٔ شمشیر بگیرند وما کومك نکنیم٭ وخود در خندق فرود آمدند و سپاهیان هیچکدام از اسپ فرود نه آمدند و میرزا دو بار از خندق برآمدند وحمله‌ها کردند٭ در همان تردّد شهید شدند٭

نمیدانم که کدام ظالمی بی رحمی آن جوان کم آزاررا به تیغ ظلم بیجان کرده ✲ کاشکی بدل و دیدهٔ من یا بسعادت یار پسرِ من (80 b) یا بخضر خواجه خان آن تیغ بی دریغ میرسید ✲ آه صد آه افسوس و دریغ هزار دریغ ✲

ای دریغا ای دریغا ای دریغ ✲ آفتابم شد نهان در زیرِ میغ —

غرض که میرزا هندال در خدمت و دلسوزئ حضرت جان سپاری کرد ✲ میر بابا دوست میرزارا برداشته در دولت‌خانهٔ میرزا آورد و بهیچ کس اظهار نکرد و یساولان آورده در دروازه نشاند و گفت — هر که بیاید و پرسد بگوئید که زخمِ میرزا کاری است و حکمِ حضرتست که هیچکس نه در آید ✲

و بعرضِ حضرت پادشاه آمده رسانید که میرزا هندال زخمی شده اند ✲ حضرت پادشاه اسپ طلبیدند که رفته میرزارا به بینم ✲ میر عبد الحی گفته که زخمِ ایشان کاریست و رفتنِ حضرت مناسب نیست ✲ حضرت فهمیده اند و هر چند که خودرا حفظ کردند نتواستند و بیطاقتی نمودند ✲

جوساهی جاگیرِ خضر خواجه خان بود ✲ حضرت خضر خواجه خان‌را طلبیده فرمودند که میرزا هندال‌را در جوساهی بُرده امانت نگاه دارید ✲ خان مُهارِ شتررا گرفته بفریاد و فغان و جزع و فزع کرده می‌رفت (81 a) که این خبررا حضرت پادشاه شنیدند بخضر خواجه گفته فرستادند که صبر باید کرد — دل من از تو پشتر می‌سوزد امّا از ملاحظهٔ آن غنیم خونخوار ظالم بیطاقتی نمی‌کنم وحال آنکه او نزدیکست غیر از صبر چاره نیست ✲ بصد افسوس و بیچاره‌گی و درد بُرده در جوساهی امانت گذاشتند ✲

میرزا کامران ظالم برادرکش بیگانه پرور بی رحم اگر آن شب نمی آمد این بالا از آسمان نازل نمی شد ✲ حضرت پادشاه بکابل خطها نوشتند ✲ بمجرّد رسیدنِ این خطها بخواهران گویا تمامی کابل بماتم سرا مانند شد و در و دیوار

براحوالِ میرزای سعید شهید گریه و فغان می‌کردند* و گلچهره بیگم در خانهٔ قرا خان رفته بودند* وقتی که ایشان باز آمدند گویا قیامت شد قایم واز گریه و غم بسیار ایشان بیمار و جنونی شدند*

از بهادرئ میرزا کامران ظالم بی رحم میرزا هندال شهید شدند* از آن روز باز دیگر نشنیدیم که در کار و بارِ میرزا کامران رشدی شده باشد بلك روز بروز تنزل کرد وابتر وضایع شد و بنوعی رو بخرابی (81 b) آورد که دیگر دولت بمیرزا کامران یار نشد وکامرانی نکرد وگویا حیاتِ میرزا کامران بلك روشنائی چشمِ میرزا کامران میرزا هندال بود که از همان شکست که گریخته راست رفت در پیش سلیم شاه پسر شیر خان* او یکهزار روپیه داده ودرین ضمن میرزا کامران عرض احوال نموده وکومك طلبید* سلیم شاه در جوابِ میرزا بظاهر چیزی نگفت امّا در مخفی گفته است که کسی که برادر خود میرزا هندال‌را بکشد به آن کومك چنوع توان داد* بلك همچوکسی‌را نا بود کردن ومعدوم ساختن بهتراست* میرزا کامران این کنگایش سلیم خان‌را شنید وبمردم خود هم کنگایش نکرد وشبی فراررا برخود قرار داده گریخت ومردم میرزا خبر هم ندانشتند* اینها ماندند* بسلیم خان که خبر شد اکثر مردم میرزارا در بندخانه حکم کرده و میرزا کامران تا به بهیره وخوش‌آب رفته بود که در (82 a) همان حدود آدم گهکهر بصد وحیله ومکر در قید آورده پیش حضرت پادشاه آورد* عاقبت الامر جمیع خوانان وسلطانین و وضیع و شریف و صغیر وکبیر وسپاهی و رعیّت وغیره که از دستِ میرزا کامران داغها داشتند در آن مجلس متفق سده بعرضِ حضرت پادشاه رسانیدند که در پادشاهی وتحکّم رسم برادری منظور نمی باشد* اگر خاطرِ برادر میخواهید ترکِ پادشاهی بکنید واگر پادشاهی میخواهید ترکِ برادری بکنید واین همان میرزا کامران است که از سببِ او در دشتِ قبچاق بسرِ مبارك ایشان چه نوع زخم رسیده

بود و به افغانان مکر و فریب داده یکی شده ومتفق شده میرزا هندال‌را کشت و اکثر چغتای از سببِ میرزا نابود شده واهل و عیالِ مردم به بند رفت و بی ناموس شد * دیگر محال نمانده که عیال و اطفالِ مردم من بعد تابِ بند و عذاب (82 b) ندارند و دیگرها بر جهنم جان و مال واهل و عیالِ مایان همه تصدّقِ یکتارِ موئ حضرت * این برادر نیست — این دشمنِ حضرت است * سخن مختصر که همه جمع شده به اتفاق بجد شده بعرض رسانیدند که — مص رخنه‌گرِ ملك سر افگنده به* * وحضرت پادشاه در جواب فرمودند که اگرچه این سخنانِ شمایان خاطرنشانِ من می کند امّا دلِ من نمی شود * همه فریاد برآوردند وگفتند که آنچه بعرض رسانیده شده است عین مصلحت است * آخرالامر حضرت فرمودند که اگر مصلحت و رضامندی همهٔ شمایان درین است پس همهٔ شمایان جمع شوید ومحضری نویسید * همه از یمین و یسار امرایان جمع شده نوشته دادند بهمان مصراع‌را — رخنه‌گرِ ملك سر افگنده به * بحضرت پادشاه هم ضرور شد *

در نواحی رهتاس که رسیدند به سید محمّد حکم کردند که هر دو چشمِ میرزا کامران‌را میل کشند * در ساعت رفت و میل کشید *

حضرت پادشاه بعد از میل کشیدن**

END OF THE MS.

---

* This line is quoted by Daulat Shāh. Cf. Mr. E. G. Browne's ed. p. 537.

** The folio which follows in the MS. (83a and 83b) has been conjecturally placed after 73b.

مطبعة دروغولين في ليپسك